Upgrading PCs
Made Easy

Upgrading PCs Made Easy

Bud Aaron
and
Alex Aaron

Osborne McGraw-Hill

Berkeley New York St. Louis San Francisco
Auckland Bogotá Hamburg London Madrid
Mexico City Milan Montreal New Delhi Panama City
Paris São Paulo Singapore Sydney
Tokyo Toronto

Osborne **McGraw-Hill**
2600 Tenth Street
Berkeley, California 94710
U.S.A.

Osborne **McGraw-Hill** offers software for sale. For information on software, translations, or book distributors outside of the U.S.A., please write to Osborne **McGraw-Hill** at the above address.

Upgrading PCs Made Easy

1234567890 DOC 9987654321

ISBN 0-07-881652-1

This book is dedicated to those whose names aren't on the cover—
Dina Aaron, Roy Aaron, Erica Aaron, and Bill Aaron—
they also serve.

Publisher

Kenna S. Wood

Aquisitions Editor

Roger Stewart

Associate Editor

Laurie K. Beaulieu

Project Editor

Kevin Shafer

Contributing Writer

James L. Turley

Copy Editor

Ann Krueger Spivack

Proofreader

Julie Anjos

Indexer

Valerie Robbins

Book Designers

Marcela Hancik
Jani Beckwith

Typesetting

Mickey Salinaro
Helena Charm
Peter F. Hancik

Technical Illustrations:

Susie C. Kim
Erick J. Christgau

Word Processing

Valerie Haynes Perry
Donna Behrens

Cover Design

Bay Graphics Design, Inc.

CONTENTS

Foreword

Do you know what the most significant decision ever made in the personal computer industry was? It was the decision made by the late Don Estridge and IBM to build the original IBM PC out of off-the-shelf parts. In a complete break with tradition and corporate policy, the only part of the original 1981 IBM PC that was made by IBM itself was the keyboard. Everything else was freely available and nonproprietary.

Today, nearly a decade later, it is hard to fully appreciate the impact of this decision. It's difficult to remember what the world was like "B.P.C." (before the IBM PC). Was there really a time when customers were "locked in" to buying all their parts, upgrades, and software from a single company? You bet there was!

After all, it was only good business. If you were IBM, Lanier, CPT, Exxon, or any of the other leading manufacturers of word processing equipment at the time, it made sense to lock in your customer base in this manner. There were a few third-party suppliers for the Apple II and for the Tandy TSR-80 line of personal computers, so the lock there wasn't quite so tight. But the stickers Tandy placed over the external screws on its equipment symbolized for me the hold manufacturers had over users.

The screws in question were the ones you had to remove to get inside the system, and the stickers advised you that doing so would void your warranty. The catch was that to undo the screws, you had to tear the stickers, a sure sign to any Tandy/Radio Shack repairman that you had crossed into forbidden territory.

Luckily, things have changed. IBM's desire and need to create a personal computer and bring it to market *fast* made the decision to use off-the-shelf parts inevitable. What neither IBM nor anyone else could have foreseen was that this single decision would create an entire industry of add-on and upgrade equipment.

Today, as you know if you read virtually any computer magazine, it is possible to buy a plain-vanilla IBM-compatible computer, and get it cheaply. You can then, in effect, design your own machine by adding various boards and other equipment to it. You're not locked in to anything.

If you need a better monitor, greater graphics capabilities, a more powerful power supply, more memory, a scanner, a mouse, a bigger and faster hard drive, a tape backup system, a different keyboard, or even a faster, more powerful processor (CPU), you can have it. You don't have to pay for capabilities until you really need them. And when the time comes that you do need them, you have lots of choices.

In fact, in most cases, there are too many choices. All you have to do is look at any issue of *Computer Shopper, PC Magazine, PC World,* or *PC Computing* to get a very real, physical idea of how many choices the typical PC owner has. In a word, it's overwhelming.

What's needed is a clear, concise guide to all that is available. And that's exactly what you'll find in this book by the father-and-son team of Bud and Alex Aaron. This book will show you what your PC upgrade options are, and, equally important, explain what to look for and what to watch out for when improving your PC. It will show you what to get, where to get it, and how to buy it at the lowest possible price.

But the Aarons go the extra mile. Bud and Alex not only take you to the door, they guide you inside so that you will also know the in's and out's of actually adding an upgrade component to your system.

This is the book everyone has been waiting for. It pulls together and presents in a single volume everything you need to know to maximize the power at your fingertips and to customize a system to your own wants and needs. Finally, someone has made it possible for everyone to claim the promise of truly "personal" computing.

Upgrading PCs Made Easy by Bud and Alex Aaron makes sense of it all. It will save you time, and it will save you money. And, after reading a single chapter, you will be convinced that it is nothing less than essential for every PC owner and user. 0

— Alfred Glossbrenner

Acknowledgments

The list of acknowledgments would make a book by itself but there are some special people we would like to thank. We would like to thank our family Dina Aaron, Roy Aaron, Erica Aaron, Bill Aaron, David Hines, David Ward, Daniel Fernandez, and others who have helped during its writing. Special thanks go to Jeff Pepper, Roger Stewart, Ann Krueger Spivack, Laurie Beaulieu, Scott Rogers, Nick Anis, and the staff of Osborne/McGraw-Hill. As many people have pointed out, it takes a substantial team effort to put a book like this together. We would also like to thank our technical editor Victor Filiba for keeping us honest providing help in many areas. Special thanks go to Jim Turley without whom this book would never have been done. The acknowledgments would not be complete without special mention of the vendors listed in Appendix A who provided material and helped in completing this book.

Introduction

This book assumes that you are a novice computer user who needs a new computer or would like to upgrade an older model. (If you are an advanced user, keep reading.) It also assumes that you would rather not be at the mercy of computer salespeople when it's time to buy a computer, or when considering options for your current computer. This books explains the terms and jargon that are part of the computer industry—terms you should be familiar with to get the most for your computer-related purchases. And although this book is geared more toward IBM PCs and compatibles, the information, tips, and general upgrade ideas can be used with other computers such as the Apple Macintosh, Commodore Amiga, and others.

This book also provides up-to-date information, sources, and tips that advanced users will find useful when upgrading. The drive tables and other appendixes provide help for anyone that gets a "hand-me-down" computer and needs to figure out what it is and what parts can be upgraded.

When you are finished with the book you will have a working knowledge of computers that will enable you to determine what can and cannot be accomplished with them. You will also be familiar with the terms used in ads and by salespeople to help you make a more knowledgeable purchase.

How This Book Is Organized

This book is split up into logical steps that build on each other as each step is completed. The book begins with an overview of computers, then covers opening the system and simple upgrades, proceeds to more advanced upgrades, and finally gives you a step-by-step guide to building your own computer.

The book covers upgrading your drives, upgrading memory, increasing the speed of your computer, adding a math coprocessor, adding a tape backup system, and discusses various backup philosophies. You'll learn how to change the power supply, upgrade the motherboard, upgrade the monitor and graphics adapter, install a new printer, and add interface ports. The book also notes what types of applications can be improved with an upgrade (this includes Computer Aided Design, desktop publishing, and other applications).

Also covered are upgrades to the software portion of your system. This includes the operating system, operating environments, memory managers, and other portions that can be enhanced so you can get the most out of your computer system. The book tells you when to upgrade your software when adding memory or upgrading to a drive that is not supported by an earlier version of DOS.

Chapters 1 through 4 give you an overview of the computer system, what makes up a computer system, and simple additions that can be made to the system. Chapter 1 covers the history and concepts behind the computer. This chapter also introduces terms that you will hear used whenever computers are discussed. Chapter 2 covers the anatomy of the computer, explaining the various parts that are used, and discussing what can and cannot be upgraded. In Chapter 3, you will actually open the computer to see how it is laid out internally. Chapter 3 also offers a variety of safety tips and ideas that should be helpful even to advanced users. Chapter 4 introduces simple upgrades and additions that will increase the usefulness of the computer system.

Chapters 5 through 8 start to get serious about upgrades. They cover adding expansion boards, drives, tape backup systems, memory chips, and math coprocessors. You'll also learn how to upgrade the case, power supply, and other external parts for more power, and greater expandability. Chapter 5 covers the process of adding expansion boards, the types of expansion buses available, and discusses memory and how it applies to the overall scheme of upgrading. Chapter 5 also discusses video adapters, and communications ports, and gives information about each. In Chapter 6, you'll learn about drives and tape backup systems—how to install them, and the different interfaces available. You also learn about configuring, formatting, and the backup software used with these devices. Chapter 7 covers adding memory to your system, be it SIMM, SIP, DIP, or any other type of memory. You also cover installation of the math coprocessor, including tips to ensure that everything is installed correctly. In Chapter 8 you get into serious modifications, including upgrading the power supply, adding accelerator cards, installing a new motherboard, installing a new processor, installing new BIOS chips, and using SETUP to configure the system.

Chapters 9 through 12 cover a wide range of subjects, including modifying and adding software, upgrading the operating system, troubleshooting and maintenance, and building your own computer. Chapter 9 covers adding and modifying your software. In Chapter 9 you add device drivers to the CONFIG.SYS file, thereby optimizing the settings for the most speed and memory. In Chapter 10, you learn how to upgrade your operating system and operating environment. Operating systems covered are MS-DOS 5.0, DR-DOS 5.0, and OS/2. Operating environments covered include Windows 3.0, Presentation Manager, DESQview, the DOS shell and DR-DOS ViewMax. Chapter 11 covers troubleshooting and maintenance. This section has a lot of tips for keeping your computer in excellent condition, plus suggestions for rescuing data on disks. Finally Chapter 12 brings everything together and explains how to build your own system. You'll get a parts list for the computer that shows alternate choices so you can customize the computer to fit the way you work.

The appendixes contain a listing of vendors, sources for a variety of parts, a source for information on adaptive computing, plus listings of hard disks and video adapters and their capabilities.

1

The Open Computer

In the world of personal computers, it seems the only thing that is constant is change. The computers themselves change constantly, and the uses for them are always increasing and evolving. In the 1960s the idea of a "personal" computer was ludicrous. In the 1970s it was an extravagance. In the 1980s it became commonplace, and in the 1990s it has become almost mandatory—at least for small businesses. What was exciting and new yesterday is mass-produced and available by mail order today.

This rapid change is a double-edged sword for many, however. On the one hand, those who could never afford a computer, or who simply had no use for one, are now finding themselves in a position to buy a computer and use it for a variety of purposes. On the other hand, those who have already bought personal computers are seeing their investments rapidly becoming obsolete, with little or no demand for an "old" computer in the resale market.

Because the personal computer industry is moving and growing so quickly, a computer that is only five years old no longer represents the state of the art—in fact, it verges on obsolescence. Even though the machine itself may still be reliable and in good working condition, it cannot perform the same kinds of work, or work as rapidly, as a new computer. Many owners of an aging personal computer may find themselves covetously eyeing next year's model at the local computer store.

Fortunately, the majority of personal computers in use today are not necessarily destined for the scrap heap after only a few short years. You have the ability to update them to keep them current with their newer counterparts. In the same way that an older car might benefit from an engine overhaul, a new set of tires, and a fresh coat of paint, many computers also can be "overhauled". That means computer owners don't necessarily have to replace the entire machine when they find themselves needing more computing power.

This book is intended for exactly those people: personal computer owners who have a good, working PC, but who have discovered that it may no longer have all the features they want. Perhaps the computer is too slow, or it does not run the latest software, or it cannot store enough data. All of these things, and more, can be changed, improved, and upgraded. In this book, you will learn what can be upgraded in your personal computer, and how to go about doing it. You'll also find some suggestions about upgrading for specific purposes, such as database management or the growing field of desktop publishing.

You'll learn what the various parts of your PC are, and what they do. You'll see how a particular upgrade might help, and what changes you can expect. You'll also see what upgrades might not be right for you and your machine.

All of the information in this book is provided in a simple, straightforward manner, without a lot of computer "buzzwords" and jargon. You are not expected to be an expert in computers or electronics. Where special terms or concepts are introduced, they will be explained right away, and as simply as necessary to get the point across. Also, this book is arranged so that each chapter deals with a particular kind of upgrade or modification. If you are not interested in a particular subject, feel free to skip over it. Those sections that are really necessary will be noted, and each chapter has complete instructions and background information for your particular upgrade.

History

In the 1950s and 1960s the first electronic computers used vacuum tubes and mechanical relays. They were huge devices that required rooms full of equipment, and consumed incredible amounts of power. Early machines used plugboards with hundreds of wires connected from point to point to *program* the computer (tell it what to do). These machines solved mathematical problems that would have taken years using slide rules or the mechanical calculators available at that time.

Newsrooms and other businesses used a machine called a Teletype. The Teletype had a rotating cylinder and a keyboard that could only type capital letters. The Teletype printed on rolls of paper, somewhat like a typewriter. It could also make punched paper tapes or send text over the telephone lines to other Teletype machines. Modern computer communication over telephone lines (via *modem*) is rooted in the Teletype and similar machines.

The punched paper tapes generated by Teletype machines were used to input programs and data for early computers; the Teletype was used extensively as an input and output device. The keyboard and tape reader were used for input to the computer and the printed paper and tape punch were used for output. It was a keyboard, display, printer, and paper tape reader/punch all in one very slow, very noisy machine.

Vacuum tubes and relays eventually gave way to transistors. They performed the same basic functions, but with considerably more speed and less electricity. Even the smallest vacuum tubes were as big as a human thumb, while early transistors were as small as a kernel of corn. Transistors represented a monumental decrease in the space and power requirements for computers and other electronic devices. (The "transistor radio" is a good example.)

Transistors are made from the chemical element silicon. Silicon is easy to produce in large quantities from simple, inexpensive ingredients like sand. It is also very smooth, and can be sculpted or "etched" into very intricate shapes. Because of the way silicon (with impurities) conducts electricity, it is known as a "semiconductor" to chemists and electronics engineers. It is this semiconducting aspect of silicon that made transistors possible.

Eventually, Texas Instruments in Dallas developed *integrated circuits,* or ICs. What TI did was put many transistors on a single piece of silicon and connect them internally to perform a specific electrical function. Continued improvement led to more functions at ever-decreasing prices. The trend towards increasing complexity and decreasing costs continues to this day.

Since TI's introduction, integrated circuits have blossomed into a multibillion dollar industry, both in the United States and in other countries around the world. Today there are literally millions of different kinds of IC devices, or chips, performing many different kinds of functions.

Perhaps the most well-known—and most complex—type of silicon chip is the Central Processing Unit, or CPU chip. Intel Corporation of Santa Clara, California developed early chips called the 4004, 4040, 8008, and 8080. The 8080 became the first Central Processing Unit used in a general-purpose computer. It was hailed as "a computer on a chip." While this may have been a premature claim by today's standards, it was very popular, and eventually became the heart of the Altair personal computer—the Model T of modern personal computers.

The Altair was introduced by a company called MITS in Albuquerque, New Mexico. It used the Intel 8080 CPU and boasted 256 bytes of memory! This new memory also used integrated circuits. The Altair computer had no keyboard, no screen, and no disk drives; it was programmed by flipping switches on the front panel to store instructions in the computer. To a dedicated computer science student, this was acceptable, but the Altair was a far cry from the convenience and power available in personal computers today.

Steve Wozniack and Steve Jobs designed their own personal computer around a CPU chip from another company. They preferred the 6502 from Mostek to Intel's 8080. They called their new computer Apple I, presumably in memory of their summers picking apples in the local orchards. (Their own company, Apple Computer Corporation, now stands where some of those orchards once were.)

After the Apple I came the Apple II. The Apple II was to become one of the biggest success stories in the electronics industry. It succeeded phenomenally with small businesses as well as schools, and made the idea of a

1

"personal" computer a reality. While MITS and other early personal computer companies eventually failed, Apple grew and grew. In 1982, computer giant IBM introduced their own personal computer, called the Model 5150, known more commonly as just the "Personal Computer" or the PC. Since that time, the terms "personal computer" and "PC" have come to mean an IBM personal computer rather than an Apple personal computer.

Open Architecture

One of the most interesting features that both the Apple II and the IBM Personal Computer shared was an *open architecture*. This means that these two computers were not "closed boxes" as many earlier computers had been. Instead, the box could be opened and new electronics could be installed at any time. In a sense, these computers were "obsolete proof" because they could be endlessly modified and tinkered with. For example a modern television set or microwave oven is a "closed architecture." That is, it may not (and should not) be opened and modified by the average user. By contrast, the Apple II and IBM PC were more like a set of Tinkertoys or Lego blocks in the hands of early personal computer users. They (the owners) could open their computers and add to them at will.

In these early days of personal computers, most PC owners were technically competent, able to make repairs or modifications to their computers to improve its speed, storage space, or other features. They would then share this knowledge with other PC owners, so that everyone's machine would improve. A computer that had an open architecture was therefore more desirable than a computer that didn't. The result of this was that computers with open architectures (like IBMs and Apples) outsold those without it.

Since the days of the Apple II and the IBM 5150, both companies have continually improved and expanded their line of personal computers. Apple has developed the Apple III, and the entire Macintosh line of computers. For their part, IBM has followed the PC with the XT, the AT, the PS/2, and several more powerful models. But the one thing that virtually all of these machines have maintained was the open architecture approach to designing computers. By allowing computer owners to customize and improve their computers to fit their needs and desires, the computer itself becomes a more useful tool.

Why Upgrade?

The computers that are popular today are designed around an open architecture. This is true of small personal computers, as well as larger, more powerful workstations, and even mainframe computers used by banks and large corporations. A computer is too large an investment to risk obsolescence. With computer hardware and software technology changing as quickly as it does, only open architecture guarantees a "growth path" to the future.

If you use a personal computer in a small business, your needs may have been very simple when you purchased the machine. Perhaps it was used for inventory control, or for word processing, or for financial calculation. Perhaps it was used for all of these things. Over time, your needs or your firm's needs may have changed. Every business strives for continued growth. Every shopowner would like to have more customers and higher turnover. Perhaps the inventory list has become much longer, the word processing developed into graphic arts and printing, and the financial spreadsheets turned into complex investment strategies. As the demands on the computer change, the computer should be able to change with them.

Certainly there are more application programs available now than there were five or ten years ago. Business applications have become more complex, and the software to handle those applications has kept pace. Many of these new software applications require much more powerful hardware to run on. There are many business applications available today that simply cannot run on earlier PC or XT class computers. They're simply too complex for such an "old" computer. So, the alternatives are clear: either forgo the newer, more powerful software, or get a better computer to run them on.

Fortunately, getting that better computer doesn't need to mean throwing out your hardware and software and starting over again. (That would really only postpone the problem—in a few years, the new computer would again be too old to keep pace with new developments in software and with your ever-increasing demands on the system.) Instead of replacing the entire computer system every few years, you can simply upgrade or replace those components of the system that you need to improve.

If your computer is too slow, you can speed up the processing power. If you need to store more information than you did before, you can upgrade you PC's storage. If you had a black-and-white screen and now you want color,

1

you can change that, too. Poor quality printouts can be improved with a new printer, graphics capabilities can be added with a new video adapter, and reliability can be increased with backup storage and power supplies. Nearly any aspect of your PC can be enhanced, improved, or modified. And you can do it a piece at a time, at your own pace as your needs and budget dictate.

Throughout the chapters of this book, you will see what parts can be upgraded, and what benefits you can get from those changes. Some of the information will be general. You will see what kinds of changes you might want to consider, or what to avoid. Other parts will be very specific, with step-by-step instructions for installing new circuit boards and cabling up printers. Not everything in this book may interest you—at least not yet. But that's the whole point of having a PC and being able to upgrade it. You never know what you might want to do in the future!

2

Anatomy of a Personal Computer System

In this chapter you'll look at the parts of a personal computer and learn a little about what each part contributes to the complete system. This will help you understand how your computer works a little better, and can be referred to when you're ready to open up your computer and identify the part or parts you may need to find.

For this chapter, the PC has been divided into four basic sections. They are your system unit (the big metal or plastic box that holds most of the parts), your keyboard, your monitor (the part that looks like a TV), and your printer or any other pieces of equipment connected to the outside of the system unit.

System Unit

The system unit is the main part of your computer. It houses the most important components that make your computer run. All the other pieces of

9

your computer system (keyboard, monitor, printer, and so on) connect to the system unit with cables.

System unit boxes don't have to come in any particular shape, size, or color, but most look very much like the original IBM PC or the IBM AT. This may seem like lack of originality on the part of the other computer manufacturers, but there is a very practical reason for this. Since the goal of the PC compatible manufacturers is to make their components work just like the IBM components, any alterations might compromise their usefulness. In the case of the system unit box, this means keeping the same shape and size so that all of the same components will fit in the same way. Figure 2-1 shows the front of a PC/XT system unit (top) and the front of an AT system unit (bottom).

While the outside of the box itself isn't very interesting, there are some features you should look at now. Your particular computer may not have all of these items on the outside, depending upon the manufacturer.

Reset Switch

This is an improvement over the original IBM equipment. When things go badly wrong, it is sometimes necessary to reset your computer. Resetting

Figure 2-1.   *The front views of two system units*

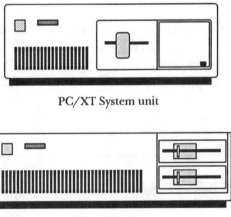

PC/XT System unit

AT System unit

a PC is *almost* like turning it off and back on, but not quite as drastic. On IBM equipment, you reset the computer by pressing the (CTRL), (ALT), and (DEL) keys all at once. This pattern was chosen because it takes two hands, and because you're not likely to do it accidentally. Unfortunately, it assumes that your keyboard is working correctly, and that some of the software inside the PC is working as well.

A push-button reset switch on the outside of the system unit allows you to reset your computer simply by pressing the button momentarily. Some PC-compatible computers offer this feature, while others do not.

Power Switch

Every computer needs an on/off switch. In keeping with IBM's role as trendsetter, this switch is usually big and orange (or red), and located on the right side of the computer, near the back. Furthermore, it is not usually marked "ON" and "OFF." Instead, it is marked with a straight line and a circle. These generic, international symbols are meant to represent on and off, respectively.

Your computer's system case may have a power switch on the front of it instead. While this can make reaching the power switch a little simpler, it can also make it too easy to turn the computer off accidentally.

Speed Switch

Another improvement that has been made over earlier IBM equipment is the addition of a CPU speed switch, often called a "Turbo Mode" switch. This is mostly a catchy advertising term, since it does not actually speed up your computer if you press it. Instead, it slows your computer down if you don't press it.

Why would anybody want this? Again, the issue of strict compatibility to IBM equipment comes up. There are many PC-compatible computers that run faster than IBM's computers do. While it is unlikely, there is a possibility that some computer programs will not work properly if the computer runs too fast. For that reason, some computers offer this switch to allow you to slow down the computer if necessary to "IBM standard" speed, or even slower.

LED Display

As an adjunct to the Turbo switch, some computers offer a two-digit numeric display. The display often uses red *light-emitting diodes,* or *LEDs.* This display is intended to indicate how fast the computer is running—the higher the number, the better. In actual fact, this number is quite meaningless. It usually displays one fixed number (say, 33) when the Turbo switch is pressed a smaller number is displayed.

Key Lock

Beginning with the IBM AT, personal computers were deemed important enough to warrant some form of security. This took the form of a lock and key on the outside of the system unit. On the AT, the keyboard is disabled when the lock is locked. As a result, anything you typed would be completely ignored. This made it possible to start the computer in the morning, turn the lock, and then walk away from it with the assurance that nobody could interrupt its operation (that is, unless the computer were turned off: the lock does nothing to protect the power switch).

Disk Drive Bays

The most obvious external feature of the system unit box is the space for the disk drives. Most PCs have space for two floppy disk drives. Others have space for three or more, and they may offer 5 1/4-inch drive bays as well as 3 1/2-inch spaces. Nearly any mixture is possible. When disk drives are not installed in all of the possible spaces, cover plates should be in place to ensure proper air circulation and cooling.

Fan Vent

Since the electronics inside your PC generate a certain amount of heat, there needs to be a fan inside to blow that excess heat out. Otherwise, the insides of your PC would "cook." While it would never get hot enough to actually melt anything or cause a fire, there are limits to the electronic components' durability. If they are operated at high temperatures for a long time, they may fail catastrophically, and your computer will need an early repair.

The fan usually blows warm air out the back of your computer's system unit. Be sure to give your PC plenty of "breathing room." If your computer sits on a desk or on the floor against a wall, don't shove it all the way back against the wall. Leave a good six inches of space between the wall and the back of your PC.

Expansion Board Openings

As mentioned earlier, one of the reasons for the popularity of personal computers is their ability to be enhanced, upgraded, and expanded. The expansion slots inside your PC (discussed later) are where that upgrading is done. Each expansion slot is given an opening into the "outside world" where you can connect other things (printers, plotters, and so on) to them. Your PC may have eight or more of these openings, or it may have none at all.

Cable Connectors

Even without any expansion cards installed, there are some devices that all computers need, and cables are necessary to connect them. One of these joins your keyboard with the system unit. The keyboard connector is usually found inside a round hole about the size of a quarter in the back of the system unit. Since it is physically mounted on the motherboard, it will always be in the same location on any PC. The connector itself has ten sockets, five of which are used. The used sockets are arranged in a lopsided circle that connect to the keyboard cable. An illustration of a keyboard cable and its connnector is shown here:

Align with the notch

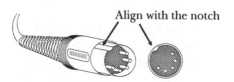

Your PC may also have serial or parallel communications ports (discussed later). On the first PCs, these were optional, but now they are often included as standard equipment. If so, there will be connectors mounted on the back of your system unit case. These connectors will generally be small and rectangular in shape, like a stretched-out letter D. These connectors, and their function, will be covered in many of the chapters that follow, and in Appendix C, "Connector Reference."

Power Connectors

Of course, your computer needs to be plugged in before it will work! Over the years, even the size and shape of the power cord has become a standard. Like everything else, this makes it easier to buy and use parts from a variety of vendors without worrying about compatibility. There should be a three-prong male power connector on the back of your PC so that you can plug it into the wall outlet, as shown here on the right:

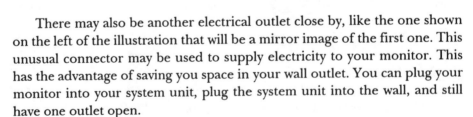

There may also be another electrical outlet close by, like the one shown on the left of the illustration that will be a mirror image of the first one. This unusual connector may be used to supply electricity to your monitor. This has the advantage of saving you space in your wall outlet. You can plug your monitor into your system unit, plug the system unit into the wall, and still have one outlet open.

Motherboard

The system unit is the basis of your computer, and the motherboard is the heart of your system unit. It holds the most important components of your system, and is one of the most expensive parts as well. Without a motherboard, the rest of your system would be worthless.

2

Your motherboard is a large printed circuit board with electronic components soldered onto it. Printed circuit boards are covered in Chapter 3, "Taking a Look Inside Your PC." In your PC, the motherboard will generally lie at the very bottom of the system unit case. It may be almost completely covered up by other parts of your computer. The power supply and the hard disk drive may be covering part of the motherboard. Figure 2-2 shows the motherboard lying at the bottom of a system case.

The CPU, the main memory, and perhaps some of the input and output functions are all located on the motherboard. Some of these components, and what they do, are described next.

Central Processing Unit

If forced to choose the single most important device in an entire personal computer system, you would have to choose the *central processing unit,* or *CPU.* The CPU is an *integrated circuit,* or *IC,* just like the dozens of other ICs in your PC, but it is much more complex than any of the others. Integrated circuits are made up of dozens to millions of transistors on a single chip of silicon not much larger than a fingernail. The silicon chip is mounted in a plastic or

Figure 2-2. *The interior of the System Unit (viewed from overhead)*

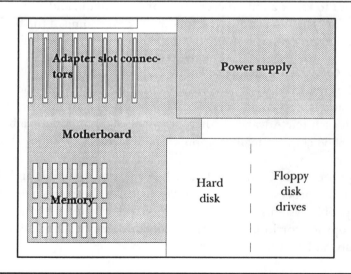

ceramic case with connections brought out to pins that are either soldered into a circuit board or plugged into a socket on a circuit board. In a very real sense, all of the other electronic devices in your PC exist to serve the CPU in one way or another.

Various types of CPU chips (also called microprocessors) have existed since the late 1970s. Today there are dozens of different kinds of CPUs from several different manufacturers worldwide. When IBM developed the Personal Computer, they chose an 8088 CPU from Intel Corporation.

The Intel 8088 was a successor to the 8080, mentioned in Chapter 1, "The Open Computer." It offered many features not found on earlier microprocessors, and so it was a good choice for the PC. After the 8088, Intel developed the 8086, the 80186, the 80286, the 80386, and the 80486. Each of these offers more speed, more power, and more capabilities than its predecessor. Any of these CPUs can be found in personal computers today. The speed and capabilities of your PC depends in large part upon which one of these CPU chips it contains.

The microprocessor is the chip that runs your software. The faster and more efficiently it can execute your programs, the faster your computer will be, and the more work you'll get done in a given amount of time. People often describe their personal computers in terms of the CPU chip, as in "I've just bought a new 386 machine." With that in mind, there are some things you might want to know about microprocessors in general, and about your CPU in particular. The discussions that follow will cover some of the basic aspects of each microprocessor, as well as some of the more vital technical details.

The 8088 CPU   This chip is used in the IBM PC and XT computers. It is also used in the great majority of PC- or XT-compatible computers, including early portable and laptop computers. The 8088 is manufactured by a few companies besides Intel. Advanced Micro Devices of Sunnyvale, California also supplies 8088 chips to many computer manufacturers, as does Harris Semiconductor.

Nippon Electric Company, better known as NEC, builds an "8088-compatible" microprocessor called the V20. Just like the companies that make PC-compatible systems, NEC has designed a device that is compatible with the microprocessor in the PC. The V20 can do some things that the 8088 cannot do, and it runs a bit faster.

As far as the PC pecking order goes, the 8088 is at the very bottom. It has only an 8-bit data bus, meaning it can move a single byte of data at a time. It also has a 20-bit address bus, allowing it a one megabyte address range. This 1 MB address limitation haunts the PC-compatible market to this day. The 1 MB limitation is the reason that MS-DOS is limited to 640 KB of work space (the other 3B4 KB is used for other purposes), and why expanded memory management was developed. These themes will be covered in more detail in Chapter 5, "Adding Expansion Boards."

The 8086 CPU The 8086 is virtually identical to the 8088. The only difference is that the 8086 has a 16-bit wide data bus, instead of one 8 bits wide. This difference is absolutely undetectable to software, so anything that runs on an 8088 will run on an 8086 as well. However, if the software requires moving 16 bits of data, the 8086 can move it twice as fast.

Because of this feature, personal computers with an 8086 CPU generally run faster than those with an 8088. How much faster depends a great deal on what software you are running. An average of about 20 percent faster might be a reasonable expectation.

The 80286 CPU This device was the first successor to the 8088 to appear in a new IBM computer (IBM never used the 8086). When the PC AT was developed, it was designed with an 80286 microprocessor. The 80286 offers many technical advancements over the 8088 and 8086. Unfortunately, very few of them were utilized when the AT was designed. Hence, the 286 is used essentially as a newer, faster 8086. Like the earlier CPUs, the 286 is also produced by AMD and Harris. NEC has developed a 286-compatible component, the V40.

The 80286 and the AT-class computers offered a large performance improvement over the earlier PC- and XT-class machines. An 80286-based PC can run from three to five times faster than an 8088-based computer. (There are probably no PC manufacturers that still design or build new 8088 PCs.) These days, the 286 is considered the "entry level" microprocessor. Many full-featured desktop PCs as well as some of the newer laptop computers use a 286.

Like the 8086, the 286 has a 16-bit data bus, so it can move 2 bytes of data at once. The address bus has grown from 20 to 24 bits. This gives the 286 a 16-Megabyte address space, but DOS only takes advantage of the first 1 MB.

In addition to these external differences, the 286 also runs at a faster clock rate than the 8086, and can execute program instructions faster. This gives AT-class computers their overall speed increase.

Perhaps the biggest enhancement made to the 286 was the addition of the *protected mode* of operation. With appropriate software, the 286 could run in this new mode and address much more memory, execute new instructions, and even run several programs at once. The advantages of protected mode are significant; unfortunately, MS-DOS does not take advantage of them, so the benefits of protected mode are not available to the DOS user.

The 80386 CPU   The next generation after the 80286 was, of course, the 80386. Until 1990, the 80386 was the top of the Intel line. Intel has dropped the "80" prefix from their processor names, and now calls the 80386 an "i386."

The i386 was a large improvement over the 286. It has a 32-bit data path, so it can move 4 bytes of data at once. It also has a 32-bit address bus, so it can directly address over 4 billion bytes of data. The 386 also runs at a faster clock rate than the 286. Finally, a very complex and powerful memory management unit was added, which improved the overall performance of the 386. The 386 also added many powerful features previously found only in minicomputers costing several time as much. All in all, the 386 was a quantum leap in microprocessor performance.

But unfortunately, as with the 286, nearly all of these features are left unused when running DOS on PC-compatible computers. For DOS users, the 386 is almost nothing more than a speeded-up 8086—almost, but not quite. There are some things that only a 386 PC can do.

Microsoft Windows version 3.0 was released in the middle of 1990. It is a popular graphic user interface. Windows 3.0 was one of the first significant programs to use the extended features of the 386 microprocessor. The operating system software OS/2 is another example of a program that really utilizes the 386's features, and AutoCAD/386 does, too.

Currently, the 386 comes in three slightly different versions. The first, and still the fastest, is the "i386 DX." The DX suffix means that this version of the 386 has a 32-bit data bus, as described earlier.

The second version is the "i386SX." This version of the 386 is exactly the same as the DX, except that the SX has a 16-bit data bus—half as wide. This means that the 386SX cannot move data around inside your PC quite as fast as a 386DX can. The overall effect to a PC system is not great, perhaps 25 percent. Apart from that, the two components are identical. It is impossible for software to tell them apart, so anything that runs on one processor will run on the other.

The third version of the 386 family is the "i386 SL." This is a special 386 processor with many of the other PC-compatible components already added to it. This feature is primarily of interest to PC manufacturers and not users. It means that the PC motherboard can be made smaller and (presumably) less expensive because many of the required components are already included with the processor. This is especially helpful for small laptop computers.

Some of the first 386DX chips used in PCs had a flaw, or a "bug" in the microscopic circuitry that performed floating-point arithmetic. This bug rarely, if ever, occurred in normal daily use, but it could cause the 386 to give the wrong answer to some obscure math problems. This problem was quickly solved, and newer 386 chips no longer have this bug. However, there are still a great number of PCs with the earlier 386 chips. If your 386 is marked with the words "For 16 bit software only" then it certainly is one of these. If, on the other hand, it is marked with two Greek letters sigma (which look like a pair of capital letters E), then it is one of the later, corrected ones.

The 80486 CPU   The i486 was introduced in 1989, and contains many improvements over the 386. The two biggest ones are the addition of a cache, and a floating-point unit, or FPU. A *cache* is a special kind of memory that is very fast. Having a cache on the same chip makes the 486 much faster than the 386.

All of the Intel processors used in PCs have had floating-point coprocessors, but the 486 is the first to have the FPU built in. *Floating-point coprocessors* are special circuits that speed up mathematical calculations (they are discussed in more detail in Chapter 7, "Adding Chips").

Numeric Processor Extension

Most PC's give you the option of installing a second processor. As amazing as that sounds, in reality it's not quite as dramatic as installing a second engine in your car. First of all, the optional second processor isn't a Central Processing Unit (CPU) like the first one, and secondly, even if it is installed, it will only work with certain kinds of software.

Every member of Intel's 8086 family up to the 80386 (but not including the 80486—more on this later) has had a matching companion processor to go with it. The secondary processor has always had the same part number as the main CPU, but with a final "7" instead of a "6." For example, the companion processor for the 80286 is an 80287. As a group, these secondary processors are called *Numeric Processor Extensions* (NPX), to use Intel's term. Most people today call them floating-point processors, or simply "math chips."

So, what does this math chip do for you? Either a great deal or nothing at all, depending on what you use your PC for. As the name might imply, the math chips are used for complex mathematical calculations. The CPU in your PC does complex mathematics very slowly.

Help comes in the form of the NPX, or math chip. If you do a lot of complex math calculations you might benefit from one of these. If you do a lot of drafting or CAD work on your PC, you almost certainly will (in fact AutoCAD requires one). The NPX chip works alongside the main CPU in your PC and handles all of the complex mathematical functions. It can do math functions 10 to 300 *times* faster than the CPU alone. Depending on your application, that can be a startling improvement.

As mentioned before, math chips are matched with CPU chips. The 8086 has its 8087, the 80286 its 80287, and the 80386 has an 80387. You cannot mix them any other way. The 80486 has no companion math chip because the math functions are built right into the 80486 itself.

Adding a math chip is a relatively simple procedure (it is covered in detail in Chapter 6). Bear in mind, though, that adding a math chip will not always speed up your computer. It only makes sense if you are doing lots of mathematical work, like graphics, drawing, or calculating. Even then, simply adding the NPX doesn't speed things up automatically. Your software must make use of the NPX for it to work.

Memory

Another part of your computer's motherboard is memory. Memory is almost as important as the microprocessor; each needs the other to work. The memory in your PC is made up of ICs.

To really understand what memory is, and what it does, you have to have a pretty good understanding of computers. Since that's not the goal here, only some basic memory-related terms and concepts will be presented. These will help you to decide when or why you might want to upgrade your computer's memory.

A microprocessor's need of memory is like a person's need for a desk. The memory is where the CPU keeps the software instructions it is supposed to execute (the program), the data values it is supposed to read, and the answers it is supposed to produce. Adding more memory is like getting a larger desk: it allows your computer to work on bigger and more complex projects.

Memory capacity is measured in units called *bytes*. Bytes measure how much information memory chips can store, just as teaspoons measure how much liquid a cup can hold. Generally speaking, one byte of memory is enough to store one letter of the alphabet. (That's not the actual, technical definition, but it's close enough.) Therefore, 8-10 bytes would hold most English words, and several thousand bytes of memory could store a small book.

Computers need to work with more than just words, though. They also work with numbers. The same byte of memory that could store one letter of the alphabet could also store any integer (whole number without fractions) between 0 and 255. Any number up to 255 times 255, or 65,535, can be stored in 2 bytes. It takes only 4 bytes to store any number up to 4 billion.

Although the byte is the main unit of measure for memory, you will also see the word bit used. A bit is a byte that has been slivered into eight equal pieces. One bit equals 1/8 of one byte. A bit is only enough storage for the numbers 0 and 1. Be careful when you see memory capacities advertised; be sure to divide all quantities of bits by eight to get bytes.

Note

The first personal computers had around 32,000 bytes of memory. Some had more than 65,000 bytes. When the IBM PC came out, it had about 65,000 bytes of memory, too. Today, this is a ridiculously small amount. Nearly any computer will have over 256,000 bytes of memory, with most having over 512,000 bytes. Newer machines have a few million!

As you can see, these numbers grow very rapidly into the hundreds of thousands and millions. There is a common shorthand way of handling numbers this large. Multiples of a thousand bytes are called *kilobytes,* after the Greek word "Kilo". Multiples of a million bytes are called *megabytes*. So, a computer with about 64,000 bytes of memory would have 64 kilobytes, abbreviated 64 KB.

Note

For obscure technical reasons, a kilobyte is not exactly 1000 bytes, but really 1024 bytes. A megabyte is really 1,048,576 bytes. But for most purposes, you simply need to remember that kilobytes and megabytes are one thousand and one million, respectively.

Memory chips are very fast, and the microprocessor in your PC reads and writes information to them all the time. Each chip holds quite a bit of information. Through the progress of the silicon companies, the amount of information that a memory chip can hold seems to double about every two years. When the first PC was built, it used memory chips that could store 65,535 bits (8192 bytes) per chip. Today, those chips would be hopelessly obsolete. PCs today are manufactured with memory chips that hold 256 K bits, 1024 K bits, or 4096 K bits (512 K bytes) per chip.

Memory chips are fast, inexpensive, and hold an immense amount of data. But there is one thing most of them can't do: they cannot store data after their power has been turned off. For this reason, most memory chips are called *volatile* memory devices. The term volatile doesn't mean that they're explosive. It refers to the fact that they "forget" when they are turned off. Memory chips come in two basic types, described next.

RAM   One of the two types of memory is RAM. RAM is an acronym for random-access memory. The memory part is easy to understand, but what is random access? This is a technical term that describes the way memory is written to and read from in your computer. It means that the microprocessor in your PC can read or write any individual byte of information it wants, no matter where it is stored in the memory. It might be helpful to think of computer memory as a big scratch pad with numbered pages. Each page contains a single byte of information. The information may be a computer instruction or it may be data the computer is going to use in the execution of a program. This type of memory is called random-access memory because you can skip from page to page at random and read the information from the page.

Note

You might understand random-access memory better if you knew its opposite–sequential-access memory. This type of computer memory (magnetic tape, for example) only allows you to retrieve information sequentially. For instance, suppose you're on a freeway and you want to get to Fourth Avenue. You may have to go past the First, Second, and Third Avenues exits first. That could be called "sequential-access exits" because you cannot jump from First to Fourth directly. If you could, you would have "random-access exits." With sequential memory, to get from one address (0) to another (4), you must first read 1, 2, and then 3 to reach 4. With random-access memory, you can read 0, then 3, then 2, or whatever in any random order you choose. With the exceptions of ROM BIOS and other ROM, the memory in your PC is RAM memory.

There are two basic kinds of RAM chips (and one special kind). The basic types are called *dynamic RAM* and *static RAM.* You will often hear these called DRAM and SRAM, respectively. (Again, you don't really need to know what these terms mean to use your computer, but learning them will help you to understand some of the material that follows. It will also help you decipher some of the sales literature you're likely to encounter.)

Basically, a dynamic RAM chip can hold more information than a static RAM chip, and it will cost less. On the other hand, static RAM chips are faster, and use less power. The vast majority of personal computers use only DRAM devices because of their lower cost. You benefit because they also provide more data storage per chip than SRAMs do. Some very high-performance PCs use some SRAM because they're faster. Some laptop computers use SRAM too, because they use less power and the laptop's battery lasts longer.

You may hear the term CMOS RAM used in connection with your PC. This is unfortunate, because CMOS does not really describe what the RAM chip does. It stands for *complementary metal-oxide semiconductor,* which describes how it is made. Many people use the term CMOS RAM to describe one particular memory chip inside AT-class computers. This is especially ironic, because most of the chips inside AT-class machines are all manufactured with the CMOS process. What people are referring to when they say this is a special SRAM in the computer with its own battery to keep it "alive" when the power is turned off. This will be covered in more detail in Chapter 8, "Serious Modifications."

A third kind of RAM chip that is just becoming popular is called *flash memory.* A flash memory chip works somewhat like a DRAM or a SRAM, but with a big advantage. Flash RAMs do not forget what you were working on when your computer is turned off. That means that any data on your computer will still be intact after the power is turned off and back on, even if you never stored it on a disk.

In fact, flash memories are being used primarily as alternatives to disk drives in some computers. Because flash memory chips are not nearly as fast as DRAMs or SRAMs, they make better disks than memory. Compared to a normal, mechanical disk drive, flash memory uses less power and takes up less space. Both of these abilities make flash memory chips very attractive to laptop computer makers.

ROM   The other kind of memory besides RAM is ROM. ROM stands for *read-only memory*. As the name might imply, your computer cannot write information into a ROM chip. What good is a memory chip that you can't store anything into?

The answer is that the term "read-only" memory isn't really true. A more accurate description would be "write once" memory. Data can only be written into a ROM chip one time. After that, it can only be read back out. No changes are allowed. This might be compared to a stone tablet, where a scribe might chisel something into it for all to read (but that no one can alter).

The major advantage of ROM chips is that they do not forget when the power is turned off, like DRAMs and SRAMs do. Anything written into a ROM will still be there after the power is turned off and back on again. This makes them invaluable devices for certain uses. In particular, your computer executes its very first instructions from a program stored in ROM chips every time you turn it on.

As with RAMs, there are two types of ROMs. They are called *PROMs* and *EPROMs*. In both cases, the "P" stands for programmable. This is somewhat of a misnomer, because ROMs cannot be written into, or programmed, by the user. The programming here refers to loading the chip with information at the factory. For EPROMs, the "E" stands for erasable. EPROM devices can be erased and programmed again. This procedure requires special programming equipment and a strong source of ultraviolet light—not something you're likely to do yourself. Nonetheless, these are terms you may hear, so it pays to know what they mean.

Built-in I/O Devices

A microprocessor is used to run programs, and the memory is used to store data. The third major piece of a computer is its input and output circuitry. Without input and output (or simply, I/O) you could never get any information into your computer or receive anything back out. I/O devices include the keyboard, disk drives, serial and parallel communications ports, and so on.

Most of these I/O circuits will reside on add-in expansion boards, covered later in this chapter. In the first PCs, nearly all of the I/O circuitry was on removable expansion boards. This had both good and bad points. On the one hand, it took up a lot of extra space. If all of the available expansion slots were occupied with expansion boards for necessary features like disk I/O, serial I/O, parallel I/O and video, there was no room left for optional features.

On the other hand, by moving most of the I/O functions to expansion boards, you could customize your computer almost any way you wanted. If you didn't like your disk controller or your video controller, you could remove it and replace it with another one. This ability to expand and upgrade is what made the PC as popular as it is (and what this book is all about).

PC makers are always striving to make their computers smaller, lighter, and less expensive. One of the trends that is developing because of this is a shift away from using expansion boards for most I/O functions, placing them on the motherboard instead. Again, there are good and bad points to this strategy. The PCs do, in fact, get lighter and smaller. In some ways, they can also run faster when functions like disk I/O are closer to the CPU.

The downside is that a PC with several I/O functions built in as part of its motherboard is inherently less expandable. For example, if your video controller is built in, you have no choice but to use that video format. To be fair, some computers do allow you to disable the onboard I/O functions and replace them with a traditional expansion board, but then you lose the advantages of having a built-in system.

What appears to be happening is that certain common, uncontroversial functions more and more frequently are built onto the motherboard. Other features that are not as "generic" are left off to let the user decide what kind to install. Disk control, serial communications, and parallel ports are commonly built into the motherboard of a PC. Video controllers are sometimes on, sometimes not. Functions like a modem or voice synthesis seldom are built in.

Power Supply

Your computer's power supply converts your house current (110 volts in North America) to the voltages that your computer needs to run. This is a completely self-contained unit, with no adjustments and no really interesting features.

Power supplies are installed in the system unit and come in several power ratings. That means different power supplies are designed to provide different quantities of electricity. Power supply prices range from $60 to $100 and up. You will probably stay with the same power supply for a long time. Figure 2-3 shows an overhead view of an open system unit. The power supply is located in the upper-right corner.

Floppy Disk Drives

There are two basic kinds of disk drives: floppy disk drives and hard disk drives. Both perform the same basic function, but go about it in different ways. Disk drives are the permanent storage of your computer. Your PC uses its memory (described earlier) to work on your data, but it must use the disk drives to store the data before you turn the power off.

Floppy disk drives are less expensive than hard disk drives, but they also store less data and operate more slowly. Floppy drives are currently much

Figure 2-3.   *The interior of an AT-style system unit*

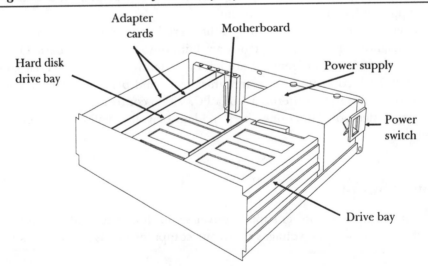

2

more common. When personal computers were new, all PCs had one or two floppy disk drives. These were the only permanent storage available.

Floppy disk drives are used to read and write to floppy disks, of course. Floppy disks (also called removable disks, or diskettes) come in two basic sizes. Although the outside of a floppy disk is square, the disk itself is round, like a record, and it turns inside this square cover. The two sizes are 5 1/4-inch diameter disks and 3 1/2-inch diameter disks.

You may change your existing floppy disk drive or add additional floppy disk drives as a possible upgrade. It is permissible (and also common) to mix 5 1/4-inch and 3 1/2-inch drives in one computer. Floppy disk drives also come in two basic "heights." The height of a disk drive has absolutely no bearing on its performance or its capabilities. It is just another example of the endless quest to miniaturize computers. Figure 2-4 shows the location and general appearance of full- and half-height floppy disk drives. The full-height drive takes up the entire space allowed for it. Half-height drives take half of the space—hence their name. Drives cost about $100 each.

Figure 2-4.   *The two types of floppy disk drives*

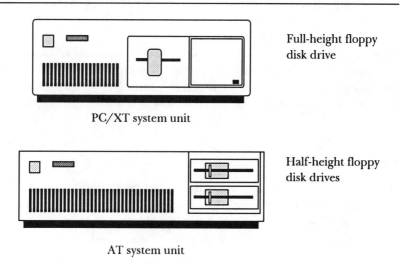

PC/XT system unit

Full-height floppy
disk drive

AT system unit

Half-height floppy
disk drives

Hard Disk Drives

Hard disk drives are the high-performance cousins of floppy disk drives. They are much faster, and they hold much more data, but they also cost more and use more power.

Hard disk drives read and write data to hard disks. These disks are permanently mounted inside the hard disk drive and cannot be removed like floppy disks. This is how they achieve their superior performance. Since a hard disk drive is a sealed unit, the mechanical tolerances can be much tighter and the disk spins much faster. Hard disk drives are also called fixed disk drives, or Winchester drives.

Note

The name "Winchester" doesn't come from the inventor of the hard disk drive, but from the man who built and sold thousands of Winchester repeating rifles in the days of the Old West. When hard disks were still new, a primary goal was to build one that could hold 30 megabytes of data and access it in 30 milliseconds. That project became known as the 30/30 project—the name of the famous rifle of a hundred years before.

Figure 2-5 shows the location and general appearance of a full-height hard disk. Hard disks also come in half-height versions. Hard disks come in capacities from 5 megabytes to a whopping 1600 megabytes (1.6 Gigabytes). Prices range from $200 to $2500 and up. The price is determined mostly by the storage capacity of the disk. Installing a new hard disk is one of the most likely upgrades you will make.

Note

Both floppy disk drives and hard disks require an adapter card called a disk controller. This controller board plugs into an expansion slot on the motherboard and is connected to the drives with cables. Controllers usually have provisions for handling two floppy disk drives and two hard disk drives.

Cables

Every part of your computer is provided with connectors and cables that allow the various parts to be connected together. External cables connect the computer to the printer and the display adapter to the display monitor. Internal cables connect the floppy disk drives and hard disk drives to the

Figure 2-5. *The Micropolis 1598-15 1.2 Gigabyte hard drive (Photograph courtesy of Micropolis Corporation)*

controller. Each individual cable will be covered in more depth in the sections on these devices.

Expansion Boards

The five or eight connectors on the motherboard (Figure 2-2) and the associated openings in the rear of the case (Figure 2-6) are called *adapter slots* or *expansion slots.* These let you expand the functions of your computer. Many of the upgrades you will make are accomplished by plugging an adapter card into these motherboard connectors or slots.

Figure 2-6.   *The rear view of a system unit*

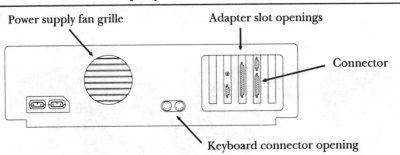

An adapter bracket attached to the adapter card matches the opening in the rear of the computer case allowing connectors on the adapter card to come out at the back of the computer. The connectors at the back provide connections to display monitors, printers, and other devices outside the system unit.

Keyboard

You use the keyboard to enter commands that tell your computer what to do, to enter text when using word processors, and generally to control the computer. You do not need to be a touch-typist to use a computer keyboard.

The Monitor

The display system consists of a monitor and a display adapter. The monitor is much like a television screen; it is your window into your system. The cost of a monitor can range from under $50 to over $3000. Even though the monitor is what you look at, the real work of displaying words and pictures is done by your video display adapter (one of the expansion boards described earlier). The cost of a display adapter can run from less than a hundred to several hundred dollars.

Upgrading your computer's video quality may require a new monitor, or a new video adapter, or both. Enhancing video quality is one of the most commonly performed of all PC upgrades, and it is covered in Chapter 4, "Simple Additions," and Chapter 5, "Adding Expansion Boards."

Printer and Other Peripherals

All of the components described so far have been either inside the PC system unit or required add-ons, like the keyboard and the monitor. There are many other devices you can add to your computer system besides these. You will probably want a printer if you don't already have one. You may want a plotter instead, in addition to the printer. Modems are used for communicating and exchanging data with other computers. All of these devices, and others, are collectively called *peripherals,* because they are on the periphery, or outside, of your PC system unit. Peripherals will be covered in Chapter 4, "Simple Additions."

Summary

In this chapter we've given you some very general information about modern desktop and laptop computers. You've learned a number of new words and should be prepared to continue with the assurance that you can identify your system unit, display, keyboard, floppy and hard disk drives, and the other major parts of your computers.

You should also have a better understanding of the various parts contained in the system unit, including the power supply, motherboard, and adapter or expansion slots, all of which will be covered in greater detail in later chapters.

3

Taking a Look Inside Your PC

In the last chapter, you were introduced to the various components that make up your PC. In this chapter, you'll actually open your system unit to see what these components look like. If opening your system makes you a bit apprehensive, don't worry—if you've ever had to put together a swing set, by comparison the operation in this chapter will be a breeze.

The goal of this chapter is not to explain the function of each component, but rather to make sure that you can identify each component. The emphasis is on recognition rather than comprehension.

Before you actually open the system, you'll look at the procedures we'll follow, see what tools you'll need, and learn a few safety measures.

Safety

Before you learn about protecting your PC, you should know about protecting yourself. Good safety rules and practices are fundamental to any new endeavor.

The good news is that there is almost nothing about your personal computer that can hurt you. Apart from dropping heavy equipment on your foot, you're a lot safer working on a PC than, say, a toaster. Even though personal computers are electrical appliances, they use such small amounts of electricity that you can reach inside without fear of electrical shock. In fact, your PC is much more liable to be harmed from a shock than you are (as you'll see in the upcoming section, "Antistatic Precautions").

There are two notable exceptions to this rule, however. The first is your computer's power supply. The power supply converts the 110 volts of electricity from your wall outlet to the low voltage your computer needs. That's right—your computer only needs low voltage, which is why there is little danger of electrical shock. The 100-volts, which *is* dangerous to you, is isolated inside the metal box surrounding your power supply. As long as you don't poke around inside the power supply or try to disassemble it, you are safe from danger. You should never tamper inside a power supply; there is no need to do so.

The second exception is your computer's monitor, or screen. This has a glass picture tube like a television set's (also called a cathode-ray tube, or a CRT). To create images, a strong stream of electrons is sprayed at the front of the tube from an electronic "gun" at the back. A very high voltage is required to make the electrons jump across this gap. Several thousand volts is common.

For this reason, you should *not* open your monitor's case. (There is nothing inside it that you could fix anyway.) The only instance where the case may need to be opened is when the access holes do not align properly with the monitor's video control knobs. Even here, you should have a trained professional make the adjustments; don't try to do it yourself.

Procedures

If you've never worked inside of a computer before, there are some rules you should know and habits you should form. There's nothing particularly difficult about working inside your PC, but there are some things that might not be obvious to you if you've never done it before. The following sections give you some pointers.

In the later chapters of this book, you'll find specific instructions for implementing many different kinds of upgrades. These supplement what you'll learn here. Be sure you have a good grasp of these basics before continuing on. You may want to refer back to this section from time to time to refresh your memory.

Make Notes

Keep a notepad and pen handy, so you'll always be able to take notes as you upgrade. Pencils are not recommended, because the pencil lead (really graphite and glue) is an electrical conductor. You don't want pieces of conductive pencil rolling around inside your computer.

You should always note (on paper) the position of anything you're about to move *before* you move it. For example, record any jumpers you're about to change, cables you want to remove, or a disk drive you're about to pull out. If you don't record changes before you make them, you'll find that even basic implements that you thought you knew will suddenly look foreign.

If you're really concerned about forgetting where something went, and you have an instant camera, take a picture! Right after you open up your computer's case but before you remove anything, take a quick snapshot. That way, there'll be no question about where a specific cable or component should go.

Antistatic Precautions

Some of the electronic devices in your computer are sensitive to extremely small amounts of electricity. That is partly what makes them so fast, and why they use so little power. (Battery-operated laptop computers, in particular, use a lot of these micro-power components.) On the other hand, it also means that these components can easily be overloaded and damaged by more electricity than they can handle.

When you walk across a carpet or pet a cat, you can easily generate hundreds or thousands of volts of static electricity, without even being aware of it. Anyone who has ever touched a metal object afterwards (like a doorknob) or another person knows hows painful this experience can be. This same charge can wreak havoc on your computer.

Before touching anything inside your computer you must be sure to discharge any static electricity in your body (and you should do this periodically as you work—every few minutes is a good rule of thumb).

You can discharge any electrical charge simply by placing your hand on a grounded metal object, such as the computer case, before reaching in. A radiator will also work, and so will most electrical appliances with metal cases, such as a table lamp or a stereo receiver. Better still, try to minimize the amount of static electricity you generate in the first place. Avoid knit or wool sweaters, fur or furry animals, walking on carpeted surfaces, and rubber or plastic toys or balloons. Once you've discharged yourself of static, try not to shuffle around any more than necessary.

Many computer supply stores sell special antistatic materials. Plastic bags and foam can be made antistatic. Some antistatic bags are dyed pink so you can identify them as such. Other antistatic bags (and foam) are black because they are fabricated with plastic and carbon. These are often used for storing and shipping circuit boards. Save these bags if you get them. You can also save or buy antistatic foam. This looks like Styrofoam, but is usually black. The antistatic bags and foam make excellent work surfaces because they prevent static buildup in your equipment while you work. Always place ICs on antistatic foam or plastic, not directly on a tabletop.

Tools

For any kind of work, there are always appropriate tools. When you are working on your PC or installing some of the upgrades discussed in this book, you will need a few tools. Fortunately, none of them are very exotic or difficult to find or to use. You may already have everything you need.

If you don't have most of the tools described in the following sections, there are complete "computer handyman" tools kits available from computer stores and hardware stores. You might even get one free by subscribing to a magazine. Also, the Jensen Tools JTK-49 PC Workstation Kit or Specialized Products Company's SPC-250C Computer Technician Kit will provide most of the tools you will ever need.

Screwdrivers

You will require a Phillips-head #2 screwdriver. (Phillips-head screwdrivers are the ones with the cross-shaped end.) You'll also want a small flat-bladed screwdriver. If you have these two, you'll be able to perform most of the up-grades in this book.

Chip Puller

A chip puller is like a small U-shaped pair of tweezers. It is usually stamped out of aluminum and has curved hooks at the very ends to grab onto the end of integrated circuits in Dual In Line (DIP) packages. If you need to remove an IC from its socket on a PC board, these little things are invaluable. They are available from most computer supply stores, and generally cost about 79 cents. In lieu of a chip puller, a small, cheap flathead screwdriver with a three-inch blade can be used instead. All you have to do is bend the blade at about a quarter inch from the tip into a 90-degree angle. This makes an excellent tool to lever out almost any type of IC.

Cleaning Materials

Computers get dirty, too. While there are very few moving parts that dust and dirt can harm, accumulating too much dust can clog your PC's fan or air filter. That makes it hard to keep the insides cool, and your PC may overheat. A lot of dust buildup inside the computer can also cause erratic or intermittent electrical problems. You can use a small one- or two-inch paintbrush to brush dirt away. Any cheap one will do. Cotton swabs are also handy for cleaning dust from hard-to-reach places. A vacuum cleaner is another easy way to remove this dirt. Be careful with a full-sized house vacuum cleaner, though. Computer stores and catalogs sell tiny battery-operated vacuum cleaners especially for computers. These items are also good for cleaning excess toner dust from laser printers or photocopy machines.

The same places that sell the little vacuum cleaners will also offer canned compressed air at about $5 per can. These are just like aerosol cans of furniture polish or air freshener, but there's nothing in them—just air. Sure, it's a lot of money, but they can keep small parts clean. Be cautious with these, too, because they can blow dust and dirt into places they shouldn't be.

Paper Clip

Here's another wonderfully low-tech computer tool. When you need to change the position of one of those tiny little DIP switches, you're going to want one of these. Unbend the paper clip until it's straight, and use the end to poke the switches into place. Nothing else works quite as well.

Opening the Case

You're ready to open the case. There's nothing very strenuous or difficult about this, but you'll want to be sure you do it right.

Caution

Before you open your computer, always turn the power switch off and disconnect the power cord from the wall outlet. This is for your own safety and for the safety of your computer. Although 110-volt household power can be lethal, it is very unlikely that you would be shocked. The greater likelihood is that you could do serious damage to your computer when plugging in adapter boards or doing other things inside the system unit with the power on.

Not all computer companies make their cases the same way. Some cases unscrew from the back, some from the sides, and some have push buttons that open the case automatically. Most of them, though, are very much like IBM's original sheet-metal cases for the PC, XT, and AT computers. This section describes the procedures for opening and closing one of these.

After turning your computer off and removing the power cord, turn the system unit around so that you can see the back of it. Next, unplug any other cables that are plugged into your computer. You probably have at least one cable that leads from the system unit to your display monitor. You may also have a cable leading to your printer, or to a modem. If you have a mouse, unplug that as well. This might be a good place to use your notepad or instant camera so that you can put everything back in place later!

Find your Phillips-head screwdriver and look for five screws on the back of the case around the outside edge. There should be a screw at each of the four corners, and a fifth one at the top, near the center. See Figure 3-1. Remove these in any order you like but read the caution below first.

Caution

Be sure you only remove the screws around the very outside edge of the back side of the case. There will probably be other screws visible on the back of the case, too. Don't remove these! These "extra" screws scattered around the back side are probably holding your power supply in place. Use Figure 3-1 to make sure you're removing the correct screws.

After you've removed all of the appropriate screws, turn your computer around again so that you can reach the front. Grab the metal case, pull it toward you, and lift it up just a little. The sheet-metal cover should come loose with minimal effort. Don't pull it completely off yet.

There may be a small metal tab or tongue inside the metal cover at the very back. This is probably what the fifth screw was attached to. Be careful when removing the cover that you don't let this metal tab scrape anything inside your computer. Be especially watchful for cables. These are particularly

Figure 3-1. *Rear view of a system unit showing the screws that hold on the cover (1) and the power supply (2)*

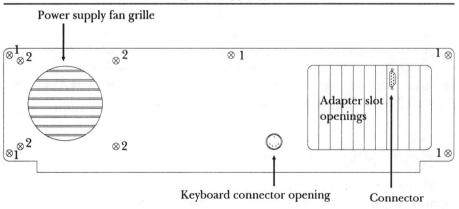

prone to snagging. You may also have to pull the sides of the case away a bit to free the cover.

After you've removed the cover, set it aside on the floor. It's best to just lay it flat, rather than standing it up on one end, so that it doesn't fall over later on.

The procedure given here for opening your case should cover the majority of PC-compatible computers available. If your machine is different, you may have to refer to your owners' manual (always a good source of information) for guidance. The Enlight 6600 case has screws at the back. Unscrewing these allows a panel to swing out and off. The front of the case "pops" off allowing access to the drive bays. The Enlight cases (covered in later chapters) usually have three or five screws. Some have hinged covers and some have pop-off front bezels. So, again, the best source of information about cover removal will be the manufacturer of the computer or the store where you bought your machine.

If you'd like to close your case now and come back to this later, see the section at the end of the chapter about closing your case.

Identification

The first step towards getting to know your PC better is learning to identify its parts. Since the system unit that you just opened is where most of your upgrades will be made, without a little bit of background you're liable to get stuck when you're ready to remove some devices, replace something, or set a switch. You have already been introduced to the major components in Chapter 2, "Anatomy of a Personal Computer System." It would probably be helpful to take a quick look at the layout of the major parts again (see Figure 3-2) now that you have opened up your case.

Reviewing the Components

If you have the computer facing you, the power supply is the metal box in the far-right corner. The power supply furnishes power to all internal

Figure 3-2.   *The interior of a system unit*

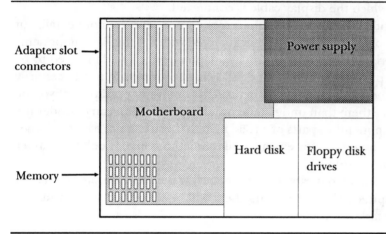

components. Two multi-colored cables run from the power supply to the motherboard in the bottom of the case. Several other cables are attached to disk drives and you will probably find one, two, or more that are not attached.

The floppy disk drives are usually located at the front right in most modern computers and the hard disk drive is located near the center of the system unit. The hard disk drive usually sits farther back in the drive bay than the floppy disk drives.

The motherboard is the large printed circuit board covering one-half to two-thirds of the bottom of the case. It's located on the bottom left and will usually have five or eight printed circuit edge connectors (you'll read about these later in this chapter) near the back of the case. Each of these connectors is associated with an opening in the back of the case. The openings are covered by a metal plate unless an adapter card is installed.

One of the adapter cards plugged into one of these edge connectors will probably have flat, ribbon cables connected to the adapter card on one end. The other end of these cables will be connected to the floppy disk and hard disk drives. This adapter card is called a *disk controller*. This card is required unless your controller is built into the motherboard.

The other required card is the *display adapter.* This adapter will have a connector to which the display cable is connected.

Later chapters will cover all of the major components in more detail, but for now, let's concentrate on getting acquainted with the smaller components on the motherboard and on the display adapters, which seldom need to be replaced except for upgrading. The following sections will not necessarily explain *what* these components do because it is more important that you be able to recogize them than understand how they work. You can consider the following components as parts of a road map that you can use to locate other components. You might, for example, see something like, "Look for jumper J3 located near resistor R11."

The components described in the next few sections are pieces that all personal computers share. Knowing them will be helpful to you no matter what upgrade task you undertake.

Printed Circuit Board

A printed circuit board is a very basic part of virtually all electronic devices anywhere in the world. Computers, video cassette recorders, radios, and televisions all rely on printed circuit boards. A *printed circuit board,* or PCB, is a flat piece of fiberglass with copper wires etched into it. The fiberglass board is usually green, and rectangular in shape. It acts as a solid platform onto which electronic components are mounted. The wires buried within the PC board are very small and slender. They carry electronic signals between the various components soldered to the PCB. A printed circuit board is usually filled with many very small holes. These holes are drilled to allow the pins of the electronic components to pass through. The holes are then filled with solder, which is a combination of tin and lead. This combination of metals melts very easily, but stays strong and solid at room temperature. Solder is used as a combination glue and electrical conductor. It holds the components in place, and it also allows the flow of electricity between components.

A printed circuit board may be very large, like the motherboard in your PC. It may also be very small, say, about the size of a business card. A PCB may have many electronic components soldered to it, or only a few.

Integrated Circuits

The electronic devices you will most commonly find soldered to a printed circuit board are the integrated circuits, or ICs, as you'll remember from Chapter 2. Integrated circuits are found in virtually all electronic devices everywhere. There are thousands upon thousands of different kinds of ICs made to perform all kinds of functions. Some are large and some are small. Some cost only a few pennies apiece, while others cost several hundred dollars.

ICs come in standard shapes and sizes so most of them look pretty similar with some slight differences depending upon their functions. Figure 3-3 illustrates a few typical-looking integrated circuits. Most are rectangular or square, and are usually black or violet. They should also have some letters or numbers printed on them (in very small print, of course!). All ICs have at least one row of metal "legs" sprouting out one edge. Many have two parallel rows. These legs are generally referred to as pins, and they conduct electricity into and out of the integrated circuit. Inside the black plastic case of the IC, invisible to you, is the silicon *chip* that actually does the work. The black plastic outside is just a holder: the real "brains" of an IC are even much smaller than this.

Figure 3-3.   *Examples of typical integrated circuits*

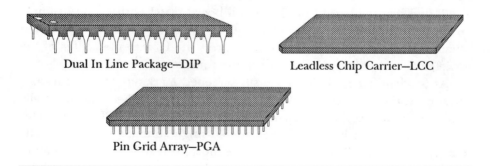

Dual In Line Package—DIP   Leadless Chip Carrier—LCC

Pin Grid Array—PGA

Orienting ICs

On circuit boards, ICs will be identified with a silk-screened designator "U" followed by a number. These designators are used to locate and identify parts on the circuit board.

Each of the metal pins on an IC is actually an electrical wire that runs inside the plastic or ceramic case to the silicon chip inside. That means that even though every pin looks the same, each one is different as far as the chip is concerned. Therefore, you must be careful about how an IC is placed on a circuit board. If you put an IC in backwards, you will almost certainly ruin it. Sometimes, you may damage other devices on the printed circuit board as well.

Fortunately, there is a simple way to tell which way an IC should be installed. A look at a DIP socket and the associated IC that plugs into it will quickly reveal that there are two ways to plug in the IC—only one way is right. If you're an engineer you'll know how to count pins and how to find pin 1, but for upgrading purposes you don't really need this information. Some of the literature you read might also refer to pin 1, but the following information is all you really need.

The motherboard or expansion board into which you will be installing ICs has a silk-screened legend imprinted on it. The outline for a DIP is a rectangular box with a half-moon indent on one end. The socket will also frequently have a half-moon cutout on only one end. If you examine the DIP closely, you'll find that it also has a half-moon cutout molded into the case. Just match the cutouts. It's as simple as that.

For other types of ICs (like PLCCs and PGAs), which come in square packages, you will find that one corner is unmistakably cut off or beveled. You'll find that the legend on the circuit board matches this shape. Simply match the chopped-off corner of the IC to the chopped-off corner of the square legend on the circuit board and press the IC into the center of the socket, unless there are instructions to the contrary.

As to identifying ICs from the silk-screened markings on the package, you'll need the three-volume IC Master. Don't despair, because you really don't need to interpret these markings. Devices like CPUs and math coprocessors are packaged in boxes or sold singly so that you know exactly what you're getting. The other ICs you're most likely to handle are memory chips, and you'll pretty much have to depend on your memory chip supplier to provide you with the proper chips to upgrade your memory. In fact, the supplier of your computer or motherboard should be able to tell you which memory chips to buy if it's not mentioned in the manuals that come with your computer or motherboard.

Resistors

Resistors are usually small cylindrical shapes with a wire coming out each end, as shown here:

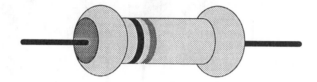

Electricity flows in one end and out the other. Unlike the more complicated ICs, resistors can be installed in either direction. The electricity will flow through them either way.

Because resistor bodies are so small, there is no way to mark identifying information on them. Many years ago, the resistor color code was developed to identify hard-to-mark devices like resistors. Each colored stripe around a resistor represents a particular number, from 0 to 9. Taken all together, the colored stripes tell a technician everything there is to know about that resistor. Fortunately, you won't have to learn this skill at all; you only need to recognize them occasionally. They are identified on circuit boards with an "R" followed by a number.

Resistors can also be packaged together into one larger package. This makes kind of an *integrated resistor* or a *resistor network*. Sometimes these are also called *terminators* or *termination resistors*.

Capacitors

Capacitors are energy-storage devices. Used with resistors, they serve mainly to smooth the voltages supplied to circuits in your computer. Capacitors are designated on circuit boards with a "C" followed by a number.

Capacitors usually have two pins. A small capacitor looks like a flat round disk, with the two wires extending from one side. Larger capacitors look like tiny cans with plastic sleeves. These have both pins at one end. Two examples of capacitors are shown here:

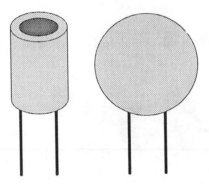

Although in this book you will not have the opportunity to install or remove capacitors, it helps to be able to recognize them.

Jumpers

Sometimes the engineer who designs a printed circuit board and selects the ICs, resistors, and capacitors to put on it will build in one or more options. These options might allow you to select between several different modes, speeds, colors, and so on. Board designers do this because they don't always know in advance how the board will be used; building in a variety of options guarantees that the board can be used optimally.

The most common way to select among these options is with a jumper. A *jumper,* or *shunt,* is simply a short piece of wire that you use to make an electrical connection. A jumper allows you to make a connection on the board without using solder. Jumpers are easy to remove and change. They are covered with plastic and often brightly colored, so they are also easy and safe to use.

In Figure 3-4 there are some jumpers shown on the PC board. The board has jumper pins, or posts, sticking straight up. A jumper is used to connect two of these pins together. By simply sliding the jumper down over two

Figure 3-4.   *Jumpers on a PC board*

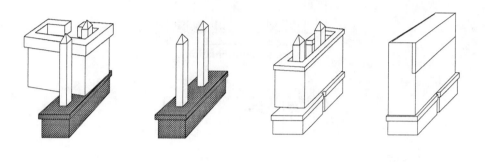

neighboring pins, you can connect them together. A metal clip inside the jumper conducts electricity between the two pins, and it also holds the jumper snugly in place. You can remove the jumper simply by sliding it back off again. The designator for jumpers is usually "J" followed by a number.

DIP Switches

Another way of selecting options is to turn tiny little switches on and off. For many years, electronic manufacturers have been able to make switches small enough to be mounted on a PC board just like ICs. In fact, they are just the same size and shape. For this reason, they are called DIP switches, because they come in a Dual In Line Package, just like many ICs do, as in Figure 3-5.

It is easy to pick out DIP switches. They are usually colored blue or red. If not, they're often black with tiny white switches, prompting some people to call them *mouse pianos*. The switches are spaced at 10 switches to the inch, so it's possible to get a lot of switches into a little space.

Each switch has two positions, on and off. But because the DIP switches are so small, it's difficult to label them. Some may have the word "ON" printed along one side, or you may see "OPEN." Open is the same as off. You might

Figure 3-5.   *DIP switches*

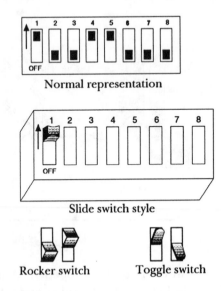

Normal representation

Slide switch style

Rocker switch   Toggle switch

also find your DIP switches simply labeled with a "1" and/or a "0." If so, 1 is the same as on, and 0 means off. No matter how they're labeled, all the switches in a DIP switch group will turn on and off the same way. In other words, what is "ON" for one will be "ON" for the others as well. Switches usually have "S" or "SW" as designators on circuit boards.

Cables

Obviously, there are a lot of electrical signals traveling back and forth inside a personal computer. Most of these signals travel through the copper wires on the printed circuit boards. But if two components are not mounted on the same circuit board, how can they "communicate" between themselves?

How can electrical signals travel between a floppy disk drive and the ICs on the motherboard that control it? To do this you need cables.

When a lot of wires need to travel from one place in your PC to another place, and they can't travel through a printed circuit board, they are grouped together into a cable. One type, called a *ribbon cable,* is a bunch of separate wires arranged in a flat, flexible cable, like a ribbon. Ribbon cables are usually either all gray or they are rainbow-colored.

While the rainbow-colored ones are certainly prettier, they both work equally well. There may be as few as two wires in a ribbon cable, or as many as 64. Each wire is separate and insulated from all the others. They are merely grouped together for convenience. Ribbon cables are *not* bi-directional. Just as with IC packages, if you plug a ribbon cable in backwards you can damage something—ribbon cable can only be connected one way. Learning to identify pin 1 on a ribbon cable is quite easy. If it's a gray-colored ribbon cable, there will always be one wire colored red or some other contrasting color. The red wire will always be on the outside of the cable (that is, at the end of the row). The red wire is wire number 1. The wire that is next to it is the second wire, and so on.

If you come across a rainbow-colored cable (they are slowly being phased out), notice the pattern of colors. It should contain exactly ten different colors. If there are more than ten wires in the ribbon cable, you should also notice that the colors repeat after every ten wires, and always in the same pattern. Usually, the pattern will start with a black wire, and then a brown own, and then a red one, and so on through all ten colors. If so, the black wire is wire number 1. If not, you'll have to look at the connector at the end of the wire.

The connectors at the end of most ribbon cables have two rows of holes that exactly match up with a row of pins somewhere else in your computer. If you look near the corners of these connectors, you will notice a small triangle, or some other kind of mark. This indicates where pin 1 of the cable connector is.

Diodes

A *diode* is a small cylindrical device that looks very much like a resistor. Diodes don't have the colored stripes that resistors have, though. Diodes are either made of clear glass or they are black. Either way, there should be one stripe running all the way around it near one end. The designator for diodes is "D" or "ZD".

Light-emitting Diodes

As mentioned briefly in Chapter 2, "Anatomy of a Personal Computer System," light-emitting diodes, or LEDs, are special diodes that light up when electricity passes through them. As such, they do exactly the same thing that a small light bulb does, but they are far more reliable than a light bulb, and use less electricity. Furthermore, they don't get hot, and they come in pretty colors. LEDs are used extensively in computers. Your floppy disk drive probably has a red or green LED that lights up every time you use a floppy disk. You may also have one in your hard disk as well.

Crystals and Oscillators

Computers, like watches, are precision instruments, and they need a good crystal to keep them running smoothly. *Crystals* are naturally occurring minerals that have an interesting property. If you apply an electric current to a crystal, it will vibrate by a very tiny amount, but at a very steady rate. The rate at which a crystal vibrates, or *oscillates,* can be controlled by cutting it to a specific size or shape. Crystals have an "X" for a designator as a rule, though others may be used.

Computer systems need an accurate and reliable oscillator like this to keep them running. Your PC is bound to have at least one crystal in it. Crystals are mounted in small metal cans, with two or more wires coming out of them. The following illustration shows two kinds of crystals:

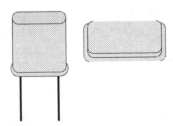

You shouldn't need to add or replace crystals in this book.

3

Connectors

There are many kinds of connectors in your PC because there are many things to connect to. The following sections look at four of the most common connectors. You will need to be familiar with these because you'll have many opportunities to plug and unplug things from these kinds of connectors.

Edge Connectors

An *edge connector* is used to hold the expansion cards in your computer. Expansion cards will be covered in detail in Chapter 5, "Adding Expansion Boards." An edge connector allows you to connect one PC board directly to another PC board. One example is the group of 5, 8, or more edge connectors on the motherboard into which expansion boards, such as disk controllers and display adapters, are plugged.

Edge connectors provide a narrow slot into which you insert the expansion board. Inside the connector, surrounding the slot, are many spring-loaded metal fingers. These hold the expansion board in place by squeezing it, and make electrical contact at the same time. To remove the expansion board, simply pull it out of the edge connector.

Edge connectors have been criticized because they become unreliable as they age. They tend to wear out as board after board is inserted and removed over and over. Modern connectors can stand many changes, but you should avoid switching your expansion boards around any more than necessary.

D-Sub Connectors

While edge connectors are found mainly inside your PC, you will find D-Sub connectors on the outside. Nearly every PC has at least a few of these. *D-Sub connectors* come with 9, 15, or 25 pins and are used for serial interfaces, parallel interfaces, video, mouse, and many others.

You will see the following connectors most frequently:

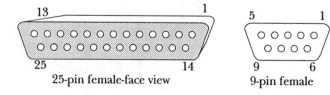

25-pin female-face view   9-pin female

The name of this connector comes from the protective cover around the outside, which is shaped like an elongated letter D. This prevents plugging a connector in backwards. The "sub" part comes from "subminiature."

The pins in a D-Sub connector are arranged in two or three parallel rows. Again, finding pin 1 is not always easy. Look for a small "1" printed near one of the corners of the connector. If you can't find it, you should refer to Appendix C, "Connector Reference." It has a summary of connector styles and numbering patterns.

Molex Connector

The Molex connector is named after the company that developed it. While there are now many companies that manufacture this kind of connector, the name has stuck. Molex connectors are used for relatively heavy-duty purposes. For your PC, this means supplying power to the hard and floppy disk drives. An end view of a typical Molex connector that might be used to connect a floppy drive to the power supply is shown here:

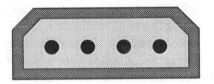

You'll find this connector inside your PC.

DIN Connector

The DIN designation stands for Deutsche Industrie Normale, and German standards bureau. There are actually many kinds of DIN-approved connectors, but there are one or two kinds in particular that you are likely to find in connection with personal computers. The one you are most likely to encounter is the keyboard connector, which uses five pins, as shown here:

Like most other kinds of connectors covered here, you cannot insert a DIN connector the wrong way. The metal shield around it is not symmetrical, so there is only one way it will fit in.

Closing the Case

When you put the cover back on, you should pull the sides apart a bit, place it over the system unit, and slide it backwards into place. Again, pay special attention to the metal tab at the rear of the case so that it doesn't snag anything. Put all of the screws back in with a screwdriver. The screws don't have to be very tight—just tight enough so that the cover won't rattle.

Summary

After covering the material in this chapter, you should be able to identify just about anything inside your PC. You should also have a good idea what tools you need to work on your computer, and how to go about opening up your computer in preparation for installing or removing circuit boards and disk drives. In the next chapter, you will learn more about other devices you can attach to your computer, such as printers and scanners. You will also find additional information on keyboards and displays.

4

Simple Additions

In this chapter, you will be introduced to some of the simplest and most basic additions you can make to your PC. That doesn't mean that these are trivial or useless alterations, though. On the contrary, the upgrades described in this chapter are among the most common and useful additions that you can make. You will learn how to add a printing device to your computer, or how to add a new keyboard or a mouse. If you are interested in upgrading your PC to a color display or adding graphics, you will find that covered here as well.

Each of the sections in this chapter deals with a particular kind of upgrade (printers, scanners, and so on). It is not necessary to read all the way through each section if it covers something you're not interested in right now. Feel free to skip ahead to the section that covers the particular upgrade or addition you have in mind.

Adding a Printer or Plotter

Nearly every PC needs a printer at some time, and there are many different kinds of printers, just as there are many different uses for them.

Some printers print very quickly, while others are quite slow. Some printers can print in multiple colors, while others print only in black. The quality of the print can differ, too, with some printers producing coarse, grainy output while others produce pages good enough to bind into a book.

The kind of printer you choose depends on what you plan to use it for, and how much you are willing to spend. There are many trade-offs that must be considered, and choices to be made. The sections that follow will give you a good idea of what choices are available to you today. With this as a guide, you can make better-educated decisions about buying and installing a printer.

There are some words that you are bound to come across when you are shopping for a printer, or comparing printer features. Some of the more useful ones are covered here.

A *character* is any printable symbol. Each of the letters of the alphabet is a character. Punctuation marks and numbers are also characters. Your printer may also be capable of printing unusual characters such as Greek letters or mathematical symbols.

A *typeface* describes the overall style of the characters. For example, the Old English script at the top of Figure 4-1 is obviously different than the print at the bottom. These are two examples of different typefaces. A typeface is a style that covers a complete set of characters—that is, the whole alphabet plus numbers and punctuation marks. Many typefaces are copyrighted and have special names like Times or Helvetica. There are typeface artists whose entire job it is to create pleasing typefaces.

Figure 4-1.   *Examples of typefaces*

𝕿𝖍𝖎𝖘 𝖎𝖘 𝖆 𝖙𝖊𝖘𝖙

and this is another

Pitch describes how far apart the characters are spaced. If you can fit 10 characters across in one inch of paper, then you are printing at 10 pitch.

A point is 1/72nd of an inch. Points are used to measure the height of a character.

A *pica* is 12 points. There are 6 picas to the inch.

A *font* is a particular style of typeface printed at a particular size (measured in points or picas). For example, 10-point Helvetica is one font, 12-point Helvetica is another, and 12-point Times Roman is a third.

A typeface is *fixed pitch* if all of the characters take up the same amount of space. For example, a typewriter prints with a fixed-pitch font—a capital letter M takes up the same amount of space as a small letter i. If you print several lines of text, one above the other, you can line up the characters vertically with a ruler, as shown here:

```
This is an example of a fixed-pitch typeface.
Notice how the characters are vertically aligned.
```

A *proportional* typeface has characters of different widths. Most serious publications—newspapers, books, and magazines—use proportional fonts. Proportional fonts are much more pleasing to read, but more difficult to print by mechanical means. The text in this book uses proportional fonts.

Kerning is the process of adjusting individual letters to reduce "white space" between them. The uppercase letters W and A are frequently used as examples of kerning. Without kerning, the space between these letters is relatively large. To improve appearance, the W and A are moved closer together. Packages like Ventura Publisher and PageMaker provide kerning tables of letter pairs to indicate the proper kerned spacing.

In the sections that follow, the various type of printers will be grouped according to the way they work. This might seem like an overly technical way to organize things, but you will see that the way a printer works affects the quality of the printing it produces.

Dot Matrix Printers

A dot matrix printer makes a good, low-cost general-purpose printer for most user's needs. They are neither very slow nor very expensive. The quality of the print they produce is, while not the best, sufficient for most purposes.

Like most other printers, a dot matrix printer prints one letter at a time, from left to right. When it finishes a line, it rolls the paper up one row, and starts printing the next row—very much like you would type a letter on a typewriter, but much faster.

There is a significant difference between a dot matrix printer and a typewriter, though. It has to do with the way the printer makes each letter. With a typewriter, there are little metal hammers for each letter of the alphabet, number, and mark of punctuation. Each hammer has the shape of a letter carved into it, and when it hits the paper, it leaves an image of the letter on your paper. In computer circles, this image is known as a *fully formed character.*

A dot matrix printer doesn't use hammers. Instead, it has a row of very fine wires with their ends pointed at the paper. The wires are arranged in a vertical row. To print a letter, the wires stick out briefly, making a row of vertical dots on the paper. Then the set of wires is moved a little bit to the right, and another row of dots is printed. This continues about five or six more times, until a single letter has been printed. The result is a very readable, if somewhat grainy, letter. The print is very easy to read, but it is obvious that it was made on a dot matrix printer. You probably would not want to use print of this quality for sending resumes, or for writing letters to important business contacts.

A 9-wire printer might form the letter C like this:

In Figure 4-2, position 1, wires 3, 4, 5, and 6 are activated to print the parts of the character shown. The printhead is then moved 1/72nd of an inch to the next position (2) and wires 2 and 7 are activated to print the next part. This continues until the complete character is formed.

While the output is not refined, dot matrix printers are among the very fastest printers available. They are also the least expensive. Between these two important considerations, dot matrix printers have become very common, and are often the printer of choice for first-time computer users. There are many companies that manufacture dot matrix printers, and prices are very competitive.

Figure 4-2. *Forming a character*

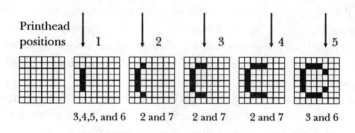

In order to combat the poor print quality that dot matrix printers produce, many printer companies developed better quality printing mechanisms in the mid-1980s. These new printers still use a matrix of dots to print, but they use more dots per square inch to improve the overall quality of the output.

Inexpensive dot matrix printers have 9 wires (pins) in a vertical row. The newer generation of printers has 16 or even 24 pins in the same amount of space. With a 24-pin dot matrix printer, it is very difficult to make out the individual dots. The printed page gives the appearance of having been typed on a typewriter. This is called *near letter quality* printing, meaning that the printed output is nearly good enough to use for writing important letters.

The fonts and other characteristics of the text are defined in the printer electronics so, again, you are restricted in the range of character sizes and typefaces you can use when the printer is in character mode. Some printers have fonts called *downloadable fonts.* These fonts are defined by software supplied by the printer manufacturer and third-party vendors. Your printer must have RAM memory to use downloadable fonts. Your choice of a font or fonts can be sent (downloaded) to the printer where they will be used by the printer to print the text you specify.

Dot matrix printers now come in 9-pin and 24-pin versions. In the 24-pin printer, the wire diameter is smaller and the wires are staggered. The *cell matrix,* or the number of squares (wires) in the grid shown in Figure 4-2, is 12 by 12. These printers are designed to improve the overall appearance in both text and graphics applications and produce near letter quality output.

Impact Printers

Probably the second most popular type of printer is the *impact printer*. These are also known as *daisy-wheel printers* or *thimble printers*. Impact printers work rather like a typewriter works, and produce excellent, letter-quality print. Impact printers were definitely the printer of choice for office and small business work until the advent of laser printers.

Impact printers use a set of fully formed characters embossed onto a metal or plastic disk and a hammer. The disk is about 4 inches in diameter and each letter or symbol is at the end of a slender rod. These rods are arranged around the outside of the disk like petals on a flower. Unlike a typewriter, an impact printer has only one hammer. To print a character, the daisy wheel is turned, and then the hammer strikes it from behind. The character on the tip of the "petal" presses against an inked ribbon, and this will leave an impression on the paper.

The wheel and hammer arrangement moves back and forth across the paper, printing each letter as it goes. The paper doesn't move from left to right like a typewriter, it only rolls up and down. Most daisy-wheel printers can print from right to left as easily as from left to right, so they print both directions across the paper—in other words, when the printer finishes one line moving from left to right, it doesn't "return" to the left margin, but just resumes typing at the right margin moving leftward. The daisy wheel is easy to remove, and most impact printers offer a variety of daisy wheels that come in different fonts.

Impact printers have the advantage of producing excellent, letter-quality print. Because they work very much like a typewriter, the printed output has a typewritten appearance. But for the same reason, impact printers are also noisy. They sound pretty much like a 250 word-per-minute typist.

Ink-Jet Printers

Ink-jet printers are an immense technological improvement over dot matrix printers. Instead of wires, the printer has a number of small nozzles that actually squirt metered amounts of ink directly onto the paper. The elimination of ribbons allows a properly designed ink-jet printer to produce excellent quality output. The printer is also much quieter than a dot matrix printer or impact printer because there is no impact at all and fewer moving parts. Ink-jet printers also tend to be smaller.

Apart from these differences, ink-jet printers are very much like dot matrix printers. In particular, the letters are still formed a dot at a time, so the output looks similar to that of a dot matrix printer. Ink-jet printers are a good choice where size, speed, or noise are a concern.

Color Printers

Color printers are not so much a different kind of printer as an option that is available for many of the printers covered so far. A number of dot matrix printers have multi-color ribbons and color printing capabilities. Some ink-jet printers have more than one ink reservoir so they can spray multiple colors at once.

If you need color, try to determine if the software packages you will be using support the color and graphics modes for the printer you are thinking of buying.

Laser Printers

The current high end of the PC printer hierarchy is occupied by laser printers. These printers produce high-quality output to go along with their high-tech name. Laser printers are capable of filling almost any printing need from simple text output to graphics, and from desktop publishing to CAD drawings.

A laser printer works on the same principle as a photocopier. Simply, a metal drum is covered with a fine black powder called *toner*. The toner is then attracted to the paper, fused to the paper using heat and pressure, and then the printed paper is ejected from the printer. The whole process takes about ten seconds per page for actual printing. Moving a graphics image to the printer in preparation for printing can take considerably longer.

In order to print legible text, the toner must only be applied to selected portions of the paper. That, in turn, requires that the toner only cover a certain portion of the metal drum. To make the toner stick to the drum in the first place, the drum is electrostatically charged, then discharged by a laser beam to form an image. The powdery toner only sticks to the resulting charged image area. The resulting image on the drum is then transferred to the paper (which is also charged) to produce the image on paper.

Theoretically, the laser can draw any arbitrary patterns on the metal drum to produce any kind of printed output you'd like: pictures, words, drawings, you name it. In practice, not all laser printers support all possible features. Also, a laser printer is technically still a dot matrix printer because of the way it forms letters and characters. But the dots are so much closer together (typically 300 DPI or dots per inch) that it's difficult to notice.

If you need the highest quality printed output possible, there are laser printers available with resolution better than the 300 DPI norm.

- The Printware 720 IQ shown in Figure 4-3 which prints at 1200 DPI.
- Beyond this are 1200, 2400, and 4800 DPI RIP (raster image processing) machines like the Linotronic 100 and 300. These are true photo typesetting machines costing well over $10,000.

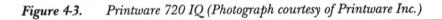

Figure 4-3.   *Printware 720 IQ (Photograph courtesy of Printware Inc.)*

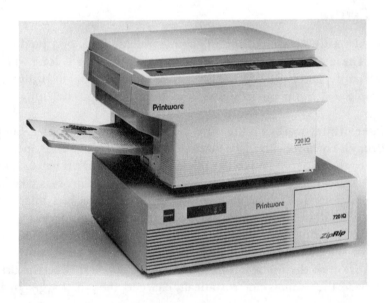

Laser printers are fast, and nearly silent. They can print text as well as graphics. The text is letter quality, and the graphics are quite sharp. The number of fonts is theoretically unlimited, again because of the nature of the laser. In practice, most laser printers offer somewhere between a few to a few dozen fonts "built in" to their internal electronics. Some can have new fonts taught to them, or downloaded. PostScript is also an option, described shortly.

Laser Printer Enhancements

There are several enhancements you can add to ordinary laser printers. Adding memory will help. Font cartridges can be added to increase the number of available fonts, and you can turn a Hewlett-Packard LaserJet printer into a PostScript-compatible printer using a plug-in cartridge.

- LaserMaster for Hewlett-Packard-compatible printers provide 800 DPI printing capabilities and up to 135 basic typefaces.

- Adobe PostScript cartridges include 35 Adobe scalable outline fonts, and come with control panel software to switch between PostScript and the printer's "native" language.

- Pacific Page PostScript cartridges include 35 scalable fonts and support Adobe Type 1 fonts and Bitstream QEM fonts.

Plotters

Plotters are an alternative to printers for drafting applications. Because they are specialized, they are unbeatable for certain kinds of work.

A *plotter* is basically a mechanical hand holding a pen. As such, they are perfectly suited for long or tedious drawing chores, such as architectural or engineering drawing. (An architectural or engineering firm will often have more plotters than printers.) Because a plotter draws with a pen instead of making marks with a collection of dots like a printer, straight lines are straighter, and curves are rounder. Also, many plotters are specially designed to hold the large sheets of paper that such drawings often require.

Hewlett-Packard, Roland, and Houston Instruments (not to be confused with Texas Instruments) are just three of the major plotter manufacturers.

They all make single-pen plotters and multi-pen plotters. The latter can plot in multiple colors and/or line widths simply by loading the plotter with different pens.

Software Compatibility

There are virtually no standards in the computer printer industry. Every manufacturer does things a little differently, often providing a mixed bag of fonts, graphics, and other capabilities for their printer. Any software that relies heavily on printed output will include *printer drivers* (software that controls the printer) for the printers it supports. The problem is there are so many printers available that it is virtually impossible for the software to supply a driver for each printer.

One answer is to design a printer so that it operates (and can use the same printer driver) as a more popular brand of printer. As it turns out, certain Hewlett-Packard, Epson, and Okidata printers are more popular than other brands. So, for example, printer company X might design their Model 5 printer to use the same software commands for boldface, underlining, and font selection as a more popular Epson model. Then, even if your software doesn't support the Brand X Model 5, it can still communicate with it by using the Epson protocol. This is known as *emulation,* and it is a common feature of many printers. Some printers can emulate several different brands and models.

PostScript

One printer standard began emerging in the late 1980s. It was developed not by a printer company, but by a software company. Adobe Systems in Mountain View, California developed a product called PostScript that is designed to act as a universal language between computers and printers. By using PostScript, the need for individual software drivers for each brand and model of printer disappears. PostScript also defines how each letter and character will look, so different printers will all print the same text exactly the same way.

For PostScript to work, both your printer and your software must support it. Currently there are many PostScript printers. Most word processing and desktop publishing applications also have PostScript "drivers" along with their more traditional printer-specific drivers.

One problem preventing the widespread acceptance of PostScript is its expense. In order for a printer to accept and "understand" PostScript commands, the printer must have its own CPU and memory for the PostScript software. Also, the printer manufacturer must pay licensing fees and royalties to Adobe for every PostScript printer they sell. This usually adds about $1000 on top of the purchase price of the printer. When a simple laser printer costs less than $3000, this represents a pretty significant increase in price.

Another drawback with PostScript is that it is slow. Because your computer must send complex PostScript commands, and your printer must subsequently interpret them, there is much more communication going on between the two of them than normal. This takes up time both on your PC and in your printer.

4

Printer and Plotter Interface

Both printers and plotters use one of two common interface techniques to connect to your computer. Your printer may have either a *serial interface* or a *parallel interface*. It may have both. A serial interface transmits characters 1 bit at a time whereas a parallel interface transmits one character (8 bits) at a time over 8 wires.

The type of communications interface will have absolutely no bearing on the capabilities of your printer. Most printers are offered with both merely for the sake of convenience. The selection of interface is up to you. There are advocates for both camps, but the best bet is to select whichever interface you have available on your computer. If you have an unused serial communication port, then select a printer with a serial interface. Ditto with the parallel port.

If it comes down to tossing a coin, you might want to lean toward the parallel interface. Parallel interfaces on a personal computer aren't good for much besides hooking up printers, plotters, and sometimes scanners whereas serial communications ports can be used for any numbers of things, including printers, plotters, scanners, modems, mice, trackballs, and many others. Also, there is a speed advantage to using the parallel interface. In short, conserve your serial ports if possible.

Installation

Hooking up a printer is a very simple matter. As always, start by turning your computer off. Also make sure the printer is completely unpacked, and that all of the plastic bags and packing foam are removed. Printers are notorious for having little pieces of Styrofoam jammed into obscure corners to prevent rattling during shipment. Be sure to carefully read and follow the manufacturer's unpacking instructions, for a piece of packing material or strapping tape can stop the printer and may damage it.

If you've selected a printer with a parallel interface, the next step is quite easy. Simply connect your parallel interface cable between the printer and your computer. On your PC, the parallel interface will be a 25-pin female D-Sub connector. This is true for all versions of the PC, XT, and AT.

Note

Don't connect a parallel printer cable to a male D-Sub connector. These are serial communications ports, not parallel ports.

After you've connected the cable, turn your PC on and wait for it to finish its normal power-up self-test routine (POST). When you get a DOS prompt, turn on the printer. As a test, you can print a simple file. Type **PRINT AUTOEXEC.BAT** and press (ENTER). This assumes that you have an AUTOEXEC.BAT file, of course.

DOS should then ask you where your printer is connected. For parallel printers, this is easy. Simply press (ENTER) again, and your file should print.

If you have a printer with a serial interface, there are a few extra steps involved. First, connect your serial interface cable between your printer and your PC. On the PC end, you need to look for either a 9-pin male D-Sub connector or a 25-pin male D-Sub connector. They're usually 25-pin connectors for PCs and XTs, and 9-pin connectors for ATs and 386 computers. Either way, it will be a male connector.

Note

Don't connect a serial printer cable to a female connector, even if it fits. These are parallel ports, not serial ports.

After you've connected the cable, turn your PC on and wait for it to finish its normal power-up self-test routine. When you get a DOS prompt, turn on the printer. Now you have to do a little software setup.

Serial ports have a lot more options than parallel ports do. This is partly what makes them so flexible. It also makes them a pain to set up for the first time. Before going any further, scan the words below to see if you're familiar with all of them.

Baud Rate   Baud rate describes how fast data can be transferred through a serial cable (kind of like miles per hour). Numbers like 1200, 2400, 4800, 9600, and 19200 are common baud rates. You want a higher number—the higher the number, the better.

Start Bit   The start bit is an extra bit of information that your computer sends to your printer to tell it that the next 7 or 8 bits are part of a character (data).

Data Bits   Data bits carry the information from your computer to your printer. Values like 7 and 8 are normal.

Stop Bit   The stop bit is the same as a start bit, but it comes at the end.

Parity   Yet another extra bit of information, this one helps to ensure that the other bits were transmitted correctly. Choices are usually even parity, odd parity, or none.

In order to start using your PC's serial port, you must first set all of these options using the MODE command. To set them, you must first know what your printer is expecting. For example, if your printer is set to receive data at 9600 baud, you must set your PC to send data at 9600 baud. You also need to know which of your PC's serial communications ports (COM1, COM2, and so on) you just connected the printer to.

Using the MODE command, you will set all of these options at once, by typing a command something like this:

MODE COM1: 9600, n, 8, 1, p

This tells DOS to configure the first serial port (COM1) to transmit data at 9600 baud, with no parity, 8 data bits, and 1 stop bn it. The final "p" is something DOS requires if you're attaching a printer.

After the first MODE command, you need to issue another one, this time to tell DOS that your printer is a serial printer and not a parallel printer.

4

MODE LPT1=COM1

Bear in mind that both of these commands are just examples. The actual command that you type may (and probably will) be different.

Now you should be ready to test your new printer. Type **PRINT AUTOEXEC.BAT** and press (ENTER). This assumes that you have an AUTOEXEC.BAT file, of course.

If you have any problems, you should review your printer's serial communications settings and make sure that they agree with your computer's settings. Also make sure that your printer is on-line and that it has paper in it. Most printers are too smart to print when they're out of paper.

Adding a Mouse, Trackball, or Light Pen

A mouse is a favorite addition to many personal computers. You may find that by using a mouse with your PC, you get more work done in less time. Some programs, in fact, require you to have a mouse.

What exactly is a mouse? A *mouse* is a small hand-held device, about the size of a bar of soap. It connects to your PC with a cable much the same way that your keyboard does. And, like the keyboard, you use the mouse to give commands to your PC or to control its actions. You can see one in Figure 4-4.

Basically, a mouse replaces the four cursor keys on your keyboard ((UP ARROW), (DOWN ARROW), (LEFT ARROW), (RIGHT ARROW)). When you move a mouse around on your desk, the cursor on your screen follows it. Move the mouse up, the cursor moves up. Move the mouse left, and the cursor moves left, too. A mouse will also have two or three buttons on it that you can press to make things happen. Just what will happen depends entirely on the software you're running. Some programs ignore the mouse completely, while others won't work without it.

With word processing software, you can use a mouse to point to a word that is misspelled, and retype it. You can also point to a word or a sentence that you want underlined or deleted, or to a word, sentence, or paragraph that you want to move elsewhere. Drafting, drawing, and CAD programs practically require a mouse so that you can draw diagrams and figures on your computer's screen—a difficult task with just four arrow keys.

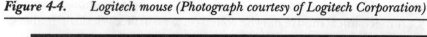

Figure 4-4. *Logitech mouse (Photograph courtesy of Logitech Corporation)*

4

Computer mice were developed at the Palo Alto Research Center, an arm of the Xerox Corporation in California. That is also where the Ethernet computer network and graphical user interfaces (like Windows and Presentation Manager) got their start. Mice were designed from the start to make computers easier to use. To a large extent, they have done this. Roughly one-third of the PC-compatible computers around the world have a mouse attached. All of the Apple Macintosh computers have one.

Selecting a Mouse

There are two basic kinds of mice, and three different ways to attach them to your computer. The two kinds are mechanical and optical. You basically use each the same way, but their mouse pads differ.

A *mechanical* mouse works by using a small metal or rubber ball inside the mouse case. As you slide the mouse on your desktop, the ball rolls and turns some shafts, which then send electrical impulses through the mouse cable to your PC. A mechanical mouse may be rolled on any surface—desktop, papers, notebook, blotter—as long at it is smooth and relatively clean. This last point is where mechanical mice can have problems. If the top of your desk is unusually dusty or dirty, the insides of the mouse will accumulate debris and will have to be cleaned often. Also, if your desk is very cluttered or very small, you may not have sufficient space to roll it around. You can get a mouse pad, which optimizes mouse movement in a small space.

An *optical* mouse works on a different principle. It has no moving parts. A light source is reflected from the surface of a special "mouse pad." The pad has special stripes on its surface. One type of stripe runs horizontally, the other vertically. The pad is a shiny, reflective square, about 8 inches on a side. The mouse only works when it is moved across this pad. Also, the mouse can only tell where it is in relation to its pad, not necessarily in relation to your desk. In other words, if you turn your mouse pad 90 degrees, the mouse will think that up is left, down is right, and so on. This can be a little confusing the first time it happens.

On the whole, it doesn't matter much which type of mouse you get. What's more important is how it feels to you. Like a keyboard, you should try out a mouse before you buy it. Get to know how it feels and how comfortable it is to use. Mechanical mice are available from Logitech, Microsoft, and Genius, among others. Mouse Systems is the primary maker of optical mice. A good mouse will cost between $50 and $100. They should all come with mouse "driver" software. Some also come with nice application programs, too.

Installation

As mentioned above, there are three different ways that a mouse might attach to your computer. If your computer has a special "mouse port" then that's where to plug it in, obviously. Another option is a *mouse controller board.* This is a circuit board included with the mouse that you must install inside your PC. Installing circuit boards is covered in Chapter 5, "Adding Expansion Boards." The third possibility is that the mouse will attach to an existing serial communications port.

It doesn't make any difference which of these three methods your mouse uses. They all function equally well. If your PC has a mouse port, you would waste the minimum amount of money and save the greatest number of expansion slots by using a compatible mouse.

There are mice available that substitute an infrared beam of light much like remote controllers for televisions. These mice, like television remote controllers, require a battery.

Note

Before installing any kind of mouse, be sure to turn your PC off. It is not necessary to unplug any of the cables in the back of your computer, unless you will be installing an expansion board.

If you have a mouse port, simply plug the mouse cable into the mouse port. The connector will only fit in one way, so turn it gently until it clicks in.

If your mouse comes with its own interface board, you will have to open your PC system unit and install the board. Please refer to Chapter 5 for more detailed instructions on installing expansion boards.

If you will be connecting your mouse to a serial communications port, locate the port you wish to use at the back of your PC. This should be either a 9-pin male D-Sub connector or a 25-pin male D-Sub connector.

Don't try to connect your mouse to a 25-pin female connector: that's a parallel port, not a serial port.

Caution

Your PC might have from one to four serial communications ports, called COM1 through COM4. While your mouse might fit any of them, not all mouse programs can work with a mouse on COM3 or COM4. If you are considering connecting your mouse to COM3 or COM4 check your mouse's manual first to be sure that it will work there.

After you've installed your mouse to the mouse port, interface board, or serial port, you will probably need to install mouse driver software. The mouse driver tells your computer and your applications programs that you now have a mouse. Read your mouse manual for any specific instructions on this point. You should also read Chapter 9, "Modifying Your Software."

Trackballs

A solution you may find more to your liking is shown in Figure 4-5. This device is commonly called a trackball. The actual device shown is Logitech's TrackMan. You might think of it as an inverted mouse. You move the ball

Figure 4-5.   *Logitech TrackMan (Photograph courtesy of Logitech Corporation)*

with your fingertips (or thumb, depending on the design) and use your thumb (or fingers) to press the buttons that surround it. The advantage is that it is stationary and thus requires less desk space to use.

You don't have as many options when installing a trackball. They usually only connect to serial communications ports. Simply follow the instructions given earlier for installing a mouse.

Light Pen

A light pen is a much less common addition than either the mouse or the trackball. With a light pen, you can "write" on your display screen using this special stylus. The light pen has a light-sensitive cell at its tip, and it can detect pixels on your screen. With the proper software, your computer can tell where you are placing the pen. The light pen works in conjunction with your display adapter. When the display beam moves under the light pen, it sends a signal to the display adapter, which can then determine the pixel location that the pen just sensed.

The secret here is the software. There are very few programs that can use a light pen. Those that do will often be sold "bundled"—that is, the software and the light pen are sold at the same time. Don't rush out and buy a light pen without the appropriate software.

Changing Your Keyboard

If your computer display is your view of the world, your access to that world is through the keyboard. You will find keyboards with different layouts and with a different feel to the keys. You will find keyboards with built-in digitizing pads, built-in trackballs, built-in bar code scanners, and even built-in voice recognition circuits.

Keyboard Layouts

There are dozens of different keyboards on the market but most will have one of two basic key layouts. It is a very good idea to try any keyboard before you buy one. Every manufacturer's keyboard feels a little different. The keys may be stiff or soft; they may click when depressed and so forth, but the only way to determine what suits you is to try as many as possible. All keyboards will be usable but one may suit you better than another.

84-Key Keyboards

When the original IBM PC was introduced, it had a keyboard with 84 keys, like the top one shown in Figure 4-6. This has since become the "standard" keyboard for PC-compatible computers. It has the familiar "QWERTY" layout in the middle, with ten function keys on the left, and the number/cursor keys on the right.

With an 84-key keyboard, you must decide whether to use the number/cursor keys for typing numbers or for moving the cursor. You can switch

Figure 4-6.   *A typical 84-key PC keyboard and 101-key AT keyboard*

PC Keyboard

Function   Typewriter keyboard   Numeric
keys   keypad

AT Keyboard

Function keys

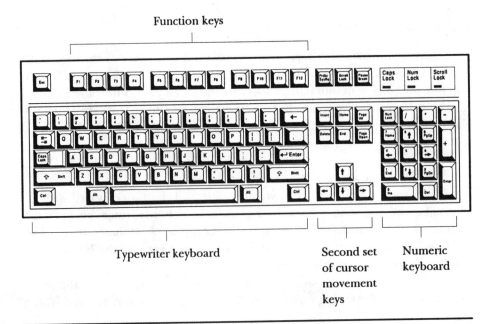

Typewriter keyboard   Second set   Numeric
                             of cursor   keyboard
                             movement
                             keys

back and forth with the (NUM LOCK) key. When (NUM LOCK) is pressed, the keyboard will type numbers, just like the top row of keys. When (NUM LOCK) is pressed again, the keys will control the cursor on your display screen.

The original IBM 84-key keyboard had no way of indicating whether the (NUM LOCK) key was pressed or not. It did not "click" into place like the shift lock on a normal typewriter, nor did it light up. The (SCROLL LOCK) and (CAPS LOCK) keys were similarly difficult to use. Fortunately, nearly every keyboard maker since that time has added three small LEDs (lights) to their keyboards so that you can tell which mode (NUM LOCK) is in. Be sure to look for these when you are shopping for keyboards.

101-Key Keyboards

The first official improvement from IBM over the 84-key keyboard came with the introduction of the Personal Computer AT. (See the bottom keyboard in Figure 4-6). It added 17 keys to the original, giving a total of 101. The additions were

- (F11) and (F12) function keys
- Four duplicate cursor control (arrow) keys
- Six duplicate editing keys
- Duplicate (CTRL) and (ALT) keys
- Duplicate mathematical functions
- Duplicate (ENTER) key

The 12 function keys were also moved to the top of the keyboard, making a row above the number keys. Moving the function keys obsoleted a lot of keyboard "templates" used to mark the significance of the keys. Most software packages now provide two templates: one for 84-key keyboards and one for 101-key keyboards.

The biggest improvement for most people was the separation of the numeric keypad and the cursor control keys. Now it is possible to use both at once.

Specialty Keyboards

You can get keyboards with built-in trackballs, built-in solar calculators, or any number of specialty devices, but the majority of keyboards have a fairly standard layout and will run from $50 to $100.

Northgate Computer's OmniKey Ultra is a good example of a specialty keyboard. It has 119 keys and puts the 12 function keys back on the left. It adds 12 keys ((F1) through (F12)), which allow you to activate a shifted function key without using the (SHIFT) key. A keycap-removal tool is provided that allows you to change the keycaps around. You can use it to implement two versions of the Dvorak keyboard layout by changing keycaps and setting a DIP switch.

Specially built Dvorak keyboards are also available for PCs. A Dvorak keyboard uses the same kinds of keys as a "QWERTY" keyboard, but they are arranged differently, for efficiency. There is a small but dedicated group of touch typists who prefer Dvorak keyboards.

The Keyboard Connector

Your keyboard requires electrical power to work, because there is a fair amount of circuitry inside it. Rather than plug your keyboard into the wall outlet, which would be bulky and a little hazardous, you merely plug the keyboard into your PC's system unit. The cable between them supplies power to the keyboard electronics, and provides wiring so that the keyboard can send and receive information to and from your PC. The cable is narrow and flexible, and the connector is usually small and round.

Like everything else, the connector style used by IBM in their original PC has been used by nearly all keyboard makers since then. This makes sense, because it allows you to swap your IBM keyboard for one you like better— hence, the keyboard makers sell more keyboards.

Installation

To change your keyboard, you must first turn your PC off. Remember, the keyboard cable supplies power to your keyboard's electronics, so yanking out the keyboard cable with the power on is just like pulling the electrical cord on any appliance: it is an invitation to failure.

There is a depression, or dent, on one side of the keyboard DIN connector that locks the connector to the matching DIN socket on the motherboard so that it can only be inserted one way. The dent is normally positioned at the top of the motherboard connector, pointing up. Just rotate the connector until it plugs easily into the keyboard socket on the motherboard.

When the keyboard cable is nice and snug, turn your PC back on. Your computer will automatically test the new keyboard as part of its POST (power-on self-test) procedure. If you have LEDs on the keyboard for (NUM LOCK) and so forth, they may blink. Finally, you should hear one or two beeps (depending on your BIOS) and your computer will start normally.

Note

Don't press any of the keys on your new keyboard while the POST is in progress. Your PC is checking to see that all keys are released, and if any key is pressed during the check, it considers that a failure.

That's all there is to it! Changing a keyboard is probably the easiest upgrade described in this book. But that doesn't mean it's not important. Many people are very possessive about their keyboards, and a PC shared by two or more people may have its keyboards swapped often.

Changing Your Monitor

Along with adding memory and upgrading a hard disk, improving the video output of a PC ranks as one of the most popular of all computer upgrades. Your PC's monitor is what you look at all day, it's where you get your information, and it enhances—or limits—your computer's software. There are lots and lots of choices, and always new developments. The latest video monitor and the most expensive display may not be right for you. Perhaps you can get by with—or maybe even prefer—something less exotic. With the information that is supplied next, you'll be better able to make those choices.

To really understand all there is to know about video monitors, you should have a little background information. In the next section, you'll pick up some valuable information about how the screen on your PC works, and what each of the important parts does. While there's no need to become an electronics expert, this section will prepare you for what is to come, and it also will help you to decipher the specifications and claims of competing monitor companies.

How Your Monitor Works

Your PC monitor looks pretty much like a small TV screen, and it should. They both work in much the same way. While that may not mean much to most people, it's sometimes nice to know that you're not embarking into completely uncharted territory. The ideas behind TV and computer monitors are pretty simple, and fortunately, you don't need to know most of the technology behind either of them.

Your PC generates words and pictures on your screen using two major components: the monitor and the video adapter card. The monitor will be covered here, and the video adapter card will be covered in more detail in Chapter 5, "Adding Expansion Boards." The monitor you can see. The video adapter card sits inside your PC's system unit case, and the two are connected via a cable.

The glass front of your monitor is coated with a special chemical on the inside, which also coats the inside of fluorescent light bulbs. It's called *phosphor*, and it glows when electrons strike it. Your monitor consists mainly of a large glass cone, lying on its side. You're looking at the bottom or wide end of the cone. The top or point of the cone is at the back of your monitor.

Inside the glass cone or cathode ray tube (CRT), towards the back end, are some interesting electronic devices that aim a beam of electrons towards the front of the monitor. This beam is very finely focused so that when it hits the front of the CRT, only a small dot on the phosphor surface will glow. If the beam is turned off, the phosphor will continue to glow for a little bit, and then fade.

To make the whole front of the monitor light up, the electron beam is moved very quickly from left to right across the face of the CRT, and from top to bottom. Even though only one little point of phosphor is being hit by electrons at any time, it takes the phosphor long enough to fade so that you don't notice; it appears that the whole thing is lit up at once. Furthermore, the front isn't lit up in a random pattern. The electron beam is carefully controlled so that it appears to draw words or pictures on the face of the screen.

The electron beam follows a regular path across your screen. From the upper-left corner, it moves to the right until it reaches the end. Then it moves down a tiny bit, and back over to the left side like a typewriter carriage moves. Then it draws the second line, from left to right, below the first one. It continues from left to right, from top to bottom, until it reaches the lower-right corner of your screen. Then it all starts over again. This process repeats from 30 to 60 times per second.

If the beam were left on during this whole procedure, the screen would appear evenly lit over its entire surface. Instead, the beam is turned on and off very quickly as it moves, so that only some portions are lit up. This is what gives the impression of recognizable letters and pictures.

If you have a black-and-white monitor, or a green or an amber monitor, all of the points of phosphors glow the same color. If you have a color monitor, the front of your CRT is coated with three different kinds of phosphor. Each dot is a triad with separate green, red, and blue dots at each location on the screen. One glows red, one green, and the other blue. There will be three electron "guns" as well, one that aims at the red dots, one at the green dots, and one that aims at the blue dots. All three beams scan across the screen at the same time.

The electronics inside your monitor handle the electron beam(s), the brightness, the contrast, and some other chores associated with displaying pictures. The video adapter card inside your computer has the job of converting your computer's commands into pictures for the monitor to display. In short, the adapter card determines what to display, and the monitor controls how it is displayed.

4

Some Display Terminology

Before going much further, there are some terms you should become familiar with. These are outlined here.

Pixel   This word is short for picture element. A pixel is one location on the screen of your monitor. An EGA display adapter can activate any of 640 spots horizontally and 400 spots vertically. Thus, there are 640 ×400 or 256,000 pixels. The number of pixels is controlled by your display adapter.

Resolution   This describes how many pixels a display adapter can display. An adapter might be able to display 1024 pixels across by 768 pixels up and down, for a total of 786,432. The more pixels the better, because it means that your PC will be able to display more complex pictures with better clarity.

Interlaced   Not all monitors paint the display in a strict left-to-right, top-to-bottom pattern. For certain technical reasons, it is often easier to display all of the odd-numbered lines first (1, 3, 5, and so on) and then go back and display the even-numbered ones. This is called *interlacing*. Monitors that display in strict 1-2-3 order are called *non-interlaced* monitors.

Dot Pitch   This term describes the size of the triads of red, green, and blue phosphor spots on a monitor's screen, measured in millimeters. The smaller the triad the better, because it means finer detail and less blurring. For example, a good monitor might have 0.31 millimeter dot pitch or smaller.

Frequency   This is a general-purpose electronics term that describes how frequently something happens. Frequency is measured in units of Hertz. Events occurring more than 1000 times per second are measured in kilohertz, or KHz. One million times per second is one megahertz or 1 MHz.

Scan Rate   The frequency at which a monitor sweeps its electron beam across the screen is called its *scan rate*. There are two important scan rates for computer monitors: the horizontal scan (left to right) and the vertical scan (top to bottom), which takes longer.

Digital   Generally, digital means that there are only two levels involved, on and off. Virtually everything inside your computer is digital. It can also be used to describe the interface between your PC and your monitor.

Analog   If it's not digital, it's analog. Analog electronics uses a smoothly varying voltage to convey information. For some tasks, analog is better suited than digital—as in the case of video monitors. Using analog signals allows a greater range of colors.

Video Modes

Different people use their PCs for different reasons, and so there are various demands made upon the PC's video output capabilities. If you use a PC strictly for word processing or for calculating financial spreadsheets, then you probably have little need for graphics or for color. If, on the other hand, you are using your PC for mechanical CAD work or for newsletter composition and layout, you'll need high-quality graphics, and maybe color as well.

To meet the disparate needs of a wide range of users, PC makers and monitor makers offer a wide selection of output options. Some are small, simple, and inexpensive, while others can cost more than the rest of the PC put together. What you need depends on what you want to do with your PC, not only now, but in the future.

As always, IBM sets the pace here. Every few years, they have introduced a new video "standard" for the Personal Computer or PS/2 family of computers. And, for the most part, all of the PC clone makers have followed suit. There are some instances, though, where renegade PC makers have developed their own video standards, and some of them have been quite successful, such as S-VGA.

The selection of a video mode depends just as much on the video adapter board inside your PC as it does on the monitor you select. For a complete discussion of text and graphics modes currently available for PCs, see the section on video adapter boards in Chapter 5, "Adding Expansion Boards." That will help you to decide if you haven't already settled on a video adapter. If you already have, then the next section will help you select the appropriate monitor.

4

Types of Monitors

There are different types of monitors that are matched to the different video display modes available for PCs (text, low resolution graphics, and so on). Some of the lower-cost monitors are built specifically to work with one or two of the popular video modes. These perform their intended purpose just fine, but they will be useless if you change your video adapter board to a new, unsupported format. Some of the newer and (naturally) more expensive monitors can support almost anything your PC can throw at it. These are essentially "obsolete proof" and paying the extra price can be like buying insurance.

When you look at monitors at the upper end of the price range, you're bound to come across the terms interlaced and non-interlaced. (These were defined earlier in this chapter in the "Some Display Terminology" section.)

Basically, an interlaced monitor is cheaper, but a non-interlaced one is more desirable. An interlaced monitor will take two passes across the screen to draw the whole picture. First, it will draw all the odd-numbered lines, and then all the even-numbered ones, "interlacing" the two to produce one picture. The advantage is that it takes twice as long, so the monitor maker can use less expensive components. The disadvantage is that it takes twice as long, so you may be able to notice a slight flickering on the screen if you have sharp eyes. Obviously, if you're even considering a monitor with enough resolution to require an interlaced display, you're going to be looking at it enough so that you should carefully evaluate it in the store before you buy.

Another set of terms you'll have to become familiar with are the two scanning frequencies: horizontal and vertical. In the final analysis, these two numbers will determine whether a given monitor will work with your video adapter board or not. Here's the rule: If the monitor's maximum horizontal and vertical scanning frequencies are both higher than the horizontal and vertical scanning frequencies produced by your video adapter, it should work. Table 4-1 summarizes the most popular video formats with the horizontal and vertical scan frequencies they use.

Nowadays, computer dealers have found that it's much easier to label monitors with the video modes they'll work with. For example, a certain monitor might say "VGA 640×480 Compatible" saving you the trouble of comparing scan rates and the like. If you're using one of the recognized "standard" PC video modes like CGA, EGA, VGA, or Hercules, you'll have no trouble at all finding an assortment of workable monitors.

Remember

Using the full capabilities of any monitor and display adapter combination requires that they both have the same upper limit of resolution and display capabilities. However, most combinations will work fine together even if these capabilities don't match exactly. If you buy a monitor capable of displaying 1024 ×768, non-interlaced images at 16.7 million colors and your display adapter is only capable of delivering 640 ×480 VGA images with 256 colors, you can always use such a combination and later upgrade your display adapter. Combinations that reverse this arrangement are also possible.

Monochrome Monitor

A monochrome monitor is any monitor that can't display colors. They can be the familiar black-and-white type, but they are often green because green is easier on the eyes. Monochrome amber monitors are also popular.

Table 4-1.   *Video Monitor Frequencies*

Type	Vertical		Horizontal	
MDA	50	Hz	18.432	KHz
CGA	60	Hz	15.75	KHz
EGA	60	Hz	15.7 to 21.8	KHz
VGA	70	Hz	31.5	KHz
S-VGA	56-70 Hz		31.5 - 48.5	KHz

A monochrome monitor usually can't display graphics, either. This isn't because of any inherent limitation of monochrome screens, but because the monochrome adapter boards available for PCs typically don't display graphics. There's little reason for the monitor manufacturers to build graphics capabilities into a monitor if the adapter card will never take advantage of it.

One exception to this is the Hercules Graphics Card. This was an early, and still popular, monochrome graphics card that also generated excellent quality text. If this is what you're using, be sure that your monochrome monitor can display graphics as well.

Digital Color Monitor

The first color monitors were introduced at the same time as IBM's Color Graphics Adapter (CGA) board. These were generally called RGB monitors, in reference to the red, green, and blue pixels used to generate the colors. The CGA board could create a 320 by 200 pixel display in four colors. While this was an improvement at the time, lines drawn at an angle looked more like a staircase than a straight line and led to the term "jaggies." Curves were worse.

These low-resolution color monitors are still popular and easy to find. They use a digital interface between the CGA display adapter and the monitor. You can identify a digital color interface by the 9-pin D-Sub connector on the CGA board and the monitor's cable. A digital color interface is also called a *TTL interface.*

Analog Color Monitor

Color monitors with an analog interface are inherently more flexible than those with a digital interface because they can display a richer collection of colors. Therefore, these monitors are currently at the top of the PC monitor pecking order. For demanding applications with high resolution graphics and/or lots of colors, you'll want a color monitor with an analog interface. You can identify the analog interface by the 15-pin D-Sub connector between the display adapter card and the monitor.

Multiple-Frequency Monitors

Many video monitors operate at a fixed horizontal and vertical scanning frequency. Because of the popularity of the PC, these are fixed at the factory to match the scanning frequencies of the various "standard" video modes: CGA, EGA, and so on. That is well and good until you decide to exchange your video adapter for a new one offering higher resolution and, inevitably, a higher scanning rate.

Enter the multiple-frequency monitor. As PC video modes multiplied and expanded, it became clear that making a monitor with a fixed scanning rate was to doom it to obsolescence within the year. The first really successful monitor to support multiple frequencies was the NEC MultiSync, and the name *multi-sync* or multi-frequency has come to mean any monitor of this type. Multi-sync monitors are able to "sync up" with many different video adapter boards. This makes them a kind of generic high-resolution solution. While a multi-sync monitor is more expensive than a fixed frequency monitor, it can save you the price of a whole new monitor should you decide to upgrade your video adapter board again.

Word Processing Monitors

Word processing monitors are distinguished from "normal" monitors in two ways: shape and color. While there is nothing in the world that says you must buy a special word processing monitor to do word processing work, there are many people who appreciate the difference enough to make these monitors a viable alternative.

One type of word processing display is a special monochrome monitor called a *paper-white display*. As the name might imply, a paper-white display is a black-and-white monitor, but the colors are reversed from the norm—that is, the background is white, and the text displayed on it is black as in Figure

4-7. This looks quite a bit like an actual printed page when you look at it. The glass screen is usually also coated with a special anti-glare coating.

The other special type of monitor is the *portrait display,* also shown in Figure 4-7. This looks like a normal PC monitor that has been tipped on its side. Since normal writing paper is longer vertically than horizontally, it makes sense to build a monitor to the same proportions. Assuming that you have the appropriate software as well, this allows you to see an entire page of text on the screen at once.

Because color is not an issue, prices for a word processing monitor are correspondingly lower than a color monitor for a given resolution. Perhaps the best known and most widely supported of these is the Wyse 700 monitor and adapter card. The monitor supports a resolution of 1280 by 800, which means you can display a full page of text under Ventura Publisher for example.

4

Figure 4-7.   *SOTA PAGE/VGA System paper-white portrait-oriented display system (Photograph courtesy of SOTA Technology)*

SOTA markets two paper-white monitors. A horizontal (normal) version called the SOTA VIEW SYSTEM provides 1664 by 1200 resolution on a 19-inch monitor screen, which allows a facing-pages view of publishing work. Figure 4-7 shows the SOTA PAGE/VGA SYSTEM, which allows a vertical view (portrait) of a page in 768 by 1024 resolution.

Display Adjustments

Your display will have at least a power switch, a brightness control, and a contrast control. Here's how to adjust contrast and brightness. Turn both controls fully counterclockwise to their lowest setting. In this control position you should see a blank screen. Turn the brightness control up until the retrace lines become visible, then turn it counterclockwise until the retrace lines just disappear. Now turn the contrast control up to a comfortable viewing level.

You may also find, usually on the back of the display, horizontal position, horizontal hold, vertical position, and vertical hold controls. The hold controls need to be adjusted if your displayed image rolls or tears. The position controls can be used to adjust the position of the image on your screen. There may also be external controls to control the vertical and horizontal size of the image.

All displays have the controls just mentioned. Some of the controls may be on the inside of your monitor, but it is strongly recommended that you do not tamper with these. The internal controls can only be adjusted with power applied and there are some high voltages that can give you some tingles and cause the hair on your arms to stand at attention. For the most part, they're more surprising than dangerous. The adjustments on high-priced monitors will frequently require very special equipment to get right.

Installation

When it comes to upgrading your PC's video output capabilities, installing the monitor is the easiest part. If you are completely overhauling your display system, changing the video adapter board will represent most of the work. That subject is covered in Chapter 5, "Adding Expansion Boards." If all you're changing is the monitor itself, the procedure is simple.

First of all, turn your PC off and unpack your new monitor. Make sure the power switch for the monitor is turned off too, and then plug it in. If there is a power outlet on the back of your PC, so much the better. Otherwise, plug your monitor's power cord into the wall. It is better to have the PC and the monitor plugged into the same wall outlet, if possible.

Attach the video interface cable between your monitor and your PC. This will be a short, heavily shielded cable with D-Sub connectors at either end. Plug it in snugly, and screw down the ends of the cable with your small screwdriver. If you have a monochrome monitor or a digital color (RGB) monitor, it will connect with a 9-pin connector. Otherwise, you'll have a 15-pin connector.

Turn your PC on and then turn your monitor on. After a short warm-up period, you should be able to see your display working. If not, adjust the brightness and/or contrast controls until you get a picture. Failing that, be sure that you've plugged your monitor into the video adapter board, and not some other expansion board with a 9-pin connector. Serial I/O ports also use 9-pin D-Sub connectors, but they are usually male connectors, and your video interface should use a female connector.

4

Adding a Scanner

A scanner is a new, relatively complex device that is becoming more and more popular all the time. Scanners are used primarily in desktop publishing applications, and also in drafting, CAD, and inventory control applications. Scanners come large and small, expensive or inexpensive, and color or black and white.

A scanner is basically the opposite of a printer. While a printer turns computer codes into printed paper that people can read, a scanner turns printed matter into computer codes that your computer can understand. You can scan printed text from magazines, pictures from newspapers, family photos, mechanical drawings, letterhead, signatures, or anything else you'd like. If you can photograph it, you can scan it.

Scanners are used to turn printed matter into a manageable form for your computer. It is possible to scan in photographs and then print them out again and again on your printer. This is a great boon for those who are publishing newsletters or advertising flyers. You could also scan in someone's original, hand-drawn artwork and use it as a company letterhead at the top of all your business correspondence. Mechanical drawings or other documents may be scanned into your computer and then stored safely on hard disk or floppy disk. A database of scanned documents can be maintained, providing a quick electronic filing system. The uses are almost limitless.

One very popular use for scanners is as an "automatic typist"—that is, a scanner may be used to scan a typed document into your favorite word processor. This is a reversal of the normal typist-word processor-printer routine. Scanning documents has saved uncounted hours of laborious typing for businesses with mountains of old paperwork that needed to be entered into a new computer system.

The scanners themselves come in a few basic types, with various combinations of features. There are many scanner manufacturers to choose from. Like some of the other upgrades covered in this chapter, scanners require special software to operate. Be sure that the software you are using, or are planning to use, supports the scanners you want and that it will provide the features you are looking for. The sections that follow cover both scanner hardware and scanner software.

Note

There are two things that scanners require a lot of: CPU speed and disk space. The speed of a scanner depends heavily on the CPU in your computer. Scanning will be painfully slow on a PC with an 8088 or 8086 CPU, but it can be quite fast on an 80386-based computer. Even black-and-white scans can take several thousand kilobytes of disk storage; color and gray-scale images can take several megabytes.

Types of Scanners

Scanners can be divided into three basic types, based on the way they handle colors. They are monochrome (black-and-white) scanners, gray-scale scanners, and full color scanners. You could just as easily divide them into two groups depending on how they are used. There are hand-held scanners and flatbed scanners. This section will take the former approach. Scanners range in price from a few hundred dollars to six figures depending on the size, capability, and purpose of the scanner.

All scanners work in basically the same manner. They examine your original picture a small piece at a time, and determine what "color" that piece is. Then they move on to the next piece. In the case of a monochrome scanner, the choice is either black or not black. In a sense, your original picture is electronically chopped up into little squares. The finer it is chopped up, the better the quality of the scanned image will be. This is called the scanner's *resolution.*

Scanner resolution is measured in dots per inch. This is often abbreviated as DPI. A resolution of 75 DPI is rather coarse; it would render grainy images. A resolution of 300 DPI is quite good. It means that the scanner takes 300 samples across every inch of your original picture. If you have 300 samples vertically times 300 samples horizontally, the scanner would take 90,000 samples in every square inch of your original picture.

4

Monochrome Scanner

A monochrome scanner can only distinguish dark from light. Such scanners can be used for line drawings or for pages of text. Banks and mortgage companies use high-speed monochrome scanners to scan important documents in what are called image retrieval systems. Line drawings can be anything from pencil sketches to large architectural or engineering drawings.

A monochrome scanner can also scan photographs, even color photographs, but the result is not always appealing. Even though black-and-white photographs like newspaper pictures are only printed in one color, they use a technique called *halftoning* that allows them to appear much more detailed. A monochrome scanner will reduce such pictures to true black and white.

Monochrome scanners are the least expensive of the three types of scanners discussed here, and usually also the quickest.

Gray-Scale Scanner

Gray-scale scanners add the necessary electronics to recognize different levels of light intensity. Such scanners are usually sensitive to 16, 64, or 256 levels of gray. That doesn't necessarily mean that the picture you are scanning must be gray also. It just means that your scanned image will be reduced to that many different shades. A 16-color scan produces recognizable images from a black-and-white photograph. A 256-level gray scan will produce very clear images, even from color masters.

Color Scanner

Color scanners are both expensive and slow but the end results are breathtaking. Color in computers, photography, and printing depends on separating three additive (red, green, and blue) or subtractive (cyan, magenta, and yellow) colors to generate a spectrum of all colors available. A color scanner must scan first through a red filter, then through a green filter, and finally through a blue filter.

Some color scanners do this by scanning the image three times, each time through a different filter; and some, like the Epson ES-300C, have three light sources (one red, one green, and one blue), and scan the individual colors in a single pass.

Note

Your scanner and the software used with it will normally allow you to select the resolution and the number of colors. For example, the resolution may be 75, 100, 200, 300, or 400 dots per inch. The number of colors available is usually 4, 16, 64, 256, or 16,777,216. That last violent leap represents the color range normally used by television frame grabbers. A frame grabber is an adapter card that can be installed in your computer and attached to a video camera, video recorder, or other video source to allow the capture of television pictures.

Flatbed Scanners

Flatbed scanners look pretty much alike on the outside. Figure 4-8 is a photo of the Epson ES-300C. Most flatbed scanners are similar in appearance but this scanner is a top-of-the-line one-pass color scanner capable of monochrome, 256 gray-scale or 16 million color operation. A number of other companies including Microtek, Canon, Dest, Panasonic, and Hewlett-Packard make monochrome and color flatbed scanners.

To use the scanner, you simply lift the cover of the scanner and lay your original face down on the glass surface underneath. Then close the cover. Your software will control the operation of the scanning mechanism. All in all, it works very much like a photocopier.

There are several full-page scanners available. These scanners scan full-page documents into the system and scan images. In a sense, they're the electronic equivalent of a copying machine or camera.

- Hewlett Packard ScanJet Plus is a flatbed, gray-scale scanner that can have an automatic document feeder (ADF) attached. (The next section discusses this feature.) This is good for OCR (optical character recognition) work where you have to scan many pages. (OCR is discussed shortly.)

- Datacopy GS Plus is a flatbed, gray-scale scanner that can have an automatic document feeder (ADF) attached.

- Microtek MSF-300Z is a flatbed, gray-scale/color scanner that can have an automatic document feeder (ADF) attached.

- Epson ES-300C is a flatbed, gray-scale/color scanner that can have an automatic document feeder (ADF) attached.

- Chinon DS-3000 is one of the most versatile scanners on the market. It can be connected to a serial port, a parallel port, or to its own interface card. It can also be plugged into a printer so that it acts like a copying machine. It has an overhead scanning element that allows you to place large books or three-dimensional objects on the platform to be scanned.

Figure 4-8. *The Epson ES-300C flatbed color scanner (Photograph courtesy of Epson)*

Figure 4-9.   *The ScanMan Plus from Logitech (Photograph courtesy of Logitech Corporation)*

Automatic Document Feed   Flatbed scanners can usually be equipped with an automatic document feed attachment that allows you to feed an entire stack of documents and scan them unattended. The time required for scanning with some devices makes this a useful addition to your scanner.

Hand-held Scanners

Figure 4-9 shows a typical hand-held scanner. A light source and sensor are enclosed in the top of the scanner. You place the scanner at the top of the material to be scanned and slowly move it down the page by hand. Rollers on the bottom of the scanner guide the operation and tell the electronics how fast or slow you are moving the scanner.

Hand-held scanners are available in monochrome, gray-scale, and color versions. Prices are normally under $500. For the casual user with a limited amount of scanning to do, these are an excellent way to get images into documents. Caere has bundled a hand-held scanner with optical character recognition (OCR) software and named the result the "Typist." You scan text, and the software converts it from an image to ASCII text that you can use with your word processor. OCR software is covered shortly.

4

Installation

With most scanners you will receive the scanner, an adapter card that fits in your computer, and one or more software packages that provide the image scanning capabilities for your scanner.

The fastest systems use special-purpose adapter cards. Most of these use parallel data transfer systems similar to the parallel printer port. In fact, many allow you to set the scanner to use the I/O addresses and the interrupt normally used by LPT2 (the port that would ordinarily take a second printer). Since many computer systems only use one printer, the use of LPT2 leaves other I/O addresses and interrupts available for other uses.

One scanner breaks the rules. The Chinon scanner provides a base on which you position the copy to be scanned. A scanning head is mounted above this and the ambient room light is used as the source of light for scanning. It also offers two methods of connection to your computer. The first is through a serial port. The serial port connection can save space inside your PC and makes the scanner easy to install but it is also very slow. The Chinon also has a parallel adapter card that speeds the operation considerably.

As with any kind of interface adapter card, you should be cautious. First read through the sections in Chapter 5 that deal with adding adapter boards.

Scanner Software

Image scanning depends heavily on software. The scanner you select will almost certainly come with special software called device drivers that will help your computer to work. You must also consider what you want to use the scanned images for after you scan them in. Make sure the drafting software, image retrieval software, artistic design software, or whatever application you have in mind will accept and manipulate the image files that your scanner will create.

There are many different ways to store graphic images on a computer. Nearly every freehand paint program for PCs uses a different file format. Scanners, too, use different formats. It is not a trivial matter to convert graphics files from one format to another, so be sure that your scanner, your printer, and your intended application programs all agree on what image file formats they will accept.

Optical Character Recognition (OCR)

Optical Character Recognition (OCR) is a technique that allows your computer to "understand" the printed text that it sees on a scanner. This is a function that most people take for granted, but it is not automatic. It is surprisingly difficult to teach a computer to recognize the alphabet and read English text. OCR is a complex and (at least today) not entirely dependable technique for scanning.

Note

Just because a page of text is scanned into a computer doesn't mean that your computer can read and manipulate the text. Your computer doesn't even know it is looking at English language writing unless you use special OCR software to translate it.

There are OCR software packages available from a number of companies. Figure 4-10 is a screen captured from Caere's WordScan Plus. This is an OCR software package that allows pages of text to be scanned and converted to ASCII files. Normally a page of text must be keyed into a computer before it can be used in word processing. OCR makes it possible to scan the images and convert the images to text.

The methods used to do such work are trade secrets for most of the companies working in this area and involve artificial intelligence to some degree. Many of the OCR software packages available have problems recognizing all characters and require a little to a lot of correction after the recognition phase is completed. None of the currently available packages work with hand-written text.

Figure 4-10. *Caere's WordScan Plus main window*

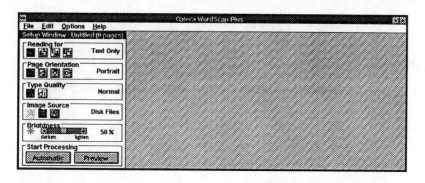

This doesn't mean that you can't scan in signatures or other hand-written items. It's just that your computer will not be able to translate hand-written words into computer text format. Untranslatable text is treated as a picture.

Gray-scale Scanning

A package called Image-In developed in Switzerland is an excellent choice for gray-scale scanning. This package has the ability to import and export a wide range of graphics image formats. You can also buy separate options. One option allows Image-In to do optical character recognition. Another provides a way to make images usable in CAD packages such as AutoCAD.

The main window for Image-In is shown in Figure 4-11 while Figure 4-12 shows the scanning window. Many of the items in this window relate to capabilities of the Epson ES-300C.

Color Scanning

When photographs are used in publishing, they require special attention. First, the photo should have good contrast, meaning that highlights should be white and shadows nearly black with a wide range of intermediate tones. All too frequently this requirement is not met and the photo must be adjusted using messy darkroom techniques. It must then be converted to a halftone before it can be printed.

Figure 4-11.   *Image-In main window*

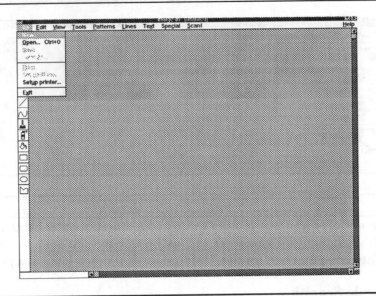

Figure 4-12.   *Image-In scanning window*

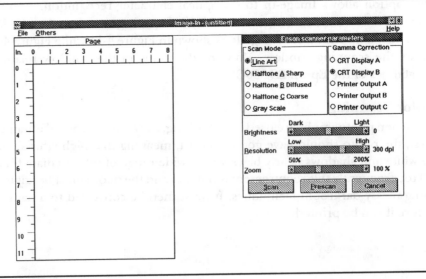

Astral's Picture Publisher is a software package that provides a darkroom on your computer. In fact, this package allows you to make adjustments to images that would be next to impossible using conventional methods.

Figure 4-13 shows Picture Publisher's main window. You can use existing images or you can scan images from almost any source including photographs. Figure 4-14 is the scanning window for Picture Publisher. The prescan feature allows a quick scan of an image. Once you have a prescan, you can crop the image to the desired size and scan only the portion of the image you need.

The dialog box in the upper-right of the screen allows a selection of calibration maps. The sensitivity of scanners varies, and Picture Publisher supplies calibration maps for various models. Essentially this means that Picture Publisher will see all pictures the same way regardless of whose scanner you are using.

Once the image is scanned or captured, you can use Picture Publisher's tools to adjust the contrast range. You can make blacks blacker, whites whiter, and change the gray levels all in the interest of producing the best picture or

Figure 4-13.   *Astral's Picture Publisher main window*

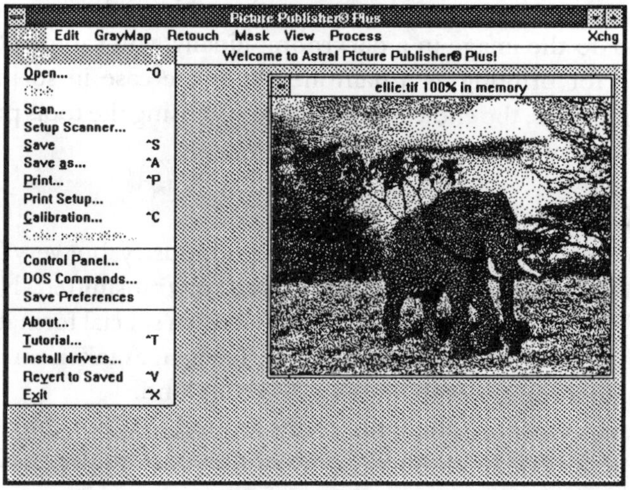

Figure 4-14.   *Astral's scanner window*

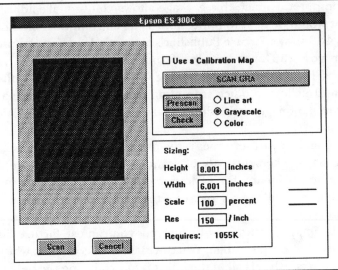

creating special effects. You can use a range of retouch tools to clean up fingerprints, do airbrushing, and lighten or darken specific parts of the image.

You can use masks to cover selected parts of the image while you work on others. You can use a range of filters to smooth edges, sharpen edges, blur images, sharpen images, and do many other things that you would find impossible to do the image in a darkroom. Finally, you can print the image or prepare it for printing as a halftone. As is the case in so many things involving computers, the choices available to you using the tools provided are limited only by your imagination.

Graphics Conversion

There are many standards in the computer industry, but very few relating to how pictures should be converted, stored, or transmitted. Nearly every publisher of graphics-oriented software uses its own special format for storing pictures. This makes it very difficult to transfer images taken on one kind of scanner, say, to a computer that uses a different kind.

Fortunately, there are some programs around that can convert graphics files from one format to another. Some of these are in the public domain, meaning they can be copied and used free of charge. While these are usually effective, they are often limited and there is no guarantee that they will work.

There are also some commercial graphics conversion programs available. One notable example is from Inset Systems. Their program, simply called CONVERT, can convert to and from no fewer than 20 different graphics file formats at last count. It would be difficult to find a format that CONVERT didn't support.

Uninterruptable Power Supplies and Power Conditioners

4

If you've used your PC for any length of time, you've probably discovered what happens when the computer gets turned off accidentally. Data can be lost and files can even be corrupted or destroyed. For even the casual user, this is an annoyance. For a serious business user, this is disastrous.

Accidentally pulling the plug or turning off the power switch is bad enough, but there are other hazards as well. Storms can shut off power without warning. Lightning can send damaging power surges through the lines. Events that cannot be predicted leave your computer defenseless.

Uninterruptable Power Supply

Fortunately, there are solutions to even these problems. To protect against sudden power failures you can get an *uninterruptable power supply* (UPS). A UPS is basically a secondary, backup power supply with a big battery to be used in case of a power failure. To make the backup supply useful, though, it needs to automatically switch on within a tiny fraction of a second, and this is exactly what a good UPS will do. It senses the amount of electrical current coming in from the power lines, and switches your computer over to battery power if it ever drops below a certain level.

To use a UPS, you simply plug your computer into the electrical outlet provided on the UPS, and then plug the UPS into the wall. The rest is automatic. Depending on the size of the internal battery, the backup power may last from a few minutes to several hours. Most UPS supplies also have outlets for your monitor and printer, so that your whole system will be operational even during a total blackout.

Power Conditioner

A much smaller and simpler device can protect you and your computer from less catastrophic events. Sometimes a power failure in a nearby town or a lightning strike can send dangerous voltage fluctuations, or *spikes,* through the power lines. If one of these spikes comes in through your wall outlet, your computer could be damaged. Any number of odd things can occur, from lost data to damaged hard disks, to ruined power supplies.

A power conditioner, or line conditioner, is a small device that you plug in between your computer and the wall outlet. While it doesn't provide you with any protection against power failures like a UPS does, it's not nearly as big or expensive, either. A power line conditioner can be as small as a pack of playing cards and they are usually quite inexpensive.

Summary

This chapter has covered the easiest additions you can make to your system—printers, plotters, a mouse or trackball, keyboard, monitor, and scanners. The next chapter goes one step further in teaching you how to add expansion boards.

5

Adding Expansion Boards

One of the features that lead to the fantastic popularity of the IBM PC was its open architecture, discussed in Chapter 1, "The Open Computer." The fact that the PC could be opened up, literally and figuratively, and new features could be added to it let computer users determine just what capabilities they needed. Every PC became, in effect, a custom computer.

The mechanism that allows you to do this is the *expansion bus*. A bus is an electrical term for a wire, or a collection of wires, that carry information. The bus allows you to add new circuit boards to your PC for serial or parallel communication, a new video adapter, more memory, or almost anything else.

Expansion Buses

To make upgrades simple, a group of circuit board connectors into which adapter cards can be plugged is installed on the motherboard near the rear apron of the computer. A metal bracket at the rear of each adapter card, called an *adapter bracket* (on the PS/2 it's called an *orb*), allows you to connect cables between the adapter cards and external devices like monitors, printers, scanners, and other peripherals.

The connectors on the motherboard nearest the rear apron are 62-pin connectors. The expansion connectors are not like the ones you've seen on the outside of your computer. These are long, rectangular connectors with 31 pins along each side. There's a deep groove, or a slot, down the middle of each connector where you insert the edge of an expansion board. An end view is shown here:

The IBM PC and XT have 62-pin connectors on the motherboard to pass information between the motherboard and the adapter cards. Eight of the pins in each slot carry data. The other 54 are for various functions like supplying power to the expansion board. The eight data pins correspond to the eight data lines on an 8088 CPU.

When the AT was released, some of the adapter slots (connectors) were enlarged with an additional 36-pin connector to allow for the 16-bit data bus of the 80286. These are called *16-bit slots* to distinguish them from the 8-bit slots of the PC and XT. To accommodate both 8- and 16-bit expansion cards, the AT motherboard had a mixture of the older 62-pin (8-bit) expansion slots and the newer 98-pin (16-bit) connectors. This combination of slots has been maintained by most PC makers to this day.

Because the 80386 CPU has 32 data lines you would naturally expect the expansion connectors to be extended once again to accommodate the larger data bus. But, since IBM has never officially introduced a member of the ISA-bus Personal Computer family with an 80386, this was never done. Therefore, only 8-bit and 16-bit PC expansion slots exist.

ISA

The 8-bit PC bus just described was never officially named by IBM. Instead, it came to be known among computer users and designers simply as the "PC bus." When new and different expansion bus architectures were developed in the late 1980s, it became clear that the bus had to be called something. So, a group of PC makers (excluding IBM) suggested the somewhat presumptuous name of "Industry Standard Architecture" or ISA. This name has stuck, although "PC bus" is still used just as often.

MCA

The reason for renaming the PC bus was the announcement by IBM of a new and improved expansion bus for their new family of computers called the Personal System/2 (PS/2) series. The PS/2 computers did not use the same expansion bus of the Personal Computer series (including the PC, XT, and AT). Instead, a new bus was developed, called Micro Channel Architecture, or simply MCA. Expansion boards that worked with the older PC bus would not work with MCA, and vice versa.

This was seen by many industry observers as a blatant case of IBM "taking their ball and going home" after they had lost a great deal of business to the PC clone makers in the U.S. and abroad. By declaring the Personal Computer family obsolete and announcing a new bus (which, it should be pointed out, requires licensing fees and royalties to be paid to IBM) it was predicted that a whole new market would appear for MCA boards, while the PC expansion business would dwindle.

Whether for good or ill, this hasn't happened—at least not yet. Micro Channel has not caught on nearly as well as IBM might have liked. Currently IBM and National Cash Register (better known as NCR) are nearly the only companies pushing MCA computers.

There are some significant technical advances in the Micro Channel Architecture that make it interesting. First of all, it provides a 32-bit data path, which makes moving large amounts of data inside your computer much faster, especially for 80386 and 80486 computers.

5

EISA

In a revolt against the perceived tyranny from IBM, a group of seven major PC makers developed an alternative to Micro Channel. This new bus is called the Extended Industry Standard Architecture, or EISA. The EISA bus (pronounced "ee-suh") allows many of the capabilities of MCA. Older ISA boards will still fit and work in a computer with EISA expansion slots. Furthermore, new EISA-compatible boards will work as well, but with the added features of the EISA specification.

Both MCA and EISA provide a built-in 32-bit data path for the first time. EISA also offers the *bus mastering* features of MCA. Technically, there is little to recommend EISA over MCA, or vice versa. But history has shown that technical superiority rarely matters in issues of commercial popularity. In the end, the computers that provide the most value to the customer for the money are usually the winners.

Proprietary Buses

Before there was EISA or MCA, when PC makers began designing the first computers with the 80386 CPU, it became clear that at least one or two of the expansion slots should have a 32-bit data path. The 80386 was the first 32-bit CPU chip used in PCs, and so this problem had never occurred before. Furthermore, IBM had not yet announced a PC with a 386 (and, as it turned out, never would), so there was no IBM "standard" to copy. Consequently, some PC makers designed their own special 32-bit expansion slots to go along with the familiar 8-bit and 16-bit slots. Most are designed to accommodate proprietary memory expansion boards. A bus that is designed and used by only one company this way is called a *proprietary bus*.

A 32-bit expansion slot allows a 386-based PC to move data back and forth at top speed to a 32-bit expansion board. In that respect, it was a good thing to have. On the other hand, since every PC maker used a different design for their 32-bit expansion slots, there was no single standard for the expansion board makers to follow. The net result was that very few 32-bit expansion boards were ever made. Each company that made a 386 PC would make one or two expansion boards for it as well, but that was all.

Memory

Your computer's memory is probably one of the most important resources you have and the most likely candidate for upgrading. The words used to describe memory can even be confusing to experts. You will hear conventional memory, reserved memory, expanded memory, extended memory, and a number of other terms. The next few pages will give you a better understanding of computer memory in general and the terms relating to memory in IBM PCs and compatibles using Intel CPUs in particular.

Note

As you read this, keep the chronology of events in mind. Many terms developed five or ten years ago aptly described equipment then; however, these terms are often still around today and are usually used inappropriately.

5

Registers

Let's start with the hardware (the motherboard, CPU, and memory chips). A binary bit can be either 0 or 1 (off or on). At the lowest level, a device called a *flip-flop* acts much like a light switch. It can be turned off (0) or on (1). The light switch uses a spring to latch it on or off—a flip-flop uses an electronic impulse to latch it to 0 or 1.

A group of flip-flops is called a *register*. The flip-flops in registers can be turned on or off individually. Here are possible combinations with a 2-bit register (two flip-flops):

00

01

10

11

Table 5-1 expands these combinations. Under "No. of bits" find 2 and read over to find 4 possible combinations. 32 bits gives 4,294,967,296 combinations.

Table 5-1.   *Possible Combinations in a Register (Depending on No. of Bits)*

No. of Bits	Possible Combinations	Address Limits by Intel CPU and # Systems
1	2	
2	4	
3	8	octal
4	16	hexadecimal (HEX)
5	32	
6	64	
7	128	
8	256	
9	512	
10	1,024	
11	2,048	
12	4,096	
13	8,192	
14	16,384	
15	32,768	
16	65,536	8080 address limit
17	131,072	
18	262,144	
19	524,288	
20	1,048,576	8086 address limit
21	2,097,152	
22	4,194,304	
23	8,388,608	
24	16,777,216	80286 address limit
25	33,554,432	
26	67,108,864	
27	134,217,728	
28	268,435,456	
29	536,870,912	
30	1,073,741,824	
31	2,147,483,648	
32	4,294,967,296	80386 address limit

CPU's Use of Memory

Your computer's memory is where instructions and data are stored during the execution of a program to make the instructions and data quickly available. Typically DOS COMMAND.COM will load your program into memory. The CPU then repeats a cycle of operations that fetch an instruction from memory, decode the instruction, and execute the instruction (the CPU may need to store or fetch data during execution). This cycle of operation is repeated until the program ends.

A register called the *Instruction Pointer* or *Instruction Program Counter* (IP or IPC) is supplied with the starting location or address of your program in memory. The IPC puts that address on the address lines of the CPU and initiates a fetch to read the first instruction into the CPU. Once the instruction is complete, the IPC is incremented and the next instruction is fetched. Some computer instructions (like JUMP or CALL) give the IPC a new starting address from which to fetch instructions.

Each location (or address) in a PC's memory is a register that stores 8 bits or 1 byte of instruction or data. Looking again at Table 5-1 you can see that 16 bits provides 65,536 combinations. Thus a CPU with 16 address lines can address 65,536 unique memory locations, each containing a byte of instruction or data. These address lines are controlled by an address register, the CPU, and the IPC.

If an instruction is being fetched, the IPC will put its contents in the address register and thus on the address lines. If data is being fetched or stored, the CPU will put the contents of some other register (which contains the address of the required data) in the address register.

From this you can see that your computer's use of *physical memory* is directly controlled by the address register connected to address lines. The address lines are the pins coming out of the CPU chip—and each CPU has a limited number of these lines. The 8080 has 16 lines, the 8088/8086 (IBM PC/XT) has 20 lines, the 80286 (IBM AT) has 24 lines, and the 80386 has 32 lines, as mentioned at the beginning of this chapter.

5

Looking at Table 5-1 again, you can see that the 8080 can address 65,536 locations or 64 KB of memory. The 8088/8086 can address 1,048,576 locations or 1 MB; the 80286 can address 16,777,216 locations or 16 MB; and the 80386 can address 4,294,967,296 locations or 4 Gigabytes. The available locations depend on the mode the CPU is in—you'll learn more about these modes shortly. Since each location contains 1 byte of instruction or data you can see that the 8080 (for example) can address 64 kilobytes of memory. Each kilobyte represents 1024 bytes but this is usually rounded down to 1000—you'll find that multiplying 64 (KB) by 1024 yields 65,536.

The 8080 CPU

The 8080 was used in early microcomputers. It has 16 address lines and can address 64 KB of memory. By today's standards that's not much memory.

Memory Maps

This is a good place to introduce *memory maps*—a method of illustrating memory (because not only neophytes have trouble keeping track!). A box 1 byte wide and a number of address locations (like 0 to 640 K) tall is used to represent how memory is used in a computer. The memory map for the 8080 is shown here:

The bottom represents location or address 0; the top represents location 65,536 (64 KB). Additional information would normally be included in the box but is not really needed here.

The 8088/8086 CPU

These two CPUs are closely related. The 8088 is used in the PC/XT and has an 8-bit-wide data path. This simply means that 8 pins on the CPU chip are used for data. The motherboard and CPU take care of fetching or storing the contents of the 16-bit registers used in the CPU. The 8086 has 16 data lines or pins. Both CPUs have 20 address lines or pins.

Segmented Addressing

When Intel designed the 8088/8086, building microcomputers on a chip was still a relatively new art and it just wasn't possible to include the circuitry to manage 32 address lines, but the need for additional memory was obvious. The answer was a scheme called *segmented addressing.* The physical memory is effectively divided into sixteen 64 KB segments. The IPC supplies the base address. The contents of a segment register is shifted by 4 and added to the IPC to make the 20 bits. This concept was—and still is—a programmer's nightmare. You needn't worry about it—just know the name.

The New Kid on the Block—the IBM PC

When IBM introduced the PC, a microcomputer with 64 KB was considered rich with memory. Projected sales were not high for the PC and few people considered that 640 KB would ever be restrictive. It seemed a reasonable arrangement to put many functions (such as display and BIOS) high in memory and leave a whopping 10 segments (640 KB) available to programs.

The PC did meet with success, and 640 KB became restrictive to such a point that it is called a "barrier"—and hundreds to thousands of programs were written that depended on a fledgling operating system called PC-DOS. From that point on it became a constant fight to retain backward and forward compatibility. Each new advance in software and hardware required that existing software and hardware not be made obsolete.

A Memory Map for the PC

Figure 5-1 shows the memory map for the PC/XT or any computer using the 8088/8086 CPU. On the left is a stack of sixteen 64 KB segments to give you a sense of scale. On the right is the memory map you will see associated with the PC.

Figure 5-1.   *A memory map for the PC/XT*

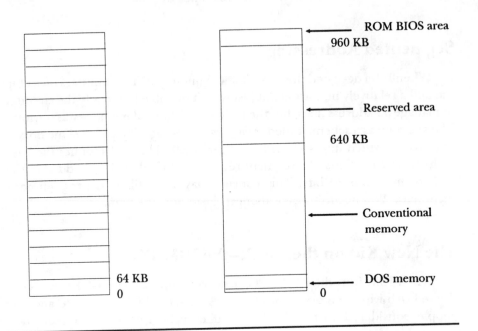

The very first addresses are called the DOS area. The first 1024 bytes of the DOS area are called *interrupt vectors*—addresses used by DOS to tell it where the programs are for display, keyboard, mouse, BIOS services, and dozens of other interrupt service programs. Still in the DOS area will be device drivers and DOS COMMAND.COM.

All of these reduce the basic 640 KB of available memory. If you add additional device drivers using *device* statements in your CONFIG.SYS file, or if you add terminate-and-stay-resident programs (TSRs) like SideKick, these are also included in the DOS memory area and further shrink the amount of memory available to applications.

Conventional Memory

Next is *conventional memory*. It is the area in memory where your application programs are loaded and from which they execute. The actual space available will depend on how much you have in the DOS area and, as mentioned earlier, can be substantially reduced by device drives and TSRs.

The reserved area is where IBM felt it was safe to put display memory and other BIOS routines (programs) while the very highest addresses (the top area) was used for the ROM BIOS.

Expanded Memory

Remember that all of this was before the IBM AT and, in some instances, before compatibles. Available applications were becoming more plentiful and larger. More TSRs were being introduced. What had been considered ample memory was becoming very restrictive. Large spreadsheets, in particular, needed more room for data.

To "fix" the problem, Lotus, Intel, and Microsoft came up with a "solution" called *expanded memory*. The full title, covered by a substantial manual, is Lotus/Intel/Microsoft Expanded Memory Specification Version 4.0, (but you'll just stick with expanded memory).

A specially designed memory card and software is required. The expanded memory hardware contains memory which *is not* directly addressable by the PC/XT. This card is installed in an adapter slot, and a device driver is provided to make the hardware think a window (called a *page frame*) is located in the reserved area. This page frame can be directed to provide access to 64 KB segments of the expanded memory as shown in Figure 5-2.

This allowed large spreadsheets to store data out of conventional memory. The result was more memory for programs to run. Program code cannot use expanded memory—expanded memory can only be used to store data.

This set the stage for still another backward/forward compatibility problem. Many programs still use expanded memory if it's available. More discussion on that soon.

5

Figure 5-2.   *Access provided to 64 KB segments of expanded memory*

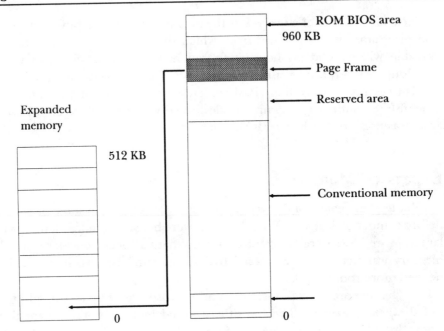

Virtual Memory

Memory availability in computers has been an issue on mainframes, minicomputers, and microcomputers for years. One of the early answers was a *swap file*. Used mostly with text editors, the swap file allows much of the text file you're working on to remain on disk. The part of the text file being edited is in memory. Most of the text file is fetched into memory as needed by the program using the swap file. But wouldn't it be nice to have large executing programs read only the needed parts of a program into memory, leaving the rest of the program on disk until needed?

The concept is called *virtual memory* and, although simple in concept, it's a real bear to implement. Most programs are written, compiled, and linked to make one large program. This large program is read from disk into memory and executed. To make virtual memory work, the link must be delayed (keeping the program in small pieces) until the program is executed. The process is called *late binding* and you'll find it in Windows and OS/2 Dynamic Link Libraries or DLLs.

The result is that the executing program loads what it needs only when it's needed. The part of the program loaded will be used, then made a candidate for discarding if it's not used for a while. If another running program needs memory, the system looks for code that is not being used and removes it from memory on a least recently used basis to make room in memory for the running program.

The system programming requirements can become extremely complex. You need to know that the process of keeping program code on disk until it is needed is called running in *virtual memory mode.*

The 80286 CPU and the IBM AT

During much of the struggle to make more memory available on PCs, a new CPU called the Intel 80286 was becoming commercially available from Intel. With improved manufacturing techniques, the 80286 was much more powerful than the 8088/8086. You might say it was two computers in one. Running in what Intel calls *real mode,* the 80286 is nothing more than a fast 8088. In fact, in this mode the 80286 only uses 20 of its 24 address lines. This mode was designed specifically to take advantage of DOS and the tremendous amount of available software until a new operating system could be developed.

80286 Native Mode

The other mode available (frequently called *protected mode,* although that's technically incorrect) is what Intel calls *native mode.* In fact, native mode is a full implementation of a multiuser, multitasking, virtual memory CPU. Virtual memory was only found on large mainframes and some minis at the time the 80286 was being developed. The 80286 splits the machine-language instruction set into operating system instructions and application program instructions.

It also offers a four-level protection scheme to protect the operating system from errant application programs and to protect application programs from each other. This kind of protection did not exist on earlier microprocessors. The name "protected mode" stems from the fact that you need only set one bit in one register (called the protected bit) to enter native mode. If you

you turn on the protected bit without setting up the other necessary elements required in protected mode (native mode), your computer will lock up and require a reset to get it started again.

To run successfully in native mode requires a lot of software preparation. This preparation includes setting up a task state segment and local and global descriptor tables for example. In addition, to make virtual memory work, the 80286 provides (in addition to the protected bit) a present bit, an accessed bit, and a dirty bit.

The *present bit* is set to 1 when the operating system loads a piece of code or data. Since it could be swapped out when it's not in use, the operating system checks the bit to see if it is still in memory when needed or must be reloaded.

The *accessed bit* is set to 1 each time the memory associated with it is accessed for either reading or writing. The operating system checks it at intervals, turns it off, and keeps a running total of the number of times the piece of code or data is accessed. This count is used to see which pieces of code or data are the most likely candidates to be discarded.

If you've changed the contents of a document, the data in memory has changed. If the operating system decided to discard that piece of memory it wouldn't be very nice if it didn't save it first. The *dirty bit* (and yes that is what Intel calls it) simply tells the operating system that a swap candidate has been changed and must be saved to disk before it's discarded out of memory. If it hasn't changed, the information can be discarded without a disk write, saving considerable time.

You can see that these preparations are so involved that we won't even try to describe them further here. They're the province of OS/2, Windows 3.0, and other very complex software that use native mode. Some idea of their complexity might be gained from the fact that when Microsoft released the beta version of OS/2 in April of 1987 they'd already put in 300 man years of work! It might also give you some insight into why OS/2 has been slow in maturing.

Extended Memory

The 80286 running in native mode makes 24 address lines available. This means (looking again at Table 5-1) that you can access up to 16 MB of memory.

To take advantage of this, every 80286 motherboard manufacturer allows you to install additional memory. That extra memory is not directly available when the 80286 is running in real mode and has been given the name *extended memory*—any memory in an 80286 (80386/80486) computer that can be addressed by the CPU running in native mode but that is not available in real mode is called extended memory. Essentially that is any memory in the 1 MB to 16 MB range on the 80286. The same definition applies to the 80386 and 80486.

With that explanation it should be clear that few DOS applications can make use of extended memory. A few software companies decided that resources were being wasted. As mentioned earlier, many programs have been written to use expanded memory—so why not write a device driver that would emulate expanded memory using the extended memory in the 80286. DESQView (QEMM.SYS), 386MAX (386MAX.SYS), Compaq (CEMM.SYS), and a number of other companies developed software drivers called *Expanded Memory Managers* to do exactly that.

Since the memory is normally unavailable to DOS, these programs set things up, switch the computer to native mode (called by most protected mode), and set up an expanded memory emulator that allows programs to think they have expanded memory available. And now that you know what protected mode means, you might as well follow the trend and call native mode protected mode.

The 80386 and 80486

The 80286 has 24 address lines available in protected mode. The 80386 and 80486 boost that number to 32 making it possible for these CPUs to address a whopping 4,000 MB or 4 Gigabytes of physical memory. In protected mode (actually native mode) these CPUs can also use virtual memory methods to address an obscene 64,000 Gigabytes or 64 Terabytes. This doesn't seem limiting at this point—but then neither did 640 KB several years ago.

These CPUs also provide other capabilities too complex to delve into in this book. OS/2 Version 2.0 is one of the first operating systems to begin making use of these capabilities.

5

Extended Memory Managers

A number of device drivers and standards have been developed or proposed to make extended memory available to programs much the way such devices were developed to emulate expanded memory. These standards still presuppose that application software will be designed to take advantage of extended memory drivers like HIMEM.SYS and others.

You'll find that a device driver called HIMEM.SYS provides you with a number of advantages in DOS 5.0. By moving DOS and device drivers to high memory (out of low DOS memory), the room left in conventional memory can reach close to a full 640 KB (637 KB). Just remember that much of this functionality is provided only by an 80386 or 80486 computer.

VCPI

An extended memory driver called Virtual Control Program Interface was developed by Phar Lap Software and QuarterDeck Office Systems. VCPI is used by Lotus 1-2-3 Release 3, AutoCAD, and Paradox.

DPMI

DPMI is the extended memory management specification used by Microsoft for Windows. Until DOS 5.0, VCPI and DPMI would not work cooperatively. In fact, you can only have one program at a time running protected mode (actually native mode) but various extended memory managers do now cooperate.

Memory in a Nutshell

Look again at Figure 5-2 for a review of conventional, reserved, BIOS, and DOS memory. Expanded memory is a hardware and software scheme that allows programs to store *data* in special memory not normally available to DOS. Application programs must be designed specifically to use such memory. Expanded memory might include a special adapter card or an expanded memory emulator on 80286/80386/80486 but it is still an artificial system unrelated to a specific CPU type.

Extended memory is any memory in an 80286 (80386/80486) computer that can be addressed by the CPU running in protected mode (native mode) but which is not available in real mode. This usually means the memory in one of these computers from address 1,048,576 up to the top of the processor's addressing capability.

Unless you become (or are) a programmer, most of these issues are just useful information. If you are adding memory to a PC/XT, you can only have 640 KB. If you need more, you will require an expanded memory card with the proper software (usually supplied with the card).

On a 80286/80386/80486 computer, it is best to install memory that is directly addressable by the CPU in protected mode (native mode). This extended memory requires the installation of a special manufacturer specific memory card or space will be provided on the motherboard. Once installed, you can use an expanded memory emulator (device driver) like CEMM.SYS, QEMM.SYS, or Microsoft's EMM386.EXE. You only need to install an expanded memory emulator if you are using software that can use expanded memory. Look at the system requirements panel on the software package.

Changing Your Video Adapter

Display adapters are installed in the system unit of your computer and work in conjunction with the monitor to furnish the output you normally work with—the computer display screen. The most reliable way to buy a display adapter is to purchase it with a monitor as a pair. The manufacturer will have checked to ensure that the two work well together.

MDA

MDA stands for *Monochrome Display Adapter*. This was the first display adapter ever used with the IBM Personal Computer family. A monochrome display adapter does not produce color. The resolution is 720 pixels horizon-

5

tally by 350 pixels vertically, but this is normally irrelevant, since it cannot produce graphics. The quality of the text, however, is quite good.

If you don't already have one of these display adapters, it would be hard to justify "upgrading" to an MDA board. Perhaps, if you currently have a CGA display, and you find the text too grainy to read (as most people do), and you have no need of graphics or color at all, you might conceivably want to add one of these to your computer. Otherwise, regard it as a museum piece.

Hercules

Hercules Computer Technology in Berkeley, California developed the first graphics adapter for the IBM PC. The Hercules graphics adapter was designed to allow early IBM monochrome displays to do graphics. The resolution remained at 720 by 320 pixels, like the MDA. Hercules software device drivers are needed for software to use the graphics capabilities of this adapter but all text-based software will work with a Hercules board just like an MDA.

CGA

The *Color Graphics Adapter* (CGA) was the first video adapter from IBM to display either color or graphics. It can display up to four colors at a time with a resolution of 320 by 200 pixels. It can also display 1 color at 640 by 200 pixels.

Neither the text nor the graphics are very good with this adapter. If you are moving from monochrome to a color display system you should consider an EGA or VGA adapter instead. Anything less will be a disappointment.

EGA

The *Enhanced Graphics Adapter* pushed the number of colors to 16 and the resolution to 640 by 350 pixels. For most modern applications, this adapter and an appropriate monitor are the minimum acceptable standards. The resolution is high enough that graphics are clear and text is sharp.

MCGA

The *Multi-Color Graphics Array* (MCGA) standard was part of the ill-fated PCjr. Resolutions are 640 by 480 in 2 colors or 320 by 200 in 256 colors. You will not see MCGA mentioned often.

VGA

In 1987 IBM introduced the *Video Graphics Array* (VGA) in their PS/2 line of computers. This was the first display adapter to use analog color signals allowing 256 continuously variable colors and a resolution of 640 by 480 pixels. The resulting display is very good, allowing near photographic image quality on your screen. The cost is only slightly more than EGA and is a very good choice for a computer system.

This standard is now very widely accepted and you will notice that many VGA adapters are available from many different companies. Most software supports VGA. Also, most VGA adapter boards support the earlier formats (EGA and CGA) as well, providing "backwards compatibility."

Super VGA

When IBM announced VGA for the PS/2 computers, dozens of manufacturers jumped to fill the void with VGA for AT-style computers. Then, as time wore on, it became apparent that IBM was not going to introduce another graphics standard in the near future, so the VGA boards makers began tweaking.

Now there's VGA and then there's VGA. Sometimes improving on the "official" IBM standard equipment backfires, if nobody supports the improvements with improved software. In this case, though, the various "Super VGA" enhancements have been very well received. A completely standard IBM VGA display is now seen as something less than optimal.

Figure 5-3 shows a SOTA VGA/16+ high-speed, high-resolution VGA card capable of 1024 by 768 resolution in 262,400 colors. It has both 9-pin and 15-pin D-Sub connectors. An optional chip provides a built-in PS/2 compatible mouse port. The card will work in either an 8- or 16-bit slot and has a

5

Figure 5-3.   *SOTA VGA/16+ high-resolution graphics adapter (Photograph courtesy of SOTA Technology)*

VGA pass-through connector at the top. (A section will be devoted to pass-through shortly.)

8514/A

Some time after VGA, IBM introduced the first display adapter to have its own CPU on it. The 8514/A display controller is an "intelligent" board offering 1024 by 768 resolution in 256 colors. This is a relatively exotic, high-performance display adapter that has not caught the public's attention. Because the display adapter has its own CPU, it is more difficult for software developers to support an 8514/A than, say, a VGA board.

XGA

The *Extended Graphics Adapter* (XGA) provides 1024 by 768 and 1280 by 1024 in 256 colors. So far, it's too new to have acquired much of a following.

TIGA

Resolutions for TIGA range from 640 by 480 to 4096 by 4096 with over 16 million colors. Figure 5-4 shows the SOTA 340i, which is a TIGA/DGIS (Texas Instruments Graphic Array/Display Graphics Interface Standard). This display adapter provides VGA pass-through, 1024 by 768 resolution in 16 million colors, and high speed for graphics and CAD operations.

The Texas Instrument 34010 graphics IC has made heavy inroads and is used in a number of high-end display adapters. The advantage is speed. The disadvantage is, again, that few software developers provide drivers for these fast, high-resolution adapters.

If your requirements are in the CAD world, these display adapters are worth considering. Some have VGA capabilities built in, others provide VGA pass-through.

5

Figure 5-4. *SOTA 340i TIGA "Intelligent Graphics System" (Photograph courtesy of SOTA Technology)*

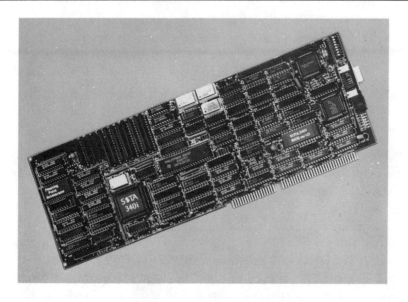

Special Monitors and Display Adapters

The VGA monitor is adequate for most operations. There are other monitors that will provide you with a larger viewing area and more display speed than the standard VGA monitor.

A list of some display adapters is provided in Appendix C, "Connector Reference." You will also find other manufacturers who provide display adapters with these resolutions. Many are not well supported with software drivers. Each new software advance requires manufacturers to provide new drivers.

- The SOTA View System in Figure 5-5 is one of several high-resolution, paper-white display systems designed for desktop publishing and CAD. This system provides 1660 by 1200 resolution and allows facing pages of legal documents to be displayed side by side (dual page).

- The SOTA 340i is a display adapter that provides up to a 1280 by 1024 pixel display. It can display 16 or 256 colors out of a palette of 16 million colors on a compatible monitor.

- The Wyse 700 is a monitor and adapter that provides a 1280 by 800 pixel paper-white monochrome display. There are video drivers for a large selection of software.

- The Rasterex GS100 in conjunction with the Rasterex Starlight board will provide you with a 1280 by 1024 pixel display. The monitor can display 256 colors out of a palette of 4096 colors.

Video Board Features

There are a couple of features that video adapter board makers advertise that may not be immediately obvious to you. Even within a relatively strict video standard, there are sometimes enhancements and improvements that can be made.

Video Memory

Most VGA adapters are provided with 256 Kbits (32 KB) of video memory installed. This memory is used to store the screen image and is modified by the computer and software as required. You can display a 640 by 480 image

Figure 5-5. *SOTA View System (Photograph courtesy of SOTA Technology)*

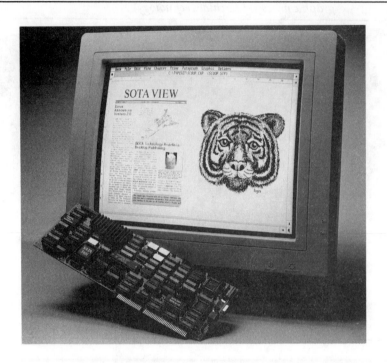

in 16 colors with 256 Kbits of video memory. Most allow an additional 256 KB to be installed for a total of 512 Kbits, which will allow 640 by 480, 256 color or 1024 by 768, 16-color operation.

Some display adapters such as Orchid Technology's ProDesigner II, shown in Figure 5-6, allow the installation of up to 1 Mbits of video memory, which boosts the display capability to 1024 by 768 with 256 simultaneous colors. This adapter and a Mitsubishi Diamond Scan 16L color monitor will probably fill your display needs for a number of years.

Pass-through

Some of the more exotic display adapters (especially TIGA) offer a feature called *pass-through*. Pass-through simply means that you must have a VGA

Figure 5-6. *Orchid Technology's ProDesigner II super VGA display (Photo-graph courtesy of Orchid Technology)*

display adapter in addition to the TIGA; a short cable is provided to connect the two together. When you run software that supports the TIGA display, the TIGA display will start working. Otherwise, the TIGA board will pass through all the display commands to your VGA board.

This allows you to use a more standard VGA adapter along with the TIGA adapter in the same computer. The reason for this is that not all software supports TIGA displays.

8-bit Versus 16-bit Slot

Most display adapters are designed to work in an 8-bit slot. Some of the higher performance ones can use a 16-bit slot as well. In these cases, the board may be plugged into an 8-bit slot if necessary. It will still function, but the graphics will be a bit slower.

Adding Input and Output Controllers

Input and output ports are your PC's links to the outside world. Your keyboard provides input to your computer, and the video adapter board and monitor are output devices. But there are other kinds of input and output devices, too. The three most common types for a PC are the serial communications port, the parallel communications port, and the game adapter port. All three of these will be covered in this section.

You've probably got a couple of input/output (I/O) ports on your PC already. Besides the necessary ones already mentioned (keyboard, monitor, disks) you should have at least one serial port and one parallel port as well. You might already be using your parallel port for a printer, and your serial port for a modem or a mouse. If you haven't already got these, then now you know what they can be used for. If you do already have them, then you may want to add more so that you can attach an extra printer or a plotter or scanner, or so that you can have a mouse and a modem.

A full complement of I/O ports would be four serial communications ports, three parallel ports, and a game adapter port. Any more than this, and you're wasting money and electricity. But once you have them, it's surprising how quickly you'll find uses for them.

5

About I/O Devices

If you've read the section earlier in this chapter about memory you have a good idea about how computer addresses work. Each byte's worth of memory is given a unique address so that the CPU can read and write data to and from each individual location. The same is true of I/O devices. Each I/O controller board will take up some amount of space in your I/O address map. And, like memory, each one must have a different address. You can't have two that overlap.

The confusing part is that the memory addresses and the I/O addresses have nothing to do with each other. For example, you might have memory at address 300, *and* an I/O device at address 300. That's not a conflict. But having two memories at address 300 or two I/O devices at address 300 would be. Remember, I/O addresses and memory addresses are different.

Also, I/O devices like to be addressed at particular locations. Your PC is designed to look for serial I/O ports, for example, at a few special addresses. Unlike memory, you can't add I/O devices haphazardly. There is a limit to how many serial, parallel, and game adapters your PC can use.

Interrupts

Another thing that sets I/O devices apart from memory devices is that I/O devices can generate interrupts. An interrupt is something that allows the I/O device to stop the CPU and make it do something else.

This might sound kind of drastic, and if it's not handled properly, it can be. But interrupts are also vital to making your computer operate efficiently. And once you understand how interrupts work, it's pretty simple to do.

There is a special wire that runs to the CPU chip in your PC called an *interrupt line.* If a special electrical signal is sent through this wire to the CPU, it will stop running the program it is currently executing and start running a different program. This new program is called an *Interrupt Service Routine,* or ISR, and it is not a normal applications program like you buy in the store. Instead, it is one of the built-in parts of DOS that you don't normally see. When the ISR program is through running, the CPU will pick up where it left off with the previous program as though nothing happened.

The whole purpose of the interrupt is to get your computer's attention and make it do something special right away. Suppose you were playing an arcade game with your PC using a joystick attached to a game adapter board. Every time you press the button on your joystick, the game adapter board will generate an interrupt. When the CPU gets the interrupt, it will start executing the ISR, and the ISR will make sure your arcade game does what it is supposed to do when you press a button.

Without interrupts, your computer might never know that you'd pressed the button. Getting an interrupt is like hearing the telephone ring. You are free to go about your business without worrying about someone calling you on the telephone because you know that it will ring if anybody does. The alternative would be to constantly stop, pick up the telephone, and listen for a voice. Obviously, it is much more efficient to let the telephone interrupt you when it needs to. The same is true of your computer.

Although there is only one interrupt signal going to the CPU chip in your PC, there are several different interrupt wires connected to the expansion slots. All of these separate interrupt wires are "bunched together" into one by a chip called the *interrupt controller.*

One of the problems with the PC and XT is a shortage of interrupt lines. They have only eight interrupt lines apiece, handled by one interrupt controller. The AT has two interrupt controllers working together for a total of 15 interrupts, but most adapter cards limit your selection to one of the first eight.

The electronics are not important—the number of interrupt lines available for upgrading is, since assigning two adapter cards to the same interrupt is a sure way to cause problems. Appendix B, "Technical Information," contains a list of available interrupts and indicates their uses.

Setting I/O Addresses and Interrupts

When installing I/O adapter cards you will usually find switches or jumpers that allow you to select the I/O address and an interrupt for the adapter card. Remember that, depending on what the card does, you will have a very limited number of choices regarding I/O addresses and interrupt assignments. Fortunately, this only makes configuring the board easier for you.

You might also get a *multifunction board.* This is a board with several I/O devices on it, like two serial ports and two parallel ports. Most multifunction cards will provide you with the ability to disable unused ports. For example, you may only need one serial and one parallel port. In this case you can disable the other two devices, making their interrupts and I/O addresses available to other adapter cards that might need them.

Serial Communications Port

A serial communications port is a good thing to have. Most PCs now have one built into the motherboard. Serial communications ports (or "com ports") are very versatile and can interface to most any peripheral. Of the three types of I/O ports covered here, the com port is the only one that could fulfill the functions of the other two.

Serial communication is a technique that allows one computer to talk to another computer, or to another device, by sending data through a single wire. This is the simplest and most widely used system of transferring data between machines in the world. That is why a serial com port is so useful.

5

The technique is called serial communication because all of the data is sent along the single wire in a continuous stream, or series. Serial communication is not the fastest type of communication possible, but it is usually fast enough for the needs of PC owners, and it has the advantage of being adaptable to a number of different situations. For example, serial ports are used to transmit data to modems, which in turn transmit data through telephone lines. The telephone system is an excellent example of a serial communication network.

You can also use your serial ports to interface to printers. Most printers and plotters offer a serial interface option. If you are considering adding a mouse to your PC you may find that it will connect very nicely to a serial communications port.

In IBM PC parlance, the serial ports are called COM1, COM2, COM3, and COM4. These are just names attached to the four possible serial ports, and have no particular significance. You will see them referred to in this manner quite often. One important bit of information to keep in mind is that COM1 doesn't mean your first serial port. Technically, it means the serial port at I/O address 3F8 that uses interrupt 4. You might have a serial port at COM2 without one at COM1. The names are shorthand for how they are configured, not when you bought them.

The names COM1 through COM4 refer to the I/O address and interrupts of the four possible serial ports. Your first serial port is not necessarily COM1.

Remember

Serial Connectors

All of the serial I/O ports used on the PC and XT look the same. They use a 25-pin male D-Sub connector. A lot of people have wondered why a 25-pin connector is necessary when data is only transmitted over one wire. The answer lies buried in a lot of history and electrical nomenclature. Basically, the serial ports on your PC conform to a standard set up by the Institute of Electrical and Electronic Engineers (IEEE), a worldwide standards organization. They devised standard number RS-232C, which governs serial interfaces. In order to cover as many bases as possible, they specified (some would say "over-specified") 25 signal pins to be used for all sorts of serial communications. Your PC only uses 10 of them.

The signal and control lines associated with the RS-232C implementation in most serial adapter cards for the IBM PC, XT, and compatibles are assigned as listed in Table 5-2.

The connectors used all have numbered pins that correspond to the pin numbers shown. Pins 10, 12 through 17, 19, 21, 23, and 24 are not used. Pins 9, 11, 18, and 25 are sometimes used in sending and receiving data through what is called a "current loop" and are seldom used in modern RS-232C communications.

On AT computers and compatibles, these nine signal lines are packed into a male 9-pin D-Sub connector. This situation frequently requires a 9-pin to 25-pin adapter, which may be supplied by vendors of some equipment—particularly mice. The connections are listed in Table 5-3. Note that the redundant GND pin has been removed.

Parallel Communication Port

After adding your serial communications port, you'll want a parallel port, too. Parallel ports aren't nearly as flexible as serial ports, but they can be just as indispensable. Parallel ports are used mostly for printer ports.

Table 5-2.   *Input or Output Signal Line Descriptions Used for the PC, XT, and Compatibles*

Pin	Input or Output	Signal Line Description
1		GND — Connected to Ground
2	OUTPUT	TxD — Transmit Data
3	INPUT	RxD — Receive Data
4	OUTPUT	RTS — Request to Send
5	INPUT	CTS — Clear to Send
6	INPUT	DSR — Data Set Ready
7		GND — Connected to Ground
8	INPUT	DCD — Data Carrier Detect
20	OUTPUT	DTR — Data Terminal Ready
22	INPUT	RI — Ring Indicator

Table 5-3.   *Input or Output Signal Line Descriptions Used for the AT and Compatibles*

Pin	Input or Output	Signal Line Description
1	INPUT	DCD — Data Carrier Detect
2	INPUT	RxD — Receive Data line
3	OUTPUT	TxD — Transmit Data line
4	OUTPUT	DTR — Data Terminal Ready
5		GND — Connected to Ground
6	INPUT	DSR — Data Set Ready
7	OUTPUT	RTS — Request to Send
8	INPUT	CTS — Clear to Send
9	INPUT	RI — Ring Indicator

A parallel port works by sending data through a collection of eight wires at once. Unlike a serial interface, a parallel interface can send an entire byte of data at once by using eight data wires. Theoretically at least, this allows your PC to send data faster than a serial port.

The PC parallel ports are called LPT1, LPT2, and LPT3. Your PC only supports three parallel ports, but this is usually ample. Like the serial ports, each parallel port has a "preferred" I/O address and interrupt that they like to use. Sticking to these preset standards will save you a lot of frustration later on.

When you start your PC and boot DOS, it assumes that you have a printer attached to the port at LPT1. For example, if you issue the PRINT command, DOS will ask you where you want to send the printed output, and if you simply press (ENTER) without changing the assignment, DOS will print to your LPT1 port (also called PRN).

All PCs, XTs, and ATs since the early days have used the same connector for their parallel ports. This is a 25-pin female D-Sub connector. It looks like the serial connector on earlier PCs, except it's female instead of male.

Game Adapter Port

The IBM Game Control Adapter was designed for use with a pair of joysticks to allow various games to be played on the PC. Many IBM PC games allow a joystick to be used if one is connected to your computer.

The game port connector is a female 15-pin D-Sub but even when the port is included on a multifunction card you will often have to buy an additional cable and the connector must be attached to an adapter bracket, which will take up slot space.

There is only support for one game port, but that's enough for two joysticks. The game port is located at I/O address 200.

Multifunction Boards

There are a number of adapter cards on the market that provide many of the most needed functions on a single adapter card. The best way to choose one is to decide what you need for your computer, then look for a card that fills most if not all of your requirements.

There are cards available that provide monochrome graphics, serial ports, parallel ports, a game port, and a clock for the IBM PC/XT and compatibles. Since many of these older machines have only five slots to begin with, this is a good card for circumstances that require these capabilities.

In fact, you can find many different combinations for many different circumstances. Just look at your requirements and the capability of your computer, decide what functions you need, and buy the card that fits those needs. The clock on these cards will be useless in an AT or compatible, but it will save resetting the time and the date on a PC or XT every time that you boot the system.

Most multifunction cards provide one or two serial ports and one or two parallel ports. Such cards will usually have one parallel and one serial connector mounted on the adapter bracket that is attached to the card. Additional connectors might be included on a second adapter bracket, which you will then have to install in a second slot, unless your computer case is one

5

of the newer types that has several 9-pin and 25-pin connector cutouts available in the back.

If you already have serial or parallel ports installed in your computer, you will have to decide which ports to disable, if any, to avoid I/O address or interrupt conflicts.

For example, say you purchase a multifunction serial/parallel card with two serial ports and two parallel ports. You already have a monochrome graphics card with a parallel port installed in your computer. Since you cannot readily use three parallel ports, you will need to disable LPT1 on your new multifunction card. Most monochrome display/parallel port cards have the parallel port permanently fixed as LPT1 and you cannot disable it. Therefore, you have no choice but to disable LPT1 on your new card. The manual that comes with the card will usually show you the switch and jumper settings necessary to do this.

Another example would be the case where you have an internal modem using COM1. In this case you would disable COM1 on your new multifunction card or you could set your modem to use COM2 and disable COM2 on the new card. The point is that any combination you use will be based on the notion of having one each of COM1, COM2, LPT1, and LPT2 available.

Many motherboards now include two built-in serial ports and one or two built-in parallel ports. Any one or all of them might also be disabled. With a case that provides I/O cutouts (holes in the back of the case designed for D-Sub connectors) separately from adapter slots, you can save at least one and possibly more adapter slots.

Installing an Expansion Board

Regardless of the function of your particular board, you can install all of them in more or less the same manner. First, give yourself plenty of space and plenty of time. When you've got the system case open, you'll need some room to work. Before you start, be sure to review the general information and antistatic precautions in Chapter 3, "Taking a Look Inside Your PC."

Before you begin installation of your board, read through the manual supplied with it and acquaint yourself with the location of various parts. You should be able to locate the switches and jumpers mentioned in the manual and you should also know what the various connectors are used for. Once you've done this, decide which functions you want to use (for a multifunction board) and which cables and adapter brackets will be required. This would be a good time to connect the cables from the extra adapter brackets, if any, to the appropriate connectors on the multifunction card.

Setting Adapter Card Jumpers and Switches

Each card you purchase will have the switches and jumpers located in different places on the card. You must review the manual to locate these and determine their purpose. Once you've done this, you can set the switches and jumpers to establish I/O addresses, memory addresses, or interrupts or to disable those ports you don't intend to use. Making a mistake will not damage anything but could result in your computer not functioning.

Opening Your Computer Case

Be sure your computer is turned off and the power cord is unplugged. Locate the slot in which you will install the new adapter card, and ensure that cables are not going to interfere with the installation. If cables are in the way, carefully note where and how they are connected, then disconnect them temporarily.

Removing the Expansion Slot Cover

Remove the expansion slot cover (Figure 5-7) using a Phillips-head screwdriver or hex nut driver of the proper size. Save this cover—if you ever decide to take the adapter card back out, you'll want this bracket to fill the empty space. Although your system might function with a missing bracket, it will eventually interfere with proper cooling and allow dirt to enter your computer.

Installing Your New Adapter Card

Install the adapter card (Figure 5-8). Carefully position the card and slide it into the computer. Be sure the adapter bracket goes into the slot at the

Figure 5-7.   *Removing the expansion slot cover*

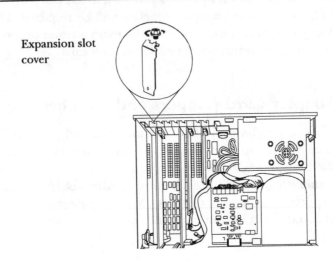

Expansion slot
cover

Figure 5-8.   *Installing an adapter card*

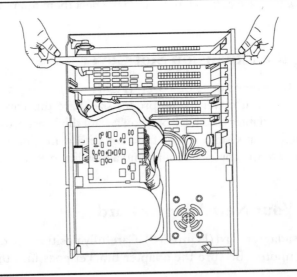

bottom rear of the case and gently but firmly press the 8-bit bus connector into the motherboard slot connector. Now align the adapter bracket. Using the screw removed earlier, attach the adapter bracket to the computer case. Tighten the screw only moderately tightly. It should not require a lot of force, and applying excessive torque could strip the threads in the computer case or on the screw. Close the case and install and tighten the screws that hold the cover in place.

Making External Connections to Your Adapter Card

Plug in the power cord and turn the power on. Your computer should boot as usual. If it does not, you will need to go back over your switch and jumper settings to see what you may have missed. Once your computer boots correctly, you can start connecting your external equipment as needed and test it to ensure that it performs the way you like.

5

Summary

That's all there is to adding the expansion boards. In this chapter, you learned enough about memory to help you understand what to buy when you need more, and how to install it. You learned how to change your video adapter and to add input and output controllers.

In the next chapter, you will see how to add more storage capacity to your PC with new floppy disk drives, hard disk drives, and tape drives.

6

Adding Storage Devices

How convenient it would be if you could store everything you needed in your computer memory to be easily and quickly retrieved right when you needed it. In the real world, storing in memory has several disadvantages, the biggest being cost. The memory chips in your PC also "forget" what's in them when the power is turned off—obviously, not acceptable behavior where your programs, data files, and years of work are concerned. This chapter discusses floppy disks, hard disks, tapes, and other options for permanent mass storage to determine what best fits your needs.

Disk Drives

Disk drives tend to be one of the more complicated parts of a PC. This means that for most users there are some aspects of disks and disk drives that are not familiar. To really understand what some of the unfamiliar words mean, and to make better-informed decisions, a little background on disk drives might be necessary. In this section, some basic terms will be defined, and the workings of a hard disk and a floppy disk will be described. The intent here is not to make you an expert, but to make you feel more comfortable in unfamiliar territory.

Basically, a disk drive is a combination of two devices that you are probably already familiar with: tape recorders and record players. Computer permanent mass storage systems use magnetic recording techniques like the audio cassette tape recorder in a stereo system. A disk drive spins a disk around like a record player on a turntable, but the information recorded on the disk is in magnetic form just as it is on a cassette tape.

Magnetic Disks

If you open up the square plastic jacket on a 5 1/4-inch floppy disk, you'll find a round plastic disk inside, as shown in Figure 6-1. This is the actual magnetic recording media that stores your information; the square cover is just for protection. The disk will be light and very thin (hence the name, floppy disk), and usually dark brown. The brown color is a result of the magnetic iron oxide in the disk. There should be one big hole in the center, about the size of a quarter, with one or more smaller holes around it.

If you open up one of the smaller 3 1/2-inch floppy disks, you'll find that it looks pretty much the same. One difference is that the center hole has a metal hub in it. The cover around the outside is made of tougher plastic.

The round plastic disk inside the square cover is made of the same stuff that cassette tapes and VCR tapes are made of. It is just a circle cut out of plastic that's been coated with a special magnetic substance. The magnetic strength of the coating on the disk is very weak (you can't use it to pick up paper clips, for instance) but it is strong enough for its purpose.

Some metals (among them iron, nickel, and cobalt) can be magnetized. The coating on the surface of both hard and floppy disks is made of material that can easily be magnetized and demagnetized. This is usually a combination of iron oxide (and other magnetic metal oxides) finely powdered and mixed with a binder much like paint. Some hard disk platters are actually plated with magnetic material to resist wear.

Electrical current flowing through a coil of wire produces a magnetic field. This principle is used to make read/write heads for disk drives. If a lot of current is passed through the head, it will magnetize the coating on the disk

Figure 6-1. *Inside a 5 1/4-inch floppy disk*

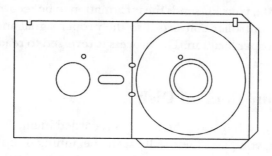

to a higher degree than if we pass a small current through it. In a reverse manner, if a magnetic field is moved past a coil of wire, a small current is caused to flow in the coil of wire. The first principle is used to record (write) information on the disk—the second to read it back.

The resulting recording on the floppy or hard disk is a very complex signal and the techniques used to record it could fill a chapter in this book. The techniques go by the name *Frequency Modulation* (FM) and *Modified Frequency Modulation* (MFM). The entire process is managed by the drive controller and drive electronics. The fact is that computer information can be sent to the controller and recorded. When requested to do so, the controller will go find the information and return the exact information (bits and bytes) that was originally recorded.

What about inside the disk drive? Once the disk is placed inside the floppy disk drive, it can be rotated by a small motor. This is just like spinning a record on a turntable. The motor spins at a constant speed, usually 300 RPM. And that's not the only similarity between a floppy disk drive and a turntable. A turntable has an arm with a phonograph needle at the end, and a disk drive has a very similar arrangement. Instead of a needle, a disk drive has a small coil called a *read/write* head at the end of the arm. The head is very small.

As the disk spins, the arm can move either in, towards the center of the disk, or out, towards the edge of the disk in discrete stops. Between the movement of the arm and spinning of the disk the magnetic head can cover every possible spot on your disk. In order to make use of both sides of the disk, there is an identical arm and head arrangement underneath the disk as well. Both arms move at once.

To record data, your PC sends the information to be recorded to the drive controller. The controller converts it to the proper signal and records it on the disk in the proper location. The process is reversed to read the data back.

Locating Your Data on Disk

On a phonograph record, the music is recorded in one long, continuous spiral. To play it, you place the needle at the beginning or outside edge, and it works its way toward the center. For a hard disk or a floppy disk, the information isn't recorded in a single spiral. Instead, it is recorded in rings. Every ring of data goes all the way around the surface of the disk, and each subsequent ring starts just inside the previous one. The rings never cross, although they are very close together (unlike records where one song can merge into the next). A floppy disk will record data in 40 to 80 separate rings. Each ring is called a *track* shown in Figure 6-2. You will hear the word track often in connection with disk drives. Hard disk drives have quite a few more tracks than floppy disks, some with more than 1000.

Each track makes a complete circle around the disk. But often your PC doesn't want to read or write that much information, so each track is divided up into smaller portions. If you draw imaginary lines from the center of your disk out to the edge (like cutting a pizza), you will have divided up each track into equal parts. These are called *sectors*. Floppy disks are usually divided up into 8, 9, or 15 sectors. Hard disks are divided up into 17 or more sectors.

Nearly every floppy disk drive has a magnetic head (called a read/write head) on both sides of the disk, so that one side isn't wasted. Hard disk drives typically hold more than one disk in them. A hard disk with four or five disks inside it is not unusual as shown in Figure 6-3. Each of these disks is divided into tracks, and each disk has a head on each side of it. So, a hard disk drive with five disks inside will have ten heads.

Tracks are numbered starting from the outside of the disk, beginning with track 0. The next track in is track 1, and so on. The innermost track on a floppy disk would be track 39 (for a 40-track disk) or 79 (for an 80-track disk). You can refer to a group made up of the same track on each disk (that is,

Figure 6-2.   *Disk tracks and sectors*

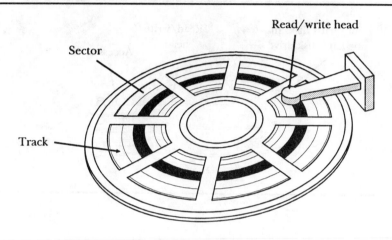

track 1 on the top disk, track 1 on the disk underneath, and so on) forming what is called a *cylinder*. This word is also used a lot. A cylinder is simply a collection of all of the tracks that lie one above another. Cylinders are numbered the same way. Cylinder 0 consists of track 0 from each side of every disk. Cylinder 79 means track 79 from all disk sides, and so forth.

When your PC records data on the disk, it also remembers where on the disk the data was stored. It does this by recording the cylinder, track, disk side (or head), and sector where the recording was made. Then, when you want to retrieve that information, it can select the proper head (disk side), place the head over the correct cylinder, and wait for the disk to turn the appropriate number of sectors.

Even though the mechanical workings inside a disk drive are pretty accurate, they're not perfect. But because the data you store is so important, it is crucial that the disk drive always be able to find any given spot on the disk, and find it quickly. For this reason, there are some built-in aids to help your PC locate your data.

Each sector holds a certain amount of data, usually 512 bytes. In addition to the data that belongs to you, each sector will also store its own *address*—that is, each sector will have a sector ID number written into it. Where does the

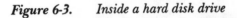

Figure 6-3.   *Inside a hard disk drive*

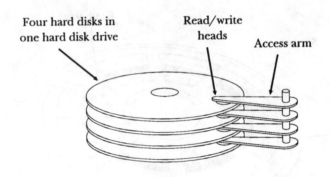

Four hard disks in   Read/write
one hard disk drive   heads
                                    Access arm

sector head come from? You put it on yourself every time you format a disk
with the FORMAT command.

Factors Affecting Disk Performance

Disk drives are an important part of your PC, no question. A hard disk
drive can make up a significant portion of the price of your PC, too,
especially if it is a large hard disk, say 100 MB or greater. When you're ready
to select a disk drive to put into your PC, you'll want to give a lot of
consideration to what you want to use the disk for, and how long you'll want
to keep it. There are two or three important measurements that you need to
be familiar with to select the best disk drive for your needs.

Disk Density

In a sense, you could say that a floppy disk drive has an infinite capacity
to store data. After all, when one floppy disk gets full, you just take it out and
put in another one. You can store information on floppies forever, as long
as you don't run out of floppies. But what really counts is how much you can
store on each individual floppy disk—the more the better.

When the IBM PC was first introduced, it had one floppy disk drive and
no hard disk. The floppy disk drive was single-sided (one head) and could

store about 160,000 bytes. Later, two-sided drives were introduced that could store 368,640 bytes of data (360 KB) on one floppy disk. That's about equal to 150 single-spaced typed pages.

Now you can get disk drives that store much more than that. If you have a 360 KB floppy disk drive, this is one area where you'll probably want to upgrade. An important point to remember here is that storage capacity depends on two things: the disk drive and the floppy disks you put into it.

A 360 KB 5 1/4-inch floppy disk drive is generally called a *double-density* disk drive. The term density refers to how densely packed the magnetic bits are on the disk surface and to the number of tracks. When the IBM AT came out, it sported a new, higher capacity 5 1/4-inch floppy disk drive that could store 1,228,800 bytes of data (1.2 MB) on a single disk. These have come to be called *quad-density,* or *high-density* disk drives.

The 3 1/2-inch drives also come in a double-density and a quad-density style. The double density 3 1/2-inch drive stores 730,112 bytes (720 KB), and the quad-density drive can store 1,457,664 bytes (1.44 MB). It is perfectly alright (and sometimes more convenient) to mix any or all of these four types of floppy disk drives in one PC, but one of each high density type is usually best.

You must be sure to use the correct type of floppy disks for each type of floppy disk drive. Even though all 5 1/4-inch floppy disks look the same, some can store 360 KB, while others can store 1.2 MB. The same is true of 3 1/2-inch diskettes. Be sure to buy and
member *use only the correct type for your disk drive(s).*

Access Time and Seek Time

Floppy disks are stable, reliable, and relatively slow. Hard disks are much faster and have a much greater storage capacity. Their only limitations are their fixed storage capacity and their higher cost. For most users, these drawbacks are easily offset by the increased speed of a hard disk.

While a floppy drive may take a second or more to read data from a disk, a hard disk drive rarely takes more than one-tenth of that time. Over the life of the average PC, that increased speed can mean a lot of extra work accomplished. But exactly how much faster is a hard disk drive?

The most time-consuming part of any disk operation, whether it be a read or a write, floppy disk or hard disk, is the time it takes to move the read/write head to the proper position. That involves mechanical movement. All the rest is electronic, and so it occurs more quickly. So, the faster the heads can move into position, the faster your PC can write new data to a disk, or read existing data from it. This is known as the disk drive's *seek time,* or *access time.*

The access time is measured in thousandths of a second, or *milliseconds.* Five hundred milliseconds is the same as one-half of one second (0.500 second). A mediocre hard disk drive might have an access time of 40 milliseconds or more. A good one might have a 25 millisecond access time, and an access time of 15 milliseconds is very good, indeed. These times are necessarily averages. It takes longer to move the heads from the very outside of the disk to the very inside, for example, than it does to move the heads only a few tracks. The average access time will give you a good overall idea of how fast the heads can move.

The difference between 15 milliseconds and 40 milliseconds may not seem very great. After all, what's a few thousandths of a second? That's less time than it takes to blink an eye. But think of this important statistic as you would the interest rate on your savings account. A few fractions may not seem like much, but when you compound it over the hours, days, months, and years that you will use your PC, it can make a very great difference. A slow hard disk can be frustrating over time.

Floppy Disk Drives

You are most likely to install an additional floppy disk drive to supplement a floppy drive you already have in your system. The two standard sizes are 5 1/4-inch and 3 1/2-inch. The 5 1/4-inch floppy drive was the PC basic size for a number of years. Most of the full-size, desktop computers still use 5 1/4-inch floppies. On the other hand, nearly all battery powered laptop computers use 3 1/2-inch floppy disk drives. When IBM introduced the PS/2 line of computers they used 3 1/2-inch floppy drives, too. That encouraged many software companies to offer programs on the smaller diskettes.

Floppy disk drives will be used for one of three reasons:

- As the only drive in your system you will use it for all program and data storage. It will also be your *boot drive*—that is, the drive from which you start your computer.

- As a drive available in addition to a hard disk drive it will be used as a means of transferring software to your hard disk drive and as a means of exchanging data between computers.

- You may also use a floppy disk drive as a means of backing up your programs and data as a precaution against loss.

You need to have at least one floppy disk drive. Having both a 5 1/4-inch drive and a 3 1/2-inch drive will make your work easier for a couple of reasons. Software is occasionally available on only 5 1/4-inch disks or only 3 1/2-inch disks. It is also possible that users to whom you will want to send disks or receive disks may not have the same disk drive size you are using. With one drive of each type these problems are eliminated. Having two drives of the *same* type makes it easier to duplicate floppy disks, while having two drives of *different* types makes it easy to alternate between disk formats.

Both 5 1/4-inch and 3 1/2-inch drives are available in a low-capacity version or a high-capacity version. The high-capacity versions of either drive will read low-capacity disks (of the same size, obviously). However, a high-capacity drive will write to a low-capacity diskette. The low-capacity drives will not read or write high-capacity disks at all. For this reason it is best to buy the high-capacity version of either drive size if your system will handle it. Table 6-1 summarizes the combinations that work.

Whether your system will handle a high-capacity drive or not depends on your computer, your BIOS, and the version of DOS you are using. If you have an older PC or XT computer, you may have to upgrade one or more of these items as well. This will be discussed later in this chapter, under the section entitled "Installation."

5 1/4-Inch Floppy Disk Drives

As mentioned previously, 5 1/4-inch floppy disk drives come in double-density (360 KB) and quad- or high-density (1.2 MB) types. The selection is up to you, although the 1.2 MB drive seems like the obvious choice. The one drawback to 1.2 MB drives is that they cannot write reliably to a low-density diskette. The low-capacity disk you make will work fine in your high-capacity drive, but it may not be readable in a low-capacity drive. If you need to

Table 6-1. *High- and Low-Capacity Workable Combinations*

Drive Type and Capacity	Read Low	Write Low	Read High	Write High
5 1/4 Low 360 KB	Y	Y	N	N
5 1/4 High 1.2 MB	Y	Y*	Y	Y
3 1/2 Low 720 KB	Y	Y	N	N
3 1/2 High 1.4 MB	Y	Y*	Y	Y

*May not be readable in a low-density drive

exchange a lot of floppies with someone else who can only accept 360 KB disks, this will pose a problem.

Apart from the issue of storage density, 5 1/4-inch floppy drives are also offered in full-height, half-height, and third-height versions. This refers to the physical dimensions of the disk drive itself, not to the size or type of disks it handles. In 1980, all floppy disk drives were about 5 inches tall. These were used in the original IBM PC and are now called *full-height* drives. Since that time, constant miniaturization has allowed PC makers to shrink the size of the disk drive without affecting its performance. If anything, the newer, smaller drives are faster and more reliable. They also use less power.

Compaq and some other computer makers have started using even smaller drives in their systems that are only about one inch tall. These so-called *third-height* drives are not as plentiful as the half-height ones, but you should have no trouble locating one—just be sure it will fit in your computer.

Even if your computer normally takes full-height drives, you may be able to install half- or third-height drives inside it. The smaller drive simply won't take up as much space. The only problem might be an aesthetic one. With the new disk drive only filling up half of the hole, you might be left with an empty space in the front of your PC, unless you get a blank filler panel. These are pretty common, and are often supplied with small disk drives for exactly this purpose.

3 1/2-Inch Floppy Disk Drives

The newer 3 1/2-inch floppy disks are rugged, small enough to fit in a shirt pocket, and do not require a protective paper sleeve. They are also considerably more expensive than 5 1/4-inch disks. The 720 KB version records 9 sectors on 80 tracks per side. The 1.44 MB version records 18 sectors on 80 tracks per side.

The only difference between the high- and low-capacity disks supplied by various disk manufacturers seems to be that the low-capacity disk case has a hole on the left side and the high-capacity disk case has a hole on both sides. Some 3 1/2-inch drives use these holes to sense the type of disk (high or low density) inserted and will automatically shift to the correct density.

Note

There is a punch available that lets you punch an extra hole in a 720 KB disk to make it look like a 1.44 disk. The punch costs close to $40 and many people report that it works. Such a procedure could save the price of the punch in a short time but use this procedure with care.

Unlike the 5 1/4-inch disk drives, 3 1/2-inch floppy drives come only in a half-height version. This makes them considerably smaller than a 5 1/4-inch disk driver overall (even a half-height one). In order to make a 3 1/2-inch disk drive fit in a 5 1/4-inch drive space, many of them are equipped with oversized mounting rails and screws. If your PC normally only takes 5 1/4-inch disk drives, this arrangement will allow you to add a 3 1/2-inch drive anyway. Even the cosmetic faceplate is the right size to fill a 5 1/4-inch hole.

6

Hard Disk Drives

Hard disk drives are the larger, faster, more expensive cousins to floppy disk drives. Although every PC must have a floppy disk drive, not everyone has a hard disk drive (although most PC users wish that they did). If you don't already have a hard disk drive (also called a Winchester disk, fixed disk, or rigid disk), then this is something you'll definitely want to consider. If you do have a hard disk drive, you may be ready for a larger one.

Hard disks do the same thing that floppy disks do: they store your programs and data. But hard disk drives are much faster than floppies, and store far more information. For professional use, a hard disk is a necessity.

Hard Disk Characteristics

So far, everything that has been discussed about floppy disk drives is true of hard disk drives, too. But there are some features of hard disk drives that make them unique. Some make hard disks more desirable, and some make them more fragile.

On a floppy disk drive, the disk spins at a constant 300 RPM and the magnetic read/write heads slide across the surface of the disk (in contact). The surface of the disk and the bottom of the head are both smooth, so no damage is done. Inside a hard disk drive, the disks spin much faster, typically at 3600 RPM. Also, the disks are made of rigid metal, or even glass. But most importantly, the read/write heads do not touch the surface of the disks. At 3600 RPM, any prolonged contact between them would quickly destroy both head and disk.

Instead of touching, the heads inside a hard disk literally fly over the tops of the disks. They ride on an amazingly thin cushion of air just over the surface. The air cushion allows the heads to get close enough to magnetize the disk's surface, but not so close that they rub and heat up. If the heads ever touch the surface of a hard disk, it's called a *head crash*. A head crash is about the worst possible thing that can happen to a hard disk drive. The heads heat up and are ruined. The surface of the disk has its thin magnetic coating scraped off, thus destroying any data that was stored there. Worst of all, the clean air inside the hard disk drive is contaminated by flying particles, probably causing the other heads to crash.

This is why you should never, ever remove the cover of a hard disk drive. Opening the cover and allowing normal "fresh" air into a hard disk is like shoveling garbage into a hospital operating room. The atmosphere inside a hard disk is many times cleaner than surgical procedures require. The drives are assembled in special "clean rooms" by skilled workers in sealed coveralls that look like spacesuits. All of these precautions are necessary to protect the delicate workings inside the drive.

Besides contamination, hard disk drives are sensitive to vibration or shock. Because the heads fly so close to the disks, it doesn't take much of a jolt to bounce them enough to cause a head crash. Although both the heads and disk are fairly tolerant, you should handle hard disk drives with care. When they are turned off, they can be lifted and moved about (but not dropped!) without much fear of damage. But when your hard disk is running, you must be especially careful not to jar it or upset it.

Be especially careful with hard disk drives. Handle them like an antique watch, and don't handle them at all when they're turned on.

Caution

Like floppy disks, hard disks must be formatted so that each sector has an identifying address written into it. But sometimes even this isn't enough. The mechanical tolerances in a hard disk drive are so fine, and the tracks spaced so closely together, that the heads can still get lost. Therefore, some hard disk drives reserve one whole side of a disk just for navigational aids.

This reserved surface is called a *servo disk*, and the data on it are called *servo tracks*. Even though all disks have two sides, of course, you may see some that advertise an odd number of sides. That's a dead giveaway that the last disk side is being used for servo tracks.

The IBM XT was the first member of the family to offer a hard disk drive. In all other respects, an XT is identical to a PC. They both run at the same speed and have all the same features. The hard disk in the XT could store 10 MB of data—quite a lot for that time, considering the floppy drive in the PC and XT could only store 360 KB. That gave the hard disk drive more than 25 times the capacity of a floppy. Today, a 10-MB hard disk is considered hardly worth the trouble to turn it on. Hard disk drives from 40 MB to 300 MB, and more, are common.

Like the floppy disk drives, hard disk drives come in full-height and half-height sizes. The early ones were all full-height, of course. As time went on, they got smaller but their storage capacity increased. Today, full-height hard drives are still popular, but only for really large capacity drives. Anything under about 100 MB is usually half-height.

Hard disk drives also shrunk to a 3 1/2-inch size, just like floppy drives. For most PCs, a half-height 3 1/2-inch hard disk drive is the most popular size. They will fit in nearly any PC, they don't use much power, and they're quiet.

6

Because the disk inside a hard disk drive can never be removed, there's no reason to mount the drive in an accessible location. Often a hard disk will be buried inside the system unit case of a PC, out of sight. It is not always obvious whether a PC has a hard disk in it or not. Today, 2 1/2-inch hard disk drives are becoming popular in battery-powered laptop computers. Prairie-Tek in Colorado makes the drive shown in Figure 6-4. The drive is a 20 MB drive with a 2 1/2-inch platter allowing a lot of data to be stored in a very small space! Although this presently represents the ultimate in refinement, most modern hard disk drives are made with the same kind of precision, and the capacity of some 5 1/4-inch drives is over 1600 MB and climbing.

You may not need this kind of capacity in your computer but it is surprising how quickly the space you do have fills up. This section addresses your possible need for a larger primary hard drive or a secondary hard drive. Most computers will handle at least two hard disk drives though this will also depend on the drive controller you have in your computer.

Figure 6-4.   *The amazing notebook computer drive (Photograph courtesy of PrairieTek Corporation)*

The first thing you really must do is assess your present and future needs in terms of the hard drive capacity you will need. If you are using your computer as a word processor to print letters and short documents you may not need a hard disk drive at all. If you intend to do desktop publishing as a single dedicated task you will probably do nicely with a 20 MB hard disk drive. On the other hand, if you intend to run two operating systems such as DOS and OS/2, develop software, do desktop publishing, and several other tasks, you may find that you are cramped with a 150 MB drive.

Look at the software you intend to use now or buy over the next year or two and find out how much disk space that software requires. A good rule of thumb is to allow 25 percent storage capacity for general overhead, beyond what your software requires. For example, if you determine that you need 50 MB of storage capacity, buy a hard disk with 70 to 100 MB of capacity. If you are doing disk-intensive chores like scanning large images, you may well need more space. Scanned images chew up hard disk space.

The possibilities for mass storage (the software appearing on the market and what it can do for you) expand almost daily and your requirements are very likely to change in this area. Ten years ago, 5 or 10 MB of hard disk storage seemed more than enough. With today's computers and software you might be surprised at how quickly a 150 MB drive begins to cramp you.

Figure 6-5 shows the present top contender for capacity. The drive is a Micropolis 1598-15 with a capacity of 1.2 gigabytes (1200 MB). There are other manufacturers with drives of similar capacity.

In any event, do use some care. A hard disk purchase can be a large part of your computer budget and deserves a reasonable amount of thought to determine your long-term as well as short-term needs before you purchase.

Disk Controllers

There are two major parts to every floppy or hard disk drive. The first part is the floppy drive or the hard drive itself. The second part is called a disk controller, which you may remember from Chapter 3, "Taking a Look Inside Your PC."

The disk controller is an adapter card that gets plugged into your PC. It occupies one of the expansion slots like any other adapter board. It also

Figure 6-5. *A Micropolis 1598-15 with a capacity of 1.2 gigabytes (photograph courtesy of Micropolis Corporation)*

connects to your hard disk or floppy disk with cables. Floppy disk drives are connected to the controller by a single 34-pin ribbon cable while hard disk drives are usually connected using one 34-pin cable and another 20-pin cable. A 34-pin cable will have 34 wires and a 20-pin cable will have 20 wires. Since both the disk drive and the disk controller board are inside your PC, the cables are buried inside your system unit case. There are usually no outside connectors on a disk controller board.

If you are adding another floppy disk drive, the controller board will probably already be in your computer, controlling your first drive. There will normally be an unused connector on the cable that runs between the controller and your first floppy drive. You can use this to connect the second drive that you are adding.

Drive controllers come in three basic flavors:

- Floppy-disk-only controllers capable of handling one, two, three, or four floppy disk drives.

- Hard-disk-only controllers capable of handling one or two hard disks.

- Hard-and-floppy disk controllers capable of handling two floppy disks and two hard disks.

To conserve computer slot space, the combination hard-and-floppy controller makes the most sense. It takes only one slot and will handle most of the drives you will ever want in your computer. If you don't mind using up the slot space, there's absolutely nothing wrong with having separate floppy and hard disk controllers and the operation of your computer will not be adversely affected.

Western Digital, Adaptec, and Ultrastor are some of the manufacturers of controllers that work well in IBM PCs and compatibles.

Disk Interfaces

In this section, you'll again enter the arcane world of computer electronics—this time conquering the subject of disk drive interfaces. As always, the intent here is not to make you into an engineer, but to give you enough background to help you make intelligent decisions about your equipment and the equipment that others are trying to sell you.

A disk interface is a method of passing data between the disk drive and your computer. There are five types of interfaces, and the more popular interfaces aren't necessarily the best or fastest. Since a disk drive must have some kind of interface on it, you must decide which kind to get. The following interfaces are listed more or less in order of their popularity in the PC world.

ST 506/412

One of the most popular of the early hard disk drives was the Model 506 from Seagate Technology. This had a 5 MB capacity, and a heavy, full-height case. It wasn't very fast, either. But it did become very popular with early PC users, and its interface to the hard disk controller—using a pair of ribbon cables—has since become an industry standard. Until very recently, virtually all hard disks in PCs used the interface that Seagate Technology pioneered. It is known simply as an ST506/412 interface.

RLL

There is a variation on the standard ST506 interface that allows you to pack betweem 50 and 100 percent more data on the exact same hard disk. Not all hard disks can do this, and even if you have one that does, you will have to change your disk controller.

The basic magnetic scheme described so far throughout this chapter is called *Modified Frequency Modulation,* or MFM recording. Using MFM, each bit of data is represented by one magnetic spot (called a *flux change*) on your disk. Recording schemes called *Run Length Limited,* or RLL, have been devised to put more information on a disk. In these schemes the precise rotational speed of the drive and precision electronics are used to allow a sequence of 2 to 7 bits to be recorded by a single flux change. This is called 2,7 RLL. Other schemes allow different numbers resulting in from 50 percent to 100 percent increase in the capacity of a given drive.

Using MFM requires one type of disk controller card and RLL requires another type. Many hard disk drives will support either MFM or RLL recording but you should check the drive tables in Appendix B, "Technical Information," to see if the drive you now have—or a drive you intend to buy—will support RLL. If you are currently using MFM recording on a 20 MB drive, for example, and that drive will support RLL, you can keep the drive and purchase an RLL controller and boost the drive capacity to 30 MB.

Don't rush out and buy an RLL controller without checking Appendix B. Most drives can be formatted for RLL and may even appear to work. But unless they are specifically designed for RLL, your data may be at risk.

Caution

MFM is the lowest density recording technique used to put data on the surface of a hard disk. If the disk can manage it, you can use a 2,7 RLL controller and increase the capacity of the disk. Without going into great detail, an RLL controller looks for patterns (a run of zeros or a run of ones) and assigns these runs a code. The code is then recorded on the hard disk. When the data is read back, these codes are translated by the controller into the proper information for the computer.

There is one step beyond this called 3,9 RLL, or ARLL, that would allow the disk capacity to be doubled over MFM. A 20 MB would allow 40 MB to be recorded on the same disk. Each step up puts a greater strain on the ability of the disk medium to handle the increased data, so if you exchange your

MFM controller board for an RLL controller board you should be aware that the result may not work reliably. *Glossbrenner's Complete Hard Disk Handbook* (Berkeley: Osborne/McGraw-Hill, 1990) contains additional details that you might be interested in.

The ESDI Interface

For a number of complex reasons, a new interface was developed to help eliminate the problems associated with the limited number of drive descriptions in BIOS tables. The ESDI (Enhanced System Device Interface— pronounced ezdee) interface again involves both the hard disk controller card and the drive itself. Both of these must be ESDI devices. More importantly, you should not assume that any ESDI controller will handle any ESDI drive.

Many ESDI controllers currently available, for example, will handle ESDI drives with data transfer rates of 10 megabits (not megabytes) per second but will not handle an ESDI drive that transfers data at 15 megabits per second. Be sure the ESDI controller you buy is capable of handling the drive you buy. Most ESDI controllers transfer data at over twice the rate of the 506.

The ESDI controller takes things a step further in allowing you to use much higher capacity drives. In particular ESDI allows you to use drives that have more than 1024 cylinders, more than 17 sectors per track, and more heads than the limit imposed by the BIOS. You will normally select drive Type 1, which is the first drive type available in the BIOS tables when setting the system up the first time, and then select sector and perhaps track translation when doing the low-level format.

Sector and track translation is used on a number of ESDI controllers including the Western Digital WD100x, Ultrastor's 12F, and various Adaptec controllers to mention the ones you are most likely to encounter.

Track translation is used to extend the capability of the system to access drives of greater that 528 MB. Track translation, like sector translation, is simply another controller trick to fool the computer. The problem is that although this works with the latest versions of DOS, track translation does not work with OS/2. Currently OS/2 still requires that a single drive be no larger than 528 MB. Most large drives will use 34 sectors (sometimes with a spare 35th sector), up to 15 heads, and 1600 or more cylinters per drive.

The ESDI interface allows for capacities into the gigabyte range and very fast data transfer rates. If you buy a drive with a 10 megabit data transfer rate you may still want to buy a controller with 25 megabit data transfer rate. Such

6

a controller will handle any transfer rate below its maximum rating. In this way, if you later decide to move up to a drive with a higher transfer rate you will not need to replace the controller.

The IDE Interface

The IDE interface (depending on who you talk to, IDE stands for Intelligent Drive Electronics, Integrated Drive Electronics or, more probably, Integrated Device Electronics) takes the entire business a step further. Developed by Compaq and Western Digital, this interface requires only a single cable. You connect the cable, screw in the drive, turn on the power, and you're ready to go.

IDE is relatively new, since it owes its existence to the latest developments in electronic miniaturization. Basically, a hard disk drive with an IDE interface has the disk controller board built in—you don't need a disk controller at all. Instead, the disk drive cable attaches directly to your motherboard.

Some manufacturers are now making adapter cards that can be used with IDE drives if the interface isn't provided on your motherboard. You install the adapter card as you would any other and attach it to your IDE drive and you're up and running.

Drives with IDE interfaces will normally be used in computers that specifically provide for the interface by having it built into the motherboard. Check your computer or motherboard manual to see if this is the case before you decide to buy an IDE drive.

The SCSI Interface

The SCSI (Small Computer System Interface—pronounced scuzzy) is a sleeper. Apple has been using SCSI for a few years and there is now a SCSI II interface standard. A major advantage of the SCSI interface is that it is not designed for a single type of peripheral; rather a mix of up to seven different peripherals can be connected to a single SCSI controller board, called a *host adapter*. With the right host adapter you could, for example, have a hard disk drive, a CD-ROM drive, a printer, a tape backup system, a scanner, and two other devices all connected to a single host adapter taking up a single slot in your computer.

The downside for IBM PC and compatible users is that there are dozens of SCSI host adapters available but they will not necessarily work with every SCSI device available.

Manufacturers of scanners, printers, disk drives, and other peripherals tend to choose a host adapter for their particular device and do not really provide for compatibility with other manufacturers' devices. When all IBM-compatible device manufacturers begin providing for other devices that might be used, this may well become the interface of choice for IBM PC and compatible users.

Installation

Installing a disk drive is a pretty simple procedure. It's part mechanical work and part electrical. Most of all, you need to allow yourself plenty of time and a good solid, uncluttered place to work. Disk drives—especially hard disk drives—are sensitive mechanical devices, and dropping them or carelessly handling them can spoil a sizeable investment in your equipment.

The physical installation of hard disk and floppy disk drives have so much in common that it is worth covering them together. The major difference involves the control cables. Floppy drives have a single 34-pin control cable, while hard disk drives have the 34-pin control cable and an additional 20-pin data cable. The control cable for hard disk drives has a different twist arrangement than its floppy disk drive counterpart.

Each control cable will manage either two floppy disk drives or two hard disk drives, but a separate 20-pin data cable is required for each hard disk drive.

6

Unpacking Your Drive

Most modern floppy disk drives are half-height drives. A 5 1/4-inch floppy drive will be wide enough to fit into a half-height drive bay. Most 3 1/2-inch drives are about 4 inches wide, 1 inch high, and 3 1/2-inches long. Since the drive is considerably narrower than the width of a drive bay, it will be supplied with a mounting kit and a new bezel or faceplate for the front of the drive.

The connectors on a 3 1/2-inch drive are also different from the standard PC connectors, so there will be a power cable adapter and a controller cable adapter with instructions for installing these parts if they are not already installed.

To install the floppy disk drive you've selected, you will need a controller, which may already be present in your computer if you are adding a second drive, a 34-pin cable, which also may already be connected to your controller if you are adding a second drive, drive rails, instructions, and possibly some software. For hard disk drive installation, you also need a 20-pin data cable.

Your new hard disk drive will usually be shipped suspended between thick blocks of foam in the middle of a very large carton. You should handle the drive as little as possible and, above all, don't drop it. Large capacity drives can be very heavy.

Caution

Mounting Your Disk Drive

The next step is to get your new drive inside your PC. The mounting method depends upon what kind of PC you have, and what kind of drive you're putting into it. Keep a pair of screwdrivers handy. Also be sure that as you slide your new drive into the PC, you don't pinch any of the large or small cables that are already in there.

Drive Mounting Screws for PCs and XTs

Drives are mounted in IBM PCs, XTs, and compatibles using small L-shaped brackets. These keep the disk drive from sliding out the front of your computer. To mount a drive in these computers, remove the screws holding the brackets on either side of the drive bay and remove the brackets. Slide the disk drive into the bay and replace the brackets using the original screws to hold the drive in place.

Drive Mounting Rails for ATs

Most modern drives are installed using rails. Depending on the drive supplier, these rails may be either metal or plastic. Figure 6-6 shows a standard metal rail with a latching spring that holds the drive in place once installed. This spring latch may not be present on some rails. The rail is shown by itself at the bottom of the figure, and mounted on a floppy drive at the top.

On floppy drives the two forward holes are used. This positions the rail further back on the drive and causes the faceplate of the drive to extend further forward. Hard drives that are installed in internal bays use the other

Figure 6-6. *Drive installation rails*

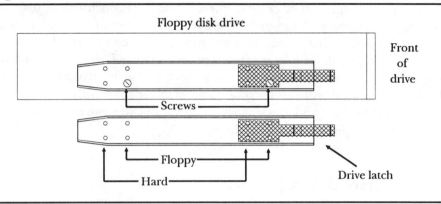

set of holes on these rails so that the drive will be far enough back to be hidden by the computer cover, as shown here:

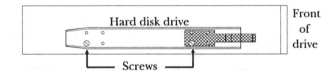

If your drive or computer has a different drive mounting system you should follow the instructions provided with that system.

Special Adapter Frames for 3 1/2-Inch Drives

The smaller physical size of 3 1/2-inch disk drives requires special mechanical adapters to make the final assembly wide enough to fit correctly in a 5 1/4-inch drive bay. These adapters take different forms from different manufacturers but usually include instructions for installation. Once the adapters are installed, the normal rails or other mounting system are installed to make the drives ready for installation in the drive bay.

Some computers have bays designed for 3 1/2-inch drives. These computers will not need the adapters; they may also have the correct control and power connectors for a 3 1/2-inch disk drive.

Note

Special Connectors for 3 1/2-Inch Drives

The power and ribbon cable connectors on 3 1/2-inch drives may be different than those on 5 1/4-inch drives. If they are, you should find a small two-wire connector that adapts the small power connector on the 3 1/2-inch drive to the larger Molex power connector used in PCs. There will also be an adapter from the pin type connector on the 3 1/2-inch drive to a printed circuit edge connector. The edge connector on this adapter and on 5 1/4-inch drives looks like Figure 6-7 and will have a keying slot to ensure that the cable is connected properly as shown in the figure.

Set the Drive Select Jumper

Once any necessary adapter hardware and rails are installed, you need to check the setting of the drive select jumper. Every disk drive has a set of drive select jumpers. These jumpers tell the drive whether it is the first, second, third, or fourth drive in the system. That way, the driver responds to read and

Figure 6-7.   *PC/XT/AT floppy drive cable*

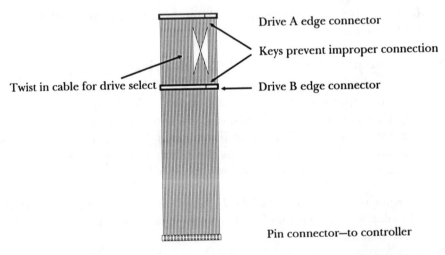

Drive A edge connector

Keys prevent improper connection

Twist in cable for drive select   Drive B edge connector

Pin connector—to controller

write commands sent to it, and ignores commands intended for the other drives (if any). Since there is no standard location for these jumpers, just look near the edge connector until you find a set of jumpers labeled DS0 or DS1 and up.

The jumpers are normally numbered DS0 (drive select 0) through DS3 (drive select 3). By inserting a jumper block on the correct pair of pins, you tell the disk drive which drive it will be. In an unusually perverse move, IBM chose to ignore these jumpers and requires a special ribbon cable instead. Therefore, all disk drives should be jumpered as though they were drive #2. If your jumpers are labeled DS0 through DS3, then insert the jumper at DS1. If your jumpers are labeled DS1 through DS4, then insert the jumper at DS2.

Checking Terminating Resistors

When an electrical signal travels down a long wire or cable, the quality of the signal can deteriorate, just as the quality of a radio transmission worsens as you move farther away from the transmitter. In the case of your PC, a cable that is only a foot long can cause this kind of degradation. To help combat the problem, you should put something called a *terminating resistor* at the end of the cable.

Most disk drives come with terminating resistors installed on their circuit boards. More often than not, you'll have to take the extra resistors off of one or more of your disk drives. You only want one set of resistors on a cable, and they must be at the end.

Now comes our problem: Terminating resistors on drives do not all look the same. Some will look like a blobby DIP (Dual Inline Package), some will be SIPs (Single Inline Packages), and so forth. Some drives will have them installed, some will not, and some will have no provisions for terminating resistors at all. (The last case is characteristic of some 3 1/2-inch drives.) Two drives with terminating resistors installed will usually work, so if you simply cannot locate the terminating resistors, you might find that everything works fine with or without them.

If you do manage to locate the resistors, remove the terminating resistor from the drive connected to the edge connector nearest the drive controller and leave the resistor installed in the drive connected to the last connector on the cable.

Remember

You should have terminating resistors installed in the last disk drive on the cable, the one farthest from the disk controller. That's not necessarily the last drive you've installed, or the last-numbered one.

Connecting the Power Cable

Now, with rails installed, terminating resistors taken care of, and drive select jumpers set, you are ready to put the drive inside your PC. If you are using drive rails, simply slide the drive part way into the drive bay, leaving enough room to make the connections required.

Holding the drive firmly, connect one of the Molex power connectors from your computer's power supply to the proper socket on the drive. You can use any available power connector from the power supply since they are all identical.

If you are connecting a 3 1/2-inch disk drive, it may have a miniaturized power connector that doesn't fit with your power cables. In that case, you should have received a short power cable adapter with your disk drive.

Connecting the Ribbon Cables

After the power cable is connected, you need to connect the data and/or control ribbon cables. If you are installing a second floppy drive or a second hard disk drive, locate the ribbon cable that connects to your existing drive. There should be an additional connector (or two) on that cable. Press one of the connectors onto the gold edge connector of your floppy drive.

There should be a slot cut into the drive's edge connector, and a key tab in the cable's connector so that it won't go on backwards. If not, you'll have to make sure that you put it on properly. Look for the colored stripe at one edge of the ribbon cable. This identifies wire #1. Now look for a small "1" printed near the gold edge connectors on your drive. Slide the connector on so that wire #1 connects to pin #1 on the drive.

Note

If all else fails, don't worry—just guess and put the connector on. Putting the ribbon cable on backwards won't damage anything. Your drive just won't work until it's promptly connected. When you turn your computer on, the access light on the disk should be off. If it is on and stays on, disconnect the connector, turn it over, and reconnect it.

Since all drive select jumpers are set to Drive #2, the floppy disk drive connected to the part of the cable with a twist in it will be drive A while the drive connected to the connector without the twist will be drive B. See Figure 6-8. The hard disk drive connected to the part of the cable with a twist will be drive C (the first hard disk) and a second hard disk drive (if installed) would be connected to the connector without a twist making it drive D.

Although 34-pin controller cables for floppy and hard disk drives look alike there is a distinct difference involving the twisted portion of the cable. The twist in the floppy disk controller cable is 7 wires wide and starts 9 wires from wire #1 (the wire on the edge of the cable with a different color). The twist in the hard disk controller cable is 5 wires wide and starts 5 wires from the opposite edge. Interchanging these cables is a frequent cause of trouble.

Caution

Cosmetic Surgery

Most PCs have faceplates covering unused drive bay openings. Remove the appropriate drive bay faceplate before replacing the cover on your

6

Figure 6-8.   *A 34-pin control cable (a) and a 20-pin data cable (b)*

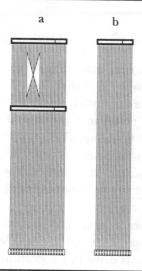

a   b

computer. Once the faceplate is removed, replace your computer cover. You are now ready to test your new disk drive.

You may need to replace the existing faceplate on the 3 1/2-inch drive with one that should be supplied with your drive kit. All of these things may have already been done but many drives still come with the parts supplied separately. Follow the manufacturer's instructions to mount the faceplate and ejector button on your drive.

Finishing Up

Once the connectors are joined, slide the drive into the drive bay until the drive latches snap into place. (Listen for a click.) Arrange the cables so they will not be snagged when you replace the cover.

Note

Some drive rails are held in place using one screw on each side of the drive. In this case the rails will not have a latch spring, and you should secure the drive using the screws that should be provided.

Some drives may have an extra wire for a ground connection that is used to connect the frame of the drive to the computer case. You can now replace the computer cover and continue with the software installation.

Preparing Your New Floppy Disk Drive

If you are installing a new hard disk drive, skip ahead to the section entitled "Preparing Your New Hard Disk Drive."

In an AT or compatible computer, restarting your system after installing a new drive will probably result in a message telling you that your CMOS configuration information is wrong. The actual content of the message will depend on the BIOS manufacturer but you will be prompted on-screen for how to get to the CMOS configuration screen. You may have to press a special combination of keys (like (CTRL)-(F1)), or you may have to run a special SETUP program from disk.

Once the configuration program has started, you will have a number of selections. For a new floppy drive, go to the selection involving drive A or drive B. If your new floppy is drive B, for example, the configuration screen will probably say something like "Not Installed" for drive B. Use the keys indicated on the screen to change this entry to reflect the size and capacity of the drive you've just installed. Next, select the option to reboot your system. Your computer should boot normally.

Testing a New Floppy Disk Drive

Once at the DOS prompt, put a disk with some files in your new drive and use the DIR command to obtain a directory for the disk. If that works, try copying a file from your new drive. If both of these tests work, you should have a fully functional floppy disk drive ready for use.

Preparing Your New Hard Disk Drive

Assuming that you have been booting your computer from a floppy disk and have just installed a new hard disk drive, your computer may spend several minutes determining that you have installed a new hard drive and that the new drive is neither formatted nor does it have an operating system installed on it. Your computer may appear to be completely locked up but give it a good five or ten minutes before you start looking for problems.

PCs and XTs do not support hard drives in the BIOS and do not have CMOS RAM. These computers require a controller with a BIOS extension built into the controller. Follow the instructions supplied with the controller to set up your hard drive.

Note

After what can seem like ages, your computer should beep and display a message indicating that your CMOS RAM configuration is wrong. It should also offer you the choice of changing your system configuration. Follow the instructions on your display to start the system configuration. Figure 6-9 is an example of one menu you may see, containing the information that can be changed in the CMOS RAM. Most menus will be very much like this one.

The lines labeled Hard Disk 1: and Hard Disk 2: are the lines you will need to change for your new hard disk. The possible entries are "Not Installed" or one of about 48 possible drive types. The type number is less important than the information listed under Cyl (cylinders), Hd (heads), Pre (the track on which write precompensation starts), Sec (the number of sectors per track), and Size (the rough capacity of the drive selected). The figures under these headings will change as you change drive types.

Figure 6-9.   *The System Configuration menu*

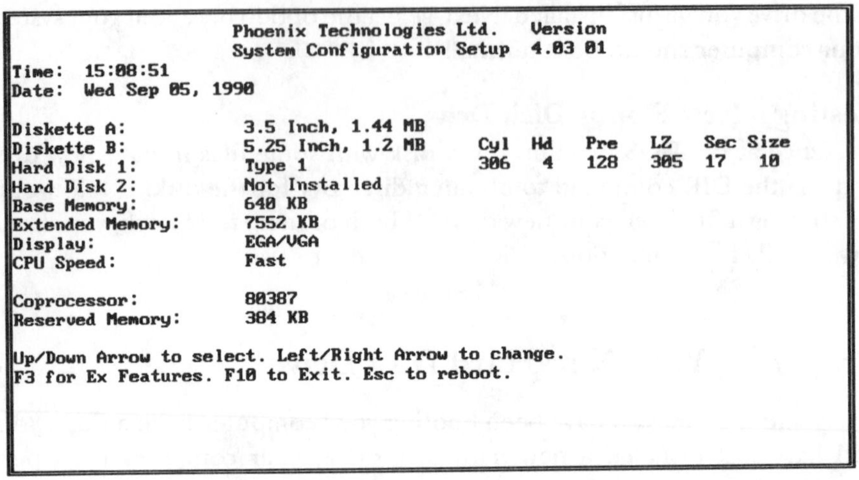

```
        Phoenix Technologies Ltd.    Version
        System Configuration Setup   4.03 01
Time:   15:08:51
Date:   Wed Sep 05, 1990

Diskette A:           3.5 Inch, 1.44 MB
Diskette B:           5.25 Inch, 1.2 MB    Cyl  Hd   Pre   LZ   Sec Size
Hard Disk 1:          Type 1               306   4   128  305   17   10
Hard Disk 2:          Not Installed
Base Memory:          640 KB
Extended Memory:      7552 KB
Display:              EGA/VGA
CPU Speed:            Fast

Coprocessor:          80387
Reserved Memory:      384 KB

Up/Down Arrow to select. Left/Right Arrow to change.
F3 for Ex Features. F10 to Exit. Esc to reboot.
```

If your drive and controller are RLL or ESDI, set the drive type to 1. This and other factors alert your system to the fact that the RLL or ESDI controller will be responsible for managing this information and the system should not consult this table.

If your drive is an MFM drive (ST506 interface) select the entry that matches the drive you have installed. You can look this information up in the drive tables in Appendix B or take it from the manufacturer's information supplied with the drive. If none of the choices matches your drive, you will find that most computers allow one or two user-defined types, usually type 47 and 48. You can fill in the information yourself using Appendix B and one of these user-defined types.

If you have a built in IDE interface on your motherboard, you must select the correct drive type from the drive BIOS drive tables. If you have an IDE controller installed as an adapter card, it must have a BIOS extension and you should select drive type 1 or follow the manufacturer's instructions.

Once you've set the information, follow the procedure (in this case press the (ESC) key) to save the configuration and reboot your computer.

Booting from the Floppy Drive

When you've set your system configuration, put a DOS boot disk in your floppy disk drive A. Again, the system may take a considerable amount of time but will finally boot from the floppy in drive A to get you to the DOS prompt. If everything has worked to this point you are ready to continue preparing your new hard disk. Use these steps to accomplish this:

1. Perform a low-level format of the drive, if required.
2. Boot your computer from a floppy disk and run FDISK.
3. Boot your computer from a floppy disk and run FORMAT.
4. Boot your computer from the new hard disk drive.

Note

If you are using DOS 4.0 or higher, your DOS diskettes may contain an "INSTALL" disk, which you should boot from to install DOS. For other operating systems, follow the manufacturer's instructions.

Low-Level Format

A *low-level format* is a procedure that places some very important and very esoteric technical information on the surface of your new hard disk. It is not something you will need to do more than once per hard disk.

Your new drive may already be low-level formatted. If it is, you can go directly to the section entitled "Running FDISK" and skip the low-level format that follows. There is no way to tell ahead of time whether your drive has been low-level formatted or not. You will need to ask your dealer.

If your disk drive and controller use an ST506 interface (which is likely), you will need a program to perform a low-level format. This program is not supplied with DOS. It is usually supplied by the drive manufacturer. You might also get a copy of Gibson Research's SpinRite II and use it with your new drive. SpinRite II does some very nice things for the management of drives that are defined in the system configuration drive tables. It will, for example, perform a low-level format on your drive without disturbing the data you have on the drive.

Low-Level Format for ESDI and RLL Controllers   RLL and ESDI controllers contain their own BIOS. This BIOS supplements your system BIOS in such a way that it takes over and manages the hard disk drive or drives attached to it. It also has a program that allows you to do a low-level of format your ESDI or RLL drive. The actual menu for this program will vary from controller to controller but Figure 6-10 shows a typical menu for an ESDI controller—the Western Digital WD1007A-WA2.

This controller will manage two hard disks with transfer rates up to 10 megabits per second and two floppy disk drives. For higher transfer rates, Western Digital has a WD1007V and a WD1009.

Adaptec and Ultrastor, among others, also make RLL and ESDI controllers. Other controllers may use different methods to do low-level formats but the principles will be the same.

Remember

Identifying Bad Tracks

Hard disk drives are like diamonds: they are very valuable, and they are rarely perfect. You may find one perfect drive in several thousand but most

Figure 6-10.   *A low-level format menu for Western Digital drive*

```
* * * Western Digital WD1007A-WA2 Initialization Utilities, Rev. 1.1 * * *

For Logical Parameter selection, type + or - for next, or <ENTER> for no change


DRIVE 0 CYLINDERS 618    HEADS 16   SPT 63
DRIVE 1 *** NONE SELECTED or NO DRIVE PRESENT ! ***

     Change Drive Types    ------> 1
     Low Level Format      ------> 2
     Surface Analysis      ------> 3
     Verify Drive          ------> 4
     Enter Defect List     ------> 5
     Exit and Reboot       ------> 6

     Enter Choice (1-6) ------>
```

hard disk drives have from 1 to perhaps 40 bad tracks. The total disk capacity represented by these bad tracks will seldom be more than 1 or 2 percent of the total disk capacity but bad tracks are a fact of life with hard disk drives.

If you have purchased a new drive, you should have received a list on paper of the bad tracks the factory found on the disk. You will need this list if you are going to do a low-level format. If such a list was not provided, a label on the drive will usually contain a similar list, which you should copy to a piece of paper for reference when you do a low-level format.

The low-level format of a hard disk takes care of a multitude of things that are only needed by the drive and controller. It will, for example, reserve a group of tracks on the drive's surface to be used as alternate tracks when a bad track is found.

Hard disks will have one or more tracks reserved for the specific purpose of maintaining information about the bad tracks on the disk. This bad track map will also tell the system what alternate tracks have been assigned as replacements for the bad track. Part of the low-level format procedure allows the entry of bad tracks or defects. When the track numbers are entered, the bad track is marked bad and an alternate track is assigned.

Let's say the track at cylinder 60, head 1 contains a defect. When this track is marked bad using the "Enter Defect List" option, the track is marked bad and an alternate track is assigned that your computer will think is still cylinder 60, head 1.

One of your DOS floppy disks will contain a program called DEBUG.EXE. Locate the disk containing this program and with that disk installed in drive A and at the A prompt (A>) type DEBUG. Your display will present you with a dash prompt. At the dash prompt type G=C800:5.

If your controller is from Western Digital, your computer will display the first three lines shown in Figure 6-10. At this point you can use the + key to examine the selections presented, or simply press (ENTER) to display the next line, then (ENTER) once more to display the menu.

The first selection on the menu (Change Drive Types) will allow you to repeat this procedure. The second selection (Low-level Format) begins the actual low-level format procedure, which can take a considerable amount of time depending on the size of your drive.

The third selection allows you to do an exhaustive surface analysis of the hard disk drive. This also takes a lot of time—4 to 12 hours is not unusual. With a 300 MB drive, the procedure could take overnight. You will not want

6

to use this option unless you suspect that your drive has developed bad tracks other than those on the bad track list.

The fourth option allows you to verify the drive format before proceeding to the fifth option, which allows you to enter the bad tracks listed in the bad track list. Once this step is complete, the sixth option allows you to quit this program and reboot.

This reboot must still be from a floppy disk but your computer should now recognize the drive immediately and the boot should be a little faster.

Running FDISK

The next step in preparing your new hard disk drive is called *partitioning,* accomplished using a program called FDISK. Partitioning allows you to assign the entire disk as one drive or divide your hard disk up into smaller, "logical" disks. For example, if you have a 60 MB disk, you can partition it as one 60 MB disk or into two 30 MB disks. These would be called drive C and drive D. For all practical purposes, you would have two separate hard disk drives, even though you really have only one hard disk inside your PC.

The version of DOS that you have may determine whether you need to partition. Versions of DOS before 3.3 cannot work with partitions larger than 32 MB. To allow the use of larger disks, partitioning is required. Even after DOS 3.3, many users prefer to partition one large disk into two, three, or four smaller logical drives. The illusion of smaller disks makes it easier for some users to keep track of files.

Having smaller disk partitions can also make more efficient use of your disk space. This has to do with the way DOS stores files. Basically, DOS can only keep track of so many different chunks of data, called *clusters.* No matter how big your disk is and no matter how little data you store in each cluster, the number of clusters remains the same. For a small disk, a cluster might be two sectors, or 1024 bytes. For a big disk, each cluster might be 16 sectors, or 8192 bytes. Each file, no matter how small, always uses up at least one cluster. (Big files take more clusters.) But that means that a tiny 5-byte file stored on a big disk will take up one 8192-byte cluster, most of which will be wasted. If this big disk had been divided up into smaller logical disks, there would be much less waste because cluster sizes are smaller.

Locate a DOS disk containing this program and, at the A> prompt, type **FDISK**. A menu similar to the one shown in Figure 6-11 will be displayed.

Figure 6-11. The DOS FDISK menu

```
                        MS-DOS Version x.xx
                      Fixed Disk Setup Program
                (C)Copyright Microsoft Corp. 1983 - 1998
                         FDISK Options

Current fixed disk drive: 1

Choose one of the following:

1. Create DOS Partition or Logical DOS Drive
2. Set active partition
3. Delete DOS Partition or Logical DOS Drive
4. Display partition information


Enter choice: [1]



Press Esc to exit FDISK
```

FDISK gives you four options. Option 1 will already be selected for you. Press the (ENTER) key to select this option.

Injudicious use of FDISK, FORMAT, and the low-level formatting tools covered thus far, can destroy the data on your hard disk. Most of these programs will warn you of the imminent loss of hard disk data but use extreme care if you have data on your hard disk that has not been backed up. You might even want to remove FDISK.COM from your hard disk as a precaution.

Caution

Setting the Active Drive

Once you've decided on a partitioning arrangement, you can follow the prompts in FDISK to partition your new hard drive to suit your circumstances. The first to partition (an example is shown in Figure 6-12) should now be set to "ACTIVE" so that DOS will recognize it as your primary hard disk drive and boot from it. Once this step is complete, you must reboot from a floppy disk once more.

6

Figure 6-12.   *The FDISK partition information display*

```
                    Display Partition Information

Current fixed disk drive: 1

Partition Status   Type    Size in Mbytes   Percentage of Disk Used
  C: 1        A    PRI DOS      383             100%




Total disk space is 384 Mbytes (1 Mbyte = 1048576 bytes)



Press Esc to continue
```

High-Level Format

At this point, your system should boot from the floppy disk in drive A almost immediately Once you have the A> prompt, type: **FORMAT C: /S**.

After appropriate warnings, the system will begin formatting your new drive C and, on completion, will transfer the most vital parts of DOS to your new drive C. Once complete, you can remove the floppy disk from drive A and reboot your computer from the hard disk drive!

Testing the New Hard Drive

Installing a new primary hard disk drive can be a rather time-consuming project. About the best thing you can say about it is that you only have to do it once. The low-level format, in particular, is usually good for the life of the drive. You may find that you will want to change your partitioning scheme, but otherwise you've just finished a "once in the life of your hard drive" operation. Enjoy!

Other Types of Disk Drives

Following is a brief list of some of the more unusual storage devices that are available for PCs. Some of these may be a little out of your range, either in price or in storage capacity. All of them are real, bona fide products built by reliable companies with thousands of happy customers. In a few years, any one of these may become standard equipment on personal computers.

Drive-and-Controller Combination Boards

The Plus Hardcard is another possibility. It plugs into an expansion slot in your computer like any other adapter card and provides a very simple way to add a hard disk.

Plus Development Corporation makes several products that you might want to consider. Figure 6-13 shows the 8- and 16-bit bus versions of the Plus Hardcard. The Hardcard comes in 20 and 40 MB versions for the PC, XT, and compatibles. The Hardcard II (Figure 6-14) comes in 40 and 80 MB versions for the AT and compatibles.

To install these drives you remove the top of your computer, plug the card into an adapter slot, load the software supplied, and you are up and running with a new hard disk drive. Plus also offers the Passport and Impulse removable hard disk drive systems.

6

Removable Hard Disks

Cumulus Corporation makes a 44 MB removable hard disk drive system that works on the IBM PC, XT, and AT; the Apple Macintosh; and the PS/2. This system uses a SCSI interface and is easy to install and to use. In addition to being fast and removable, it allows you to transfer data files between other systems with a cartridge drive.

The cartridges are about $150 apiece, making them a good drive choice for many applications. This is also an excellent way to make fast, safe backups. The IBM and Macintosh external drives are shown in Figure 6-15 along with the IBM PC and PS/2 host adapter cards. The Macintosh computer has its own SCSI interface and does not require a host adapter.

Figure 6-13.   *Plus Development Hardcards (Photograph courtesy of Plus*
                 Development Corporation)

Figure 6-14.   *The Plus Hardcard II 80 MB drive (Photograph courtesy of Plus*
                 Development Corporation)

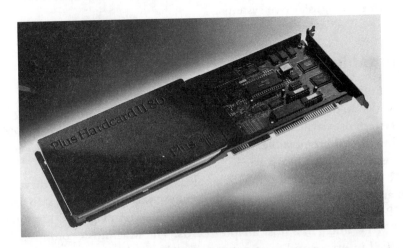

Figure 6-15.   *Cumulus SILHOUETTE 44 MB removable hard disk drive*
(Photograph courtesy of Cumulus Corporation)

There are other companies that make similar units but Cumulus supplies a formidable array of backup tools to go with its drives. The drives cost about $1500. The initial cost of the drive is rather high but, when you amortize the cost of the cartridges and when you consider that this is a high-quality hard disk drive, the cost per MB is very reasonable.

Using a removable hard disk as a backup medium has some advantages over using floppies or tape. For one, you can simply copy the files you want to back up from your hard drive to your removable drive with no fuss and no special software. That makes it easy to retrieve backed-up files later on. A removable hard disk is also handy in very sensitive or secure applications. You can simply remove the hard disk at the end of the day and lock it in a safe. Some government offices require this procedure.

CD ROM Drive

A compact disk (CD) player in a stereo system uses optical media. In this type of medium, music is digitally recorded on the disk using a laser beam.

An audio CD can only be played—it cannot be recorded. An equivalent device used on a computer is called CD ROM, for *Compact Disk, Read-Only Memory*.

Optical disk media is recorded with a laser beam that actually deforms the disk in a controlled way by melting tiny pits in the shiny surface of the disk. Instead of a magnetic recording that can be accidentally erased or destroyed by a magnet, CD ROM disks are not erasable. The result is a very permanent and stable recording.

CD ROM disks are becoming popular as a way to distribute large collections of data in a compact form. Some current examples are English literary works in computer-readable form, sales catalogs complete with color illustrations, and large software releases.

WORM Drive

While a CD ROM disk drive cannot be written to at all, there is another kind of optical disk that you can write to, albeit in a limited fashion. These were given the unfortunate name of WORM disks, for *Write Once, Read Many*.

Several manufacturers supply optical disk systems based on the MAXTOR 400/800 WORM drive, which is also a removable cartridge drive with 400 MB of storage per side. The problem is, once it's written, data cannot be erased. Data can be deleted but it won't free up the space that was being used. If the data you delete took up 100 MB, you will have only 300 MB of usable space left on the cartridge afterward.

These drives are used mostly for archival storage of scanned images that banks and courts want to be permanent. The drives cost between $3000 and $5000. The cartridges cost about $250 each. This is not a recommended medium for general backup, but the fact that it offers nearly a infinite storage life makes it ideal for some purposes.

Erasable Optical Disks

Magneto-optical or erasable optical disks are another optical medium that can be written to using a laser beam, but in this instance, you can write to it over and over. The structure of the disk is very complex; but basically, the application of a steady magnetic field allows the laser beam to repeatedly write to the disk by melting and remelting the plastic in a controlled way. The result is much like regular hard disks except that the recording uses tiny pits in the plastic surface.

The recording process uses both a magnetic field and laser beam. Reading data only requires the laser. A magnetic field by itself will not disturb the data. Therefore, your information is nearly as secure as with a CD ROM drive or a WORM drive.

Pinnacle Micro in Irvine, California offers a 3 1/2-inch magneto-optical drive and disks. An internal version of the drive costs $2995 and uses a SCSI interface. The cartridges store 128 MB and cost $129 each. Procom Technology, Inc. in Costa Mesa, California offers a 5 1/4-inch drive called MEOD. These drives make perfect backup devices.

High-Capacity Floppy Disks

Computer users have known for several years that floppy disks can hold more data than is currently stored on them. The key is positioning the heads accurately over each track. Most floppy disks have either 40 or 80 tracks. More tracks than this requires new technology.

High-capacity hard disks reserve one side of one disk for navigational information called servo tracks. Servo tracks have an electronic signal recorded by the drive maker in precise locations at the time of manufacture. The signal on the tracks is used by drive electronics to center the head over the track much as a swinging door is centered by springs. An electronic circuit called a *closed-loop servo system* positions the heads by seeking the strongest signal from the servo track.

A company called Brier Technology has developed a coating method for floppy disks called the Flextra system using what they call Twin Tier Tracking or T3. The first layer of magnetic material is designed to be used as a servo track. A second coat of material is the data recording media. The result is a 3 1/2-inch disk that looks exactly like regular 3 1/2-inch disks but is able to store 21.4 MB of data.

This technology has been put to use by Q/Cor in the Stor/Mor drive shown in Figure 6-16. The disks hold 25 MB unformatted and 21.4 MB formatted. The drive and SCSI host adapter as shown costs $895. The disks are $25 each which, in terms of dollars per megabyte, works out to about the same price as ordinary 3 1/2-inch disks. Later on, the drive will be able to read 720 KB, 1.44 MB, or 21.4 MB disks, making this a universal replacement for a standard floppy disk drive. The nice part is that at the 21.4 MB capacity, access times are comparable to those of low-end hard disk drives.

Tape Drives

Another type of storage device is the tape drive. Tape drives have some advantages and some disadvantages when compared to disk drives. On the one hand, they can store quite a bit more data than all but the largest and most expensive hard disk drives, while costing a whole lot less. On the other hand, tape drives are very slow, and they cannot be used for normal "online" storage at all. That means that tape drives are really only good for making backup copies of your programs and data.

As backup devices, tapes are very good. A tape cartridge has a terrific capacity, as already noted, and they are compact and easy to use. Most of the

Figure 6-16.   *The Stor/Mor disk drive, media, and host adapter (Photograph courtesy of Q/Cor Corporation)*

time, you can back up your files to a tape with little or no effort on your part. Tapes are reliable, and they are inexpensive.

Tape drives are somewhat like floppy disk drives, in that the tape itself is removable. That means you can have as many tapes as you like. There are two basic types of tape drives, based on the size of the cartridge. The smaller ones use tapes exactly like audio cassette tapes. The larger ones use tapes that are more the size of a paperback book.

The tapes come in capacities ranging from 20 MB to over 2200 MB or 2.2 gigabytes. The backup speeds run from just under 1 MB per minute to almost 7 MB per minute. The tape drives cost from $350 to over $1000. Each tape will cost from $20 to $40 or more. You can get a tape drive to mount inside your PC, like a floppy drive, or an external tape drive.

Because tapes drives are used exclusively for making backups, most are provided with fairly extensive software to automate your backup procedure. With the software installed, you can leave your computer running and, at a preset time of day or night, the software will take over and do an unattended backup. The type and amount of software provided by each manufacturer differs so much that it would be impossible to go into details here but good documentation is usually provided with your drive and software.

Tape backup software is required because DOS does not "talk" to tape drives. For example, you can't simply copy files from disk to tape with a DOS COPY command. There are no tape drivers in DOS and DOS knows nothing about tape drives. Therefore, special tape backup software is required, and it should be supplied with the tape drive when you buy it.

You should also bear in mind that, because tapes aren't handled as a normal part of DOS, you can't exchange tapes with another PC user the way you exchange floppy disks. Even if you both have the same kind of tape drive and use the same size tape cartridges, you still may not be able to read each other's tapes. You can only exchange tapes if you are using the same tape backup software as well. This tends to reinforce the notion that tapes are solely for personal backups, and not a means to distribute or exchange data.

Figure 6-17 shows the interior of an average magnetic tape cartridge. Tape motion is controlled by an endless plastic belt. The belt and tape are driven as a unit by the capstan motor under considerable tension. This keeps the tape tightly wound on the takeup and supply reels and is the only reliable way to move the tape. Tapes vary in length but fairly standard ones are about 1500 feet long—that's about a quarter of a mile! The tape is also very thin.

6

Figure 6-17. *Internal view of a standard tape cartridge*

1. Belt guide
2. Tape supply reel
3. Aluminum base
4. Tape guide pins
5. Tape guide
6. Read/write head—part of tape drive
7. Rubber covered capstan roller—part of tape drive
8. Capstan drive motor—part of tape drive
9. Light sensing unit—part of tape drive
10. Right angle mirror mounted on tape cartridges
11. Tape guide
12. File protection lug
13. Arrow shows forward tape motion
14. Recording tape—oxide coating out
15. Belt guide
16. Tape takeup reel
17. Belt roller
18. Endless-loop composition tape control belt

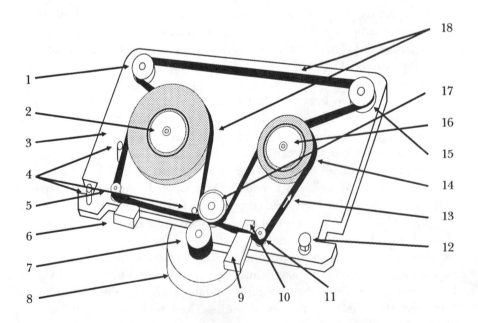

When you consider that the tape drive moves 1500 feet of fragile, thin tape from one spool to the other in something under a minute, records 18 to 26 tracks or more on 1/4 inch wide tape, and must start and stop in milliseconds, it's surprising that they work as well as they do.

Installing a Tape Drive

Tape drives are available in either external or internal versions. If your system has only one floppy disk drive, an internal unit is probably best. The drive is installed like a regular floppy disk drive and uses the drive B floppy disk drive connector making the installation very simple. Just install rails, slide the drive into place, connect the drive B floppy disk connector, and connect a power connector. Closing the case completes the installation.

Tape drive units are also available with SCSI interfaces. Such drives require a slot for the SCSI host adapter and proper cabling according to the manufacturer's instructions.

Tip

Your tape drive can tell when it has reached the end of a tape by trying to shine a light through it. (Near the end of the reel, there are holes in the tape to make this work.) If the light gets dirty, it might not see the end of the tape coming, and can unwind it right off the reels.

If this happens, it is difficult–but not impossible–to respool the tape. First, clean the inside of your tape drive so it doesn't happen again. You can use a cotton swab to dust off the light source and light sensor. To fix the tape, remove the screws under the aluminum base and lift the plastic housing off. One or the other of the reels will be empty. Turn the full reel and feed off a small amount of tape.

Carefully feed the loose end of the tape between the empty reel and the tape control belt. As you turn the reel, both reels will turn together. Guide the tape around the empty reel keeping it as flat as possible against the reel until you have one or two turns on it. Once the tape is anchored with one or two turns hold the full reel still and then gently take up the slack in the tape. Don't reel the tape too tightly–just enough to take up the slack.

Now reassemble the tape cartridge and put it in the drive. Most tape drives automatically retension tapes by winding them to the end-of-tape hole on one end, then back to the end-of-tape hole on the other end. At this point, your tape should be ready to use again.

6

Making Backups

Floppy and hard disks are precision magnetic storage media; as such they are constantly at risk. With a tape of your favorite music, a small glitch in the signal recorded on the tape might go unnoticed. If a similar glitch occurs on a floppy or hard disk, your PC may not be able to read a stored file. If that same glitch occurs on a critical track, the entire disk may be unusable until it is reformatted.

The reliability of floppy and hard disk media is getting better but you simply cannot rely upon any single copy of your hard work. You must make backups. (A backup is simply a second copy of a file.) You might even want to make a third copy of really critical material.

There are many different ways to make backup copies of your important data. How you decide to go about it, and how often you do it depends on you. But however you do it, do it.

Caution

Making backups is like buying insurance. People may not want to bother but often in retrospect dearly wish they had. PCs work so smoothly that it hardly seems worth the effort–that is, until the day you get the message "Sector not found reading drive C." With that message you've usually lost only one file. The error messages that have incredible pucker-power are "General failure error reading drive C" or, at boot up, "Hard disk failure." If you have six months of hard work stored on the offending disk, it's as good as gone–forever. Naturally, these kinds of messages usually occur at the most inconvenient times. The point is very simple: it costs you far less time to make backups than it does to try to reproduce your work.

Full Backup

A full system backup means copying everything. Copy everything on every disk to either another set of disks, or to a tape. If you have more than one hard disk, or if it's a big one, this might take you awhile. But you'll never have to worry about whether or not a particular file has been backed up.

Making full backups all the time can be wasteful. If you are like most PC users, roughly three-quarters of your files are programs or data files that never change. Backing up the same file over and over is pointless. Assuming that you have at least one good copy of a never-changing file somewhere, you shouldn't have to back it up again.

Incremental Backup

Incremental backups are backups of selected files. Such a backup might consist only of changed files or of some selected files. You will always have the originals and (hopefully) a working copy of all your programs. You will also have a floppy disk copy of DOS. In the event of a hard disk failure, these can always be restored from the copies you have.

If you make floppy disk copies of any work you create, such as letters and spreadsheets, you are relatively close to a safe system without the added burden of making full backups. You should also keep copies of your CONFIG.SYS files, AUTOEXEC.BAT files, and other configuration files. With these files on floppy disk, you can normally restore most of the work on a hard disk.

Shadow Backup

Shadow backup is for super critical operations. Two hard disk drives are used. The main drive works as a normal hard disk drive. The shadow drive mimics every read and write operation. Should the main drive fail, the shadow drive will take over just as if it were the main drive with an appropriate warning telling you your main hard drive has failed. With such an arrangement you can continue your work until you take the necessary action to fix your main drive.

An example of good use for shadow backup would be capturing stock market ticker data where it is imperative that no data is lost. If PCs were used on NASA shuttles they would almost certainly use shadow backup.

Shadow backup capabilities are provided by Cumulus and other manufacturers. The Cumulus SILHOUETTE 44 MB removable drive is capable of working in shadow mode.

Backing Up New Programs

The first step to making backups is to protect expensive software that you've just purchased. Virtually every software vendor suggests that you use a program like DISKCOPY to make a duplicate set of working disks copied from the program disks they supply. You use these working disks to do software installation to your hard disk and keep both the original disks *and* the working copies in a safe place away from heat and magnetic fields. This practice makes it a fairly sure bet that should something happen to one copy, you will have another available.

Other programs are specially copy-protected, making them nearly impossible to duplicate. In these cases, the software company will either provide you with a duplicate set of disks right out of the box, or they'll have a special disk duplication program for you to use. By all means, take advantage of this.

Backing Up with Floppy Disks

The nicest part about floppy disk backups is that you already have a floppy disk drive in your computer and a DOS program called BACKUP.EXE. You will need about one high-density (1.2 MB 5 1/4-inch or 1.44 MB 3 1/2-inch) disk per 1 MB of hard disk you intend to back up. The extra capacity on the disks makes the total number of disks required somewhat less than that figure. It will take about three minutes per disk to make a backup.

With this in mind, backing up a completely full 20 MB hard disk will take about 20 disks and around an hour of your time. Since full floppy disks must be removed and empty disks inserted, you must be present for the backup. Using floppy disks is effective and only requires that you buy disks, so for small systems it's probably the best choice.

The BACKUP command works like this:

BACKUP {*source*} {*destination*} [/s][/m][/a][/f:*size*][/d:*date*][/t:*time*] [/L:*pathname*]

/s	Backs up subdirectories
/m	Backs up only files changed since the last backup
/a	Adds backed-up files to an existing backup disk
/f:*size*	Formats the target backup disk(s)
/d:*date*	Backs up only files modified since {date}
/t:*time*	Backs up only files modified since {time}
/L:*pathname*	Creates a log to record the backup operation

From this you can see that typing BACKUP C: A: /s at the DOS prompt will back up everything on drive C to floppy disks in drive A. That includes your subdirectories and the files in them. When BACKUP fills one floppy disk, it will ask you to insert another one. You can use floppies with old files on them, which BACKUP will erase. BACKUP will not erase subdirectories on the floppy disk, though, so the best procedure is to use newly formatted floppy disks.

You can see from the options in the help listing shown earlier that many other options are available. You can back up only files that have changed since the last backup, add files to an existing backup set, back up files created since a particular date or a particular time, and others. You could, for example, use BACKUP C: A: /s /m /a to add to an existing set of backup diskettes (/a) all files on your hard disk, including subdirectories (/s), that have changed since your last backup (/m).

Note

Obviously, a set of backup disks isn't any good unless you can restore them in time of need. The complement to the DOS BACKUP command is the RESTORE command. It works like this:

RESTORE {*drive*}: {*pathname*}[/s][/p][/b:*date*][/a:*date*][/e:*time*]
[/L:*time*][/m][/n]

/s	Restores all subdirectories
/p	Prompts before restoring read-only or modified files
/b:*date*	Restores only files modified on or before {*date*}
/a:*date*	Restores only files modified on or after {*date*}
/e:*time*	Restores only files modified on or before {*time*}
/L:*time*	Restores only files modified on or after {*time*}
/m	Restores only files modified since the last backup
/n	Restores only files that no longer exist on the disk

Notice that many of the same options are available that are available under the BACKUP command.

All in all, the BACKUP and RESTORE programs supplied with DOS aren't very good. In particular, it's too easy to get the source and destination drives reversed and wind up writing over your backup disks by accident. There are other programs available that do a much better job of backing up your disk. One example is FASTBACK from 5th Generation Systems in Louisiana. FASTBACK allows you to use normal floppy disks, just like the DOS BACK-UP, but it compresses the data before it is placed on the disks, thus increasing storage capacity and reducing the number of disks you need. Also, if you have two floppy disk drives, FASTBACK will alternate between them, so that you can swap disks in one drive while FASTBACK writes compressed data to the other. Finally, FASTBACK uses the DMA (Direct Memory Access) controller chip in your PC to speed things up even more.

Different Backup Philosophies

Philosophy may seem a strange word to describe computer backups but there is a problem with any backup operation. It is time-consuming and basically nonproductive. As such, it is very easy to become complacent. Modern hardware functions so smoothly that it's hard to imagine it failing— but it does fail and at the most unexpected times. Following are five different backup "philosophies" presented for your consideration. Pick the one you feel you can live with.

Backup System 0

Backup system 0 is making no backups at all. If you don't bother to make copies of your new program disks, don't periodically save your files, don't keep backup disks or tapes in a safe place, then you can't look for help when it all crashes one day and you're left with nothing but a pile of expensive hardware (there's no help available for this situation).

Backup System 1

Backup system 1 recycles the same backup media. Let's say you have a backup set of 20 floppy disks. You make a backup to these. A week later you use the same disks to make another backup. During the time you are making the new backup all your files are at risk because if the hard disk fails during the backup, you have no backup.

Backup System 2

A safer backup procedure uses two sets of disks or tapes. You back up to one set one week, the second set is used for a backup the second week, and the first set is recycled in the third week. In this way you always have one fairly recent backup of your files. You may lose some files if a failure occurs while you're making the latest backup but you won't have lost your entire file system.

Backup System 3

An even safer philosophy uses three sets of disks or tapes so that you always have at least two "live" backups while making a third. It makes a good middle-of-the-road backup philosophy for most small-to-medium operations.

Backup System 4

There are a number of professional backup philosophies that are normally spelled out in considerable detail by the manufacturers of tape and cartridge backup systems. It may seem, at first blush, that the manufacturer is trying to sell you backup media but this is really not the case. If your computer is the hub of a network and you are the administrator of that network, losing one file can present a major headache.

So, although the professional backup philosophies may seem like overkill, it really does make good sense in critical operations. Here's a look at one recommended system.

Week 1   Make a full backup of your system on Friday. Label the media "Week #1" and add the date. Store the media in a safe place. At the end of each day except Friday back up all changed files, and label the media with the particular day—"Monday," "Tuesday," and so on with the date. Store these in a safe place.

Week 2   Again make a full backup of your system on Friday using new media. Label the media "Week #2" and add the date. Store the media in a safe place. At the end of each day except Friday back up all changed files, but in this case (and in all the following cases) you can reuse the media—"Monday," "Tuesday," and so on with the date.

Week 3   Make a complete backup of your system on Friday using new media. Again make daily backups as just described.

Week 4   Make a complete backup of your system on Friday. Label this cartridge with the month and store it. At this point you will have four sets of

Weeks 5 through 8   Repeat the steps starting with Week #1, but you can now begin writing over the earlier weekly media starting with the oldest. When you make your month-end cartridge, use new media.

Weeks 9 through 12   Use new media for the second and third month backups, then begin writing over the media for the oldest month's backup. Once the system is running you will have three weekly sets of media, three monthly sets of media, and four to six daily sets depending on your backup week. Continue the schedule by writing over the oldest media in each new period.

If this all seems like overkill, consider John Doe who wrote a very important letter a month ago, then accidentally erased it from the system. With the backup regiment just described you have a pretty good chance of finding this lost letter even though the loss was neither your fault nor the fault of the system. It all comes down to how important it is to you to keep your file systems safe and retrieve a specific document.

Summary

Backing up your software is probably one of the most important things you can do—and it is probably one of the most neglected. It seems both nonproductive and time-consuming, but the fact is that a disaster can strike at any time and wipe out anything from minutes to months of your hard work. How much can be salvaged depends entirely on your backup philosophy. It usually takes only one major disaster to make a computer user exquisitely conscious of the need to back up.

In this chapter, you saw several types of backup media and several systems that use those media. You also learned that as speed and capacity go up, so does the price of both the drives and the media. On small systems, a good floppy backup is probably the least expensive and most effective for the money although you will still have to invest a little time in the process.

In the next chapter, you'll learn how to add individual chips.

7

Adding Chips

Adding chips to your PC, while not difficult, is one step up from the easier additions of the expansion boards and storage devices you've seen thus far.

This chapter discusses the various types of memory chips available (the ones you'll use depends entirely on the manufacturer of your motherboard), and then looks at installing a math coprocessor chip.

Adding Memory Chips to Your Motherboard

Like money, memory is one of those things that you can never get enough of. Early PCs couldn't handle more than 64 KB. Even that was seen as overly generous on the part of the engineers and more than any sane user would ever need. Now with Windows and OS/2, 2 MB—32 times as much—is the *minimum* requirement.

The craze for more and more memory began from the very start. Prices for solid-state memory chips, or RAM, have constantly decreased since personal computers were introduced. As memory became cheaper, people bought more of it. As PCs held more and more memory, programmers wrote bigger and bigger programs. As programs got bigger, people needed more memory to run them, and so it goes.

Depending on your particular PC, there may be a limit to how much memory you can add. A very early IBM PC peaks out at 512 KB. All PC computers are limited to 640 KB of "conventional" memory (see Chapter 5, "Adding Expansion Boards") before you must start adding expanded and/or extended memory. Some PCs allow you to add memory chips directly to the motherboard. Others make you use memory expansion boards. Still others use a kind of combination: memory modules that are inserted in special sockets on the motherboard.

The selection of RAM depends on several things. First, RAM can be installed on the motherboard (the first 1 MB usually is) or it can be on an adapter board. Two additional criteria are access speed and the "package" of chips used. Early machines used mostly DIPs (Dual Inline Package) on the motherboard or DIPs on an adapter board. The disadvantage of memory on an adapter card is that you must use up one of your expansion slots.

The present trend is to use SIMM (Single Inline Memory Module) with an occasional motherboard using SIPs (Single Inline Package). SIPs are much like SIMMs except they have pins that fit into a socket. SIMMs and SIPs have the advantage of not taking up adapter slot space.

The motherboard manufacturer decides the organization of the chips you can install. As a result you will have to rely on the motherboard manufacturer's information to determine what type of memory chips to buy for your computer.

Remember

You will see the terms RAM (Random Access Memory) and DRAM (Dynamic Random Access Memory) used interchangeably. This does not mean you have two types of memory—just that memory chips or modules may be called by either name. Your computer's main memory is made up of Dynamic Random Access Memory, which is usually shortened to RAM.

Data and Parity

As you already know from previous experience or from reading the earlier chapters, a byte consists of 8 bits. A bit may be either a 1 or a 0. No other choices are allowed. A byte may be any value between 0 and 255. Most of the time, storage capacity is measured in bytes. A thousand bytes is a kilobyte and a million bytes is a megabyte.

The DRAM chips in your PC are usually 1 bit "wide." That means that each chip is responsible for one of the 8 bits in each byte of memory. One DRAM chip stores the first bit, the next DRAM chip stores the second bit, and so on. Therefore, it takes eight DRAM chips to store the complete byte.

How can you tell when a DRAM chip goes bad? The answer is, you can't—at least you can't be really sure. If each bit of data can only be a 0 or a 1, there's a 50/50 chance that any given bit might be wrong. In order to add a little security and certainty to the DRAM in your computer, PC makers add an extra ninth bit to each of the other eight and call it the *parity bit.*

The parity bit works by storing an extra bit of data that is meant to "guard" the other eight. It does this by remembering whether there is an even number or an odd number of 1s stored in the other eight data bits. If there is an even number of 1s, the parity bit will store a 1 also. If there is an odd number of 1s, the parity bit will store a 0 instead. When your computer writes to memory, the number of 1s is tallied, and that information is stored in the parity bit automatically. When your computer reads from that location again, the number of 1s is again counted and compared against the data stored in the parity bit. If they're different, then your computer deduces that something must have happened to the DRAM in the meantime, presents an error message on the screen, and quits.

Memory Chip Capacities

Early PCs used 16 kilobit (not kilobyte) chips arranged in banks of 9 chips. There were four banks, which meant that you could have a maximum of 64 KB (now it's kilobytes) of memory on the board (16 kilobit chips times 8 chips—remember one out of the nine is the parity bit—times four banks divided by 8 bits/byte). Later machines could hold one to four banks of 64 kilobit chips for a maximum of 512 KB—or as an alternative, two banks of 256 kilobit chips and two banks of 64 kilobit chips totaling 640 KB, the most memory a PC can use for DOS programs. Figure 7-1 indicates the parity chip (P) for a total of eight data chips for each bank of memory.

7

Figure 7-1.   *The parity chip in a common layout of motherboard memory*

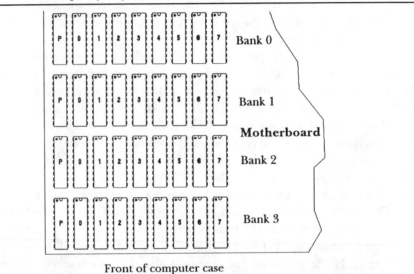

Front of computer case

Figure 7-2 shows the possible combinations of 16 kilobit chips to have 16, 32, 48, or 64 KB. You might see this arrangement on very low-cost PCs. In the same figure you can see all the possible combinations using 64 kilobit chips. Modern PCs and XTs are most likely to use combinations of 64 kilobit and 256 kilobit chips, shown at the bottom of Figure 7-2.

ATs and compatibles can usually take four banks of 256 kilobit chips (for a total of 1024 KB or 1 MB) and some newer motherboards allow 1 megabit chips in each of the four banks for a total of 4 MB of memory.

You should be aware that your motherboard may have jumpers that need to be changed if you add or change memory. Again, the variations are so wide that you can only rely on the documentation provided with your motherboard or computer.

Memory Chip Speeds

Access speed is another major factor in the selection of memory. The memory you add must be fast enough to keep up with the speed of your

Figure 7-2. *Layouts using 16 K chips, 64 K chips and 256 K, and 64 K chips*

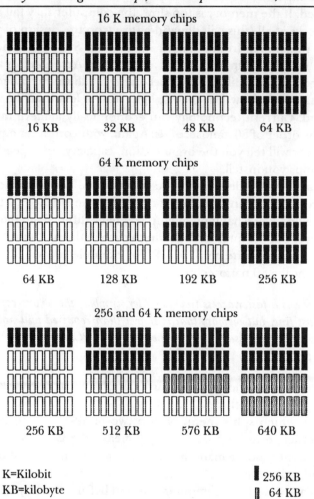

computer. For example, you cannot yank the memory chips from your 4.77 MHz IBM PC and put them in a 16 MHz 286 machine—your system may not run.

If the computer is to run at its top speed, it must be able to access memory at that speed. If the memory is too slow, the computer may fail to work properly if it works at all (this will depend entirely on the design of your PC).

You'll remember from Chapter 6, "Adding Storage Devices," that the speed of a memory chip is called its access time. Access times are measured in nanoseconds. Incredibly, a nanosecond is a billionth of a second. To give you an idea of just how fast that is, light travels less than 12 inches in one nanosecond. Current technology can economically achieve memory access times on the order of 80 nanoseconds. Again, your computer or motherboard manufacturer will tell you the organization, capacity, and speed required for memory chips you install.

You can usually determine the access time for a particular chip by carefully reading the information printed on the surface of the chip. The numbers telling you what type of chip you have differ from manufacturer to manufacturer but the number following a dash in the part number will usually tell you the speed of the chip. A –12, for example means 120 nanoseconds while a –8 means 80 nanoseconds.

Note

Memory that has a faster access time (smaller number) than your computer requires will work just fine, but memory that is slower than required will not work. Buying faster memory than necessary will not speed up your PC, however; you are limited by your PC's speed.

Some computer and motherboard manufacturers use tricks to allow the operation of slower, cheaper memory. They may use a technique called *interleaving*, which splits memory into two banks and alternates between them. Another term, *wait states*, simply means the CPU must wait between memory accesses. Some manufacturers use a combination of both the interleaving and wait states.

This is all part of the computer's design before you buy it; the terms are covered here just to familiarize you with them. Since you have no control over either item, just understand that computer ads may talk about interleaving memory and make statements like "0 wait states", which is what you want. Interleaving is a perfectly rational and acceptable way to access memory. Allowing wait states is not. The manufacturers will also tell you in their documentation what organization, speed, and packaging you need to add memory to your system.

Figure 7-3.   *A DIP memory chip*

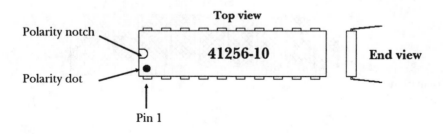

Polarity notch

Polarity dot

Top view

41256-10

End view

Pin 1

Memory Chip Packages

There are three basic types of DRAM chips, based on the way they are shaped: DIP, SIP, and SIMM. There is no real difference between how they work. One type of DRAM is no better than the other, but your PC will be built to accept only one or two kinds.

DIP Packages

Figure 7-3 shows a typical DIP (Dual Inline Package) memory chip. The term Dual Inline refers to the fact that each chip has two parallel rows of pins lined up on either side of the chip. These chips must be installed in a particular way and pin 1 on the chips is designated by a polarity notch, a circular depression or a combination of both. You will also find that either the chip socket or the motherboard will have a corresponding notch on the socket or a printed legend on the motherboard to indicate the orientation of the chip.

SIP and SIMM Packages

Many manufacturers have begun using *memory packages.* These are memory chips installed on small circuit boards. They come in two styles, called SIMMs (Single Inline Memory Modules) or SIPs (Single Inline Packages). Both kinds are shown in Figure 7-4. SIMMs contain nine memory chips and have printed circuit edge connectors. Some SIMMs use two 1 megabit chips and

Figure 7-4.   *SIMM and SIP memory modules*

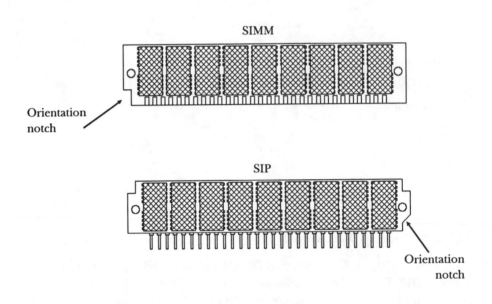

one 256 kilobit chip for a total of three chips instead of nine. SIPs are virtually identical except that they have pins like a DIP does. The orientation notches are shown in Figure 7-4. Other notches are simply part of the circuit board design and have no purpose.

Your motherboard may provide for SIMMs, SIPs, DIPs, or a combination of types of package.

Installing DIP Memory

Chips installed in reverse or with crumpled pins are the most likely causes of problems when installing chips, so take a minute to review the procedure for installing DIPs. First, you will find that the pins on new chips are splayed out at a slight angle as illustrated in Figure 7-5. They are manufactured this

Figure 7-5. *Adjusting the pins on a DIP*

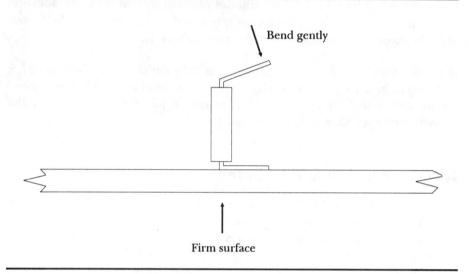

way to accommodate automatic insertion machines but this can pose a problem when inserting the chips by hand.

You can make them easier to install by bending the pins slightly. You do this by grasping the chip firmly at each end between your thumb and forefinger. Position the chip with all of the pins on one side against a firm surface like a table and apply enough pressure to bend in all the pins on one side just a little until they're perpendicular to the chip body. Turn the chip over and repeat the procedure for the pins on the other side. You will develop a feel for how much pressure to exert. The pins should bend at the body of the IC, not at the tips of the pins.

If you've done the job correctly, the pins should now be perpendicular to the chip and parallel to each other. The chip will be much easier to insert in the motherboard sockets. This procedure will also help prevent pins from being crumpled underneath the chip or splayed out to the side of the socket. If either of these things happens and you don't correct it, your computer will work erratically—if it works at all.

In the PC, XT, and some AT computers, memory is arranged on the motherboard in four banks. The amount of memory will vary. The location of this memory area is fairly common but with the advent of SIMMs and SIPs the layout has changed on newer motherboards.

Caution

Experience has shown that regardless of how carefully you check the orientation when installing chips you might still occasionally get one installed backwards. Double-check the orientation of the chips you install to be certain that they have been installed correctly. Better yet, have someone else check for you.

Installing SIP and SIMM Memory

Both the SIP and SIMM type memory devices are easier to install than DIPs. First of all, there are more memory chips on each SIP or SIMM module so you won't have to install as many devices. Plus you won't have as many fragile pins to deal with—none at all if you're using SIMMs.

Consult your PC's manual regarding the location of memory on your motherboard. It will show you which memory sockets you should use first, second, and so on. You may also have to move some jumpers around after the memory has been installed.

Adding a Math Chip

As powerful as the CPU chip in your PC is, it cannot do everything. One thing that it is particularly slow at is complex mathematics. This is a little ironic, for most people think of computers as a kind of super-fast calculator.

Your PC's slow execution of complex mathematics is sufficient for most applications. After all, how much math is involved in a word processing program? But if you are using your PC for mechanical drafting, CAD, graphics, or any of a number of other complex applications, you need advanced mathematical capabilities to speed the processing time. For this reason, there is a family of special-purpose math chips that you can add. Adding a math coprocessor can speed up some programs by as much as 2500 percent. That's 25 *times* faster than running without the math coprocessor.

Math coprocessors plug into a socket provided for them on the mother-board. They are usually offered as an option rather than standard equipment because they are expensive, and most software can run without it, and many PC users will never need a math coprocessor.

Although certainly not a memory chip, the math coprocessor is one other chip that you install in your motherboard. There is a special math coprocessor chip for each CPU found in a PC. The part number is similar to the part number for the CPU, plus 1. The math coprocessor for the 8086 CPU is the 8087. The 80286 uses the 80287 coprocessor, and the 80386 uses the 80387. There is an 80387SX for use with the 80386SX. Intermixing is not allowed; you must use only the matching coprocessor for your CPU, with one exception: the 80386 can work with an 80287 if necessary.

The 80486 has math coprocessor functions built in so there is no math coprocessor for this CPU, although Intel has indicated that it might make 80486s available with the internal math coprocessor disabled.

The coprocessors come in different speeds, just like the CPU chips do. For example, there are 16 MHZ, 20 MHz, 25 MHZ, and 33 MHz versions of the 80387 available. Be sure to purchase a coprocessor that matches the speed of your CPU. A faster or slower coprocessor won't work.

Besides the "official" coprocessors from Intel, three other companies, Weitek, IIT, and Cyrix also manufacture math coprocessors. Each of their coprocessors is different, but all of them are faster than Intel's components—in some cases, three to four times faster. They are also more expensive than Intel counterparts. Cyrix and IIT manufacturer 80387 "clone" chips that fit right into the 80387 socket and run 80387 software without modification, but they run faster.

Weitek, on the other hand, makes a completely incompatible part. You cannot use a Weitek (pronounced WAY-tek) coprocessor unless your PC is designed to accept one. Also, your software must be compatible with the Weitek part.

Note that whatever coprocessor you use, it will not magically speed up your entire system. First of all, it only accelerates mathematical functions, so unless you are using math-intensive software, forget it. Secondly, unless your software is designed to take advantage of a math coprocessor, even the math functions won't improve. Fortunately, exactly the programs that would benefit most from a math chip are the ones designed to support one. Programs like AutoCAD are a good example.

7

Installing a Math Coprocessor

Virtually all motherboards provide an empty socket for the math coprocessor. It doesn't cost the PC maker anything, and it gives you the opportunity to add a math chip later. Sockets for the 8087 and 80287 are usually DIP sockets; you will need to observe the orientation requirement when installing them. For the most part the installation is straightforward. You may need to set a jumper or a switch on the motherboard, and the CMOS RAM configuration may need to be changed once the coprocessor is installed.

The 80387 and its substitutes require some special consideration. These chips come in a square ceramic PGA (Pin Grid Array) package with a lot of pins. Pressing one into its socket can require considerable pressure. If your motherboard flexes badly, it could be damaged. You also run the risk of having the coprocessor improperly installed. If this is the case, you should first remove your motherboard from the computer and place it on a solid tabletop before proceeding.

An 80387 can cost over $500. It is possible to install them in any of four different orientations. Only one of the four is right—any of the other three will destroy your math coprocessor when you turn the power on *and it is not*

Figure 7-6.   *Orientation of an 80387 chip*

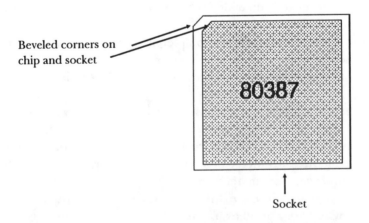

Beveled corners on
chip and socket

Socket

repairable! So, you will find one corner of the 80387 cut off at an angle. You will also find corresponding marks on your motherboard (see Figure 7-6). Orient the chip with the beveled corner toward the beveled mark on your motherboard and install the chip in the center of the socket. Press it very firmly into place and double-check the installation to be sure the chip is correctly oriented and fully seated.

If you have any qualms about this procedure, have someone familiar with coprocessor installation help you. Don't guess! The odds are 3-to-1 against you. If you buy the chip through an Intel dealer, Intel's instructions will also help.

ution

When you start your computer after installing a math coprocessor, your computer may tell you the configuration is wrong and ask if you want to correct it. The exact messages will depend on your particular PC. Use the appropriate procedure to start your configuration program. This might involve pressing a special sequence of keys (like (CTRL)-(F1)), or running a SETUP program from floppy disk. There will be an entry on the screen for "Math Coprocessor." Set the option to "Installed" and reboot your computer. Everything else is automatic.

Summary

This chapter showed you how the three types of DRAM or RAM chip packages—DIP, SIP, and SIMM—vary in their organiztion from motherboard to motherboard. You cannot change the layout that the manufacturer of your CPU uses; however, you need to be aware of the layout to upgrade.

You've also seen that, while many users will never need a math coprocessor, if you use CAD, graphics, or any number of other complex applications, a math chip can speed up your work by as much as 2500 percent. You can easily install a math chip by plugging it into a socket on your motherboard.

In the next chapter, you'll see some serioius modifications.

7

8

Serious Modifications

This chapter covers some of the major changes you could make to your PC. These are not necessarily drastic measures, but they do require more than the average amount of patience and care. The rewards are also greater. Rather than toss out an old PC that is on its last legs, you could upgrade the power supply, the motherboard, and/or the CPU. You'll have a completely new PC in the same old case, you will know that you've saved a lot of money, and you will keep your investment in your disk drives and other peripherals.

Changing the Power Supply

A power supply converts the high-voltage alternating current that comes from your wall socket into the steady flow of low-voltage direct current required by the electronics inside your PC. In the U.S., wall sockets provide about 110 volts of electricity. Your PC runs on only 5 volts—less than the voltage provided by four D batteries. But the supply of electricity must be constant and reliable, something batteries can't always provide.

There are two reasons why you might want to replace the power supply in your PC with a new one: Either your original one has broken or it doesn't provide enough power. If you have a small PC without a hard disk or if you have an older PC, it is not uncommon for the power supply to be overloaded after you've added a new hard disk or tape drive. A power supply can only generate so much power, and early PCs had power supplies just big enough to provide juice for the base equipment. Adding a lot of extras like a power-hungry hard disk drive can tax them.

There isn't much to know about power supplies, except the term *wattage*. A watt is a unit of measure for power, like inches or bytes. Technically, 1 watt is 1 volt times 1 amp. Keep this tidbit in mind, because sometimes power supply manufacturers don't advertise the wattage directly; instead they may list volt/amps or VA. The more watts your power supply produces, the better.

The general placement of parts within your system unit should follow a pattern characteristic of most PCs and compatibles. If you are facing the front of the system unit, the power supply is located at the right-rear corner. In front of the power supply are the disk drive bays. The motherboard lays on

Figure 8-1.   *The Silencer AT-style 200-watt power supply (Photograph courtesy of PC Power and Cooling)*

the bottom and the adapter cards are plugged into the motherboard near the left side.

PC Power and Cooling in Bonsall, California manufactures the Silencer AT power supply (Figure 8-1 shows it from the back side). This is a typical power supply although shapes will vary a little. The power switch is located on the left in the figure. It is a big red or orange paddle switch. As you can see, four corners on the back have captive nuts with star washers. Four screws are inserted into these captive nuts through the rear of the system unit and the star washers help make good electrical ground connections with your case. The cooling fan grille is top center and the two AC power connectors are at the lower left. There's a male power connector for your power cord, and a female socket for you to plug in another peripheral, like your monitor.

Just above the female power connector is a switch that allows the selection of 110- or 220-volt operation. 110-volt alternating current (VAC) is for North American use. 220-VAC is for overseas use. Many countries especially in Europe use 220 volts. If your new power supply has this switch, be sure to set it correctly for your locale.

Do not attempt to disassemble the power supply. There are no replaceable parts inside and you may inadvertently damage something. There are also sheets of insulating paper that must be properly positioned to provide protection for both you and your computer. At $35 to $70, even the manufacturers don't repair power supplies—they simply replace them.

ution

Not shown in the figure is the "octopus" of wires coming out of the right side. There should be two big motherboard connectors (normally labeled P8 and P9) and two or more smaller 4-pin connectors for your disk drives. Figure 8-2 is a diagram showing wire colors, voltages, and orientation for these connectors. Note that the disk drive power connectors are lopsided so they can't be connected backwards.

The big motherboard connectors are a different matter—it is possible to interchange the two connectors with disastrous results. It is difficult but also possible to reverse them end for end. So pay particular attention to the wire color code. If the wires on your power supply are coded as in the diagram, connecting them as shown will be safe—double-check the power supply manufacturer's directions in any case.

8

Figure 8-2.   *Power supply connectors*

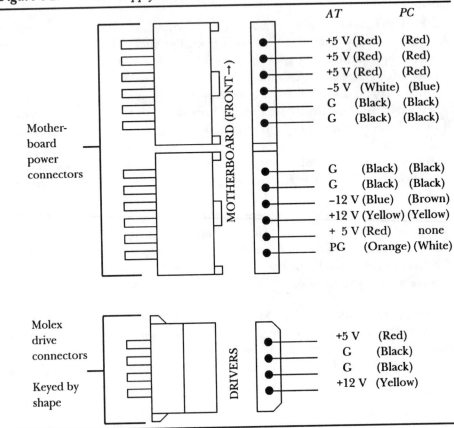

If you have a standard PC-type metal case, there will be two metal tabs, about 3/4 of an inch square, that are punched up through the bottom of your system unit. These tabs engage two holes in the bottom of the power supply as part of the power supply attachment. To remove a power supply, remove the four screws holding it to the back of the system unit, slide the power supply toward the front, and lift it out. To install a new power supply, make sure the tabs are in the holes on the bottom of the power supply and then slide it back against the rear of the system unit. Then install and tighten the four screws.

Accelerator Cards

Your PC/XT display, keyboard, pointing device, and hard disk can still be used while you boost the system unit to an AT-compatible 80286 or 80386 capability. You do this using cards called *accelerator* cards or you can change the motherboard. Even if you find you must change the case and power supply, much of what you already own can be transferred to your upgraded machine.

The basic decision you must make is between installing an accelerator card or changing the motherboard. The relatively low cost of accelerator cards make them a good choice in many instances. Several manufacturers make accelerators that give you an 80286, 80386SX, or full 80386DX computer. These cards come with various amounts of memory installed and with various memory upgrades.

nember

When Intel released the 80386 CPU chip it had a 32-bit wide address bus and a 32-bit wide data bus. This CPU changed its name to 80386DX and comes in 16, 25, and 33 MHz speed versions. To reduce costs, Intel later released the 80386SX. Like the earlier 8088, which had an 8-bit data bus, and its bigger brother the 8086, which had a 16-bit data bus, the 80386SX was reduced to a 16-bit data bus from 32.

From your computer's point of view, there is no difference between an 80386SX and an 80386DX. The difference in bus width is taken care of by hardware on the motherboard so the only real difference you might notice is that the SX part runs a little slower.

Upgrading an 8088/8086 Motherboard

Figures 8-3 through 8-5 show several SOTA products designed to plug into your IBM PC/XT motherboard. The 286i Universal Accelerator (Figure 8-3) converts your PC/XT to an 80286 AT. This card plugs into an adapter slot. After removing the 8088 CPU, connectors are used to connect the card to the 8088 socket.

The SOTA 386si (Figure 8-4) is an 80386SX-based accelerator that plugs into an adapter slot in your PC. Both of these cards work with the piggy-back memory board shown in Figure 8-5. This memory card allows up to 8 MB of additional RAM to be added to your 286i or 386si card. Either of these cards

8

Figure 8-3.   *SOTA 286i accelerator card (Photograph courtesy of SOTA Tech-nology, Inc.)*

Figure 8-4.   *SOTA 386si accelerator card (Photograph courtesy of SOTA Tech-nology, Inc.)*

Figure 8-5. *SOTA memory/16i memory expansion card (Photograph courtesy of SOTA Technology, Inc.)*

with their additional memory will allow you to run OS/2 and other software that requires an 80286 or 80386 computer.

Another excellent choice of accelerators is Intel's Inboard 386/PC. This is a full-length card with an 80386DX CPU and support for an 80387DX math coprocessor. It has several memory options; your result with Inboard 386/PC is an 80386 computer in a PC/XT case.

Upgrading an 80286 Motherboard

You can turn your 80286-based AT or compatible into an 80386 computer quite easily with an accelerator or, again, you could change the motherboard. Motherboard changes from 286 to 386 or 486 usually work well because the case and power supply will normally be very compatible with the new motherboard.

Cumulus Corporation and SOTA both make small circuit cards that plug into your 80286 CPU socket to turn your AT computer into an 80386SX. The

8

Cumulus card shown in Figure 8-6 is under 3 inches square and works in a large number of 80286 AT computers including Compaq and some PS/2 computers. The SOTA Express/386 shown in Figure 8-7 is a similar product. Both support the 80387SX math coprocessor.

Once again, Intel makes the Inboard 386 for 80286-based AT and compatible computers. The Inboard 386 uses an 80386DX and supports the 80387DX math coprocessor. The Cumulus card is available for most 80286-

Figure 8-6.   *The Cumulus 386SX card (Photograph courtesy of Cumulus Corporation)*

Figure 8-7. *The SOTA Express/386 (Photograph courtesy of SOTA Technology, Inc.)*

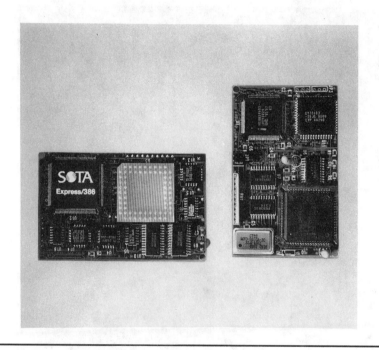

based ATs and compatibles. It is also available for the Compaq Deskpro 286 and Tandy 3000.

Motherboards

Replacing a motherboard is just about the most involved, far-reaching alteration you can make to your PC. In a very real sense, changing your motherboard means changing your PC. You might keep the power supply, the disk drives, and the case, but the real brains of your PC will be different. And this is exactly what a lot of users want.

Figure 8-8.   *A 386SX/16 Baby AT motherboard—the Orchid Privilege 386SX*
                    (Photograph courtesy of Orchid Technology)

Replacing the motherboard is not an easy upgrade, but it is one that can boost the performance of your computer immensely. Replacing the motherboard might also allow you to increase the amount of memory you can install (by providing extra SIMM or SIP sockets) or increase the number of expansion slots available for add-on boards.

You will find a bewildering variety of motherboards available as upgrade products so look carefully before deciding. This section will examine two motherboards from Orchid Technology. The first is a small motherboard called the Privilege 386SX shown in Figure 8-8. The second is a full-sized AT board called the Privilege 386/33C shown in Figure 8-9. The first one is called a *Baby AT* board because it is designed to fit into an IBM PC/XT chassis instead of an AT case. It will also fit nicely in smaller cases called "small footprint cases" because they take up less space on a desktop.

Figure 8-9.   *A 386/33 full-sized AT-style motherboard–the Orchid Privilege 386/33C (Photograph courtesy of Orchid Technology)*

8

These two boards have some very desirable features. The Baby AT board has two serial ports, one parallel port, a floppy disk controller, and an IDE (Intelligent Drive Electronics) hard disk controller built in. This saves at least two slots. It also has SIMM (Single Inline Memory Module) memory on the motherboard. This allows 4 or 16 MB of memory and saves another slot. For these reasons, it makes an ideal motherboard choice for a wide variety of applications. The conventional location of adapter slots, power supply connectors, keyboard connector, and memory should help you identify these areas on other motherboards.

The Orchid Privilege 386/33C is an excellent choice of motherboard for high-powered applications. Along the left edge is a 32-bit adapter slot. This would be used for a 32-bit memory card but could also be used as an 8-bit slot. Another 8-bit slot is followed by five 16-bit slots and a final 8-bit slot. The connectors between that and the BIOS ROM are the power supply connectors. The keyboard connector is above the BIOS chip. At the top right are two serial ports and a parallel port.

The four banks of nine chips on the lower left of the motherboard are RAM chips. These can be either 1 megabit or 4 megabit chips allowing either 4 or 16 MB of total memory. Beside them in the center are four SIMM memory sockets allowing an additional 4 or 16 MB of memory. The Intel 80386 CPU is a bit left of center with a math coprocessor socket beside it and a cache memory controller below. (See Chapter 2, "Anatomy of a Personal Computer System," if you want to review cache.)

RAM

The selection of RAM depends on several things. First, RAM can be installed on the motherboard (the first megabyte usually is) or it can be installed on an adapter board. Two additional criteria are access speed and the package used. Early machines used mostly DIPs (Dual Inline Package) on the motherboard or DIPs on an adapter board. The disadvantage of memory on an adapter card is that you use up one of your expansion slots.

The present trend is to use SIMMs with an occasional motherboard using SIPs (Single Inline Package). SIPs are much like SIMMs except that they have pins that fit into a socket. (See Chapter 7, "Adding Chips," to look up SIMMs and SIPs.) SIMMs and SIPs have the advantage that they don't take adapter slot space. They are also more expensive than DIPs.

BIOS

American Megatrends, Inc (AMI), Award, and Phoenix are three major BIOS developers aside from IBM. You will usually find two chips somewhere on your motherboard with labels belonging to one of these companies. All three license their BIOS to manufacturers to be "burned" (programmed) into EPROMs. The programs that make up the BIOS may also be supplied under license to the manufacturer who can make modifications to suit the computer or motherboard.

If you are buying from a small dealer who assembles machines, it would not be out of place to ask where the BIOS is obtained. It could save you the potential embarrassment (and legal problems) of finding that you have bootlegged BIOS ROMs. Look for the official-looking labels on the ROM chips when buying them.

Keyboard BIOS

This chip is not frequently mentioned but it must be purchased along with the main BIOS. The three chips (two main BIOS chips and one keyboard BIOS chip) are made to work together. You may find that you can buy a regular BIOS and have an existing keyboard BIOS chip work with it but it's really not worth the risk of incompatibility. So if you decide to buy a new BIOS, be sure to ask about the keyboard BIOS.

Changing Your BIOS ROMs

The following material may be of value if you intend to install a new set of BIOS chips. The chips are available from Wholesale Direct (see Appendix A, "Vendor List," for the complete address).

8

Phoenix BIOS Chip Sets

The following is a sample of the ROM BIOS chip sets offered by Phoenix.

Phoenix 286—Version 3.10

2-chip set
100 percent IBM compatible
setup in ROM
supports up to 25 MHz speeds
supports 101/102 Key Keyboards
supports 360k, 1.2 MB, 720k, and 1.44 MB floppy drives
full Novell and Netware Support
28-pin EPROM

IBM AT Replacement (this is only for genuine IBM brand ATs)

2 chips with setup disk
supports 48 different types of hard drives plus 2 user definable hard drives
supports 360k, 1.2 MB, 720k, and 1.44 MB floppy drives

XT 8088—Version 2.52

100 percent compatible
supports 360k, 720k, and 1.2 MB drives
supports 48 different types of hard drives plus 2 user definable hard drives
supports NEC V20 and V30 processors
complete power-on self-test and diagnostics
28-pin EPROM

Patterson Labs Turbo XT (Phoenix)—Version 2.13

100% IBM compatible
works with all XT turbo systems
supports NEC V20 through V50 processors
complete power-on self-test and diagnostics
supports 360k, 1.2 MB, and 720k floppy drives

supports 48 different types of hard drives plus 2 user definable hard drives
28-pin EPROM

Phoenix 386—Version 1.10

2-chip set
100 percent IBM compatible
setup in ROM
supports ESDI and RLL drives
supports 48 different types of hard drives plus 2 user definable hard
drives also available for 386SX and Chips and Technology Motherboards
28-pin EPROMs

Phoenix PC-1—Version 2.52 (This is only for the original IBM- AT)

supports 360k, 1.2 MB, and 720k 3 1/2-inch floppy drives
boot up time will be 50 percent faster
BIOS will automatically determine memory size
24-pin EPROMs

American Megatrend Inc. (AMI)

AMI offers the following chip sets:

- AMI XT
- AMI IBM XT
- AMI 1.44 ADDON (uses extra ROM socket on XT to allow 1.44 MB drives)
- AMI 286 (generic)
- AMI 286 C&T
- AMI 286 VLSI
- AMI 386 (generic)
- AMI 386 SX

8

- AMI 386 C&T
- AMI 386 COMPAQ
- AMI 386 Intel

All feature:

support for 360k, 720k, 1.2 MB and 1.44 MB floppies
complete setup in ROM, EGA, and VGA support
built-in diagnostics in ROM
Novell and Netware support and compatible
supports 48 different types of hard drives plus 2 user
definable hard drives
100 percent IBM compatible
supports speeds up to 25 MHz, supports 0, 1, or 2 wait
states
full OS/2 support

AMI BIOS PLUS provides the following in a ROM.

Standard Features

- Field-proven, extensively used
- Built-in CMOS setup utility with support for 46 predefined hard disk
  drive types, a user, definable drive type, 3 1/2-inch floppy disk drive
  support and enhanced keyboard

Options

- A Diagnostics program superior to the IBM Advanced Diagnostics
  program with special enhancements and a user-friendly interface

or

- Extended SETUP program for Extended CMOS registers in C&T

- 386 and New Enhanced AT (NEAT) 286 chipset based motherboards

or

- Extended SETUP program for G2 386 chipset EPROM registers

Installing the AMI BIOS

The rest of this chapter is devoted to detailed instructions for installing a new set of AMI BIOS ROM chips. Even if you aren't using a BIOS from AMI, these steps may be helpful to you. Be sure to read through the entire procedure before beginning to prevent being stranded halfway through because you've forgotten a tool you need.

Before you begin the installation be sure that

- Your system is turned off
- You are working on an antistatic surface

AMI BIOS PLUS comes in 256 Kbit ROM chips (32K bytes). Hence make sure that when you plug in these ROMs that the switch on the System Board is set to indicate 256K chips.

Sometimes your BIOS will be supplied in one ROM chip and sometimes in two. If you have two chips, your ROMs will probably be labeled "ODD" and "EVEN." Ensure that the ODD and EVEN BIOS chips go into the proper sockets and that the pins are oriented correctly.

Failure to follow these guidelines could result in permanent damage to the ROM chips. AMI will not replace any BIOS that has been damaged due to improper installation or handling.

aution

8

Carefully remove the old ROM chip(s) from your PC motherboard with a chip removal tool or a small screwdriver. Set them safely aside in case you need them later. Straighten the pins on the new ROM chip(s) as discussed in Chapter 7, "Adding Chips." Place the new ROM in the socket from which you took the old ROM, and press firmly in place. Power up the system and wait for the BIOS to show some activity on the screen.

Identifying the Type of BIOS

The reference number in your BIOS will let you know the type of BIOS on your system. The reference number is displayed in the following format:

ABBB-NNNN-MMDDYY-KX

These can be deciphered as follows:

A   stands for one of the following:

D   for BIOS with Diagnostics
S   for BIOS with Setup program
E   for BIOS with Extended Setup program

BBB   stands for one of the following:

C&T   for C&T 386 chipset
NET   for C&T NEAT chipset
286   for standard 286, VLSI, G2 286 boards
SUN   for Suntac 286 board
PAQ   for Compaq compatible 386 board
INT   for Intel compatible 386 board
AMI   for AMI 386 motherboard
G23   for G2 386 board

MMDDYY   stands for the BIOS release date in Month/Day/Year format

KX   stands for the AMI keyboard BIOS version number

Please note the reference number at the bottom of the screen. Keep this number written down in a safe place. If you need to call AMI's customer support personnel, they will want to know this number.

Memory Test Bypass

The BIOS performs diagnostics of the system and displays the size of the memory being tested. You can bypass the memory test by pressing the (ESC) key. This option is useful when the memory on the system is quite large. Watch for the message that says

Press <ESC> Key to bypass MEMORY test

on your screen.

Using Setup/Diagnostics/Extended Setup options

Immediately after the memory test, you will get one of the following three prompts on the screen depending upon the type of BIOS you have.

Press <DEL > key if you want to run SETUP Utility.

Press <DEL> key if you want to run SETUP or DIAGS.

Press <DEL> key if you want to run SETUP/EXTD-SET.

Press the (DEL) key to get into the Setup mode. Note that the (DEL) key will get you into the Setup mode only if the above message is displayed on the screen. When you press the (DEL) key a menu appears on the screen giving you these options:

- Going to system boot
- Running the CMOS Setup program
- Running the advanced diagnostics program or Extended Setup program depending upon the type of BIOS you have.

Use the (UP ARROW) and (DOWN ARROW) keys to set the highlighted cursor on the option you want to select and use (ENTER) to select the option.

Setting the Board Clock Speed and Wait States

The AMI BIOS allows you to change clock speeds and wait states through the keyboard at any time. The key combinations and their functions follow:

Key Combinations	Meaning
(CTRL)-(ALT)-(•)	Switch to high speed; a block cursor indicates the switch-over
(CTRL)-(ALT)-(-)	Switch to low speed; a line cursor indicates the switch-over

Each type of motherboard has a different means for changing speed from high to low. Your BIOS has to be configured by AMI for your board to support

8

speed switching from the keyboard. You are required to furnish the speed switching technique for your motherboard to AMI at the time you order the BIOS. Since the speed switching technique depends on the type of motherboard and machine you have, you should check your motherboard manual. The key combinations just listed are the most prevalent techniques.

Errors Reported by AMI BIOS

The AMI BIOS performs various diagnostic tests at the time the system is powered up. Whenever an error is encountered during these tests, either you hear a few short beeps or see an error displayed on your monitor. If the error occurs before the display is working, the system reports the error by giving a number of short beeps.

If the error is *fatal* (that is, if it keeps your computer from working), the system halts after reporting the error. If the error is *non-fatal*, the process continues after reporting the non-fatal error.

Fatal Errors Through Beeps   These errors are conveyed through a number of beeps in an infinite process but there is enough time between two subsequent sets of error beeps to discern the number in each set.

Beeps	Meaning
1	DRAM refresh failure
3	Base 64 KB RAM failure
4	System Timer failure
5	Processor failure
6	Keyboard Controller—Gate A20 error
7	Virtual Mode Exception error
9	ROM-BIOS Checksum failure

Non-Fatal Errors Through Beeps   These errors are reported as one long beep followed by a number of short beeps.

Beeps	Meaning
3	Conventional and extended test failure
8	Display test and display vertical and horizontal retrace test failed

Fatal Errors Through Display When these errors are displayed, the screen is cleared and the error message display is followed by a line saying "SYSTEM HALTED."

Display	Meaning
CMOS INOPERA-TIONAL	Indicates failure of CMOS shutdown register test
8042 GATE-A20 ERROR	Error in getting into protected mode
INVALID SWITCH MEMORY FAILURE	Indicates memory switch failure
DMA ERROR	Indicates DMA controller page register test failed
DMA #1 ERROR	Indicates DMA Unit 1 register test failed
DMA #2 ERROR	Indicates DMA Unit 2 register test failed

Non-Fatal Errors That Give Setup Option Once these errors are reported, you are given a chance to run the SETUP program. These errors commonly occur after changing your system.

Display	Meaning
CMOS battery state low	Indicates failure of CMOS battery or failure in the set and Checksum tests
CMOS system options not set	Indicates failure of CMOS battery or failure in set and Checksum tests
CMOS Checksum failure	Indicates that the CMOS battery is low or a failure in set and Checksum tests
CMOS display type mismatch	Indicates failure of display verification
CMOS memory size mismatch	Indicates a System Configuration and setup failure
CMOS time & date not set	Indicates System Configuration verification error and timer setup error
C:Drive Failure	Indicates a System Configuration verification and hard disk setup error

Non-Fatal Errors That Don't Give Setup Option The causes of these error messages are usually hardware-related.

8

Display	Meaning
CH-2 timer error	Indicates channel 2,1,0 timer test failure
Keyboard error	Indicates keyboard test failure
KB/Interface error	Indicates keyboard test failure
Display switch setting not proper	Indicates display type verification error
Keyboard is locked .... Unlock it	
FDD controller error	Indicates System Configuration verification error in floppy disk setup
HDD controller failure	Indicates System Configuration verification error in hard disk setup
C:Drive error	Indicates hard disk setup failure
D:Drive error	Indicates hard disk setup failure
D:Drive failure	Indicates hard disk setup failure

CMOS Setup Options

The Setup screen requires you to set the following:

- Date
- Time
- Floppy drive A type
- Floppy drive B type
- Hard Disk Type For Drive C
- Hard Disk Type For Drive D
- Type Of Display Card
- Presence of keyboard
- Scratch RAM option

The Setup screen also displays the following:

- Amount of real and extended memory
- Presence of numeric coprocessor
- A calendar

To set one or more of the options with SETUP, select the one you want by using the following keys:

Key	Action
(ENTER)	Moves the selection bar
(LEFT ARROW) and (RIGHT ARROW)	Move the selection bar
(PGUP) and (PGDN)	Scroll through possible settings
(ESC)	Exits and saves new settings
(CTRL)-(ALT)-(DEL)	Exits without saving settings

Date and Time Setup   The first entry in the Setup screen is the current date. A calendar has been provided to make this easier for you. Press the (PGUP) or (PGDN) key to select the appropriate value for the month, date, and year.

The procedure for setting the time is similar to that for setting the date. The time is 24-hour time so don't be alarmed when hour 13 shows up on the screen. Simply highlight either the hours, minutes, or the seconds and press the (PGUP) key or (PGDN) to step through the numbers. (To convert the displayed time to ordinary time, subtract 12 from the hours 13:00 to 24:00, and add P.M. if you wish to. For example, 13:00 is really 1:00 P.M .)

Floppy Disk Drive Setup   Drives A and/or B may come up as one of the following types:

360 KB 5 1/4-inch drive
1.2 MB 5 1/4-inch drive
720 KB 3 1/2-inch drive
1.44 KB 3 1/2-inch drive
not installed

Use the AMIGEN program, which you can buy with the AMI BIOS, to bypass the checking for the devices you do not have in your system.

Also note that you should use AMI Keyboard BIOS Version 8 or D or E to configure your system as a NOVELL nondedicated file server.

Hard Disk Drive Setup   Drives C and D are the hard drives in the system. No fewer than 46 drive types have been defined by AMI. If for some reason your particular drive is not one of the 46 predefined types, simply scroll down

8

type 47 and enter the following drive specifications: cylinders, heads, WPcom, LZone, and sectors. WPcom (Write Precompensation) is used to write the shorter tracks that are located toward the center of the drive and LZone (Landing Zone) is the area on the drive where the heads will park when the power is turned off. Consult the documentation you received with the drive for the specific values that will give you optimum performance.

Table 8-1 lists the 46 predefined types. Match your hard disk drive to one of the types shown, or select type 47.

Display Type Setup   The next option is the primary display selection. Its options are as follows:

Monochrome (MDA)
color 40 x 25 (CGA)
color 80 x 25 (CGA)
EGA or VGA
not installed

Table 8-1.   *The 46 Drive Types Predefined by AMI*

Type	Cylinders	Heads	WPcom	LZone	Capacity
1	306	4	128	305	10 MB
2	615	4	300	615	21 MB
3	615	6	300	615	31 MB
4	940	8	512	940	64 MB
5	940	6	512	940	48 MB
6	615	4	NONE	615	21 MB
7	462	8	256	511	31 MB
8	733	5	NONE	733	31 MB
9	900	15	NONE	901	115 MB
10	820	3	NONE	820	21 MB
11	855	5	NONE	855	36 MB
12	855	7	NONE	855	51 MB
13	306	8	128	319	21 MB

Table 8-1. The 46 Drive Types Predefined by AMI (continued)

Type	Cylinders	Heads	WPcom	LZone	Capacity
14	733	7	NONE	733	44 MB
15	000	0	000	000	00 MB
16	612	4	ALL CYLINDERS	663	21 MB
17	977	5	300	977	42 MB
18	977	7	NONE	977	58 MB
19	1024	7	512	1033	61 MB
20	733	5	300	732	31 MB
21	733	7	300	732	42 MB
22	733	5	300	733	31 MB
23	306	4	ALL CYLINDERS	336	10 MB
24	925	7	ALL CYLINDERS	925	56 MB
25	925	9	NONE	925	72 MB
26	754	7	754	754	46 MB
27	754	11	NONE	754	72 MB
28	699	7	256	699	42 MB
29	823	10	NONE	823	71 MB
30	918	7	918	918	55 MB
31	1024	11	NONE	1024	98 MB
32	1024	15	NONE	1024	133 MB
33	1024	5	1024	1024	44 MB
34	612	2	128	612	10 MB
35	1024	9	NONE	1024	80 MB
36	1024	8	512	1024	71 MB
37	615	8	128	615	42 MB
38	987	3	987	987	25 MB
39	987	7	987	987	60 MB
40	820	6	820	820	42 MB
41	977	5	977	977	42 MB
42	981	5	981	981	42 MB
43	830	7	512	830	50 MB
44	830	10	NONE	830	72 MB
45	917	15	NONE	918	115 MB
46	000	00	000	000	00 MB

8

Keyboard Setup   The keyboard setup is the next option. You may either choose to enable or disable the keyboard test during Power-On Self-Test by selecting keyboard as "Installed" or "Not Installed".

Scratch RAM Option   The final option is the setting of the scratch RAM. The purpose of this option is to save the user definable drive type 47, and to translate 80386 LOADALL opcode for programs such as OS/2, RAMDRIVE, and so on.

If Shadow RAM is not enabled, the parameters of the drive must be stored in normal RAM, but the integrity of the data must be maintained. You have the following options:

- The BIOS can use 100 bytes at address 30:0
- The BIOS can reduce the size of the base memory by 1024 bytes

The normal choice is 1. If you are not using drive type 47 or not running programs such as OS/2 or RAMDRIVE, this RAM will never be used. In this case you may leave the value as 1.

AMI BIOS and Keyboard Clock Switching

AMI BIOS supports clock switching through the following keyboard key combinations:

Key Combinations	Action
CTRL - ALT - +	Changes the system speed to high
CTRL - ALT - -	Changes the system speed to low

However, for the AMI BIOS to be able to change speed, there has to be support from the hardware. The protocol used by the AMI BIOS is either clock switching through the keyboard controller or clock switching by programming hardware registers.

Clock Switching Through the Keyboard Controller   To support clock switching through the keyboard controller, the clock line to the CPU should be connected through a keyboard controller pin so that when the status of the keyboard controller pin changes from high to low the speed of the processor is also changed accordingly. This type of clock switching is supported in the following motherboards or chip sets.

- C&T 286 AT chipset
- ZYMOS 286
- G2 286
- VLSI 286
- INTEL 386
- VIA 286
- 386SX

If you have trouble with clock switching on your board, check to see that the AMI BIOS you are using is configured for clock switching for your board. Also, problems may mean that you are not using the AMI keyboard BIOS. To use a keyboard BIOS other than AMI, the AMI BIOS has to be customized for that keyboard BIOS.

Summary

This chapter introduced you to a few of the major operations that may be required to optimally upgrade your PC—including upgrading your power supply, your motherboard, using BIOS or RAM on a motherboard or an adapter card, and AMI BIOS.

The next chapter shows you the second step to any upgrade—modifying your software.

8

9

Modifying Your Software

There's a saying that no job is finished until the paperwork is done. In the case of upgrading PCs, paperwork might be changed to "software." Many of the hardware upgrade procedures described in this book require more than just bolting on a new device and turning on the electricity. In order to get the full value of your new hardware, you often have to install new software or modify existing software as well. In this chapter you will see what is involved and how to go about it. You may be pleasantly surprised at how easy it is to complete the software requirements of your upgrade.

Device Drivers

A *device driver* is a small program (a driver) that helps your PC to use new hardware (a device) that you've added. Some upgrades require a device driver and others don't. Much of the hardware for upgrades described in this book will come with device driver software, which you will be required to install. Sometimes installing the physical device is easier than installing the device's driver. In this section, you'll learn a little bit about device drivers and how to install them and make them work.

While the details of device drivers are notoriously complex, the concept behind them is pretty simple. When you add a new device to your PC, like a mouse, your PC needs to know how to communicate with it. DOS can handle a lot of things, from hard disks and floppy disks to printers, keyboards, and different kinds of monitors. But it can't be expected to know how to use every possible device that's out there. If Company X develops a new type of tape drive that's unlike any other, there is little chance that DOS will know how to communicate with that tape drive. So, Company X supplies additional software along with the tape drive. The new software supplements what DOS already knows about tapes (which is almost nothing), so that your PC can make the tape start and stop, rewind it, and read and write data to it. That software is the device driver.

A device driver is often just one file supplied on a diskette. By convention, device driver files often have the .SYS extension to the filename. Other times, device drivers will include a whole disk full of software. In the case of the hypothetical tape drive given earlier, Company X might supply a device driver, a tape diagnostic program, a hard disk backup program, an install program, and some sample batch files.

Your new upgrade device should have instructions for installing any device drivers supplied with it. There may even be an automatic program that installs the device driver for you. In either case, always follow the manufacturer's instructions regarding device driver installation.

In the absence of any other guidelines, feel free to store the device drivers anywhere on the disk that you like. You may want to create a special subdirectory on your disk specifically for device drivers. Then be sure that you have made any modifications to both your CONFIG.SYS file and AUTOEXEC.BAT file that may be required.

Changing CONFIG.SYS and AUTOEXEC.BAT Files

Every time you turn your computer on or *soft boot* it by pressing (CTRL)-(ALT)-(DEL), your PC starts a bootstrap routine. A *bootstrap* is a procedure that "wakes up" your PC in a controlled and orderly manner. There is a certain sequence of things your PC must do in order to begin working properly. The sequence includes activities like starting the hard disk spinning and testing the memory chips. You have probably already noticed that it takes nearly a minute from the time you turn the power switch on until the time you can enter the first command. The bootstrap accounts for a lot of this time.

The term bootstrap comes from the old saying "pulling yourself up by your bootstraps," meaning to get started without any outside help. The ROM BIOS inside your PC contains the bootstrap procedure. After the bootstrap program is finished, your PC needs to load and run an operating system program. This is usually DOS, although there are other operating systems that run on PCs, such as Unix or OS/2. The bootstrap program is designed to search drive A, then drive C to find the operating system.

If you have a hard disk, your PC will boot DOS from your hard disk. You may already know that if you place a diskette in the floppy drive, your PC will boot DOS (or at least try to) from the floppy disk instead. Only after checking the floppy disk drive and failing, will your PC boot from the hard disk. (Booting from a floppy would also allow you the opportunity to run a different operating system without reformatting your hard disk, although caution should be used since the new operating system might be unable to read your hard disk or could damage files.)

To boot an operating system from a disk, the bootstrap program is designed to search the very first sector of that disk for some special data. If it is there, that data tells your PC what kind of operating system is on the rest of the disk. You create this special boot sector every time you format a disk with the /S option, or when you run the SYS program. If the data is not there, the bootstrap program searches the first sector of the next disk, and so on. If it never finds a good boot sector, you will see the message "Non System Disk Or Disk Error, Strike Any Key To Retry."

Assuming that the boot sector is found, your PC will begin to load DOS into memory. After DOS is loaded, your computer is almost ready to run; there are only two more steps. DOS looks for two special files on the disk called CONFIG.SYS and AUTOEXEC.BAT. You can affect your computer's bootstrap procedure and how your computer runs by changing these files. The following sections will show you how—and why.

9

Your CONFIG.SYS File

During the bootstrap, DOS looks for a file with the name CONFIG.SYS. If this file exists, it will be loaded and any instructions in it will be executed before continuing. If the file does not exist, DOS will skip this step and proceed to the next step. Your PC will only look in one place for the CONFIG.SYS file; it must be in the root directory (not in a subdirectory) of the disk it booted from. For example, if you are booting from a floppy disk, a CONFIG.SYS file on your hard disk will not be found. Also, the name must be exact. A file called CONFIGUR.SYS won't work either.

What does the CONFIG.SYS file do? Basically, it allows you to specify any special software or hardware that you have installed in your PC. In this sense, "special" doesn't necessarily mean anything very exotic, just something that requires a device driver. For example, if you have a mouse, you'll probably need to say so in your CONFIG.SYS file.

Your CONFIG.SYS file is simply a list that you create specifying the device drivers that you want loaded. You might have device drivers for a mouse, an expanded memory card, a scanner, or for Windows 3.0. Many of the hardware upgrades described in this book are supplied with device drivers. Simply storing the device driver files on your hard disk isn't enough. DOS has to know where to find them. Otherwise, DOS would have to search your whole disk, and wouldn't know a device driver file when it found one. You have to tell DOS what device drivers you have and where they are stored.

Creating and maintaining your CONFIG.SYS file is pretty easy. It is simply a basic text file (also called an ASCII file). That means that it is normal, human-readable words, not weird hexadecimal numbers or programming commands. You can create this file with whatever text editor you happen to have and you must be sure to save it in ASCII format. If you don't have a word processor at all, you will learn how to create this file without one in the upcoming section entitled, "Editing Without an Editor." When, at some later date, you're ready to change your CONFIG.SYS file, you can edit it just as you would edit any other document or text file.

Of course, you have to follow some rules when creating or changing your CONFIG.SYS file. You can't write just anything into it. There are very well-defined ways to tell DOS what you want. The next four sections cover the commands used most often that you can put in this file.

Changing FILES Parameter

Even though you can have virtually any number of files on your disks, DOS can only "open" a few at once, meaning it can only read or write to a few files simultaneously. For most users today, a low number is fine, but many application programs will ask you to increase the number of open files. To do that, create a line in your CONFIG.SYS file that looks like this:

FILES={n}

Of course, you should replace the {n} with a number between 1 and 64—20 is about average.

Changing BUFFERS Parameter

When DOS reads from a file on disk, it keeps a copy of the data it read in your memory. This memory is called a *disk buffer,* or just a *buffer.* The advantage is that if DOS has to read from that file again soon, the data may already be in memory. That saves the system from having to reread from the disk, which saves you a lot of time. The same thing applies when writing to the disk. If DOS needs to write to the same file frequently, it will just write to memory instead, and write to disk when it is finished.

DOS allows itself only two buffers for an IBM PC/XT and three buffers for an IBM AT. You can increase this by creating a line that says

BUFFERS={ n}

where {n} is a number between 1 and 99—a value of 15 or so is a good guess. Many application programs, like dBASE, will recommend a number for you. If you have many programs that all suggest increasing this value, you may want to try using the largest number suggested.

Don't add them all together! Having too many buffers can be just as slow as having too few.

ution

9

Each buffer takes up 512 bytes (one sector) of memory. BUFFERS=10, therefore, will use 5 kilobytes of memory, BUFFERS=20 will use 10 kilobytes, and so on. If the average access time for your hard drive is 30 milliseconds or less, increasing the number of buffers may not result in a noticeable improvement in speed. You may want to experiment with different numbers to see if buffering helps or slows your system down.

Changing DEVICE Parameter

The real reason most people need to change their CONFIG.SYS file is to load device drivers. To load a device driver, just give the whole name of the device driver file, including the disk drive and the path where you stored it. For example,

DEVICE=C:\MOUSE\MOUSE.SYS

will load a device driver for a mouse, (presumably) from drive C:, in the subdirectory called MOUSE. If you have more than one device driver to load, simply add another line for each one. You may wind up with several lines that all start with "DEVICE=."

Some device drivers need to have certain options set. In these cases, you will usually follow the name of the device driver with *option switches*. These switches are nothing more than letters and/or numbers that select options, set addresses, or other parameters. This example,

DEVICE=A:\DRIVER.SYS /D:5 /T:80 /H:2 /N

sets four options. What the options do depends on your device driver.

Changing LASTDRIVE Parameter

This tells DOS how many disk drives you have. Normally, this is not an issue, but sometimes if your PC is part of a network of PCs you might need to add this to your CONFIG.SYS file. It looks like this,

LASTDRIVE={ *x*}

where {*x*} is really a letter of the alphabet that specifies the last drive that you have access to. For a standard XT or AT, this would be C.

This should cover most situations you will encounter. There are other things that CONFIG.SYS can be used for. For a more complete description, you should refer to the DOS manual that came with your computer. Note that you don't have to use all of these commands in your CONFIG.SYS file. You may only need one or two. Put in what you need and ignore the rest.

If you put something in this file that DOS doesn't understand, your PC will print "Unrecognized command in CONFIG.SYS" on your screen and continue. The line with the offending command in it will be ignored but the rest of the file will be read normally. For example, the fifth line in this file

```
FILES=10
BUFFERS=20
DEVICE=C:\MOUSE\MOUSE.SYS
DEVICE=C:\DEV\QEMM.SYS /e:1200 /f:3
* This loads my expanded memory manager
DEVICE=C:\WINDOWS\SYSTEM\HIMEM.SYS
```

will be ignored. This allows you to add comments to your CONFIG.SYS file if you want to, as long as the error messages don't bother you.

Keep in mind that your computer will try to load and run your new CONFIG.SYS file the next time you boot, and every time thereafter. If your new CONFIG.SYS file doesn't do what you wanted, your computer may not work properly. For example, if you specify a bad filename for the COMSPEC parameter, your computer won't boot at all! Be cautious and always keep a working copy of CONFIG.SYS handy.

Always keep a backup copy of DOS on diskette, and never modify the CONFIG.SYS file on the backup copy. If you ever create a bad CONFIG.SYS file on your hard disk and can't boot, you can use the backup copy to boot DOS until you fix the new CONFIG.SYS file.

ution

In the examples just given, the words are typed in uppercase. That is not a requirement. DOS doesn't pay any attention to the case you use, as long as the spelling is exactly as shown. Also, don't leave any spaces between words unless the manual that comes with your device driver software tells you to add spaces.

Your AUTOEXEC.BAT File

As the very last step in booting, your PC looks for another special file called AUTOEXEC.BAT. Like the CONFIG.SYS file, this file must be in the root directory of the disk you booted from; otherwise your PC won't find it

9

and won't use it. If the file is found, DOS will execute all of the commands in it as the final step of the bootstrap procedure.

If you are familiar with .BAT (for batch) files, then you know that they allow you to create a list of commands for your computer to execute. You can name a batch file nearly anything you like, and, by simply typing the name of the file, you can set a whole sequence of programs in motion. Many people use batch files to repeat a much-used sequence of commands.

The AUTOEXEC.BAT file is a batch file just like any other. The only difference is that if DOS finds a file with this name, it will execute it for you, without your asking. Because it is a normal batch file in all other respects, it can contain one command or a whole list of commands. It can start your favorite program for you, and it can start other batch programs. You can use the AUTOEXEC.BAT file to start an applications program automatically just by turning on the computer. This is especially useful when the computer is used by untrained or novice PC users. They may never see DOS or a DOS prompt at all.

Even though the rules for AUTOEXEC.BAT are the same as for all other batch files, by convention there are some commands that only appear in AUTOEXEC.BAT. These are usually system commands that you only want to execute once per day. Below is a brief summary of typical commands that you may want to add to your AUTOEXEC.BAT file.

Setting the DATE and TIME

If your PC has a real-time clock, it will always keep the correct date and time, even when the power is turned off. On the IBM AT computer, a real-time clock (RTC) was standard equipment. On the PC and XT computers, you could only get an RTC by adding one on an expansion board. If your PC has no RTC, then DOS will ask you for the correct date and time every time you boot, *unless* you have an AUTOEXEC.BAT file.

If DOS finds AUTOEXEC.BAT, it inhibits its normal query about the date and the time. This is an important point to keep in mind, especially if you don't have an RTC. You can use the existence of this file to simply silence those questions if you want to. More likely, you will want to set the date and time in your AUTOEXEC.BAT file. If you have a PC/XT style of computer, simply add the two following lines to the very beginning of your AUTOEXEC.BAT file.

DATE

TIME

If you add these two lines, DOS will appear to ask for the date and time in the normal manner.

Changing Your DOS Prompt

If you have gotten tired of the standard C> prompt, you can change it at any time with the PROMPT command. Traditionally, people do this only once by adding PROMPT to AUTOEXEC.BAT. For example, to change the prompt to print the word "Hello!" followed by a greater-than sign, enter this:

PROMPT Hello!$g

You can change the prompt to be almost anything you want. For ideas, refer to the PROMPT command in your DOS manual. The most commonly used prompt command is

PROMPT PG

Setting Environment Strings

Some programs have an odd way of letting you set options. Instead of running a configuration program or an install program, they use something called *environment variables,* or *environment strings.* These are simply special words that you define. When the program runs, it looks for these words, and behaves accordingly. For example, a word processing program might need to know what type of video adapter you have (CGA, EGA, VGA, and so on). Rather than set this in a configuration menu, you might need to define an environment string like this:

SET VIDEO=EGA

The SET command is a normal part of DOS. You can use it at any time. It is easier to take care of environment variables at boot time by defining them in your AUTOEXEC.BAT file. Then you can forget about them for the rest of the day.

9

Changing Your Search Path

When you type something—anything—at the DOS prompt, DOS assumes that you are typing the name of a program that you want to run. After you press (ENTER), here's what happens. First DOS checks to see if you've typed the name of one of the dozen or so "built-in" DOS commands like TIME or COPY. (Notice that there are no program files called TIME or COPY that come with DOS.) If it finds no match, DOS will check the current disk directory where you are logged on. If, for example, you are currently working in the \WORD\LETTERS subdirectory and you type **FOO** then DOS will look for a file called \WORD\LETTERS\FOO. (First it will look for ...FOO.COM, then ...FOO.EXE, and, last, ...FOO.BAT.) Finally, if there is no match, DOS will check the rest of your search path.

A *search path* is a list of disks and subdirectories that you want DOS to search through when you want to run a program. You define a search path with the PATH command (another built-in DOS function). It is customary to place a PATH command in your AUTOEXEC.BAT file. A typical entry might look like this:

```
PATH=C:\;D:\;C:\DOS;C:\UTILS;C:\WORDPROC\SYSTEM;C:\VIEW;D:\GAMES
```

Actually, this is a fairly long PATH specification. It would tell DOS to search no fewer than seven subdirectories on two disks before giving up. If DOS does exhaust the entire search path without finding the name you typed, you'll get the "Bad Command or File name" message.

There are an infinite number of things that you can do with your AUTOEXEC.BAT file. Because this file is executed automatically every time you boot (hence, the name) you can also get yourself into a lot of trouble with it. Be careful about what you type, and always keep a backup copy of a working AUTOEXEC.BAT handy in case things go wrong. Unlike CONFIG.SYS, you *can* abort a batch file. Press (CTRL)-(BREAK) right away, as your system boots, to abort AUTOEXEC.BAT. When DOS asks "Abort batch file? (Y/N)" answer by pressing (Y).

Editing Without an Editor

If you find yourself needing to create a CONFIG.SYS or AUTO-EXEC.BAT file and you don't have a word processor handy, there are two courses of action: you can use EDLIN, the abominable text editor supplied free with DOS (and worth every penny), or you can type the text directly into a file. For the first option, refer to the chapter on EDLIN in your DOS manual. If you choose the second option, follow these instructions.

To create a file and enter text directly into it, simply type the following command at the DOS prompt:

COPY CON \CONFIG.SYS

and press (ENTER). The first word is "COPY" the familiar file copying program. But in this case, you will not copy from one file to another; instead you will copy from the keyboard (CON) to a file (\CONFIG.SYS). Just as in a normal copy, if the file doesn't already exist, COPY will create it for you. If it does exist, COPY will delete the old one. You may want to make a backup copy of CONFIG.SYS and AUTOEXEC.BAT before you start, by entering in the following:

COPY \CONFIG.SYS \CONFIG.BAK
COPY \AUTOEXEC.BAT \AUTOEXEC.BAK

This will ensure that you have a working file to fall back on.

After entering the COPY command to begin a new file, you can start typing your text. Be sure to type carefully because you have no editing tools. (This is like typing on a typewriter again.) You can use (BACKSPACE) to correct typing mistakes, but once you press (ENTER) you are finished with that line.

Type each line exactly as you want it, and press (ENTER) after every line. After you've finished the last line, press the (F6) key. This will add a ^Z ((CTRL)-(Z)) character to the end of the file. DOS uses ^Z to tell when it has gotten to the end. After pressing (F6), press (ENTER) one last time.

9

That's it! You've created a new file. You may want to use the TYPE command to review it and be sure that everything works fine. If it doesn't, you'll need to start over from the beginning.

Changing SETUP Parameters

Sometimes loading device drivers and changing the CONFIG.SYS and AUTOEXEC.BAT files is not enough. There are some changes that you can make to your PC that require an additional step. This involves changing the battery-backed CMOS RAM in your PC.

The CMOS RAM is not found in PC- and XT- class computers. It first appeared in the IBM AT and has since been designed into nearly all 286, 386, and 486 computers. *CMOS RAM* is a special memory chip that is attached to a battery to keep it "alive" even when the power is turned off. (By the way, CMOS is pronounced like "sea moss" and is not the best description of this chip, but it is the one everybody uses. Technically, CMOS is a manufacturing process used in making the IC chips and nearly all of the chips in your PC are made with the same CMOS process.) If you have one in your computer, that is what enables it to always know what day it is even when the PC has been turned off for several weeks.

The CMOS RAM also keeps track of several important system parameters, like how many disk drives you have, what types they are (3 1/2-inch or 5 1/4-inch, for instance), and whether or not you have a math coprocessor installed. Every time your computer boots it refers to this information so that it can start up, or initialize, each of these devices properly. If you change any of these devices you must be sure to change the information stored in the CMOS RAM as well. Usually if there are any changes, the computer itself will prompt you to update the CMOS RAM the next time you boot it up. When it checks the equipment in your PC it will find a discrepancy and suggest that you correct it.

Exactly how you go about changing the contents of the CMOS RAM depends on what brand of PC you own. If it is an IBM computer, you will need to find the "Utility/Diagnostic" disk, put it in floppy disk drive A, and reboot your computer. Let your PC boot from this floppy disk instead of the usual procedure. Then, you must run the program called SETUP. When

SETUP is running, you will see a collection of options. Many Compaq computers use a very similar procedure.

If you have any of a number of other brands of PC, you may have a built-in SETUP program. In these machines you simply press a certain combination of keys (CTRL-F1, for instance) and the SETUP screen will appear. This is especially handy because you don't have to locate a special disk.

A third type of computer will only let you execute the SETUP program if your PC determines that something is wrong as it boots up. During the bootstrap procedure, your PC will display "CMOS RAM Error" or something similar, and tell you what key to press to initiate the SETUP procedure. If you don't press the appropriate key, or if you wait too long to press it, you lose your chance. In that case, turn the power off, wait a few seconds, and turn it back on again.

Once you get your SETUP or configuration program started, you must change the appropriate values to make your computer work properly. You are usually given the opportunity to select two types of floppy disk drives, two types of hard disk drive, whether or not you have a math coprocessor, how much conventional memory you have, and the correct date and time of day. You may also be able to set the amount of expanded memory, extended memory, wait states, or other more esoteric features of your PC. For these latter parameters, don't change anything unless you have very clear instructions on how to do so from the PC maker or the maker of your upgrade equipment. Fiddling around with wait states and chip set options is a quick way to crash your computer.

When you have set the option or options that you want, be sure to save the new setup in your CMOS RAM. Most configuration programs give you the choice of either tossing out all your changes and quitting or of saving the changes in CMOS RAM. Read over everything once again to make sure it's right, and then save it. If your PC doesn't boot itself automatically afterwards, turn the power off and reboot it yourself.

Summary

This chapter showed you how to use device drivers, the CONFIG.SYS file, and the AUTOEXEC.BAT file to complete the software end of your hardware

9

upgrades. You also learned how to change CMOS RAM in your PC to affect your system's parameters—or the setup of your PC.

In this chapter, you modified existing software to accommodate hardware upgrades. In the next chapter (Chapter 10, "Upgrading Your Operating System and Environment"), you'll upgrade the software itself.

10

Upgrading Your Operating System and Environment

Operating system upgrades can give you advantages that are just as great as the advantages you get from adding hardware. A new operating system is usually cheaper and easier to install too. Before you add an enormous new hard disk drive or a new tape backup, be sure that your current operating system can handle them. Sometimes you'll need to update your operating system to make full use of a new peripheral.

In this chapter, you'll learn about operating systems and environments. Operating systems such as DOS, OS/2, and UNIX control and manage your display, keyboard, and disk drives. Operating *environments* such as COM-MAND.COM, DOSSHELL.EXE, and Microsoft Windows are placed between you and the operating system to allow you to take control of your computer via the keyboard and display. You'll see what is available in the world of PC operating systems. If you have an old version of DOS, you might be surprised at what the new versions have to offer. Or, if you've never used one of the new graphical user interfaces with windows you're in for a treat.

Operating Systems

Like the conductor of an orchestra, the software that comprises your operating system is what keeps your computer's many parts operating in harmony. Your operating system controls the overall operation of your computer, overseeing and manipulating hardware and software to make the system do what you ask it to do. The basic choices you have for operating systems for PC/XT/AT and compatibles are IBM or Microsoft DOS, OS/2, or UNIX/XENIX.

There are other less well-known systems including Digital Research's DR-DOS, the PICK operating system, and PC-MOS. These systems have their following, but they just do not have a large enough customer base to draw the widespread applications developer support that DOS, OS/2, and UNIX/XENIX have.

DOS

DOS (Disk Operating System) software provides a cushion between you and the hardware in your computer. In addition to managing your display, keyboard, mouse, floppy disk drives, hard disks, and printers, it provides a shell (called COMMAND.COM) that allows you to enter the commands needed to create files, erase files, copy files, format floppy disks, copy disks, and perform many other system services.

DOS is by far the most popular operating system for all PC/XT/AT computers. Probably 95 percent of all IBM-compatible computers are running some version of DOS. If your goal is to make your PC as compatible as possible with others' machines, and to take advantage of the huge selection of applications programs available, then you will want to stay with DOS (which is pronounced to rhyme with "moss").

When the IBM Personal Computer was first developed, it was offered with a choice of three different operating systems. The first PC customers could choose either CP/M86, UCSD P-System, or PC-DOS Version 1.0. CP/M (which stands for Control Program/Monitor) was the most popular operating system for personal computers at that time. The second choice was an operating system developed at the University of California at San Diego for writing computer programs using the computer language Pascal (hence the name UCSD P-System). The third choice, PC-DOS, was a complete newcomer.

IBM contracted with the relatively small Microsoft software company in Redmond, Washington to develop their new operating system. Once developed, DOS was sold by both IBM and Microsoft. IBM called their version PC-DOS, for Personal Computer Disk Operating System. Microsoft's version was virtually the same, but they called it MS-DOS, for Microsoft. Today, these two names are used interchangeably by nearly everybody except IBM's and Microsoft's attorneys. Technically, only IBM can sell PC-DOS. Everybody else sells MS-DOS.

Almost as soon as it was offered, computer users bought PC-DOS with the Personal Computer much more often than CP/M86 (to everybody's great surprise because CP/M was popular at that time, with a great number of applications programs, while DOS was completely new and had no applications at all). In fact, DOS was based very heavily on CP/M, and the similarities (file naming conventions and the prompt, for example) showed. This was an intentional move to make learning DOS easier for users who were already familiar with CP/M. DOS still bears a strong similarity to CP/M, a fact that many contemporary users curse.

Over the years, DOS has changed. Some changes have been minute, while others have been quite dramatic. At the same time, DOS 1.0 users could still use the same commands in DOS 5.0 that they've been using for years with the first DOS version.

If you are using one of the earlier versions of DOS, say, Version 2.0 or earlier, you should seriously consider upgrading your operating system. More and more, new application programs require that you have a current version of DOS on your computer. Hanging on to an old version may be keeping you from realizing the full potential of your PC.

At the very least, upgrade to Version 3.1 of DOS (though DOS 5.0 is preferable). Currently, there are more users with Versions 3.1, 3.2, and 3.3 than all other versions combined. For some reason, the PC world seems to have reached a plateau around DOS Version 3.3. It has become sort of a *de facto* standard version. Virtually all applications programs work with DOS 3.3, while many do not work with DOS 2.0, and very few will work with DOS 1.0 or 1.1.

10

The New Look of DOS

Early versions of DOS had only the standard A> prompt from which all commands were executed. DOS 4.x and DOS 5.0 have added an additional *shell* (besides COMMAND.COM). The word shell is used to describe any software that manages your interaction with the operating system. It acts as a "Shell" around the operating system, allowing you to interact with and give commands to the operating system. Up until DOS 4.0, the shell was a program called COMMAND.COM, and it printed the familiar A> prompt.

Figure 10-1 shows the shell (DOSSHELL.EXE) for DOS 5.0. Like Windows and Presentation Manager, DOS 5.0 provides pull-down menus, a directory tree, file lists, and other nice features that make DOS easier to use. DOS 4 is very similar in appearance.

DOS Shell

DOS Version 4 was the first to provide a shell using *graphics* as well as text. Although not as attractive or functional as Graphical User Interfaces (GUI) such as Windows, it provides an easier way to navigate directories and use DOS (more on GUIs later). When you enter a graphic DOS shell you see

Figure 10-1.　　*The DOS 5.0 shell*

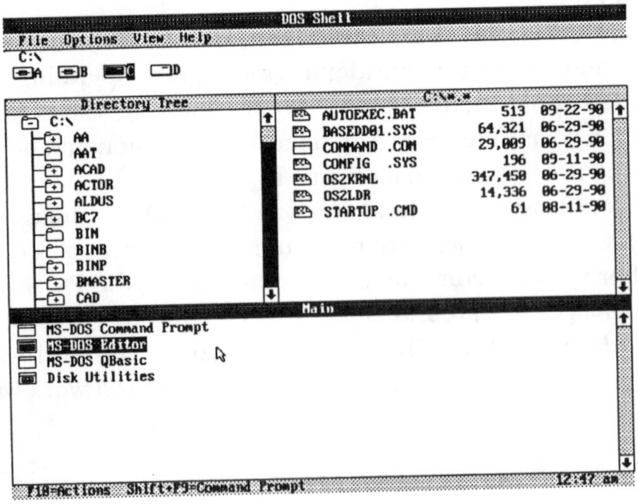

across the top of the sreen a *marque* or title bar. Below that is the *menu bar* (IBM calls it an *action bar*). The menu bar in Figure 10-2 shows File, Options, View, Tree, and Help. If the screen pointer is moved (using the mouse) to touch one of these and the mouse button is clicked, a menu drops down with a list of additional actions. This is called a *pull-down menu.*

Figure 10-3 shows one of the pull-down menus associated with the file system. Note the list of choices displayed in the menu and the arrow pointer used to select them. The dialog box shown here

is used to set up programs that can be run from the Main window.

Figure 10-2.   *A DOS shell*

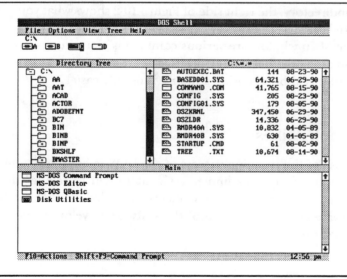

Figure 10-3.   *A DOS shell pull-down menu*

Icons (or small pictures) representing the floppy disk drives and hard disk are displayed under the menu bar in Figure 10-2. The directory tree, also shown in Figure 10-2, is under the drive icons. A plus sign in the icon indicates that it contains additional subdirectories. If the icon is empty (no plus sign), the subdirectory contains only files (or it may be empty). You can point to one of these icons and click the mouse button to display a list of the files contained in the subdirectory; the right side of Figure 10-2 shows what you would see if you clicked on the C:\ directory.

In the Main window are various commands you can run from this DOS shell. You can add other commands to this list and you can use the keyboard to do all of this although using a mouse is usually easier.

DOS Look-Alikes

Because of the stunning success of the DOS operating system, naturally other software companies immediately attempted to "clone" this piece of software just as innumerable companies have copied the IBM hardware. Like the hardware companies, some of the software developers met with more success than others.

You might want to look at Digital Research's DR-DOS 5.0 and earlier versions, since they developed CP/M the precursor to DOS. DR-DOS 5.0 is very similar to MS-DOS 5.0, including its new user shell. PC-MOS is another example of a DOS look-alike operating system. It allows you to run multiple tasks at once, something that MS-DOS normally cannot do.

OS/2

When IBM announced the Personal System/2 line of computers and declared that Personal Computers and PC-DOS were obsolete, they also introduced a new operating system to go along with them. It was called Operating System/2 or OS/2.

The first version of OS/2 was released in 1987 as OS/2 Version 1.0. It is an advanced operating system that was designed specifically to fully use the capabilities of the 80286, 80386, and 80486 CPUs. OS/2 is the first operating system to really take advantage of the protected mode of these microprocessors, putting it in a class with operating systems for much larger computers. (If you need to review protected mode, see Chapter 2, "Anatomy of a Personal Computer System.") OS/2 allows you to run many programs all at the same time. It can do more for the user than DOS but the sheer size and complexity of the operating system and the sluggish turnout by software developers supporting OS/2 slowed its market acceptance. The next few years should see the release of OS/2 2.0 and, a little later, 3.0 (or possibly NT, for "new technology").

OS/2 can be used as a character-based system (from a prompt line entering keyboard commands) like DOS, but is most likely to be used with the Presentation Manager GUI shell shown in Figure 10-4. Several program manager windows and the Task List are shown in this figure.

OS/2 provides a new filing system called the High Performance File System (HPFS) that allows filenames of up to 255 characters. You could, for example, have a file called "My letter of May 10, 1991 to my great Aunt Tillie."

A look at the Group-Applications window in Figure 10-5 will give you an idea of the range of available applications that are already available for OS/2. Figure 10-6 shows the OS/2 Presentation Manager File Manager window. You might see the similarities between this and the DOS shell mentioned earlier.

10

Figure 10-4.   *The OS/2 Presentation Manager Task List*

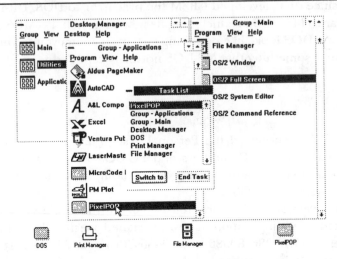

UNIX and XENIX

One of the grandparents of multiuser, multitasking operating systems is AT&T's UNIX. This operating system has been around on mainframes for many years. The Santa Cruz Operation (SCO) (in cooperation with Microsoft) developed a version of UNIX for use on PCs. They called the operating system XENIX and have spent a number of years enhancing it for use on PCs.

In the past few years several other companies have "ported" AT&T's UNIX to the PC but SCO XENIX, which now implements a superset of AT&T UNIX, is probably the most complete and powerful UNIX version available for the PC.

You'll find UNIX very expensive when compared to DOS or OS/2 and it's normally found in networked systems used with mainframe computers.

Operating Environments

Over the last few years there has been a lot of attention paid to something called an *operating environment*. An operating environment is a powerful shell.

Figure 10-5.   *Some OS/2 applications*

Figure 10-6.   *The OS/2 File Manager*

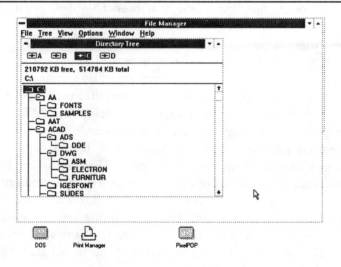

10

It is not a new operating system, but a new way of using an existing operating system. It provides extended capabilities, ease of use, printer management facilities, file management facilities, and memory management. The intent is to give the user a more comfortable way to work with the computer.

There's no denying that some people have difficulty using computers. A lot of the responsibility lies with the operating system and the commands it uses. MS-DOS and most other operating systems in use today were developed by computer scientists and engineers for use by other computer scientists. (This is especially true of Unix .) In an effort to make personal computers easier to use and more "user-friendly," some companies have developed elaborate operating system shells. These "environments" change the whole look of the computer in an attempt to make the system easier to understand and more accessible to the average person.

DOS made a small improvement in user-friendliness over CP/M because it used more logical words for commands, like COPY instead of CP/M's PIP or the MODE command instead of a STAT command. But these are minor changes, merely window dressing. For years, people have been trying to make a truly different kind of computer system, one that anybody could use without needing help.

At the Palo Alto Research Center (PARC) in California in 1981, Xerox Corporation thought they had found an answer. They developed a computer with an operating environment called SmallTalk. With SmallTalk, commands were represented by pictures on the screen. To carry out a command, the user could point to the picture, and the command would execute. Disk files were also represented by pictures, and they were also selected by pointing to them. In fact, it was possible to operate the computer without ever touching the keyboard at all. The computer mouse was developed at PARC specifically for the purpose of "pointing" at pictures on the screen.

The first really mass-produced computer to use the concept of SmallTalk was the Lisa computer, which was released in 1983 by Apple. For various reasons, the Lisa wasn't very popular, although the operating environment was a big hit. Apple stuck with the idea, and later introduced the Macintosh, "the computer for the rest of us." Today, there are several versions of the Macintosh computer, all using the same SmallTalk-inspired operating environment. That operating environment is probably the single biggest reason for the popularity of the Macintosh.

New Environments for the PC

For all of the reasons just mentioned, there are now several different operating environments available for IBM-compatible PCs. Most of them are pretty similar—they all take their inspiration from the work done at PARC. But remember that an environment is *not* an operating system. You still run DOS, and keep all of your DOS application programs. Operating system environments, or shells, change the way DOS looks, but *not* what it can do.

Because most of these new operating environments use pictures instead of words to convey information, they are called *graphical user interfaces*. The graphics part is obvious. You are the user, and an *interface* is something that acts as a buffer between two things, in this case you and your computer operating system. You will see graphical user interface abbreviated as GUI, which is pronounced (by those who insist on reducing all phrases to the minimum number of syllables) as "gooey."

The concept of representing ideas with pictures is an ancient one, but carrying it out successfully isn't always easy. A GUI uses icons to represent various functions, commands, or files. The idea is kind of like a rebus puzzle that you may have done as a child. For example if you saw the following,

you should have no trouble reading, "I like/love my bread."

would read "I can see."

The principle is simple: Put images (icons) on the screen that represent tasks to be done. (One of the best known is the image of a trash can pointed to when the user wants to "throw out" files.) The user uses a pointing device (like a mouse) to indicate the image, presses a button, and the program or

10

action starts. Add menus that appear when you move to a certain area of the screen, and *scroll bars* (like the sliding volume control lever on a radio) that allow you to move back and forth to parts of the text or image that are not currently on the screen and you have a full-fledged GUI.

The whole intent of using GUIs is to make the operation of the computer as simple as possible. One buzzword used extensively in GUI circles is "intuitive." That means that the meaning or purpose of a given icon should be obvious; you should be able to guess its use through intuition. Theoretically, the perfect GUI would require no owner's manual at all. You should be able to look at it and know intuitively what to do.

Some people swear by graphical user interfaces; others swear at them. For many, they do exactly what they are intended to do. They make the PC much easier to use than it would otherwise be. Other users see a GUI as a hindrance to their work. If you're already familiar with DOS (their argument goes), why put up a layer of software between you and it? Besides, running a GUI takes up a large chunk of your PC's memory and CPU power. To some extent, using a GUI will slow down your computer because it will spend more of its time drawing pictures and less time getting your work done. Whether or not this is a fair trade is a matter of personal taste.

Microsoft Windows 3.0

Microsoft Windows started life when the PC/XT and early ATs were prevalent. These early versions of Windows were very slow, partly because of the slow hardware. Figure 10-7 shows the MS-DOS Executive screen that was used to start programs and manage files. With the release of Microsoft Windows Version 3.0, the entire picture changed radically.

Years of improvement have led to an operating environment that surpasses many GUIs currently available for ease of use, functionality, and power. Not only do you have a superior GUI but you still have the underlying power of DOS, which gives you the best of both worlds.

Windows 3.0 splits the old Windows DOS-Executive window into a File Manager (Figure 10-8) and a Program Manager (Figure 10-9). A broad range of high-quality applications software already exists for Windows, and many of the same people who have made thousands of applications available for DOS are rapidly converting those applications to work with Windows 3.0.

Figure 10-7. *The MS-DOS Windows Executive*

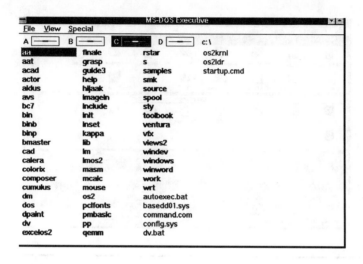

Figure 10-8. *The Windows 3.0 File Manager*

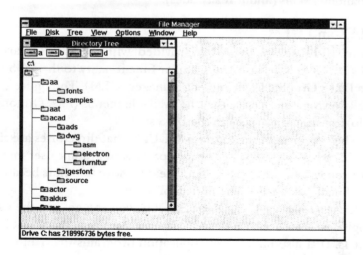

10

Figure 10-9.   *The Windows 3.0 Program Manager*

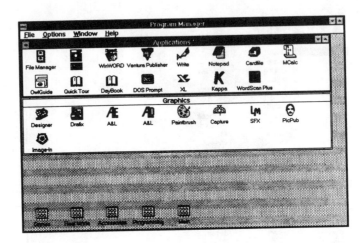

To give you an idea of the richness of 3.0, Figure 10-10 shows the Klondike solitaire game that comes with Windows 3.0. Please note that the cards are displayed in full color. The game is actually recommended to sharpen your mouse handling skills (and it really does).

ViewMAX and GEM

Figure 10-11 shows the GUI provided with Digital Researh Incorporated's DR-DOS 5.0. It provides similar functionality to the DOS 5.0 shell but uses DRI's Graphic Environment Manager (GEM). The figure shows an open pull-down menu. Notice that the available menus (File, Options, View, and Help) are similar to those in the DOS shell.

This shell is closer to the Macintosh GUI in that directories are shown as folders laid out on a "desktop." The nice part about graphic user interfaces is that once you've used one, you can quite easily move to others because of the common SmallTalk ancestry behind all of them.

For those who have MS-DOS or PC-DOS, you can get just the user shell from Digital Research. It is called GEM and it runs with DOS, just like most other GUIs. DRI also has several application programs that run with GEM.

Figure 10-10. *Windows 3.0 Solitaire*

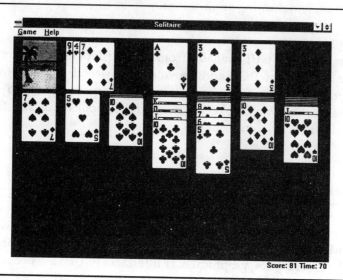

Figure 10-11. *Digital's ViewMAX shell*

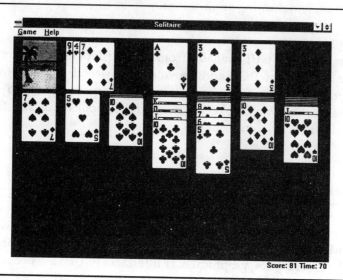

These include word processing, desktop publishing, filing, organizing, image manipulation, and drawing applications.

DESQview

DESQview is another GUI, available from Quarterdeck Office Systems. It runs with most versions of DOS and provides a powerful and easy-to-use user environment. There are no special applications program to run with DESQview. Rather, you can keep your current applications and DESQview will "launch" them for you from the user shell.

Summary

You learned some history on the most popular operating system, DOS, and saw what the various versions can do for you. You learned about OS/2 and UNIX. You saw how graphical user interfaces (GUIs) are becoming more prevalent in operating systems, and how Microsoft Windows, ViewMAX, GEM, and DESQview can alter your operating environment to make your computer easier to use.

11

Troubleshooting and Maintenance

Working on your computer can sometimes be like working on an English sports car: you always seem to have spare parts left over when you're done. (Perhaps if you work on it often enough you'll have enough parts for two!) Obviously, this shouldn't happen, and you should make every effort to find out where the spare screws, washers, cables, or jumpers came from before embarking on a more complex troubleshooting mission. This is where taking notes or instant pictures can save the day.

If you've exhausted all the possibilities and your PC still doesn't work right, try some of the suggestions in this chapter. They are culled from years of collective experience, and one of them may hold the secret to your PC's sudden demise.

Symptoms and Diagnosis

The first thing to find out is what exactly your PC isn't doing now that it used to do before. Does the fan start spinning when you turn on the power? Does the monitor show any signs of life? Do the disk drive access lights come on? Do they ever go off? Does your computer beep in an unfamiliar manner? The answers to questions like these should be clear in your mind before you go any further. The point at which your computer starts to malfunction can often tell you where the problem lies.

For example, if the fan doesn't spin, the problem may be with your power supply, not the disk drives, monitor, or DOS. On the other hand, if the power-on self-test (POST) suddenly declares that you have a memory error after you add a new disk drive, then perhaps a DRAM chip got worked loose from its socket while you were working. A DRAM chip may also have been damaged by static electricity.

It is easy to forget to plug something back in after working inside your PC. Make sure that all of the cables inside the system unit are back where they belong. There should be a little 4-wire power cable connected to each and every disk and tape drive. There should also be at least one ribbon cable firmly connected to each disk and tape drive—some disks get two. Are all the jumpers back in place? Did you remember to plug your keyboard back in? How about the video cable to your monitor? And are the monitor and your PC both plugged into the wall outlet?

If you are really baffled about the cause of the problems, try undoing whatever you just did. For instance, if you've just changed your video adapter card, try taking it out and putting the old one back in. If your computer starts working again, then the problem must be in the new card. Check and double-check any DIP switches or jumpers it might have.

If putting the system back to its original state doesn't help, then something must have been disconnected, forgotten, or damaged in the process. Look for bent pins on ICs, screws that aren't tight, boards that are bent slightly or don't fit well, or cables that have been pinched or creased.

11

Power On

One of the most frustrating problems is when you turn on your PC and nothing happens. This usually signals a very basic problem somewhere. Fortunately, these can also be the easiest problems to fix. The classic is forgetting to plug something in—or, if it is plugged in, it is plugged into a switched outlet and the switch is turned off.

Dampness

There is a strange problem that we've noticed with some of our computers that appears to be associated with high humidity. On damp mornings we turn on the computer and absolutely nothing happens. Our answer is a hair dryer. A minute or so on low heat directed into the power supply fan outlet and the computer starts as if nothing had happened.

The real point is, if your computer doesn't always start, don't panic. It's not always a total disaster. In fact it may only signal a transient glitch. With the equivalent of millions of transistors and dozens of other devices that must all get going just right, temporary failures do occur. The first answer is—try again.

Switching on the Power Too Quickly

PC power supplies don't like to be turned on and off a lot. After you turn your PC off, wait at least ten seconds (count to ten slowly) before turning it back on. If you just "flip" the power switch off and back on in one quick motion, some power supplies simply won't turn on again. The result will seem to be a dead system. Just turn the computer off, wait a few seconds, and turn it on. If you have a hard disk in your PC, wait until you hear the hard disk drive spin all the way down to a stop. Then turn the power back on. This will save wear on your power supply and will also extend the life of your hard disk drive, too.

Using a Speaker and the Display

If a fatal error occurs before the video display adapter is initialized, the BIOS will let you know through a series of error beeps. Use the system speaker to listen for the number and duration of the beeps, then look at the BIOS error messages to see what type of error it lists. If the fatal error occurs after the display is initialized, the error will be displayed on the screen.

Manufacturing Diagnostics

AMI and others provide diagnostic functions in their BIOS that are useful in the manufacturing of boards. When pin 32 on the keyboard controller is grounded, the BIOS goes through the POST (power-on self-test) continuously. The POST is repeated until either the power is switched off or the BIOS finds a fatal error on the motherboard. Error conditions can be monitored from the speaker or from the display, if the display is working. It is not necessary to connect the keyboard, video, or disk controller cards to run the manufacturing diagnostics.

Using an LED Connected to Port 80h

When the BIOS goes through the power-on self-test, it outputs a series of values at different points in the BIOS to port 80h to indicate its progress. If an LED is connected to this I/O port, it will blink in what looks like a Morse code pattern. Your PC may already have such an indicator installed on the motherboard. If not, connecting one is too complicated a procedure to attempt without intimate knowledge of PC hardware.

In case of an error, the LED will show the area where the problem exists. Table 11-1 is a sequential list of the checkpoints and the meanings associated with them.

11

Table 11-1. *A Sequential List of Checkpoints and Their Associated Part*

Checkpoint	Meaning
01	NMI disabled and 286 reg. test about to start
02	286 register test over
03	ROM checksum OK
04	8259 initialization OK
05	CMOS pending interrupt disabled
06	Video disabled and system timer counting OK
07	CH-2 of 8253 test OK
08	CH-2 of delta count test OK
09	CH-1 delta count test OK
0A	CH-0 delta count test OK
0B	Parity status cleared
0C	Refresh and system timer OK
0D	Refresh link toggling OK
0E	Refresh periods ON/OFF 50 percent OK
10	Confirmed Refresh ON and about to start 64 K memory
11	Address line test OK
12	64 K base memory test OK
13	Interrupt vectors initialized
14	8042 keyboard controller test OK
15	CMOS read/write test OK
16	CMOS checksum/battery check OK
17	Monochrome mode set OK
18	Color mode set OK
19	About to look for optional video ROM
1A	Optional video ROM control OK
1B	Display memory R/W test OK
1C	Display memory R/W test for alternate display OK
1D	Video retrace check OK
1E	Global equipment byte set for video OK
1F	Mode set call for Mono/Color OK
20	Video test OK
21	Video display OK
22	Power on message display OK
30	Virtual mode memory test about to begin

Table 11-1.   *A Sequential List of Checkpoints and Their Associated Part*
                 (continued)

Checkpoint	Meaning
31	Virtual mode memory test started
32	Processor in virtual mode
33	Memory address line test in progress
34	Memory address line test in progress
35	Memory below 1 MB calculated
36	Memory size computation OK
37	Memory test in progress
38	Memory initialization over below 1 MB
39	Memory initialization over above 1 MB
3A	Display memory size
3B	About to start below 1 MB memory test
3C	Memory test below 1 MB OK
3D	Memory test above 1 MB OK
3E	About to go to real mode (shutdown)
3F	Shutdown successful and entered in real mode
40	About to disable gate A-20 address line
41	Gate A-20 line disabled successfully
42	About to start DMA controller test
4E	Address line test OK
4F	Processor—in real mode after shutdown
50	DMA page register test OK
51	DMA unit-1 base register test about to start
52	DMA unit-1 channel OK, about to begin CH-2
53	DMA CH-2 base register test OK
54	About to test flip/flop (f/f) latch for unit-1
55	If latch test both unit OK
56	DMA unit 1 and 2 programmed OK
57	8259 initialization over
58	8259 mask register check OK
59	Master 8259 mask register OK, about to start slave
5A	About to check timer and keyboard interrupt level
5B	Timer interrupt OK
5C	About to test keyboard interrupt
5D	ERROR ! timer/keyboard interrupt not in proper level
5E	8259 interrupt controller error
5F	8259 interrupt controller test OK
70	Start of keyboard test

Table 11-1. *A Sequential List of Checkpoints and Their Associated Part (continued)*

Checkpoint	Meaning
71	Keyboard BAT test OK
72	Keyboard test OK
73	Keyboard global data initialization OK
74	Floppy setup about to start
75	Floppy setup OK
76	Hard disk setup about to start
77	Hard disk setup OK
79	About to initialize timer data area
7A	Verify CMOS battery power
7B	CMOS battery verification done
7D	About to analyze diagnostics test results for memory
7E	CMOS memory size update OK
7F	About to check optional ROM C000:0
80	Keyboard sensed to enable SETUP
81	Optional ROM control OK
82	Printer global data initialization OK
83	RS-232 global data initialization OK
84	80287 check/test OK
85	About to display soft error message
86	About to give control to system ROM E000:0
87	System ROM E000:0 check over
00	Control given to int-19, boot loader

Other Possible Culprits

If your LED does not show any of the checkpoints listed in Table 11-1, there is a good chance that you have one of the following problems:

- BIOS ROMs are bad (unlikely)
- Even and odd ROMs are interchanged (possible)
- BIOS ROMs are plugged in backwards (and therefore possibly damaged)

Problems with Your Disk

If your problem is related to a new disk drive, look at the following sections. If your disk seems to be working alright, but occasionally loses data or complains about "Sector Not Found" or "General Failure" you might try one of the many disk diagnostic programs on the market.

Disk Diagnostic Programs

There are several disk diagnostic programs available that can ferret out some of the more esoteric problems with your hard disk or floppy disk. The Norton Utilities from Peter Norton Computing in Santa Monica, California is one good example. It provides a wealth of hard disk and floppy disk exploration programs. They also offer Disk Doctor, which can diagnose, and even fix, many common disk ailments.

Spin Rite is available from Gibson Research, and it provides a large assortment of disk-related tools. It can also be used to change the interleave on your hard disk, providing better performance. (Interleaving was covered in Chapter 7, "Adding Chips.")

The Mace Utilities from Paul Mace Software in Ashland, Oregon is yet another well-regarded set of hard disk fixer-uppers.

Floppy Drives

Floppy disk drives are electromechanical devices, meaning that they have both electrical and mechanical parts. The mechanical parts do get dirty, especially if they are not covered. Whenever you find yourself with the PC system cover open, take a few moments to blow the dust off the disk drives. If you want, you can buy a little can of compressed air from your computer store, but blowing the dust off yourself may work just as well.

You might also want to take a cotton swab and remove any dust or debris from the write-protect light and sensor. This is a tiny little light that shines through the write-protect notch of your diskettes to see if there's a write-protect sticker there. If the light shines through, then it must be okay to write on or erase the disk. No light, no writing, or erasing. If the light or the sensor gets dirty, your PC might think that all of your floppy disks are write-protected. (You'll see more on this later in this chapter, in Figure 11-1 and Figure 11-2.) By the way, that's also why you can't use transparent tape as makeshift write-protect tabs.

Disk Drive Lights Stay on

If the red or green access light for a disk drive comes on when you turn on the power and stays on, it usually means that you have connected the drive's ribbon cable backwards. Don't worry—this is a classic mistake and it doesn't do any damage to the disk drive. Simply turn off your PC, open the cover, and turn the cable around the other way. Pay attention to the colored stripe on the ribbon cable that identifies pin 1.

Hard and Floppy Drive Controller Cables

Although 34-pin controller cables for floppy and hard disk drives look alike, there is a distinct difference involving the twisted portion of the cable. The twisted portion of the floppy disk controller cable is seven wires wide and starts nine wires from pin 1 (the wire on the edge of the cable with a different color). The twisted portion of the hard disk controller cable starts five wires from the opposite edge and is five wires wide. Interchanging these cables is a frequent cause of trouble.

Drive Select Jumpers

There are four pairs of drive select jumpers on most disk drives. You place a jumper across one pair of pins, and leave the others unconnected. This is supposed to allow you to attach up to four disk drives to the same ribbon cable, allowing the drives to use the position of the jumper to tell which of the four your computer is talking to. So much for theory.

Since all drive select jumpers in an IBM PC are set to drive 2 (as opposed to drive 1), the floppy disk drive connected with a twist in the cable is drive A while the drive connected with no twist is drive B. The hard disk drive connected to the controller cable connector with a twist will be drive C and a second hard disk drive (if installed) would be connected to the connector without a twist, making it drive D.

If it sounds complicated, try this: first of all, be sure you use the correct cable. The drive connector with a twist is connected to the drive you want to be the lowest lettered drive—drive A for floppy disk drives and drive C for hard disk drives.

Memory Errors

Memory errors can be difficult to solve. Normally DRAM failures are a good reason to take your PC into the local computer service shop for an examination. If you like, you can try to solve the problem yourself by checking for loose components or swapping DRAM chips.

Loose Components

In electronics, there is a phenomenon known as "chip creep." Basically the theory is that the heating and cooling of the IC devices eventually causes them to work themselves out of their sockets. It is therefore a good idea to put socketed ICs snugly in their place by pressing them into their sockets when you are experiencing trouble.

The contact between the lead on the chip and the socket connector is subject to moderate corrosion from dust and other household contaminants. The act of pressing the chip back in can wipe the connection and improve the contact. In some instances it might even be helpful to remove the IC and reinsert it. This would give all pins fresh contact.

Swapping DRAM Chips

During your POST you might see a message indicating a memory failure. You might also see the dreaded "Parity Error, System Halted" message, sometimes without warning. Both of these indicate the same thing—that there may be some problem with your DRAM.

11

There is no way to tell a good DRAM chip from a bad one just by looking at them, so forget that idea. If you are lucky enough to have some extra DRAM chips around, your best bet is to swap them with some of the DRAM chips in your PC. The more chips you swap, the better your odds of catching the bad one. Ideally, you would swap them all at once.

Memory chips rarely fail but you may find a bad one in newly purchased chips. SIPs and SIMMs are replaced as a unit but motherboard mounted DIPs are another matter. You can use a trick we call "walking the chips."

Let's say you had the first two banks of RAM full on your motherboard and you just bought an additional bank that causes your computer to quit or give error messages. The first step is to remove the bank just added. Next, remove a single chip from bank 0 and replace it with one of your new chips. If the computer starts and runs as it did before, you can set that chip aside as probably good.

Repeat the procedure with the remaining chips that you just bought. Since bank 0 is critical, one of your just purchased DRAMs will probably cause the computer to fail. Set that chip aside as bad and buy a new one. Now install the new bank and things should work.

You can use variations of this technique to locate chips that have failed in use. Simply remove all chips but bank 0. Make sure that the chips in bank 0 are working by starting your computer. (Be sure to set the jumpers or switches for the proper amount of memory.) Now walk the remaining chips as just outlined until you find the bad chip.

If the problem persists, you probably have not yet removed the bad chip. With patience, you can continue swapping chips until you find the bad one. Getting a parity error doesn't necessarily mean the parity chip is bad and it probably isn't a problem unless it persists or occurs frequently.

Maintenance

This section covers some general maintenance issues that you should know about. These issues are mostly common sense. There's no special equipment that your computer needs to stay running for years and years, but a little care and the occasional cleaning will prolong its life. Read over the suggestions listed here and see how many of them can become habits.

Figure 11-1.   *The write-protect notch*

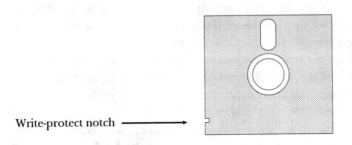

Write-protect notch ──────────►

Cleaning the Write-Protect Sensor

Your 5 1/4-inch floppy diskettes were designed to allow you to protect valuable information. A notch on the left side (Figure 11-1) is provided. If this notch is not covered, you can write to and read from the diskette. With it covered, you can only read from the disk. An attempt to write to a diskette with a write-protect tab in place will result in a "disk is write-protected" message.

The device that accomplishes this is a lamp and photosensor in the drive on the left side as shown in Figure 11-2. Some floppy disk drives exhibit a problem in that this sensor collects dirt and dust. The problem is very evident when you insert a floppy disk that is not write-protected and get a write-protect error. If this happens, you can usually clear the problem by blowing a little air into the drive towards the left side. This usually clears up the problem but a small cotton swab would do a better job and ensure that the problem won't reoccur soon. Still better would be to remove the drive and clean the assembly if it's accessible.

Floppy Disk Error Messages

There are two things to check when you start getting odd error messages on floppy disk operations. The first is that the magnetic medium may be binding in the plastic jacket around 5 1/4-inch diskettes, and the second is

Figure 11-2.   *The write-protect problems*

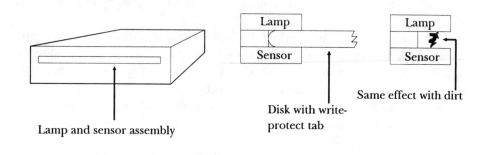

Lamp and sensor assembly

Disk with write-protect tab

Same effect with dirt

the rails supporting your carriage head may be dirty. Check the disk first because it's easier to fix. If the disk already moves freely, check the carriage head rods.

Checking the Disk

Remove the floppy disk. Hold the jacket in one hand; slip two fingers through the hub hole and see if the media rotates freely in the jacket. It is possible that the jacket has been crimped and is binding the media so that it will not turn.

This problem can be fixed. Carefully slip your thumbs into the plastic jacket at the hub hole and gently expand the jacket to free the medium. If this doesn't work, you can always extract the media and use your emergency jacket (explained shortly) to make a backup copy.

Cleaning the Head Carriage Rails

The head carriage may be supported by two metal rods. If you turn a floppy drive upside down and look near the back, you will see two cylindrical rods about 1/4 inch in diameter, spaced about an inch apart (if your drive uses this system of head positioning).

The read/write heads are positioned using these rods as guides either by a screw mechanism or by a tape band driven by a stepping motor. The rods accumulate dirt over several months and the heads no longer move smoothly. You will start getting odd error messages when trying to read or write to floppy disks.

To check this, carefully grasp the head carriage and move it back and forth on the tracks. If the movement is stiff, take a cotton swab and moisten it with a light sewing machine oil. Clean and lightly lubricate the exposed parts of the rod, move the heads to the other end, and repeat. Then move the heads back and forth to distribute the lubricant until the heads move more freely. This will normally fix the problem and save you from spending $70 to $120 to buy a new drive.

Both of these problems can be virtually eliminated using the CASE-200. The door that closes in front of all the drives keeps them fairly dust free. This should greatly extend the life of these electromechanical components.

An Emergency Jacket

If freeing the jacket around your 5 1/4-inch floppy disk didn't work, try making an emergency jacket. Take a spare floppy disk and, using a sharp craft knife, carefully slit the top edge of the diskette (on the end opposite the data windows) just as you might open an envelope. This slit should be as straight and clean as possible. The inside of the plastic jacket has a soft, white felting that you should try not to bunch with the knife. (You might want to do one now for practice and save it so it's all ready should a crisis occur.)

Puff the jacket open and remove the magnetic medium. It's made of a plastic material that can withstand very high temperatures so it is seldom damaged by either hot coffee or the hot sun. Throw the medium away and save the plastic jacket as your emergency jacket.

Now, in a similar manner, carefully remove the medium with your data on it from the damaged jacket. If it's been spilled on, wash the medium gently using warm water and dishwashing detergent, then rinse it thoroughly. Dry it by blotting it between paper or cloth towels. Be sure it is clean and dry before inserting it in your emergency jacket. Once inserted in the emergency jacket you should be able to copy it to a good floppy disk.

11

Don't attempt to simply cut the end of the emergency jacket off with a pair of scissors. This will shorten the jacket and it may not seat correctly in your drive.

Caution

Rescuing 3 1/2-Inch Floppy Disks

A similar technique can be used to rescue a 3 1/2-inch floppy disk. The hard covers of this disk are held together with plastic welds at four points. The approximate location of two of these welds is shown in Figure 11-3. Use a narrow screwdriver blade wedged between the two halves of the jacket to break these two welds.

Carefully separate the jacket at the end opposite the metal slide and remove the medium. Again you have an emergency jacket. In a similar fashion, carefully remove the medium from the damaged floppy disk and put it into your emergency case and try to copy this to a good disk. In both cases, be sure the medium is clean before you insert it in the drive. Dirty media could transfer unwanted residue to your drive heads.

High-density (1.44 MB) diskettes have a square cutout on each side of the case at the end opposite the metal slide. Be sure your emergency case matches the density of the floppy disk you are trying to rescue.

Caution

Watch Those Hub Rings!

Low-density 5 1/4-inch floppy disks have a reinforcing ring around the hub hole. The reason is simple: Closing the drive lever on a disk that has no hub ring and is slightly off-center will crinkle and damage the hole and the disk will not be readable. Carefully reseating the disk will usually allow the disk to be read but the hub hole is already damaged. You should probably make a copy and throw the damaged disk away.

Early low-density disks and many of the new high-density (1.2 MB) disks have no hub ring. The solution is to joggle the drive lever gently as you close it to coax the disk into alignment.

Figure 11-3. *3 1/2-inch emergency jacket*

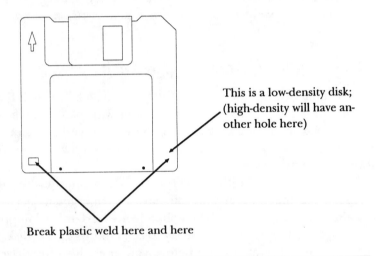

This is a low-density disk; (high-density will have another hole here)

Break plastic weld here and here

A Cleaning/Dusting System

For the most part, personal computers don't require much maintenance. One thing you should do at regular intervals, though, is to dust off the computer and keyboard. Keyboards can accumulate dust and other particles in between the keys, which may lead eventually to irregular or erratic operation.

Also pay attention to your computer's cooling vents and keep them free of dust or obstructions. A quick wipe with a soft cloth is sufficient. Avoid solvents, cleaners, or any fluids. They can mar the finish of your computer's cabinet or cause erratic electrical problems because of static electricity.

Don't Block Air Vents

If your computer system has air vents, pay attention to where they are when you place the system on a desk or in a rack. The vents are there for a reason, and each one should have at least four inches of clearance to allow

11

good airflow. If your system has a fan as well, give it a good six inches of unobstructed room so the computer will not overheat.

Turn Down the Brightness When Not in Use

Like television screens, computer display monitors have a brightness control. Some people like their screens brighter than others do, and working conditions sometimes necessitate turning the brightness up. When the computer is not used for an extended period, it is a good idea to turn the brightness down or to turn the monitor off completely.

A video display screen works by shooting a constant stream of electrons at a glass screen. The inside of the glass is coated with phosphor, which glows when struck by these electrons. The phosphor coating can be made to glow white, green, amber, or many other colors, depending on the type of monitor. Over time, however, the phosphor loses its ability to glow and becomes dimmer. The longer the phosphor is exposed to electricity, the faster it deteriorates. Usually this takes several years and it happens so gradually that no one notices.

By turning down the brightness of the screen when no one is using it, you can greatly prolong the life of your computer monitor. Here's a simple test: Turn off your monitor for a few minutes and look away from it. Then, look back at the blank screen. If you can see a pattern in the glass, your monitor's phosphor coating has already begun to "burn in." You may want to think about replacing the monitor.

Don't Turn Power On and Off Repeatedly

You should not make a habit of turning your computer on and off rapidly like a light switch. This is particularly true if your computer has a hard disk drive. Quickly switching the power on and off several times can cause the computer's power supply to overheat and can damage the hard disk drive. After you've turned your computer off, always wait several seconds before turning it back on again. Listen to your hard disk spin down when you turn your computer off. The hard disk should stop spinning before you turn the computer on again.

Don't Eat or Drink Near the Keyboard

The best way to keep your computer clean and running well is to keep it from becoming gummed up in the first place. Avoid the urge to set a cup of coffee on top of the monitor or to eat a sandwich while leaning over the keyboard. Crumbs accumulate and eventually can cause keyboard malfunctions. Liquids, on the other hand, tend to cause more immediately apparent failures.

Summary

This chapter covered various symptoms of malfunction, and how you use these symptoms to diagnose and fix your PC and disks. You also saw that your PC and your disks last longer if regularly cleaned and maintained, and protected from various hazards.

12

Building Your Own PC

Often the equipment you buy comes in pieces. The backyard swing set, exercise benches, tricycles, and many other items arrive unassembled with a sheet of instructions telling you how to put them together. Assembling a computer may be easier than assembling a tricycle—and you now have a book of instructions. This chapter tells you how to assemble a computer, giving you a real example. If specific equipment is mentioned, it's not because it's always better but because the brands given are popular ones that many readers use. The general procedures will apply to almost any components of a PC.

A capsule version of the process follows: You'll open the case and remove the hardware inside. Next, test fit and install the power supply, if it isn't preinstalled. Test fit and install the motherboard. Test fit and install a single floppy disk drive. Install and connect the drive controller. Install the graphics adapter. Make a thorough visual inspection.

Close the case and connect the monitor and keyboard. Connect the power cables to the display and the computer. Turn the display on and allow it to warm up. Turn on the computer. This is jokingly called a "smoke test" and smoke is what you don't want to see or smell. You may smell warm varnish and plastic, which shouldn't be cause for alarm.

Depending on your video display and BIOS, you should begin to see meaningful information on your display including a memory test that is part of the power-on self-test (POST). Once you get this far, the rest is quite easy.

Tip

Your monitor will take a minute or two to warm up. You should turn it on first so it can be ready to present a display. If everything is normal, you will see a flashing cursor in the upper-left corner of your display screen almost immediately. If the cursor does not appear after a few seconds, turn your computer back off right away and recheck your entire installation. The lack of a cursor does not indicate a disaster but to be on the safe side go back and check each installation step.

When the POST runs successfully you will continue by configuring your computer and booting your operating system. At this point you will have a basic working computer and can continue in the knowledge that any problems will be introduced by items you add.

Selecting a Case

At one time your choice of cases was limited to a PC/XT case or an AT case. You will still find these but you will also find a variety of other case styles including so-called "small footprint" cases (these take up little room on your desktop), tall vertical cases, short vertical cases, and a number of others. The case you choose depends on where you want it located, how much space you have, and, to some extent, the motherboard you use. There are too many variations to list here, but in general, the manufacturer of the case determines the motherboard size you can use.

It will also depend on the number of drive slots you need. If you intend to have one floppy disk drive and one hard disk, you can use almost any case. If you plan to add additional items like a tape backup, a second floppy disk drive, or similar items, you will need to buy a case with enough drive bays.

The case in the first example system is the Enlight EN-6600 shown in Figure 12-1. This case is also available from JDR Microdevices in San Jose, California, as their CASE-200. JDR's price at this writing is $499.95, which includes a 250-watt power supply. The case has five half-height drive bays

Figure 12-1. *The Enlight EN-6600 case (Photograph courtesy of Enlight Corporation)*

behind a door that you can close to protect them from dust. It also has space for two hard disk drives on a handy sliding tray, so you shouldn't run out of drive space.

Selecting a Power Supply

The first PCs contained a 65-watt power supply. Power supplies are now available in 135-, 150-, 200-, 250-, and 330-watt sizes. The CASE-200 (EN-6600) shown in Figure 12-1 comes with a 250-watt supply that accounts for about $130 of its cost. A 135-watt power supply will easily handle several adapter cards, a floppy disk drive, and a hard disk. It will probably handle any additional adapters you install.

Selecting the proper power supply wattage is usually a guess. Catalogs and advertisements don't normally tell you how much power the various pieces of a computer require. If you know exactly what components you will have in your computer, you can contact the various manufacturers or dealers and get the power requirements for each piece from them. You can then total up the requirements and buy a power supply of the right wattage but this is not really necessary.

Here's a rule-of-thumb. For small cases, get a 135- to 150-watt supply. The CASE-200 comes with a 250-watt power supply. A CASE-200H is also available with a 330-watt supply. You should probably get at least a 250-watt power supply for any vertical case that handles six or more half-height drives.

Selecting a Keyboard

The selection of a keyboard is a very personal thing. Your basic choice is either an 84-key PC keyboard (not recommended) or a 101-key keyboard. The 101-key keyboard is often called an "enhanced layout" keyboard or an AT keyboard, but all 101-key keyboards are functionally identical. If any differences exist for a particular keyboard, the differences will be detailed in the keyboard manual. For example, some manufacturers place the (ESC) key and/or the 12 function-keys differently.

The cost for a keyboard can be anything from $50 up. Since the keyboard has no provisions for upgrading, you will probably find that the keyboard you buy will move with you from machine to machine. Don't skimp on this item unless you are a two-finger, five-word-per-minute typist.

Selecting a Motherboard

Now comes the most important part. You can buy motherboards for anything from $50 for a 8088 PC motherboard to $4000 and up for an 80486

AT motherboard. If you're going to use your computer to do simple text editing or word processing you can build an adequate PC compatible for around $300 but you should strongly consider at least an 80286-based motherboard.

With motherboards, as with all PC components, you might consider checking your local newspaper for the next computer swap meet in your area. These are excellent places to hunt out real bargains.

ote

80286, 80386, 80386SX, Full-Sized, or Baby

At this writing, a 12.5-MHz MCT-M286-12 baby AT motherboard from JDR costs $199.95. A baby 386SX 16-MHz motherboard will cost about $400. A good choice is the MCT-386MBC-33 33-MHz motherboard from JDR or the Orchid Privilege 386-33C. The JDR board is $1495 without memory. JDR also has an 80486 motherboard at $2999 without memory. Since the 80486 has the math coprocessor built in, it is not an extra item that you'll have to shell out for later, which makes the $2999 price look much better. Either the 80386-33 or the 80486 are the top-of-the-line motherboards for present-day computers.

Memory Considerations

Memory will cost extra; you can estimate it at about $50 per megabyte if you purchase wisely from many chip suppliers or at a swap meet. You can expect to pay about $100 per megabyte from JDR and other mail order vendors. The advantage of buying from JDR, Jameco, or other well-known suppliers is service and the convenience of a single source. Memory prices fluctuate wildly (mostly down) and you may well find that the longer you wait the cheaper DRAM will be.

Try to buy a motherboard with SIMM sockets for memory instead of adapter card memory. Most motherboards provide that capability now and more are coming around to it. You can expand memory to 16 MB on many motherboards using SIMMs without using valuable slot space.

Math Coprocessors

Math coprocessors are expensive. They provide the extra clout needed to make some math-intensive programs run better. Some programs, like AutoCAD, require them. They can run anywhere from under $100 for an Intel 8087 to $650 for a 33-MHz Intel 80387.

Cyrix makes the FastMath, which will work at many times the speed of the Intel chip. It costs about $1200 and fits directly into the 80387 socket. Many motherboards also provide for a still more powerful chip made by Weitek.

The Weitek chip is also more expensive than Intel's and also offers greater performance. But unlike the Cyrix or IIT "clones," it does *not* run Intel software. If you are buying a Weitek coprocessor, be sure that your software is really going to use it. Some programs don't.

Selecting a BIOS

Among the more popular BIOS suppliers are Phoenix, AMI, and Award. Your motherboard will probably come with one of these already installed depending on the motherboard supplier. What you will notice is different messages and different methods of handling the power-on self-test (POST) including the messages you see on the screen. Chapter 7 "Adding Chips," provides more information on your BIOS.

Selecting a Battery

The PC/XT uses switches on the motherboards to tell the BIOS what equipment is available in the computer. If you change the amount of memory, change from a monochrome to a color display, or add a floppy disk drive, you must set these switches to tell the system software about the changes.

The AT substitutes a small memory chip called a CMOS (Complimentary Metal Oxide Semiconductor) RAM. (This was covered in Chapter 2, "Anatomy of a Personal Computer System.") The system configuration is now stored in CMOS RAM and a small battery keeps the CMOS RAM and computer date/time clock running when the system is turned off. This way, your computer date and time are always correct (well, almost always correct).

of the POST involves reading the contents of the CMOS RAM to determine what devices are available in the system.

Many new motherboards are using a newer component that houses the clock, CMOS RAM, and the battery all in one IC. On these motherboards you will not find a separate battery.

Selecting Input/Output Adapters

The number of serial and parallel ports you need will depend on your system and the peripherals you use. The Orchid Privilege 386-33C motherboard has two serial ports and one parallel port built in. In this chapter's system, these can be mounted in the 9-pin D-Sub and 25-pin D-Sub openings in the back of the case. This saves at least one expansion slot. The motherboard does have some switches—one thing these do is determine how many serial and parallel ports are enabled (or working).

Selecting a Floppy Disk Drive

You can elect to install one or two floppy disk drives in a normal system. More than two requires an extra floppy disk controller and special software. You could have either 5 1/4-inch drives supporting 360-KB or 1.2-MB capacities, or 3 1/2-inch drives supporting 760-KB or 1.44-MB capacities. Floppy drives will cost about $100 each although they can be found for considerably less if you hunt around. The example system will have one 5 1/4-inch, 1.2-MB drive and one 3 1/2-inch, 1.44-MB drive.

Selecting a Hard Disk Drive

JDR and Jameco have a broad selection of hard drives. You might also consider a Micropolis drive kit. The kits include hard disk, controller, cables, mounting rails, and everything you will need to complete the installation. A 157-MB ESDI drive kit is $1049; a 338-MB drive kit is $1799.

This chapter's example system will use a 667-MB ESDI drive ($2499) and a Western Digital WD1007V-SA/SE hard and floppy drive controller board. If you can afford the extra capacity, get the big drive—like the keyboard and motherboard, you can move it from system to system, and you'd be surprised how fast hard disks fill up. The drives have many years of useful life.

Selecting a Display and Display Adapter

Get at least a VGA-quality display. The display and adapter can be purchased for as little as $499 from JDR and you might find them for less elsewhere. The fact is CGA and EGA just don't have the resolution to run today's graphics-intensive software. Our example system will use the Orchid ProDesigner II VGA and a Mitsubishi Diamond Scan 16L displaying 1024 by 768 resolution. The ProDesigner II VGA was one of the first adapters to have 1024 by 768 Windows 3.0 drivers available.

Selecting a Pointing Device

Figures 12-2 and 12-3 show two of many pointing devices you might purchase. There are many others available, and, like your keyboard, this is a very personal choice. Many manufacturers are only now looking at the ergonomics of pointer design. Some are so badly designed that people have to use two hands—one for the ball and one for the buttons on a trackball.

The TrackMan is meant to be a thumb-operated ball. The fingers are then free to actuate the buttons making operation much like a mouse. Logitech offers several different versions of their best-selling mice. One of the nice features of a Logitech mouse it that it can emulate (or copy) the operation of virtually any other mouse on the market, so it is guaranteed to work with any of your software.

Figure 12-2.   *The Logitech mouse (Photograph courtesy of Logitech Corp.)*

Figure 12-3.   *The Logitech TrackMan (Photograph courtesy of Logitech Corp.)*

Deciding on an Operating System

You will find MS-DOS 5.0 and Windows 3.0 to be an ideal combination for much of your work. The system in this example is capable of running other operating systems like OS/2, UNIX, or Xenix; but these operating systems are more useful to networking and other high-end operations.

DESQView 386 is an operating environment you should consider if you are using many programs that don't run under Windows. In fact, DESQView, DOS, and Windows 3.0 work very well together in the latest versions. Windows 3.0 will run in "Enhanced 386 mode" with DESQView's memory manager QEMM.SYS installed and running, and that is a major accomplishment.

Building a Power Tower

This section describes the assembly of a vertical floor-standing computer that should be good for many years of use. Most of the assembly methods will apply to just about any system and you are welcome and encouraged to substitute parts that suit your needs.

The Shopping List

This system will use the following parts:

- Enlight EN-6600 case and power supply (JDR's CASE-200)
- Privilege 386/33C motherboard
- Two two serial ports (built-in)
- One parallel port (built-in)
- 4 MB of built-in RAM plus 4 MB of RAM on SIMMs
- Cyrix FastMath coprocessor
- CORE International 667-MB hard disk drive
- Western Digital WD1007V-SA/SE (or WD1009) drive controller

- 5 1/4-inch 1.2-MB floppy disk drive
- 3 1/2-inch 1.44-MB floppy disk drive
- Floppy disk drive controller cable
- Orchid ProDesigner II VGA display adapter
- Mitsubishi Diamond Scan 16L monitor
- Keyboard

12

The case comes with a power cord and a box of miscellaneous parts. Set the power cord aside and open the box of parts. You should find an instruction sheet, 10 drive rail assemblies, a small bag containing red insulating washers, and a bag of miscellaneous parts as follows:

- 1 gray cable and wire holder
- 2 keys for the keyboard lock
- 4 white snap-in motherboard standoffs
- 12 black rubber drive cushions
- 9 1/4-inch hex brass standoffs
- 20 3/16-inch flat-topped Phillips drive mounting screws (English)
- 20 3/16-inch flat-topped Phillips drive mounting screws (metric)
- 12 hex-head screws for mounting the brass standoffs
- 24 3/8-inch hex-head/Phillips screws

Sort out and identify these parts. You may want to save the packing material and to store leftover parts for future use. The number of pieces supplied may vary from our list.

Metric screws may thread into English holes or nuts but the fit will be loose and sloppy. An English screw can be forced into a metric nut or hole but it will damage the threads. If you're only going to put the screw in once, this may be marginally acceptable in the absence of an alternative.

Here's another way: Try a screw in the nut or hole. If it threads in easily all the way and only snugs up on the last turn, you probably have the right screw for the job. If it is difficult to turn don't force it. Try another size or thread type. If the screw threads in a turn or two and then becomes very tight there are two possibilities. Either the threads are damaged or the screw is the wrong size or thread pitch.

In the long run, it's more or less up to your mechanical judgement. If it feels right, it probably is. If it feels wrong, it probably is wrong. Just take it slowly and don't force things unless you have no alternative and you think force will work.

Workspace and Tools

Find a convenient place to work. It's easier to have your case at eye level, but this will require a fairly tall table or workbench. You should have adequate light that you can direct into the interior of the case when needed. You will also find a small flashlight very handy because once the motherboard is installed part labels can be very hard to read without it.

You will need the following tools:

- A #2 Phillips-head screwdriver or a nutdriver
- A small flat-blade screwdriver
- A place to keep small parts (a plastic dish works well)

Opening the Case

Figure 12-4 shows the back of the CASE-200. Remove the three screws indicated and slide the removable panel (the door) toward the back of the case. Save the screws. You may have to bump the door with the heel of your hand to move it. With the door far enough back (say, about 1/2 inch), it will swing out. The door is mounted on hinges as shown in Figure 12-5. The door can be lifted up to disengage the hinge pins. Set the door aside until needed.

Removing Front Panel

Using a flat, thin-blade screwdriver, carefully remove the snap-on, plastic front panel. The panel is held in place by six expanding spring fittings that plug into corresponding holes in the case. Set the front panel aside until you need it.

Figure 12-4.   *The back of the EN-6600 case*

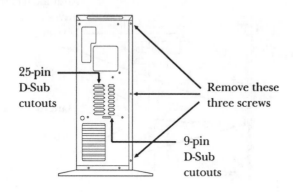

25-pin
D-Sub
cutouts

Remove these
three screws

9-pin
D-Sub
cutouts

Removing the Hard Drive Tray

The EN-6600 (CASE-200) is designed to hold several internal drives as shown in Figure 12-6. One drive is shown on the drive tray. An additional drive can be installed on the tray and a half-height drive can be installed near the top of the case. You could also put hard drives in any of the five available half-height slots.

Figure 12-5.   *The case hinge assembly*

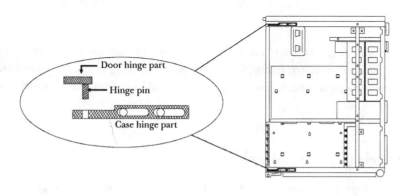

Door hinge part

Hinge pin

Case hinge part

Figure 12-6.   *The case interior*

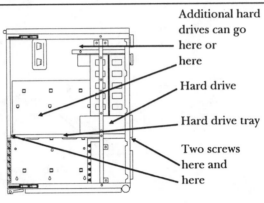

Additional hard
drives can go
here or
here

Hard drive

Hard drive tray

Two screws
here and
here

Remove the two hex-head screws in line with the keyboard connector at the rear of the case, as indicated in Figure 12-6. Remove the two hex-head screws holding the drive tray at the front. Slide the hard drive tray out and put it aside for now. This allows access for motherboard installation.

Caution

There are sharp, undressed metal edges on many computer cases. There are also sharp pins on the solder-side of circuit boards. With some care these should never be a problem. Some suggest using a file to dress sharp case edges. This might be a little dangerous. Even if the case is empty, the metal filings are difficult to remove and metal filings in disk drives or between pins on circuit cards could do extreme damage to your computer.

You may want to sort out the jungle of wires and look over the interior of the case. You can, for example, lay the wires coming from the power supply over the back of the case. You can also sort out and find the connector ends of other wires.

Preparing the Motherboard

Although this chapter's example uses the Orchid Privilege 386/33C Cache motherboard, there are many other AT boards that you could use. The principles and details are much the same. This board has some advantages. Two serial ports and one parallel port on the motherboard save at least one slot and the board provides 4 MB in the normal memory location with 4 SIMM slots. You can also get an expansion memory board that uses DIPs. Maximum expansion is to 16 MB.

aution

Many of the ICs in your computer can be destroyed or badly damaged by static electricity. Before you handle any static sensitive components, always touch a metal surface such as your computer case. Also, when installing adapter cards, touch some metal part of the computer case. This will prevent static damage in most instances.

Experience shows that the problem is not as great as labels might lead you to believe but for safety's sake, leave adapters in their antistatic bags until they are ready for use and handle parts by the edges. Don't pass them from person to person. If someone else must handle the part, put the part down and have the other person touch some grounded surface before they pick it up.

A combination of DIP memory (4 MB standard) and SIMMs (4 MB possible) allows up to 8 MB without using an expansion memory board. Most software will run very well in 8 MB of RAM, and this saves a slot. The slots saved by motherboard serial and parallel ports and motherboard memory saves two slots. For those who want it, a memory expansion board will boost total memory to 16 MB. Memory DIPs or SIMMs must have an 80-nanosecond access time. The SIMMs should be organized as 1 megabit by 9.

Read the manual that comes with your motherboard and become familiar with the location of various parts, particularly switches, jumpers, and external connectors. In this section some of that information will be duplicated and expanded upon, particularly as it applies to installing this board in the CASE-200.

Overview of the Privilege 386-33c

Figure 12-7 shows the components you are interested in. When you install the motherboard the end with the adapter slot connectors will be referred to as the back. The end with W13, 14, 15, and 16 will be at the front of the chassis; this will be called the front of the motherboard. For now, look the motherboard over and locate the various items shown in Figure 12-7.

The serial and parallel port connectors are at the upper-right corner of the motherboard. Every pin 1 is indicated by a black square. Cables supplied

Figure 12-7.   *The layout of the Privilege 386-33C motherboard*

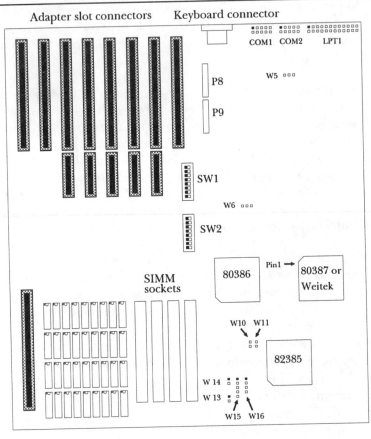

with the motherboard will be used to bring these out at the back of the cabinet. The keyboard connector is located at the top of the figure. P8 and P9 are the motherboard power connectors. Switches SW 1 and SW 2 are in the center. The various jumpers and connectors are labelled W with a number.

The 80386 CPU and 82385 are shown as "roadmap" items to help you locate the jumpers and connectors. The 80387 is shown properly oriented for this motherboard, but please do check the documentation that comes with your motherboard. Placements do change from one manufacturer to another.

Figure 12-8. Switch 1 details

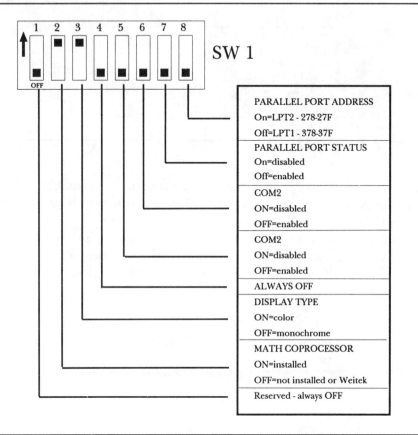

SW 1

PARALLEL PORT ADDRESS	On=LPT2 - 278-27F
	Off=LPT1 - 378-37F
PARALLEL PORT STATUS	On=disabled
	Off=enabled
COM2	ON=disabled
	OFF=enabled
COM2	ON=disabled
	OFF=enabled
ALWAYS OFF	
DISPLAY TYPE	ON=color
	OFF=monochrome
MATH COPROCESSOR	ON=installed
	OFF=not installed or Weitek
Reserved - always OFF	

Setting the Switches

Begin by setting the switches SW 1 and SW 2. Switch 1 (SW 1), toward the back of the motherboard, sets up parallel ports, serial ports, math coprocessor, and display type. Figure 12-8 shows the switch set for this computer. It also shows the various options. If you want to disable the parallel port, or one or both of the serial ports, simply set the corresponding switch position (5, 6, or 7) to ON. If you are not going to install a math coprocessor, set switch position 2 to OFF, and if you have a monochrome display, set switch position 3 to OFF.

Figure 12-9.   *Switch 2 settings*

Switch 2 (SW 2) sets up the memory configuration. The Switch 2 settings for this installation are shown in Figure 12-9 but you may have another configuration (see Table 12-1).

The table shows the possible setting for the first four positions of SW 2. Position 5 should be ON if SIMMs are used (as it is in this case) OFF otherwise. Position 6 is always ON. Positions 7 and 8 can be in either position but they are shown OFF.

Setting Jumpers

There are four jumpers that must be checked and possibly set. They are W5, W6, W10, and W11. Use the default settings. If you want to use different settings, check here to see how to set W5, W6, W10, and W11.

W5
1-2 = disable
2-3 = enable

Enables Fast A20 gate
(default)

W6
1-2 = COM1 at 3F8
      COM2 at 2F8
2-3 = COM1 at 3E8
      COM2 at 2E8

Alternate serial port address
(default)

W10
IN = enabled
OUT = disabled

Pipeline

(default)

W11
IN = enabled
OUT = disabled

DRAM controller
(default)

Table 12-1.   *Memory Size Switches for the First Four Positions of Switch 2*

	4 MB	8 MB	12 MB	16 MB
1:	ON	ON	OFF	OFF
2:	ON	OFF	ON	OFF
3:	OFF	OFF	OFF	OFF
4:	OFF	OFF	OFF	OFF

W5 is a three-position jumper located near the COM1 and COM2 connectors. W6 is a three-position jumper located to the left and down. W10 and W11 are two-position jumpers to the right of the SIMM sockets near the front edge. W5 and W6 should have a jumper installed connecting pins 1 and 2. W10 should either not have a jumper (OUT) or the jumper should be hung from a single pin. W11 should have a jumper connecting pins 1 and 2 (IN). These are the factory settings and you shouldn't have to change them.

Installing Simm Memory

With the switches and jumpers properly set it is time to install 4 MB of RAM SIMMs. Place the motherboard with the 32-bit connector slot away from you. The 32-bit slot is the connector near the DIP RAM chips. The 80387 socket should be toward you. The SIMMs must be installed in a certain order or those already installed will prevent others from being installed. The procedure is illustrated in Figure 12-10.

Take the first SIMM, face the chips away from you with the notch down and on the right. Slide the SIMM into the socket holding the SIMM at a 45 degree angle toward you. Seat it fully into the socket and carefully stand it straight up. The two locking parts of the socket (one on each end) will spread apart and should snap back in place to secure the SIMM. Also two horns will engage the holes on either end of the SIMM, locking it in place. (Removing a SIMM is done by spreading the locks on either side and tipping the SIMM back until it disengages.) Now, install the three remaining SIMMs.

Next install the Cyrix FastMath or the 80387 math coprocessor. Pay particular attention to the cut-off or beveled edge and a similar marking on the circuit board. This chip can be installed four different ways but only one is right! Installing it incorrectly will irreparably damage a chip costing over $500, so do pay attention to the markings.

ution

Figure 12-10.   *Installing SIMM memory modules*

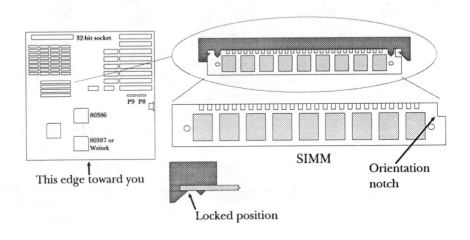

Look the motherboard over to double-check that you've completed switch settings, jumper setting, installed the SIMMs correctly, and installed the math coprocessor. Your motherboard should now be ready for installation in the case.

Installing the Motherboard

Again place the motherboard with the keyboard connector away from you and refer to Figure 12-11. On the left you will see three holes—one near you, one in the middle, and one at the rear. In the center you will see three more holes. The holes at the front and rear are surrounded by square solder pads. The center hole is like the ones on the left. There is a center hole on the right that will not be used.

You probably received some hardware with your motherboard but we will use the hardware supplied with the case. First, locate four white plastic standoffs. Press one from the bottom of the motherboard through each of the four holes indicated in the figure. The horns should spring out and latch the standoffs in place, as shown, in Figure 12-12.

Figure 12-11. *Mounting hole locations*

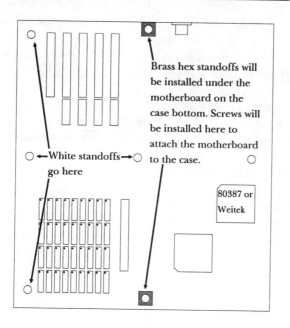

Brass hex standoffs will be installed under the motherboard on the case bottom. Screws will be installed here to attach the motherboard to the case.

←White standoffs→ go here

80387 or Weitek

Figure 12-12. *Standoff details*

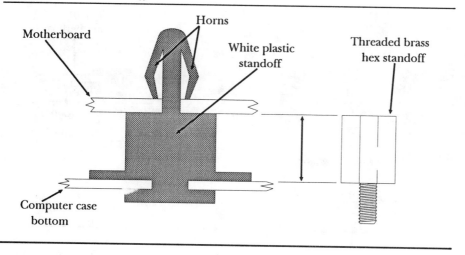

Horns

Motherboard

White plastic standoff

Threaded brass hex standoff

Computer case bottom

Make a trial fit of the motherboard in the case. The four standoffs should engage the three slotted holes near the bottom of the case and one slotted hole in the middle as shown in Figure 12-13. The top edge of the board should slide into three white plastic fixtures, which will support that edge. Be sure the board fits correctly and that no wires are trapped under it. This is just a trial fit to see that everything is going to work right.

Note

You may find that the board does not fit into the top rear plastic fixture because components are in the way. You can remove the motherboard and, using a pair of cutters, trim the overlapping part enough to allow the motherboard to seat properly. A side view of these fixtures is shown in Figure 12-13 (circled). Trim the part that extends over the top of the motherboard.

Note the location of the two holes in the case that are directly under the front and rear holes in the motherboard. You need to mount brass standoffs in these holes to supply the final support for the motherboard and to provide

Figure 12-13.   *Motherboard mounting details*

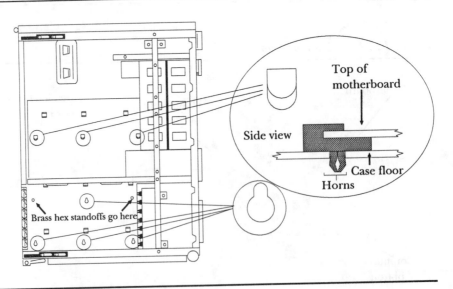

an electrical ground to the case. Once you're satisfied with the trial fit, remove the motherboard and install the two brass standoffs.

Thread them into the indicated holes in the case and tighten then snugly. Reinstall the motherboard and gently lift the components near each hole—you're lifting just enough to be sure the standoffs are engaged. Look through the holes in the motherboard above the brass standoffs and be sure they are fairly well aligned.

Remove two slot covers and temporarily install two adapter cards, one at or near the top and one at or near the bottom of the case. You do not need to install screws in the adapter cards, just ensure that the motherboard alignment is right and that the screws you might install in the adapters would be installed. Check the alignment of the motherboard and install a screw from the top of the motherboard into each brass hex standoff. Tighten the screws snugly to anchor the motherboard.

ote

The metal brackets on adapter cards that attach to the rear of the case seldom fit perfectly. You will often find that you must push and pummel them gently to get the holes to line up. This is a normal occurrence and should not be cause for alarm. Just get the alignment as nearly correct as you can.

Making the Final Connections

At the back of the case you will find eight 9-pin D-Sub connector cutouts and 25-pin D-8 Sub cutouts (refer back to Figure 12-4). Remove the covers from two of the 9-pin cutouts and one 25-pin cutout. Replace the screws in the covers. Since you may want to replace them, save them with your extra hardware.

The Privilege motherboard package should contain two narrow 9-pin ribbon cables and one 25-pin ribbon cable. Use the nuts and brass hex standoffs (provided with the case) to mount the serial and parallel D-Sub connectors to the back of your computer as shown in Figure 12-14. Label the serial connectors COM1 and COM2 on the back of the case.

Connect the ribbon cable pin connector for COM1 to J1 on the motherboard as shown in Figure 12-15. Be sure the odd-colored wire on the edge of the ribbon cable is on the pin 1 side of J1. The pin 1 position on J1 is indicated with a black square on the drawing. In a similar manner, connect the COM2 pin connector and the LPT1 pin connector.

Figure 12-14.   *Installing D-Sub connectors*

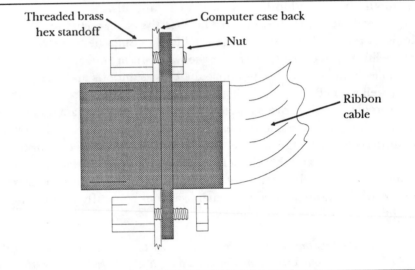

Figure 12-15.   *Connecting motherboard power*

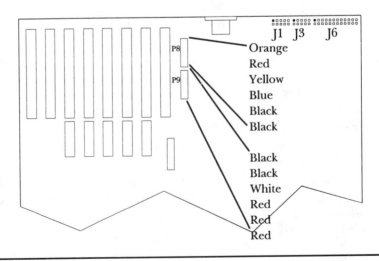

Connecting Motherboard Power

Still referring to Figure 12-15, connect the power supply cable labeled P8 to the P8 connector on the motherboard. The orange wire should go toward the top (toward the keyboard connector or nearest the back of the case). You may need to press the power supply connector very firmly against the lip of the mating motherboard connector as shown in Figure 12-16. In a similar manner connect P9.

W13 —Turbo Led Connector

W13 is the Turbo LED (light) connector. This would normally be connected to an LED in the case control panel. The CASE-200 uses a numeric display to show a low and a high CPU clock speed. You could hook it up to display "33" for cosmetics but it's not really important and is really more trouble than it's worth in this installation.

Note

The word turbo implies supercharging, but let's look at the history of the term. Early PC/XT computers ran at a CPU clock speed of 4.77 MHz. Some compatible motherboards were developed that would run at 8 MHz. This higher CPU clock speed was called "turbo mode."

Figure 12-16. *Motherboard power connector details*

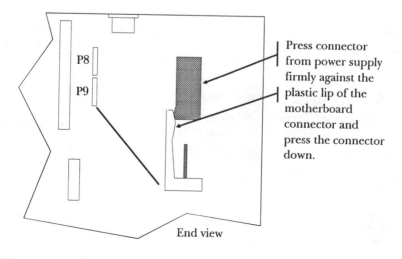

Press connector from power supply firmly against the plastic lip of the motherboard connector and press the connector down.

End view

Many software packages depended on the CPU clock for timing. Messages were presented, for example, that were displayed long enough to read at 4.77 MHz, were displayed for only half as long at 8 MHz. To accommodate this software, these computers had a switch that allowed the selection of either 4.77 or 8 MHz and a lamp that indicated which mode the computer was in—thus the terms turbo mode lamp and a turbo mode switch.

Most modern software uses timing that is not dependent on the CPU clock speed so you will probably never need to change the speed of your 80386 computer, but in case you do, you have a selection of 8 MHz or 33 MHz with the Privilege motherboard. Nowadays, the speed is changed using the keyboard; you don't have to open the case to do it.

The CASE-200 provides a push button turbo switch on the case front panel (connected by the blue, yellow, and black group of wires) but it is not used. Speed changes are accomplished via the keyboard with the AMI BIOS installed on the Privilege motherboard.

W14 —Reset Connector

W14 is the reset connector. A 2-pin reset connector from the back of the case control panel has two white wires and should be connected to W14. Orientation is not important.

W15 —Power Indicator and Keylock Connector

W15 is the power indicator and keylock connector. The mating connector comes from the rear of the case control panel at the top of the case. The connector has five positions. Connect the CASE-200 connector to W15 with the brown wire (pin 1) toward the rear of the case.

W16 —the Speaker Connector

Connect the speaker connector (attached to the speaker at the lower front of the case) to W16 with the red wire (pin 1) toward the rear of the case. You may need to reorient the speaker for these wires to reach.

Connecting the Auxiliary Fan

The CASE-200 provides an auxiliary fan at the bottom of the case to improve cooling. A two-wire Molex connector from the power supply should be connected to the mating connector from this fan.

This completes the motherboard installation steps. Your computer is nearly ready to apply power and take the first steps toward full operation.

Installing the Floppy Disk Drives

Refer to Chapter 5, "Adding Expansion Boards," to install one 3 1/2-inch and one 5 1/4-inch floppy disk drive in the top two bays. The order of installation is not important and depends on your preference. Figure 12-17 shows an enlargement of the control panel at the top of the CASE-200.

Installing the Hard Drive

Figure 12-18 shows a top view of the drive tray provided with the CASE-200. Hard disks can be installed in either location shown at the bottom. Put a thick black rubber washer at each of the four holes provided for mounting as shown in the inset in Figure 12-18. Set the drive on these and tighten the screws snugly.

Figure 12-17. *The control panel*

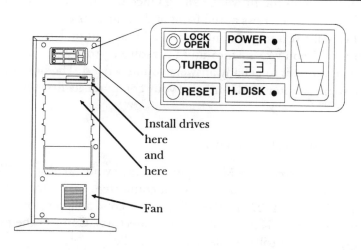

Figure 12-18.   *The hard disk drive tray from EN-6600*

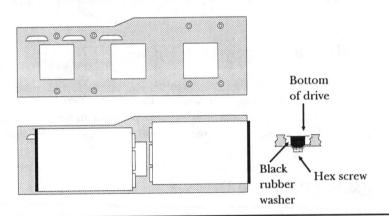

Carefully slide the drive tray partly into its position. Be sure that the rails on the bottom engage the plastic guides. Now comes a tricky part. The W13 through W16 connectors will just barely clear the edge of the tray. Carefully press the wires out of the way and slide the tray in until the widest part is over these connectors.

Continue sliding the tray in and, as you do, move the motherboard power connector wires out of the way. With a little juggling and cajoling, the tray should fit, although the fit will be snug. Once the tray is all the way in, you can reinstall the two screws at the front and in the rear of the drive tray.

At this point you might want to take a break and look over what you've done so far. If you've run into any unresolved problems, check with the appropriate vendors to get any answers you may need. The next step will be to install some adapter cards and give your computer its first test.

Connecting Drive Power

Now it's time to connect Molex connectors to your two floppy disk drives. For the first tests, leave the hard drive unconnected. Install the hard/floppy drive controller (WD1007 or WD1009) in the second adapter slot down under the hard drive tray (16-bit slot with two connectors). Connect the pin end of the floppy drive controller cable to the controller.

You can route the cable through one of the large holes in the hard drive tray or route it around the tray. Connect the cable edge connectors to the drives. The connector nearest the end should be connected to the drive you want to be drive A.

Installing the Display Adapter

Install the ProDesigner II display controller in the third slot from the bottom of the case. This is the first 16-bit slot on the motherboard. Again make a careful visual check of the work you've done.

That First Test

Rehang the side panel on the case. When you close it, it will be about 1/2 inch back of its seated position. Make sure it is fully closed and bump the door forward until it is flush with the front of the case. Make sure that the top two plastic bay covers have been removed from the plastic front panel and install it by bumping it into place with the heel of your hand. From the front, your computer should now look like Figure 12-19.

Figure 12-19.   *Front views of the finished case*

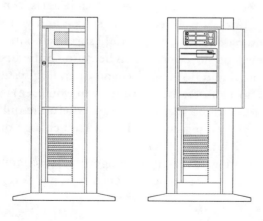

Connect a power cord to your computer and to your display monitor. Connect the display adapter to the display using the cable provided. Plug in the display monitor and computer. Turn the display monitor on to allow it to warm up.

You will want to use your ears, nose, and eyes for the next step. Turn on the computer power switch. The green POWER light should come on. There should be *no* noise coming from your computer. Within a few seconds a flashing cursor should appear in the upper-left corner of the display screen.

If you have a quiet computer, a POWER light, and a flashing cursor on the screen, leave the computer on for a few minutes to be sure all is right with the world; then turn the display and computer off and continue with the final steps.

Connecting the Hard Disk

Open the side panel and, referring again to Chapter 5, connect the hard disk control and data cables. Also connect one of the Molex power connectors from the power supply to the hard disk power connector. Again close the computer, and turn on the display monitor and the computer. This time you should hear the hard disk "spin up," which means you're on your way.

Software Installation

Your computer will be very confused when it starts its new life. You may see many strange things displayed on the screen and you may have several false starts but ultimately everything should sort itself out.

Your system will be slow to function because, in the first place, the hard disk is not formatted and does not have an operating system installed. The BIOS is going to do a lot of fiddling (which you won't see) to try and sort out this problem. There will be very long delays where the only thing you have on the screen is the flashing cursor. This will all change once everything is configured, but until it is, be patient.

If the periods of inactivity stretch longer than five minutes or more, try pushing the reset button, pressing keyboard keys, and turning the computer off, waiting a few seconds, and then back on again. If you push reset or turn the power off, again allow some time.

With everything working, you must run the ROM-based BIOS Setup utility to configure the system. A special Orchid feature is the Insert key (INS) interrupt that preconditions your BIOS RAM memory to accept system configuration information when you run the BIOS Setup utility. This feature is helpful for recovering from those times when your system reacts in unexpected ways or refuses to boot.

(INS) Key Interrupt Procedure

Press the (INS) key while you turn on your computer and keep it pressed until the following BIOS logo screen appears on your display monitor:

```
386-BIOS (c) 1989 AMI
Version XXX
0000KB Memory Count
```

The system should start and display a memory count. After it finishes, the following screen will appear:

```
"INS" key pressed, CMOS data ignored
CMOS system options not set
RUN SETUP UTILITY
Press [F1] to Resume.
```

If this screen does not appear, leave the power turned on and hold the (INS) key down while you press the reset button on the front of your computer to force the screen to appear.

Keyboard Selectable Options

The following are keyboard options built into your BIOS:

Key Sequence	Function
(ESC)	Bypass the system's memory test
(DEL)	Runs the system's SETUP program
(CTRL)-(ALT)-(+)	Puts your system in high-speed mode
(CTRL)-(ALT)-(-)	Puts your system in low-speed mode
(INS)	Preconditions your system configuration

BIOS Setup Utility

Press the (F1) key and you will be offered two choices:

EXIT FOR BOOT
RUN CMOS SETUP

Use the (↓) to select RUN CMOS SETUP, then press (ENTER). A screen similar to that in Figure 12-20 will appear on your monitor. The BIOS Setup utility screen shown contains 11 different fields that should reflect the configuration of your computer system. They are Date, Time, Floppy Drive A,

Figure 12-20. *The configuration screen for AMI BIOS*

System Configuration Setup (C) Copyright 1985–1990 American Megatrends Inc.

Date(mn/date/year):Wed, May 10 1989

Time(hour/min/sec): 00:49:36 . . . . .

Floppy drive A   : 1.2 MB,5 1/4" .

Floppy drive B   : 1.44 MB, 3 1/2 . . . .

Base memory size: 640KB
Ext. memory size: 1024KB
Numeric processor: Installed . . . . . .

	Cyln	Head	WpCom	LZone	Sec	Size
Hard disk C: type: 2	615	4	300	615	17	20 MB . . . . .
Hard disk D: type: Not Installed . . .		. . . .				

Primary display   : VGA or EGA . .

Keyboard   : Installed . . . .

Shadow RAM: BIOS and Video . . . .

Cache Controller: Enabled . . . . . .

CPU Speed: High . . . .

↓,↑ :Select Entries . . . .

←→: Change Entries . . . .

F10: Exit . . . .

ESC:Reboot . . . .

Help Message . . . . . +

Help Screen for each Entry · + ·

Floppy Drive B, Hard Disk C, Hard Disk D, Primary Display, Keyboard, Shadow RAM, Cache Controller, and CPU Speed.

To select a data field, or specific elements within a data field, use the ⊤ and ⊥ keys. To scroll through the options available for each data field, use the ← and → keys.

To help you through your selections there is a Help screen, located at the lower right within the setup screen, which changes each time you enter a different data field. The Help screen contains option information for each data field.

Date Use the ⊤ or ⊥ keys to select the month name, the day date number, and the year date number. Once selected you can scroll through the available options using the ← and → keys. Enter today's date.

Time This is the real-time, 24-hour clock setting for your computer system. Use the ⊤ or ⊥ key to select the hour, minute, or second. Use the ← and → keys to change the selected item. Enter the current time.

Floppy Drive A This field defines one of the four standard floppy drives that you may install in your system. The options are 360 KB 5 1/4-inch, 1.2 MB 5 1/4-inch, 720 KB 3 1/2-inch, 1.44 MB 3 1/2-inch, or Not Installed. Again use the ← and → keys to indicate the drive installed as Drive A:.

Floppy Drive B Same options as Floppy Drive A. Hard Disk C This field allows you to select from the standard 46 fixed disk configurations and, additionally, provides options 47 and 48 where you may specify the parameters of late-model, hard drives (for example, RLL or ESDI) that are not already in the table. "Not Installed" is also an option. If you specify the wrong hard disk, your computer will beep during boot-up and stop. If you specify a hard disk that doesn't exist, your screen will display a drive failure message. In either case you must run the BIOS Setup utility again and specify the hard drive that is installed in your computer. See Appendix C "Connector Referece," for most available options. If you've installed the 667 MB drive suggested, select Type 1.

Hard Disk D Same options as Drive C. Primary Display This field defines the primary—often the only—video display adapter connected to your com-

Primary Display   This field defines the primary—often the only—video display adapter connected to your computer system. The options are Monochrome, Color 40x25, VGA or EGA, Color 80x25, or Not Installed. Set to VGA or EGA.

Keyboard   This field contains only two options: Installed and Not Installed. Not Installed tells the system that no keyboard is attached, which allows the system to boot on systems with no keyboard (such as file servers). Set this to the Installed option.

Shadow RAM   Shadow RAM causes the BIOS software to be copied to RAM memory where it will execute faster. This feature may increase the speed of some applications by as much as 300 percent! The options for this field are Disabled, BIOS, and BIOS and VIDEO. The disabled option uses no system memory to shadow BIOS. The BIOS option enables shadowing of your system's BIOS. The BIOS and VIDEO option enables shadowing of both your system's BIOS and your video card's BIOS. Set to BIOS and VIDEO for the best performance.

Cache Controller   This field contains two options: Enabled or Disabled. Usually Enabled is selected in order to achieve maximum performance. Set this to Enabled.

CPU Speed   This field contains two options: High and Low. When the CPU speed is set to High, your system will run at the full 33 MHz. If it is set to Low, the system will run at 8 MHz. Set to High.

When you have finished selecting the options that define the configuration of your computer system, press the (ESC) key.

The Help screen will contain the question

Write data into CMOS and reboot (Y/N)?

Press (Y), and then (ENTER). The configuration will be written to CMOS RAM and your computer will restart.

The final step is to insert a floppy disk containing the operating system of your choice. This will usually be DOS. Your computer should boot and present you with a prompt. Follow the instructions in Chapter 5 to low-level format your hard disk if it is required, partition it, format it, and copy the

Summary

You now have one of the most powerful tools in the computer industry. This chapter showed you how to select the various parts and then assemble them all into a "Power Tower."

12

A

Vendor List

This appendix lists a number of vendors that supply a wide range of upgrade material. Suppliers of computers, motherboards, and math coprocessors are listed separately first. An alphabetical listing of a variety of vendors follows. All addresses and phone numbers were checked for accuracy and were correct at the time of printing.

Computers

ACER\ALTOS
401 Charcot Ave.
San Jose, CA 95131
(408) 922-0333

ALR (Advanced Logic Research)
9401 Jeronimo
Irvine, CA 92718
(714) 581-6770

AST Research, Inc.
16215 Alton Parkway
Irvine, CA 92718
(714) 727-4141

Austin Computer Systems
10300 Metric Blvd.
Austin, TX 78758
(512) 339-7932

Bristol Research Corp.
1000 Brioso Dr.
Costa Mesa, CA 92627
(714) 642-3373

Compaq Computer Corp.
20555 S.H. 249
Houston, TX 77070
(713) 370-0670

CSS Laboratories, Inc.
1641 McGaw Ave.
Irvine, CA 92714
(714) 852-8161

Cumulus Corp.
23500 Mercantile Rd.
Cleveland, OH 44122
(216) 464-2211

Dell Computer Corp.
9505 Arboretum Blvd.
Austin, TX 78759
(512) 338-4400

DTK Computers, Inc.
15711 E. Valley Blvd.
City of Industry, CA 91744
(818) 333-7533

Epson America, Inc.
2780 Lomita Blvd.
Torrance, CA 90505
(800) 922-8911

Everex Systems, Inc.
48431 Milmont Dr.
Fremont, CA 94538
(415) 498-1111
(800) 821-0806

GoldStar Technology, Inc.
3003 N. First St.
San Jose, CA 95134-2004
(408) 432-1331

HeadStart Technology, Inc.
2070 S. Leapwood
Carson, CA 90746
(213) 217-1300

Hewlett-Packard
16399 W. Bernardo Dr.
San Diego, CA 92127
(619) 487-4100

NCR Corp.
1601 South Main St.
Dayton, OH 45479
(513) 445-7478

A

NEC Technologies, Inc.
1414 Massachusetts Ave.
Boxborough, MA 01719
(508) 264-8000

Tandy (Radio Shack)
700 One Tandy Center
Fort Worth, TX 76102
(817) 390-3549

Televideo Systems, Inc.
P.O. Box 49048
San Jose, CA 95161-9048
(408) 954-8333

WANG
One Industrial Ave.
Lowell, MA 01851
(508) 459-5000

WYSE Technology
3471 N. First St.
San Jose, CA 95734
(800) GET-WYSE

Zenith Electronics
1900 N. Austin Ave.
Chicago, IL 60639
(312) 745-2000

Motherboard Suppliers

ACC Micro Electronics Corp.
3295 Scott Blvd. #400
Santa Clara, CA 95054
(408) 980-0622

American Computer Products
511 Vally Way
Milpitas, CA 95035
(408) 946-9746

American Digicom
1233 Midas Way
Sunnyvale, CA 94086
(408) 245-1580

American Megatrends, Inc.
1346 Oakbrook Dr. #120
Norcross, GA 30093
(404) 263-8181

American Micronics
3002 Dow Ave. #224
Tustin, CA 92680
(714) 573-9005

American Suntek International
2313 Chico Ave. #1
S. El Monte, CA 91733
(818) 575-8458

Amptron International
2445 Lilyvale Ave.
Los Angeles, CA 90032
(213) 221-3135

A-Tronic Computer
15703 E. Valley Blvd.
City of Industry, CA 91744
(818) 333-0193

A

BEC (Babtech Enterprises Corp.)
205 O'Toole Ave. #E
San Jose, CA 95131
(408) 954-8828

BTC Corp.
4180 Business Center Dr.
Fremont, CA 94538
(415) 657-3956

Cache Computers, Inc.
46714 Fremont Blvd.
Fremont, CA 94538
(415) 226-9922

Cambridge Graphic Systems
17517 Fabrica Way #E
Cerritos, CA 90701
(714) 521-0867

CDC Enterprise, Inc.
2992 E. La Palma #D
Anaheim, CA 92806
(714) 630-4633

Chicony America
1641 West Collins Ave.
Orange, CA 92667
(714) 771-6151

Commax Technologies, Inc.
2031 Concourse Dr.
San Jose, CA 95131
(408) 435-5000

C2 Micro Systems, Inc.
1205 Fulton Place
Fremont, CA 94560
(415) 683-8888

CUI
1680 Civic Center Dr. #101
Santa Clara, CA 95050
(408) 241-9170

DCM Data Products
610 One Tandy Center
Fort Worth, TX 76102
(817) 870-2202

Deico Electronics, Inc.
2800 Bayview Dr.
Fremont, CA 94538
(415) 651-7800

DTK Computers, Inc.
15711 E. Valley Blvd.
City of Industry, CA 91744
(818) 333-7533

Eureka Computer
9940 Business Park Dr. #185
Sacramento, CA 95827
(916) 361-8084

Exima Trading Co.
1700 Wyatt Dr. #1
Santa Clara, CA 95054
(408) 970-9225

A

Greenleaf International
136 S. Wolfe Rd.
Sunnyvale, CA 94086
(408) 735-7056

GS Technology
777 E. Middlefield
Mountain View, CA 94043
(415) 968-3400

Hawk Computers
2050 Bering Dr.
San Jose, CA 95131
(408) 436-8999

Hung Pang America Corp.
36-25 Union St. #D
Flushing, NY 11354
(718) 445-3469

Informtech International, Inc.
3349 S. La Cienega Place
Los Angeles, CA 90016
(213) 836-8993

Integrated Computer Communications
8 East Lawn Dr.
Holmdel, NJ 07733
(201) 946-3207

Jac Technology Corp.
6800 Orangethrope Ave. #E
City of Buena Park, CA 90620
(714) 228-1633

Joindata Systems
14838 Valley Blvd. #C
City of Industry, CA 91746
(818) 330-6553

Kanix, Inc.
13111 Brooks Dr. #F
Baldwin Park, CA 91706
(818) 814-3997

Key Power, Inc.
11853 E. Telegraph Rd.
Santa Fe Springs, CA 90670
(213) 948-2084

Lang Chao Group Corp.
9940 Business Park Dr. #185
Sacramento, CA 95827
(916) 361-8084

Legatech Computers
789 S. San Gabriel Blvd. #D
San Gabriel, CA 91776
(818) 309-2941

Liuski International
10 Hub Dr.
Melville, NY 11747
(516) 454-8220

Magic Computer Co.
13177 Ramona Blvd. #B
Irwindale, CA 91706-3937
(818) 813-1210

A

Mandax Computer, Inc.
14935 N.E. 95th St.
Redmond, WA 98052
(206) 867-1973

Matrix Digital Products, Inc.
1811 N. Keystone St.
Burbank, CA 91504
(818) 566-8567

Metra Info Systems, Inc.
935 Benicia Ave.
Sunnyvale, CA 94086
(408) 730-9188

Micro Channel Technology
3518 Arden Rd.
Hayward, CA 94545
(415) 670-0633

Micro Informatica Corp.
99 S.E. 5th St.
Miami, FL 33131
(305) 377-1930

Micron Technology, Inc.
Mail Stop 607
2805 E. Columbia Rd.
Boise, ID 83706
(208) 386-3800

Micronics Computers, Inc.
330 E. Warren Ave.
Fremont, CA 94539
(415) 651-2300

Monolithic Systems Corp.
7050 S. Tucson Way
Englewood, CO 80112
(303) 790-7400

Monterey Electronics, Inc.
2365 Paragon Dr. #D
San Jose, CA 95131
(408) 437-5496

Multi-Pal International
17231 E. Railroad St. #500
City of Industry, CA 91748
(818) 913-4188

Mylex Corp.
34551 Ardenwood Blvd.
Fremont, CA 94555
(415) 683-4600

Nic Technology, Inc.
2106 Ringwood Ave.
San Jose, CA 95131
(408) 434-9595

Pantex Computers, Inc.
8730-A Westpark Dr.
Houston, TX 77063
(713) 780-8187

PC Designs, Inc.
2504 N. Hemlock Circle
Broken Arrow, OK 74012
(918) 251-5550

A

PC House
841 E. Artesia Blvd.
Carson, CA 90746
(213) 324-8621

PMC
940 E. Dominguez
Carson, CA 97746
(213) 324-1144

Ratek Computer Systems
1201 Shaffer Rd.
Santa Cruz, CA 95061
(408) 458-1110

SKV International, Inc.
43232 Christy St.
Fremont, CA 94538
(415) 623-8820

Solotek Computer Supply
47400 Seabridge Dr.
Fremont, CA 94538
(415) 438-0160

Standard Computer Corp.
12803 Schabarum Ave.
Irwindale, CA 91706
(818) 338-4668

Sys Technology, Inc.
10655 Humbold St.
Los Alamitos, CA 90720
(213) 493-6888

Tang Computer, Inc.
2934 N.W. 72nd Ave.
Miami, FL 33122
(305) 599-9904

Tangent Technology, Inc.
1141-B Westminister Ave.
Alhambra, CA 91803
(818) 300-0101

Tseng Labs, Inc.
10 Pheasant Run
Newtown, PA 18940
(215) 968-0502

Unitron Computer USA, Inc.
736 Stimson Ave.
City of Industry, CA 91749
(818) 333-0280

USVideo
One Stamford Landing
62 Southfield Ave.
Stamford, CT 06902-9950
(203) 964-9000

Visi-Tron, Inc.
1805 Springdale Rd.
Cherry Hill, NJ 08003
(609) 424-0400

Wave Net, Inc.
22750 Hawthorne Blvd. #207
Torrance, CA 90505
(213) 791-2860

A

Wedge Tech, Inc.
1587 McCandless Dr.
Milpitas, CA 95035
(408) 263-9888

Win Computer Technology, Inc.
47671 Fremont Blvd.
Fremont, CA 94538
(415) 770-8772

Xtron Computer Equipment Corp.
716 Jersey Ave.
Jersey City, NJ 07310
(201) 798-5000

Math Coprocessors

Advanced MicroDevices, Inc.
901 Thompson Place
P.O. Box 3453
Sunnyvale, CA 94088-3453
(408) 732-2400
80C287-10 80EC287-10

Cyrix Corp.
P.O. Box 850118
Richardson, TX 75085
(800) 327-6284
FastMath 83D87-33

Integrated Information Technology, Inc.
2445 Mission College Blvd.
Santa Clara, CA 95054
(408) 727-1885
2C87 3C87

Intel Corp.
1900 Prairie City Rd.
Mail Stop FM2-18
Folsom, CA 95630
(916) 351-2747
80287XL-10 80387DX-33 i486-25

Weitek
1060 E. Arques Ave.
Sunnyvale, CA 94088
(800) 468-3167
Abacus 3167-33 Abacus 4167-25

A

Adaptive Computer Sources

IBM
National Support Center for Persons with Disabilities
P.O. Box 2150
Atlanta, GA 30055
(800) 426-2133 Voice and TDD
(404) 238-4806 TDD
Listings of equipment for people with disabilities

Alphabetical List of Vendors

Here is a list of some upgrade vendors. The asterisk (*) next to some vendor's names indicates a previous mention in this appendix. This list includes only one or two specialty hard disk manufacturers; for the most part those are listed in Appendix C, "Connector Reference." You will also find display adapters and monitors listed there.

This list is part of a frequently updated database. To get the latest version on floppy disk, see the coupon in the back.

3X USA Corp.
299 California #304
Palo Alto, CA 94306
(800) 327-9712
(415) 327-3944 FAX
3X-Link 16

5G Corp.
4131 Spicewood Springs Rd. A-2
Austin, TX 78759
(800) 333-4131
(512) 345-9843
(512) 345-9575 FAX
The Complete XT Upgrade

Ad Lib
220 Grande-Allee East #850
Quebec, Ontario
Canada, G1R2J1
(418) 529-9676
Ad Lib music card

Adobe Systems
P.O. Box 7900
Mountain View, CA 94039-7900
(415) 961-4400
PostScript font cartridge

AlarmCard
14700 N.E. Eighth St. #100
Bellevue, WA 98007
(206) 747-0824
AlarmCard

Alcom, Inc.
2464 Embarcadero Way
Palo Alto, CA 94303
(415) 493-3800
EasyGate Lanfax

Alfa Power, Inc.
20311 Valley Blvd. #L
Walnut, CA 91789
(714) 594-7171
(714) 595-4863 FAX
Power supply

Alps America
3553 N. First St.
San Jose, CA 95134
(800) 825-2577
(408) 432-6000
LED printer

Amdek Corp.
3080 Bristol St.
Costa Mesa, CA 92626
(714) 850-9973
CD-ROM drives

American Data Tech., Inc.
44 W. Bellevue Dr. #6
Pasadena, CA 91105
(818) 578-1339
SmartFax

American Micronics, Inc.
3002 Dow Ave. #224
Tustin, CA 92680
(714) 573-9005
Accelerators

American Power Conversion
350 Columbia St.
Peace Dale, RI 02883
(800) 443-4519
(401) 789-3710 FAX
Power Primer

A

Ampro Computers, Inc.
990 Almanor Ave.
Sunnyvale, CA 94086
(408) 522-2100
(408) 720-1305 FAX
80286 board

AOX, Inc.
486 Totten Pond Rd.
Waltham, MA 02154
(617) 890-4402
Accelerators

Appian Technology
P.O. Box 96098
Bellevue, WA 98005
(206) 649-8086
Graphics adapters

Applied Data Communications
14272 Chambers Rd.
Tustin, CA 92680
(714) 731-9000
(714) 838-7172 FAX
Rewrite/erase optical disk drive

Archive Corp.
Data Storage Division
36 Skyline Dr.
Lake Mary, FL 32746
(800) 237-4929
Archive XL tape backup system

Aslan Computer Corp.
10922 Klingerman Ave. #4
S. El Monte, CA 91733
(818) 575-5271
(818) 575-0394 FAX
Power supplies

Associates Computer Supply Co.
3644 Tibbett Ave.
Riverdale, NY 10463
(212) 543-3364
Power board 386

ATI Technologies, Inc.
3761 Victoria Park Ave.
Scarborough, Ontario
Canada, M1W 3S2
(416) 756-0718
(416) 756-0720 FAX
Complete line of modems, Messenger, VGAWonder

AT&T
1 Speedwell Ave.
Morristown, NJ 07960
(800) 247-1212
AT&T Fax Connection

Best Power Technology, Inc.
P.O. Box 280
Necedah, WI 54646
(800) 356-5794 Ext.3864
UPS

B.G. Micro
P.O. Box 280298
Dallas, TX 75228
(214) 271-5546
(214) 271-2462 FAX
Switches, speech board, and more

Brooktrout Technologies, Inc.
110 Cedar St.
Wellesley Hills, MA 02181
(617) 449-4100
TR112, Fax-Mail

Brother International Corp.
200 Cottontail Ln., South Vantage Ct.
Somerset, NJ 08875-6714
(908) 356-8880
Intellifax

Bus Computer Systems, Inc.
135 W. 26th St. 8th Fl.
New York, NY 10001
(212) 627-4485
(212) 627-9884 FAX
Keyboard

CAD & Graphics
1301 Evans Ave.
San Francisco, CA 94124
(800) 288-1611
Trackball, plotter

Calculus Distribution (formerly Faxpoint International)
168 Northeast 20th Court
Wilton Manors, FL 33305-1087
(305) 563-3326
Facsimile Pac

Calculus, Inc.
522 Mercury Dr.
Sunnyvale, CA 94086-4018
(408) 733-7800
SuperFax

Capital Equipment Corp.
76 Blanchard Rd.
Burlington, MA 01803
(800) 234-4CEC
(617) 273-1818
OS/RAM32

CATi, Inc.
16840 B Joleen Way
Morgan Hill, CA 95037
(408) 778-CATS
(408) 778-9975 FAX
Motherboards

Central Point Software, Inc.
15220 N.W. Greenbrier Pkwy. #200
Beaverton, OR 97006
(503) 690-8090
PC Tools Deluxe 5.x

CH Products
970 Park Center Dr.
Vista, CA 92083
(619) 598-2518
RollerMouse, Mach series, Gamecard, and more

Chartered Electronics, Inc.
260 E. Grand Ave. #18
So. San Francisco, CA 94080
(415) 875-3636
ProFax

Cheetah International, Inc.
7075 Flying Cloud Dr.
Eden Prairie, MN 55344
(800) 243-3824
Motherboards and music

Chinon America, Inc.
660 Maple Ave.
Torrance, CA 90503
(213) 533-0274
ScanFax

A

Chips for Less, Inc.
P.O. Box 816216
Dallas, TX 75381-6216
(214) 416-0508
Chips

Choice Technology Group, Ltd.
5415 Oberlin Dr.
San Diego, CA 92121
(800) 767-7656
DeskFAX, DFX9600

CIE America
2515 McCabe Way
P.O. Box 19663
Irvine, CA 92713-9663
(800) 877-1421
Printers

The Complete PC, Inc.
1983 Concourse Dr.
San Jose, CA 95131
(408) 434-0145
The Complete Fax, The Complete Communicator

Computer Peripherals, Inc.
667 Rancho Conejo Blvd.
Newbury Park, CA 91320
(805) 499-5751
(805) 498-8848 FAX
The ViVa24 Modem

Corollary, Inc.
17881 Cartwright Rd.
Irvine, CA 92714
(714) 250-4040
Accelerators

Covox, Inc.
675 Conger St.
Eugene, OR 97402
(503) 342-1271
The Voice Master Key System II

C-Tech Electronics
2515 McCabe Way
P.O. Box 19673
Irvine, CA 92713-9673
(800) 347-4017
Printers

Cumulus Corp.
23500 Mercantile Rd.
Cleveland, OH 44122
(216) 464-2211
Computers, drives, and memory

Dakota Microsystems
301 E. Evelyn Ave.
Bldg. A
Mountain View, CA 94041
(800) 999-6288
(415) 967-2302
PowerSave, UPS on a Card

Data Products
6200 Canoga Ave.
Woodland Hills, CA 91365
(800) 624-8999 Ext. 545
Printers

Data Race, Inc.
11550 I-10 W.
San Antonio, TX 78230
(512) 558-1900
PC Race Fax

Delkin Devices, Inc.
1940 Garnet Ave.
San Diego, CA 92109
(619) 273-8086
Clock chip

Departmental Technology, Inc.
P.O. Box 645
Andover, NJ 07821
(201) 786-6878
TC! Power, extended memory software

DeskFAX (Choice Technology Group, Ltd.)
5415 Oberlin Dr.
San Diego, CA 92121
(800) 767-7656
DFX9600

Diversified Technology
An Ergon Co.
112 E. State St.
Ridgeland, MS 39158
(800) 443-2667
The DTI 386 CAT-KIT

DRS Power Products
2065 Range Rd.
Clearwater, FL 34625
(800) 284-0345
(813) 447-4369 FAX
Power supply

Eclipse Computer Solutions
One Intercontinental Way
Peabody, MA 01960
(508) 535-7510
Accelerators

Edsun Laboratories
564 Main Street
Waltham, MA 02154
(617) 647-9300
Accelerators

Electronic Specialists, Inc.
171 S. Main St.
Natick, MA 01760
(800) 225-4876
Kleen Line Communications enhancer

Emco Maier
2757 Scioto Parkway
Columbus, OH 43221-2134
(614) 771-5996
(800) 521-8289
(614) 771-5990 FAX
Computer controlled lathe

Emerson Computer Power
3300 S. Standard
Santa Ana, CA 92702
(714) 545-5581
(800) BACK-UPS
Accupower units, UPS

Enertronics Research, Inc.
1801 Beltway Dr.
St. Louis, MO 63114
(800) 325-0174
(314) 421-2771
Aurora 1024 graphics board

Enlight Corp. USA *
345 Cloverleaf Dr. #2B
Baldwin Park, CA 91706
(818) 369-9898
(818) 369-4709 FAX
Cases

A

Epson America, Inc. *
2780 Lomita Blvd.
Torrance, CA 90505
(800) 922-8911
Scanners

Everex Systems*
48431 Milmont Dr.
Fremont, CA 94538
(415) 498-1111
(800) 821-0806
EverFax

Fast Technology
3204 Fairlane
Tempe, AZ 85282
(602) 438-0889
Boards

Fifth Generation Systems
10049 N. Reiger Rd.
Baton Rouge, LA 70809
(800) 873-4384
(504) 291-7221
Mace Gold

Focus Electronic Corp.
9080 Telstar Ave. #302-304
El Monte, CA 91731
(818) 280-0416
(818) 280-4729 FAX
Tower case, keyboards, mouse

Fremont Communications Co.
46309 Warm Springs Blvd.
Fremont, CA 94539
(415) 438-5000
(415) 490-2315 FAX
FAX 96 card

Galacticomm, Inc.
4101 S.W. 47 Ave. #101
Fort Lauderdale, FL 33314
(305) 583-5990
(305) 583-7846 FAX
The Major BBS

Gama Computers, Inc.
6210 S. Country Club
Tucson, AZ 85706
(602) 741-9550
Accelerators

Gammalink
133 Caspian Ct.
Sunnyvale, CA 94089
(408) 744-1430
GammaFax

Gazelle Systems
42 N. University Ave. #10
Provo, UT 84601
(800) 233-0383
(801) 377-1288
OPTune

Gibson Research Corp.
22991 La Cadena
Laguna Hills, CA 92653
(714) 830-2200
SpinRite II

Global Computer Supplies
2318 E. Del Amo Blvd.
Compton, CA 90220
(213) 635-8144
Computer furniture

A

GoldStar Technology, Inc.*
3003 N. First St.
San Jose, CA 95134-2004
(408) 432-1331
(408) 737-8575
Monitors

Hauppauge Computer Works, Inc.
91 Cabot Ct.
Hauppauge, NY 11788
(800) 443-6284
80386 Motherboards, 32-bit RAM boards

Hayes MicroComputer Products
P.O. Box 105203
Atlanta, GA 30348
(404) 449-8791
Hayes JT Fax, modems

Helix Software Co.
83-65 Daniels St.
Briarwood, NY 11435
(718) 392-3100
(800) 451-0551
Headroom

Hercules Computer Technology, Inc.
921 Parker St.
Berkeley, CA 94710
(800) 532-0600 Ext. 190
Hercules graphics card

Houston Computer Services
11331 Richmond Ave. #101
Houston, TX 77082
(713) 493-9900
Octacomm/IR

IBM*
National Support Center for Persons with Disabilities
P.O. Box 2150
Atlanta, GA 30055
(800) 426-2133 Voice and TDD
(404) 238-4806 TDD
Listings of equipment for people with disabilities

I Lon USA, Inc.
31238 Via Colinas #D
Westlake Village, CA 91362
(818) 991-4330
(818) 991-4331 FAX
Cards, mouse, joy stick

Image Systems
2515 McCabe Way
P.O. Box 19743
Irvine, CA 92713-9743
(800) 347-4027
Printers

Inset Systems, Inc.
71 Commerce Dr.
Brookfield, CT 06804
(800) 828-8088
Hijaak 1.1C and Inset screen capture software

Integrated Information Technology, Inc.
6200 Canoga Ave.
Woodland Hills, CA 91365
(800) 624-8999 Ext. 545
The IIT-2C87

Intel PCEO*
5200 N.E. Elam Young Pkwy.
Hillsboro, OR 97124-6497
(800) 538-3373
Connection CoProcessor

A

International Computers & Telecommunications
15235 Shady Grove Rd #303
Rockville, MD 20850
(301) 948-0200
Perfect Menu

Iomega Corp.
1821 W. 4000 S.
Roy, UT 84067
(800) 777-6649
Bernoulli drives

Jaton Corp.
556 Milpitas Blvd.
Milpitas, CA 95035
(408) 942-9888
Boards

JC Information Systems Corp.
44036 S. Grimmer Blvd.
Fremont, CA 94538
(415) 659-8440
(415) 659-8449 FAX
Complete line of boards

JDR Microdevices *
2233 Samaritan Dr.
San Jose, CA 95124
(800) 538-5000
MCT-FaxM

Jensen Tools, Inc.
7815 S. 46th St.
Phoenix, AZ 85044-5399
(602) 968-6231
(602) 438-1690 FAX
Toolkits and diagnostic equipment

Kensington
2855 Campus Dr.
San Mateo, CA 94403
(415) 572-2700
Expert Mouse, Master Piece Power Center

Kimpsion International
4701 Patrick Henry Dr. #401
Santa Clara, CA 95054
(408) 988-8808
(408) 988-8809 FAX
Controllers

Klever Computers, Inc.
1028 W. Maude Ave.
Sunnyvale, CA 94086
(408) 735-7723
Accelerators

Konan Corp.
(Fast Technology)
3204 S. Fairlane
Tempe, AZ 85282
(602) 438-0889
Accelerators

KP Electronics
4141 Business Center Dr.
Fremont, CA 94538
(415) 490-0300
Enclosures

KYE
12675 Colony St.
Chino, CA 91710
(714) 590-3940
(714) 590-1231 FAX
(800) 456-7593
Genius Mice

A

LaserMaster Corp.
7156 Shady Oak Rd.
Eden Prairie, MN 55344
(612) 944-9330
Laser printer enhancements

Logitech, Inc.
6505 Kaiser Dr.
Fremont, CA 94555
(415) 795-8500
Mice, trackball, and hand scanners

MegaDrive Systems
1900 Ave. of the Stars #2870
Los Angeles, CA 90067
(213) 556-1663
(800) 322-4744
Removable hard drives

Merritt Computer Products, Inc.
5565 Red Bird Center Dr. #150
Dallas, TX 75234
(214) 339-0753
(214) 339-1313 FAX
SafeSkin

Mextel Corp.
159 Beeline Rd.
Bensenville, IL 60106
(800) 888-4146
AutoKey

Micro Way
P.O. Box 79
Kingston, MA 02364
(508) 746-7341
FastMath 386/Accelerators

Microchip Technology
2900 N.W. 72 Ave.
Miami, FL 33122
(305) 592-5739
(305) 592-5738 FAX
286 board

MicroSolutions
132 W. Lincoln Hwy.
DeKalb, IL 60115
(815) 756-3411
Megamate

MicroTek Lab, Inc.
680 Knox St.
Torrance, CA 90502
(213) 321-2121
Scanners

Moniterm Corp.
5740 Green Circle Dr.
Minnetonka, MN 55343
(612) 935-4151
DTP Monitors

Multi-Industry Technology
West:
14741 Carmenita Rd.
Norwalk, CA 90650
(213) 921-6669
(213) 802-9281 FAX
East:
777 Durham
Edison, NJ 08817
(201) 906-9206
(201) 906-9209 FAX
Computer wholesaler

A

Multisoft Corp.
15100 S.W. Koll Pkwy, #L
Beaverton, OR 97006
(503) 644-5644
(800) 283-6858
Super PC-Kwik, Power Pak, disk cache

National Computer Accessories
769 N. 16th St.
Sacramento, CA 95814
(916) 441-1568
Cables and more

Natural MicroSystems
8 Erie Dr.
Natick, MA 01760-1313
(800) 533-6120 Ext. 255
Watson Voice Mail System

NEC (Nippon)
1255 Michael Dr.
Wood Dale, IL 60191-1094
(708) 860-9500
Monitors

Newer Technology
1117 South Rock Rd. #4
Wichita, KS 67207
(316) 685-4904
Accelerators

New Media Graphics
780 Boston Rd.
Billerica, MA 01281
(508) 663-0666
Video systems

Northgate Computer Systems, Inc.*
13895 Industrial Park Blvd. #110
Plymouth, MN 55441
(800) 526-2446
(612) 943-8181
OmniKey keyboard

Numonics
101 Commerce Dr.
Montgomeryville, PA 18936
(215) 362-2766
Mice and graphics tablets

OAZ Communications
48420 Kato Rd.
Fremont, CA 95438
(415) 226-0171
NetFax Manager

Octave Systems
1715 Dell Ave.
Campbell, CA 95008
(408) 866-8424
KeyTrak, keyboard with trackball

Omnium Corp.
1911 Curve Crest Blvd.
Stillwater, MN 55082
(715) 268-8500
PC Fax System 1.6

O'Neill Communications, Inc.
8601 Six Forks Rd.
Raleigh, NC 27615
(800) 624-5296
Lawn Network

Ontrack Computer Systems, Inc.
6321 Bury Dr. #16-19
Eden Prairie, MN 55346
(800) 752-1333
(612) 937-1107
Disk manager

Optronics Technology
P.O. Box 3239
Ashland, OR 97520
(503) 488-5040
Desktop stereo

Orchid Technology *
45365 Northport Loop West
Fremont, CA 94538
(415) 683-0300
Display adapters / motherboards

Overland Data
5600 Kearny Mesa Rd.
San Diego, CA 92111
(619) 571-5555
(619) 571-0982 FAX
Reel 9-Track Genius

Pacific Data Products
9125 Rehco Rd.
San Diego, Ca 92121
(619) 552-0880
(619) 552-0889 FAX
Plotter in a Cartridge, PacificPage PostScript Plug-in
(25 in one fonts on cartridge), PacificPage Personal edition

Pacific Image Communications
1111 S. Arroyo Pkwy. #430
Pasadena, CA 91105
(818) 441-0104
SuperFax

Panasonic Communications & Systems Co.
Two Panasonic Way
Secaucus, NJ 07094
(201) 348-7000
FX-BM89 Fax Partner Plus

Para Systems, Inc.
1455 LeMay Dr.
Carrollton, TX 75007
(800) 238-7272
(214) 446-7363
(214) 446-9011 FAX
UPS

PC Power & Cooling, Inc. *
31510 Mountain Way
Bonsall, CA 92003
(619) 723-9513
(619) 723-0075 FAX
Complete line of power supplies

Perceptive Solutions, Inc.
2700 Flora St.
Dallas, TX 75201
(800) 343-0903
(214) 954-1774
(214) 953-1774 FAX
HyperStore-1600 dual mode caching disk controller

The Periscope Co., Inc.
1197 Peachtree St.
Plaza Level
Atlanta, CA 30361
(404) 875-8080
(404) 872-1973 FAX
Boards

Perstor Systems, Inc.
1335 S. Park Lane
Tempe, AZ 85281
(602) 894-3494
Controllers

Peter Norton Computing, Inc.
2210 Wilshire Blvd. #186
Santa Monica, CA 90403
(800) 365-1010
(213) 319-2000
Norton Utilities

Phar Lap Software, Inc.
60 Aberdeen Ave.
Cambridge, MA 02138
(617) 661-1510
(617) 876-2972 FAX
Phar Lap 386 DOS Extender

Polaroid Corp.
784 Memorial Dr.
Cambridge, MA 02139
(617) 577-2000
Polaroid Pallete

Polywell Computers
61-C Airport Blvd.
So. San Francisco, CA 94080
(415) 583-7222
Accelerators

PRC Tech, Inc.
9460 Telstar #1
El Monte, CA 91731
(818) 350-8810
(818) 350-8922 FAX
Vertical systems

Prime Solutions, Inc.
1940 Garnet Ave.
San Diego, CA 92109
(800) 847-5000
(619) 274-5000
Disk Technician Pro

Prodem Technology America
1643 Stardust Ct.
Santa Clara, CA 95050
(408) 984-2850
Modems, fax cards

Productivity Software
1220 Broadway
New York, NY 10001
(212) 967-8666
PDR + 2.0

PSI
851 E. Hamilton Ave.
Campbell, CA 95008
(800) 622-1722
(408) 559-8544
Math Coprocessors

QMS
1 Magnum Pass
Mobile, AL 36618
(205) 633-4300
Laser printers

Qualstar Corp.
9621 Irondale Ave.
Chatsworth, CA 91311
(818) 882-5822
Storage drives

A

Quantum Software Systems, Ltd.
175 Terrence Matthews Crescent
Kanata, Ontario
Canada, K2M 1W8
(613) 591-0931
QNX networking

Quarterdeck *
150 Pico Blvd.
Santa Monica, CA 90405
(213) 392-9851
(213) 399-3802 FAX
Manifest 1.0

Qume Corp.
500 Yosemite Dr.
Milpitas, CA 95035
(408) 942-4000
Printers

Radio Shack
700 One Tandy Center
Fort Worth, TX 76102
(817) 390-3549
Computer

Renaissance GRX
Appian Technology
P.O. Box 96098
Bellevue, WA 98005
(206) 649-8086
Graphics adapters

RIX Softworks, Inc.
18553 MacArthur Blvd. #200
Irvine, CA 92715
(714) 476-8266
RIX graphics

A

Savin Corp.
9 West Broad St.
Stamford, CT 06904
(203) 967-5000
SavinFax SB-2000

Seiko Instruments USA
1144 Ringwood Court
San Jose, CA 95131
(408) 922-5900
Monitors

Sigma Designs
46501 Landing Parkway
Fremont, CA 94538
(415) 770-0100
DTP Monitors

Singapore Technology
260 E. Grand Ave. #18
So. San Francisco, CA 94080
(415) 875-3636
ProFax

SL Waber, Inc.
520 Fellowship Rd. #306
Mt. Laurel, NJ 08054
(800) 634-1485
(609) 866-1945 FAX
Power protection, UPS, and SPS

SoftLogic Solutions
1 Perimeter Rd.
Manchester, NH 03101
(800) 272-9900
(603) 627-9900
Disk Optimizer

Software Directions, Inc.
1572 Sussex Turnpike
Randolph, NJ 07869
(800) 346-7638
Print Q

The Software Link, Inc.
3577 Parkway Lane
Norcross, GA 30092
(800) 766-LINK
(404) 448-5465
(404) 263-6474 FAX
The UnTerminal UnNetwork

SOTA Technology, Inc. *
559 Weddell Dr.
Sunnyvale, CA 94089
(408) 745-1111
Display adapters, accelerators

Specialized Products Co.
3131 Premier Dr.
Irving, TX 75063
(214) 550-1923
Toolkits and diagnostic equipment

SpectraFAX Corp.
209 S. Airport Rd.
Naples, FL 33942
(813) 643-5060
Personal Link 2.0

Superior Electric
383 Middle St.
Bristol, CT 06010
(203) 582-9561
(203) 589-2136 FAX
Power supplies

Symantec Corp.
10201 Torre Ave.
Cupertino, CA 95014
(408) 253-9600
SUM II

SYSGEN, Inc.
556 Gibraltar Dr.
Milpitas, CA 95035
(800) 821-2151
Bridge products

System Diagnostic Software *
6945 Hermosa Circle
Buena Park, CA 90620
(714) 994-7400
System Sleuth

Tall Tree Systems
2585 E. Bayshore Rd.
Palo Alto, CA 94303
(415) 493-1980
(415) 493-7639 FAX
JLaser 5 printer controller

Tallgrass Technologies
11100 W. 82nd St.
Overland Park, KS 66214
(913) 492-6002
FileSecure 1300 cartridge

Tatung
2850 El Presidio St.
Long Beach, CA 90810
(213) 979-7055

A

Techno
2101 Jericho Turnpike
New Hyde Park, NY 11040
(516) 328-3970
(516) 326-8827 FAX
Prototyping Machines, routers

Technology Power Ent, Inc.
46560 Fremont Blvd. #118
Fremont, CA 94538
(415) 623-9162
(415) 623-9462 FAX
33 MHz 386 motherboard

Tecmar, Inc.
6225 Cochran Rd.
Solon, OH 44139
(800) 624-8560
(216) 349-1009
MicroRAM

The Complete PC, Inc.
1983 Concourse Dr.
San Jose, CA 95131
(408) 434-0145
The Complete Fax, The Complete Communicator

The Periscope Co., Inc.
1197 Peachtree St.
Plaza Level
Atlanta, GA 30361
(404) 875-8080
(404) 872-1973 FAX
Boards

The Software Link, Inc.
3577 Parkway Lane
Norcross, GA 30092
(800) 766-LINK
(404) 448-5465
(404) 263-6474 FAX
The UnTerminal UnNetwork

TG Computers, Inc.
KP Electronics
4141 Business Center Dr.
Fremont, CA 94538
(415) 490-0300
Enclosures

Timeworks, Inc.
625 Academy Dr.
Northbrook, IL 60062
(708) 559-1300
DOS Rx

Touchbase Systems, Inc.
160 Laurel Ave.
Northport, NY 11768
(516) 261-0423
(516) 754-3491 FAX
WorldPort modems

Traveling Software, Inc.
18702 N. Creek Pkwy.
Bothell, WA 98011
(800) 662-2652
(206) 483-8088
Battery Watch II, LapLink Mac III, DeskLink

A

Tripp Lite
500 N. Orleans
Chicago, IL 60610
(312) 329-1777
(312) 644-6505 FAX
LAN Battery backup

TVM
1109 W. 9th
Upland, CA 91786
(714) 985-4788
Monitors

US Robotics *
8100 N. McCormick Blvd.
Skokie, IL 60076
(800) DIAL USR
(708) 982-5010
Complete line of modems

USVideo, Inc.*
1 Stamford Landing
62 S. Field Ave.
Stamford, CT 06902-9950
(203) 964-9000
(203) 964-1824 FAX
Video info

Vatek USA, Inc.
4636 Mac Beth Ct.
Fremont, CA 94555
(415) 794-6721
Color-Mouse

Ventek Corp.
31336 Via Colinas #102
Westlake Village, CA 91361
(818) 991-3868
(818) 991-4097 FAX
Color-Mouse

VideoLogic, Inc.
245 First St.
Cambridge, MA 02142
(617) 494-0530
Digital Video Adapters

Wedge Tech, Inc.
1587 McCandless Dr.
Milpitas, CA 95035
(408) 263-9888
(408) 263-9886 FAX
Complete upgrade material

Wetex International Corp.
1122 W. Washington Blvd. #D
Montebello, CA 90640
(213) 728-3119
Systems and drives

White Crane Systems
8560 Holcomb Bridge Rd. #103-W3
Alpharetta, GA 30202
(404) 594-8180
AutoImport

A

Willow Peripherals
190 Willow Ave.
Bronx, NY 10454-3518
(212) 402-9500
Frame grabbers

Wyse Technology
3080 Bristol St.
Costa Mesa, CA 92626
(714) 850-9973
Terminals, CPUs, and monitors

Xerox Imaging Systems
185 Albany St.
Cambridge, MA 02139
(617) 864-4700
MicroFax 2.1 and other products

Xetel Corp.
8100 Cameron Rd.
Austin, TX 78753
(800) 388-7466   Ext. 14
SIMMs and SIPs

Xircom
26025 Mureau Rd.
Calabasas, CA 91302
(818) 884-8755
(818) 884-1719 FAX
Pocket LAN adapters

Zenith
2150 E. Lake Cook Rd.
Buffalo Grove, IL 60089
(708) 808-5000
Miscellaneous hardware

Z-Nix Company, Inc.
211 Erie St.
Pomona, CA 91768
(714) 629-8050
Mouse

A

BIOS and DOS Source

Wholesale Direct, Inc.
15247 N.E. 90th Street
Redmond, WA 98052
(206) 883-0227
(206) 882-2801 FAX

The following are just a few products offered by Wholesale Direct, Inc.

Microsoft MS-DOS 4.01 with GW-Basic

This is the newest version of one of the best operating systems for your computer. New features include self-install, menu shell, and partitions larger than 32 MB. This version supports file caching, expanded memory support, and window screens. Bundled with the product are the *User's Reference Manuals.*

Phoenix AT 286 BIOS

This AT 286 Version 3.10—with 100 percent compatible BIOS—includes a complete two-chip set with ROM setup. It supports up to 25 MHz processing speeds. It comes with power-on self-test and boot diagnostics and supports internal and external 720 KB or 1.44 MB, 3 1/2-inch disk drives. This version supports 101/102 key keyboards. Full NOVELL and NETWARE support is also included.

Phoenix XT BIOS

This XT Version 2.52—with 100 percent compatible BIOS—is the new standard of the industry. It supports INTEL 8086 and 8088 processors and NEC V-20, V-30, and V-40 processors. Complete power-on self-test and boot diagnostics are included. It supports internal and external 720 KB, 3 1/2-inch disk drives. Full NOVELL and NETWARE support is included. This is easy to install!

Phoenix AT 386 BIOS

This AT 386 Version 1.1—with 100 percent IBM-compatible BIOS—is a complete two-chip set with setup in ROM. With full OS/2 compatibility, it supports up to 25 MHz speeds. This version supports internal and external 720 KB or 1.44 MB 3 1/2-inch disk drives. Full NOVELL and NETWARE support is included, as well as extended hard disk tables, including support for ESDI and RLL drives.

Smartdriver

Some BIOS versions do not support the new 1.44 MB floppy drives. This handy software driver eliminates that problem and gives your PC/XT/AT system full access to your new floppy drive. It's easy to use. MS-DOS 3.2 or above is required.

Paterson Labs XT Turbo BIOS

This is a good bet for turbo systems. It's 100 percent IBM compatible. It supports NEC V-2—V-50 processors and has keyboard switchable clock speeds. it also includes a power-on self-test and boot diagnostics, which automatically determines function and system configuration. This most recent version supports 1.2 MB, 360 K, and 720 K floppy drives.

Smartclock

This accurate, real-time clock does not take up a valuable slot. Smartclock installs in any 28-pin EPROM socket, and automatically updates the time and date every time you turn on your computer so you never have to enter the time and date again. It's compatible with virtually all MS-DOS computers and fits all IBM PS/2 computers. The manual and all necessary software are included, as is a 30-day money-back guarantee.

A

B

Technical Information

Hard Drive Heads, Tracks, and Cylinders

The entries in this section are intended mostly for entries in BIOS drive tables and for drive capability information. The following list explains the column heads for the tables in this section.

Hds	Heads in the drive (BIOS entry)
Cyls	Total number of cylinders (BIOS entry)
RW	Track for start of Reduced Write current
WP	Track for start of Write precompensation (BIOS)
Form	Height (full-height, half-height, or special)
Size	Platter diameter
Int.	Interface (ST412, ESDI, SCSI, SCSI-2, IDE)
Rec.	Record method (MFM, RLL (2,7), ARLL (3,9), or...)
Sec	Sectors (nominal—no translation)
Cap	Capacity (formatted)
AA	Average access time

Alps
3553 N. First St.
San Jose, CA 95134
(408) 432-6000
(800) 825-2577

Model #	Hds	Cyls	RW	WP	Form	Size	Int.	Rec.	Sec	Cap	AA
DRND10A	2	615	616	616		3.50	ST412				
DRND20A	4	615	616	616		3.50	ST412				
DRPO20A	2	615	616	616	Half	3.50	Alps/ST 412				
DRPO20D	2	615	616	616	Half	3.50	SCSI/ST 412				
DRPO20L	2	615			Half	3.50	Alps			21	71
DRPO20Q	2	615			Half	3.50	SASI			23	86
DRQO40A	4	615			Half	3.50	Alps			43	56
DRQO40D	4	615			Half	3.50	SCSI			43	56
DRRO40C	2	1195			Half	3.50	PC AT			43	28
DRRO40D	2	1265			Half	3.50	SCSI			45	28
DRR100C	4	1465			Half	3.50	PC AT			105	28
DRR100D	4	1465			Half	3.50	SCSI			105	28

Ampex Corporation
401 Broadway
Redwood City, CA 94063-3199
(415) 367-2011

Model #	Hds	Cyls	RW	WP	Form	Size	Int.	Rec.	Sec	Cap	AA
PYXIS7	2	320	132	132		5.25	ST412				
PYXIS13	4	320			Full	5.25	ST412				
PYXIS20	6	320			Full	5.25	ST412				
PYXIS27	8	320			Full	5.25	ST412				

Areal Technology, Inc.
2075 Zanker Rd.
San Jose, CA 95131
(408) 954-0360

Model #	Hds	Cyls	RW	WP	Form	Size	Int.	Rec.	Sec	Cap	AA
BP-100	2	1720			Half	3.50	SCSI/PC AT			105	47
BP-200	2	3400			Half	3.50	SCSI/PC AT			200	47

Model #	Hds	Cyls	RW	WP	Form	Size	Int.	Rec.	Sec	Cap	AA
BP-50	1	1720			Half	3.50	SCSI/PC AT			50	47
MD-2050	2	819			Half	3.50	SCSI/PC AT			50	47
MD-2100	2	1638			Half	3.50	SCSI/PC AT			100	47

Atasi (also Priam)
2323-B Owens St.
Santa Clara, CA 95054
(408) 436-8872

Model #	Hds	Cyls	RW	WP	Form	Size	Int.	Rec.	Sec	Cap	AA
AT3020	3	635	0	0			ST412				
AT3033	5	645	0	0	Full	5.25	ST412				
AT3046	7	645	645	320	Full	5.25	ST412				
AT3051	7	704	704	350	Full	5.25	ST412				
AT3053	7	733	733	365	Full	5.25	ST412				
AT3075	8	1024	1025	1025	Full		ST412				
AT3085	8	1024	1025	1025	Full	5.25	ST412				

BASF Corp.
Crosby Dr.
Bedford, MA 01730
(617) 271-4000

Model #	Hds	Cyls	RW	WP	Form	Size	Int.	Rec.	Sec	Cap	AA
6185	6	440	220	220			ST412				
6186	4	440	220	220			ST412				
6187	2	440	220	220			ST412				

Bull Worldwide Information Systems
300 Concord Rd.
Billerica, MA 01821
(508) 294-6000

Model #	Hds	Cyls	RW	WP	Form	Size	Int.	Rec.	Sec	Cap	AA
D530	3	987	987	987			ST412				
D550	5	987	987	987			ST412				
D570	7	987	987	987			ST412				
D585	7	1166	1166	1166							

B

Cardiff
(no longer making drives)

Model #	Hds	Cyls	RW	WP	Form	Size	Int.	Rec.	Sec	Cap	AA
F-3053	5	1024				3.50	ST412				
F-3080	5	1024				3.50	ESDI/SCSI				
F-3127	5	1024				3.50	ESDI/SCSI				

Control Data Corp.
8100 34th Ave. South
Minneapolis, MN 55440
(612) 853-8100

Model #	Hds	Cyls	RW	WP	Form	Size	Int.	Rec.	Sec	Cap	AA
94354-125	7	1072	1073	1073							
94354-160	9	1072	1073	1073							
94354-200	9	1072	1073	1073							
94354-230	9	1272	1273	1273							
BJ7D5A	4	670	671	128		5.25	ST412				
BJ7D5A	5	670	671	128		5.25	ST412				
BJ75DA	5	733	734	128		5.25	ST412				
94155-21	3	697	698	128		5.25	ST412				
94155-25	4	697	698	128		5.25	ST412 WREN 1				
94155-28	4	697	698	128		5.25	ST412				
94155-36	5	697	698	128		5.25	ST412				
94155-38	5	697	698	128		5.25	ST412 WREN 1				
94155-48	5	925	926	128		5.25	ST412 WREN 2				
94295-51	5	989	990	128		5.25	ST412 WREN 2				
94155-57	6	925	926	128		5.25	ST412 WREN 2				
94155-67	7	925	926	128		5.25	ST412 WREN 2				
94155-77	8	925	926	128		5.25	ST412 WREN 2				
94155-85	8	1024	1025	128		5.25	ST412 WREN 2				
94155-86	9	925	926	128		5.25	ST412 WREN 2				
94205-51	5	989	990	128		5.25	ST412				
94335-100	9	1072	1073	300		3.50	ST412				

Model #	Hds	Cyls	RW	WP	Form	Size	Int.	Rec.	Sec	Cap	AA
94155-135	9	960	961	128		5.25	ST412 WREN 2				
94205-77	5	990	991	128		5.25	ST412 WREN 2				
94355-150	9	1072	1073	300		3.50	ST412				
94156-48	5	925	926	128			ESDI WREN 2				
94156-67	7	925	926	128			ESDI WREN 2				
94156-86	9	925	926	128			ESDI WREN 2				
94156-101	5	969	970	128		5.25	ESDI WREN 3				
94166-141	7	969	970	128		5.25	ESDI WREN 3				
94166-182	9	969	970	128		5.25	ESDI WREN 3				
94186-383	13	1412	1413	128		5.25	ESDI WREN V				
94186-383H	15	1224	1225	128		5.25	ESDI WREN V				
94186-442	15	1412	1413	128		5.25	ESDI WREN V				
94216-106	5	1024	1025	128		5.25	ESDI WREN 3				
94356-111	5	1072	1073	1073		3.50	ESDI SWIFT				
94356-155	7	1072	1073	1073		3.50	ESDI SWIFT				
94356-200	9	1072	1073	1073		3.50	ESDI SWIFT				
94171-300	9	1365	1366	1366		5.25	SCSI WREN 4				
94171-344	9	1549	1550	1550		5.25	SCSI WREN V				
94181-574	15	1549	1550	1550		5.25	SCSI WREN V				
94211-106	5	1024	1025	1025		5.25	SCSI WREN 3				
94221-190	5	1547	1548	1548		5.25	SCSI WREN V				
94211-209	5	1547	1548	1548		5.25	SCSI WREN V				
94351-128	7	1068	1069	1069		3.50	SCSI SWIFT				
94351-160	9	1068	1069	1069		3.50	SCSI SWIFT				
94351-200	9	1068	1069	1069		3.50	SCSI SWIFT				

B

Model #	Hds	Cyls	RW	WP	Form	Size	Int.	Rec.	Sec	Cap	AA
94351-200S	9	1068	1069	1069		3.50	SCSI SWIFT				
94351-230S	9	1272	1273	1273		3.50	SCSI SWIFT				

Cerplex
3332 E. La Palma Ave.
Anaheim, CA 92806
(714) 632-7500

Model #	Hds	Cyls	RW	WP	Form	Size	Int.	Rec.	Sec	Cap	AA
CAST10203E	3	1050	1051	1051		5.25	ESDI				
CAST10304	4	1050	1051	1051		5.25	ESDI				
CAST10305	5	1050	1051	1051		5.25	ESDI				
CAST14404	4	1590	1591	1591		5.25	ESDI				
CAST14405	5	1590	1591	1591		5.25	ESDI				
CAST14406	6	1590	1591	1591		5.25	ESDI				
CAST24509	9	1599	1600	1600		5.25	ESDI				
CAST24611	11	1599	1600	1600		5.25	ESDI				
CAST24713	13	1599	1600	1600		5.25	ESDI				
CAST10203S	3	1050	1051	1051		5.25	SCSI				
CAST10304S	4	1050	1051	1051		5.25	SCSI				
CAST10305S	5	1050	1051	1051		5.25	SCSI				
CAST14404S	4	1590	1591	1591		5.25	SCSI				
CAST14405S	5	1590	1591	1591		5.25	SCSI				
CAST14406S	6	1590	1591	1591		5.25	SCSI				
CAST24509S	9	1599	1600	1600		5.25	SCSI				
CAST24611S	11	1599	1600	1600		5.25	SCSI				
CAST24713S	13	1599	1600	1600		5.25	SCSI				

C. Itoh Technology
2515 McCabe Way
P.O.Box 19657
Irvine, CA 92713-9657
(714) 660-0506

Model #	Hds	Cyls	RW	WP	Form	Size	Int.	Rec.	Sec	Cap	AA
YD-3530	5	731	732	732			ST412				
YD-3540	7	731	732	732		5.25	ST412				

Model #	Hds	Cyls	RW	WP	Form	Size	Int.	Rec.	Sec	Cap	AA
YD-3042	4	788	789	789		5.25	SCSI				
YD-3082	8	788	789	789		5.25	SCSI				

CMI - Peripheral Repair Corporation
9233 Eton Ave.
Chatsworth, CA 91311
(818) 700-8482

Model #	Hds	Cyls	RW	WP	Form	Size	Int.	Rec.	Sec	Cap	AA
CM3426	4	612	612	612	Half	5.25	ST412	MFM	17	20	85
CM5205-C	2	256	256	256	Full	5.25	ST412	MFM	17	4.4	90
CM5206	2	306	307	256			ST412	MFM	17	5.0	90
CM5410-C	4	256	256	256			ST412	MFM	17	8.9	90
CM5412	4	306	306	306	Full	5.25	ST412	MFM	17	10	90
CM5616-C	6	256	256	256	Full	5.25	ST412	MFM	17	13	90
CM5619	6	306	306	306	Full	5.25	ST412	MFM	17	15	90
CM6426	4	615	256	256	Full	5.25	ST412	MFM	17	20	39
CM6426S	4	640	256	256	Full	5.25	ST412	MFM	17	20	40
CM6640	6	640	640	256	Full	5.25	ST412	MFM	17	30	39

Cogito Drives

Model #	Hds	Cyls	RW	WP	Form	Size	Int.	Rec.	Sec	Cap	AA
CG-906	2	306	128	128	Half	5.25	ST412				
CG-912	4	612	307	307	Half	5.25	ST412				
PT-912	4	612	307	307	Half	5.25	ST412				
PT-925	4	612	307	307	Half	5.25	ST412				

Comport
3096 Orchard Dr.
San Jose, CA 95134
(408) 432-0911

Model #	Hds	Cyls	RW	WP	Form	Size	Int.	Rec.	Sec	Cap	AA
2040	4	820			Full	3.50	ST412				43
2041	4	820			Full	3.50	PC AT				37
2082	6	820			Full	3.5	SCSI				37

B

Conner Peripherals, Inc.
3081 Zanker Rd.
San Jose, CA 95134
(408) 433-3340

Model #	Hds	Cyls	RW	WP	Form	Size	Int.	Rec.	Sec	Cap	AA
CP-340	4	788			Half	3.50	SCSI			40	37
CP-342	4	805			Half	3.50	ST412				
CP-344	4	805			Half	3.50	ST412				
CP-2020	2	653			Half	3.50	SCSI			21	31
Kato CP-2024	2	653			Half	2.50	PC AT/XT			21	31
CP-3020	2	636			1-in	3.50	SCSI			21	35
CP-3022	8	636			1-in	3.50	PC AT			21	35
CP-3024	4	615	615	615	1-in	3.50	IDE	2,7RLL	17	21	35
CP-3040	2	1026			1-in	3.50	SCSI	2,7RLL	40	42	33
CP-3044	5	980	980	980	1-in	3.50	IDE	2,7RLL	17	43	33
CP-3100	8	776			Half	3.50	SCSI		33	105	33
CP-3104	8	776	776	776	Half	3.50	IDE	2,7RLL	33	105	33
CP-3114	8	833			Half	3.50	ST412			112	33
CP-3180	6	833	833	833	Half	3.50	SCSI	2,7RLL	33	84	33
CP-3184	6	833	833	833	Half	3.50	IDE	2,7RLL	33	84	33
CP-3200F	8	1366			Half	3.50	SCSI	2,7RLL	38	213	24
CP-3204	8	1348			Half	3.50	ST412AT			210	27
CP-3204F	16	683	683	683	Half	3.50	IDE	2,7RLL	38	213	24
CP-3209F	8	1366			Half	3.50	MCA	2,7RLL	38	213	24
Stubby CP-4024	4	615	615	615	Quar	3.50	IDE	2,7RLL	34	21	39
Stubby CP-4044	5	980	980	980	Quar	3.50	IDE	2,7RLL	38	43	39
Hopi CP-30100	4	1524			1-in	3.50	SCSI	2,7RLL	39	120	27
Hopi CP-30104	8	762			1-in	3.50	PC/AT	EISA	39	120	27
Hopi CP-30109	4	1524			1-in	3.50	MCA		39	120	27

1-in = 1-inch low profile
Quar = quarter height

Core International
7171 North Federal Highway
Boca Raton, FL 33487
(407) 997-6055

Model #	Hds	Cyls	RW	WP	Form	Size	Int.	Rec.	Sec	Cap	AA
AT 32	5	733				5.25	ST412				
AT 30	5	733				5.25	ST412				
AT 40	5	924				5.25	ST412				
AT 63	5	988				5.25	ST412				
AT 72	9	924				5.25	ST412				
OPTIMA 30	5	733				5.25	ST412				
OPTIMA 40	5	963				5.25	ST412				
OPTIMA 70	9	918				5.25	ST412				
AT 32	5	733				5.25	ST412				
AT 30	5	733				5.25	ST412				
AT 40	5	924				5.25	ST412				
AT 63	5	988				5.25	ST412				
AT 72	9	924				5.25	ST412				
OPTIMA 30	5	733				5.25	ST412				
OPTIMA 40	5	963				5.25	ST412				
OPTIMA 70	9	918				5.25	ST412				
HC 40	4	564				5.25	ESDI				
HC 90	5	969				5.25	ESDI				
HC 150	9	969				5.25	ESDI				
HC 260	12	1212				5.25	ESDI				
HC 310	12	1582				5.25	ESDI				

Digirede
Brazil

Model #	Hds	Cyls	RW	WP	Form	Size	Int.	Rec.	Sec	Cap	AA
W525/50	5	1024				5.25	ST412			50	35
W525/85	9	1024				5.25	ST412			85	36
W525R/125	8	1024				5.25	ST412			128	36
W525/140	11	1224				5.25	ST412			140	38
W525/190	15	1224				5.25	ST412			191	38
W525R/240	15	1024				5.25	ST412			240	36
W525E/380	15	1224				5.25	ESDI			382	26
W525E/410	8	1632				5.25	ESDI			410	22
W525S/410	8	1632				5.25	SCSI			361	22

B

Digital Equipment Corporation
Storage Group
146 Main St.
Maynard, MA 01754-2571
(508) 493-5111

Model #	Hds	Cyls	RW	WP	Form	Size	Int.	Rec.	Sec	Cap	AA
YD-3530	5	731	732	732			ST412				
YD-3540	7	731	732	732		5.25	ST412				
YD-3042	4	788	789	789		5.25	SCSI				
YD-3082	8	788	789	789		5.25	SCSI				
RA70	11	1507				5.25	DEC			350	27
RF30	6	1331				5.25	DEC			200	29

Disctron
(no longer making drives)

Model #	Hds	Cyls	RW	WP	Form	Size	Int.	Rec.	Sec	Cap	AA
DSCTRN503	2	153	128	128	Full	5.25	ST412				
DSCTRN504	2	215	128	128	Full	5.25	ST412				
DSCTRN506	4	153	128	128	Full	5.25	ST412				
DSCTRN507	2	306	128	128	Full	5.25	ST412				
DSCTRN509	4	215	128	128	Full	5.25	ST412				
DSCTRN512	8	153	128	128	Full	5.25	ST412				
DSCTRN513	6	215	128	128	Full	5.25	ST412				
DSCTRN514	4	306	128	128	Full	5.25	ST412				
DSCTRN518	8	215	128	128	Full	5.25	ST412				
DSCTRN519	6	306	128	128	Full	5.25	ST412				
DSCTRN526	8	306	128	128	Full	5.25	ST412				

DMA Technologies
60 E. 42nd St. #1100
New York, NY 10165
(212) 687-7115

Model #	Hds	Cyls	RW	WP	Form	Size	Int.	Rec.	Sec	Cap	AA
306	2	612	612	400			ST412 REMOV				
360	2	612				5.25	ST412				106
370	2	1224				5.25	ST412				93
371	2	1224				5.25	SCSI				93

DZU
Bulgaria

Model #	Hds	Cyls	RW	WP	Form	Size	Int.	Rec.	Sec	Cap	AA
ISOT 5502C	5	977				5.25	ST412			51	48
SM 5509	7	615				5.25	ST412			45	53

Edisa Infomatica
Brazil

Model #	Hds	Cyls	RW	WP	Form	Size	Int.	Rec.	Sec	Cap	AA
ED 71204	6	1643				5.25	SCSI			162	26
ED 71408	12	1643				5.25	SCSI			323	26

Elcoh
(no longer making drives)

Model #	Hds	Cyls	RW	WP	Form	Size	Int.	Rec.	Sec	Cap	AA
DISCACHE 10	4	320	321	321			ST412				
DISCACHE 20	8	320	321	321			ST412				

Elebra
Brazil

Model #	Hds	Cyls	RW	WP	Form	Size	Int.	Rec.	Sec	Cap	AA
W320	4	612				3.50	ST412			25	73
W530	3	925				5.25	ST412			30	36
W540	5	925				5.25	ST412			48	36
W560	7	925				5.25	ST412			67	36
W580	9	925				5.25	ST412			86	36

Espert
(PTI - Korea)

Model #	Hds	Cyls	RW	WP	Form	Size	Int.	Rec.	Sec	Cap	AA
EP-340A	3	1040				3.50	PC AT			41	33
PT338	6	615				3.50	ST412			38	43
PT351	6	820				3.50	ST412			51	43
PT357R	6	615				3.50	ST412			57	43
PT376R	6	820				3.50	ST412			77	43

B

Flexdisk
Brazil

Model #	Hds	Cyls	RW	WP	Form	Size	Int.	Rec.	Sec	Cap	AA
DISCACHE 10	4	320	321	321			ST412				
DISCACHE 20	8	320	321	321			ST412				
FX 325	4	615				3.5	ST412			26	56

Fuji Hitech
47520 Westinghouse Dr.
Fremont, CA 94538
(415) 651-0811

Model #	Hds	Cyls	RW	WP	Form	Size	Int.	Rec.	Sec	Cap	AA
FK301	4	306			Half	5.25	ST412				
FK302-13	2	615			Half	5.25	ST412				
FK302-26	4	615			Half	5.25	ST412				
FK303-52	8	615				3.25	ST412			51	48
FK305-26	4	615	615	615	Half	5.25	ST412				
FK305-26R	4	615	615	615							
FK305-39	6	615	615	615							
FK305-39R	6	615	615	615							
FK309-26	4	615				3.50	ST412			26	73
FK309-39R	4	615				3.50	ST412			38	73
FK309S-26R	4	615				3.50	SCSI			23	55
FK309X-26	4	615				3.50	PC XT			21	73
FK311-26	4	615				3.50	ST412			25	69
FK311A-26R	2	615				3.50	PC AT			21	37
FK311A-50R	4	615				3.50	PC AT			43	37
FK311S-50R	4	628				3.50	SASI/SCSI			42	39
FK312A-53R	4	615				3.50	PC AT			43	37
FK312S-53R	4	652				3.50	SCSI			40	37
FK313S-130R	8	840				3.50	SCSI			100	28
FK314S-90R	4	1116				3.50	SCSI			90	33

Fujitsu America, Inc.
3055 Orchard Drive
San Jose, CA 95134-2022
(800) 626-4686
(408) 432-1300

B

Model #	Hds	Cyls	RW	WP	Form	Size	Int.	Rec.	Sec	Cap	AA
M2225AD	4	615	615	615		3.50	ST412			26	93
M2225D2	4	615	615	615		3.50	ST412			26	43
M2226D2	6	615	615	615		3.50	ST412			38	43
M2227D2	8	615	615	615		3.50	ST412			51	43
M2230AS	2	320	320	320			ST412				
M2233AS	4	320	320	320			ST412				
M2234AS	6	320	320	320			ST412				
M2235AS	8	320	320	320		5.25	ST412			27	91
M2230AT	2	320	320	320							
M2233AT	4	320	320	320							
M2241AS2	4	754	754	754		5.25	ST412			31	38
M2242AS2	7	754	754	754		5.25	ST412			55	38
M2243AS2	11	754	754	754		5.25	ST412			86	38
M2243R	7	1185	1185	1185		5.25	ST412			130	33
M2243T	7	1185	1185	1185		5.25	ST412			86	33
M2244C/E	5	823	823	823		5.25	ESDI			86	33
M2244S/SA/SB	5	823	823	823		5.25	SCSI			63	33
M2245C/E	7	823	823	823		5.25	ESDI			120	33
M2245S/SA/SB	7	823	823	823		5.25	SCSI			90	33
M2246C/E	10	823	823	823		5.25	ESDI			172	33
M2246S/SA/SB	10	823	823	823		5.25	SCSI			130	33
M2247E	7	1243	1243	1243		5.25	ESDI			181	26
M2247S/SA/SB	7	1243	1243	1243		5.25	SCSI			138	26
M2248E	11	1243	1243	1243		5.25	ESDI			285	26
M2248S/SA/SB	11	1243	1243	1243		5.25	SCSI			220	26
M2249E	15	1243	1243	1243		5.25	ESDI			389	26
M2249S/SA/SB	15	1243	1243	1243		5.25	SCSI			303	26

Model #	Hds	Cyls	RW	WP	Form	Size	Int.	Rec.	Sec	Cap	AA
M2261E	8	1658	1658	1658		5.25	ESDI			415	24
M2261H/HA/HB	8	1658	1658	1658		5.25	SCSI			357	24
M2611S/SA/SB	2	1334	1334	1334		3.50	SCSI			45	33
M2611T	2	1334	1334	1334		3.50	PC AT			45	33
M2612S/SA/SB	4	1334	1334	1334		3.50	SCSI			91	33
M2612T	4	1334	1334	1334		3.50	PC AT			90	33
M2613S/SA/SB	6	1334	1334	1334		3.50	SCSI			137	33
M2613T	6	1334	1334	1334		3.50	PC AT			135	33
M2614S/SA/SB	8	1334	1334	1334		3.50	SCSI			182	33
M2614T	8	1334	1334	1334		3.50	PC AT			180	33

GoldStar Technology Inc.
3003A North First St.
San Jose, CA 95134-2004
(408) 432-1331

Model #	Hds	Cyls	RW	WP	Form	Size	Int.	Rec.	Sec	Cap	AA
GSH-3026	4	615				3.50	ST412			25	73
GSH-3040	8	615				3.50	ST412			52	53

Hewlett-Packard
Disk Storage Systems Division
Boise, ID 83707
(208) 323-2332

Model #	Hds	Cyls	RW	WP	Form	Size	Int.	Rec.	Sec	Cap	AA
7957B	4	1269				5.25	HP-IB			81	25
7957S	4	1572				5.25	SCSI			107	25
7958B	6	1552				5.25	HP-IB			152	25
7958S	6	1572				5.25	SCSI			161	25
7959B	12	1572				5.25	HP-IB			304	25
7959S	12	1572				5.25	SCSI			323	25
9153	2	1400				3.50	HP			40	85
9262B	6	1552				5.25	HP-IB			152	25
9263B	12	1572				5.25	HP-IB			304	25
97532D	4	1643			Full	5.25	SCSI			108	26
97532E	4	1583			Full	5.25	ESDI			129	25
97533D	6	1643			Full	5.25	SCSI			162	26
97533E	6	1583			Full	5.25	ESDI			195	25
97536D	12	1643			Full	5.25	SCSI			323	26

Model #	Hds	Cyls	RW	WP	Form	Size	Int.	Rec.	Sec	Cap	AA
97536E	12	1583			Full	5.25	ESDI			389	25
97544D	8	1447			Full	5.25	SCSI			331	23
97544E	8	1457			Full	5.25	ESDI			396	24
97544P	8	1447			Full	5.25	SCSI-2			331	23
C2233S	5	1511			Full	3.50	SCSI-2	2,7RLL		234	21
C2234S	7	1511			Full	3.50	SCSI-2	2,7RLL		328	21
C2235S	9	1511			Full	3.50	SCSI-2	2,7RLL		422	21

Hitachi Corp.
401 West Artesia Blvd.
Compton, CA 90220
(213) 537-8383

B

Model #	Hds	Cyls	RW	WP	Form	Size	Int.	Rec.	Sec	Cap	AA
DK301-1	4	306				3.50	ST412				
DK302-2	4	615				3.50	ST412			25	93
DK302-3	6	615				3.50	ST412			38	93
DK312C-20	10	1076				3.50	SCSI			209	28
DK312C-25	12	1076				3.50	SCSI			251	28
DK502-2	4	615				5.25	ST412			26	93
DK511-3	5	699	256	256		5.25	ST412/SCSI			36	38
DK511-5	7	699	256	256		5.25	ST412/SCSI			51	38
DK511-8	10	823				5.25	ST412/SCSI			85	31
DK512-8	5	823			Full	5.25	ESDI/SM D			86	31
DK512-12	7	823			Full	5.25	ESDI/SM D			120	31
DK512-17	10	823			Full	5.25	ESDI			172	31
DK512C-8	5	819			Full	5.25	SCSI			73	31
DK512C-12	7	819			Full	5.25	SCSI			102	31
DK512C-17	10	819			Full	5.25	SCSI			146	31
DK512S-17	10	823			Full	5.25	SMD			172	31
DK514-38	14	903			Full	5.25	ESDI			382	24
DK514C-38	14	898				5.25	SCSI			322	24
DK514S-38	14	903				5.25	Mod. SMD			382	24
DK521-5	6	823				5.25	ST412			51	33
DK522-10	6	823				5.25	ESDI			103	33
DK522C-10	6	819				5.25	SCSI			87	33
DK524-20		1105				5.25	ESDI			200	33
DK524C-20		1105				5.25	SCSI			169	33

Hyosung Computer
Korea

Model #	Hds	Cyls	RW	WP	Form	Size	Int.	Rec.	Sec	Cap	AA
HC8085	8	1024				5.25	ST412			85	33
HC8128	8	1024				5.25	ST412			128	33
HC8170E	8	1024				5.25	ESDI			171	33

IBM
Old Orchard Rd.
Armonk, NY 10504
(914) 765-1900

Model #	Hds	Cyls	RW	WP	Form	Size	Int.	Rec.	Sec	Cap	AA
0661	14	949				3.50	SCSI-2			371	19
4956-G10 (40 MB)	7	733				5.25	ST412			40	48
4956-G10 (72 MB)	7	582				5.25	ESDI			72	38
4965-E00	7	582				5.25	ESDI			72	38
5363-P10	7	580				5.25	ESDI			68	38
5363-P20	7	914				5.25	ESDI			106	36
5364-001	7	733				5.25	IBM/ST412			42	48
5364-003	7	580				5.25	ESDI			66	38
6150-115	7	582				5.25	ESDI			85	38
6150-13X	7	915				5.25	ESDI			114	36
6150-4300	15	1224				5.25	ESDI			310	30
6156-001	7	915				5.25	ESDI /Remov.			114	36
671-284	11	1225				5.25	ESDI/SCSI			284	30
671-387	15	1225				5.25	ESDI/SCSI			387	30
7012-320 (#2120)	8	920				3.50	MCA			120	31
7012-320 (#2540)	14	949				3.50	SCSI			320	19
7013-520 (#2500)	8	1632				5.25	SCSI			355	24
7541	4	612				3.50	MCA			31	47
7561	6	762				3.50	MCA			61	35
8525-001,004	4	610				3.50	MCA			20	88
8530-001,E01	4	612				3.50	MCA			31	47
8530-021	2					3.50	PS/2-30			20	35

Model #	Hds	Cyls	RW	WP	Form	Size	Int.	Rec.	Sec	Cap	AA
8530-E31						3.50	PS/2-30			30	35
8550-031	4	612				3.50	MCA			31	47
8550-061	6	762				3.50	SCSI/MC A			61	35
8560-041	7	733				5.25	ST412			45	48
8560-071	7	583				5.25	ESDI			70	38
8565-061	4	920				3.50	SCSI/MC A			60	31
8570-121,B21	8	920				3.50	SCSI/MC A			120	31
8573-031	2	920				3.50	SCSI			30	27
8580-111	7	915				5.25	ESDI			115	36
8580-311	15	1225				5.25	ESDI			314	30
8580-A31,321	14	949				3.50	SCSI-2			320	19
9371-10	14					3.50	SCSI-2			295	19
9371-PS/2	14	949				3.50	SCSI-2			320	19
9404-B10	15	1223				5.25	SCSI			316	30
9404-C10	14	949				3.50	SCSI-2			320	19
WD-325	4	612				3.50	ST412			25	88
WD-387	6	762				3.50	SCSI			60	35
WD-387G	4	920				3.50	SCSI/MCA			60	31
WD-387P	4					3.50	SCSI/PC AT			80	27
WD-3158	8	920				3.50	SCSI			120	35
WD-3158G	8	920				3.50	SCSI/MCA			120	31
WD-3158P	8					3.50	SCSI/PC AT			160	27
WDI-325	4	612				3.50	PC AT			21	88
WDL-320	2					3.50	PS/2-30			27	35
WDL-330	2	920				3.50	PS/2-30/MCA			42	31

IMI
(no longer making drives)

Model #	Hds	Cyls	RW	WP	Form	Size	Int.	Rec.	Sec	Cap	AA
5006	2	306	307	214			ST412				
5012	4	306	307	214			ST412				
5018	6	306	307	214			ST412				

ISOT
Bulgaria

Model #	Hds	Cyls	RW	WP	Form	Size	Int.	Rec.	Sec	Cap	AA
CM 5508	4	306				5.25	ST412			12	93
ES 5300	4	153				5.25	ST412			6	93

B

JVC Information Products Co.
2903 Bunker Hill Lane # 102
Santa Clara, CA 95054
(408) 988-7506

Model #	Hds	Cyls	RW	WP	Form	Size	Int.	Rec.	Sec	Cap	AA
JD-E2825P	2	581					PC AT/SCSI			21	32
JD-E3848V	2	862				3.50	PC AT/SCSI			42	37
JD-E3896V	4	862				3.50	PC AT/SCSI			85	37

Kalok Corp.
1289 Anvilwood Ave.
Sunnyvale, CA 94089
(408) 747-1315

Model #	Hds	Cyls	RW	WP	Form	Size	Int.	Rec.	Sec	Cap	AA
KL320	4	615				3.50	ST412			25	48
KL330	4	615				3.50	ST412			38	48
KL332	4	615				3.50	SCSI				
KL341	4	676				3.50	SCSI			43	38
KL343	4	676				3.50	PC AT			43	37
KL386	6	815				3.50	PC AT			87	33

Kyocera
1321 Harbor Bay Parkway
Alameda, CA 94501
(619) 576-2600

Model #	Hds	Cyls	RW	WP	Form	Size	Int.	Rec.	Sec	Cap	AA
KC 20A	4	616				3.50	ST412			25	73
KC 20B	4	615				3.50	ST412			25	70
KC 30A	4	616				3.50	ST412			38	73
KC 30B	4	615				3.50	ST412			38	70
KC 40GA	2	1075				3.50	PC AT			41	38

La Pine
(handled by Kyocera)

Model #	Hds	Cyls	RW	WP	Form	Size	Int.	Rec.	Sec	Cap	AA
3522	4	306	307				ST412				

Model #	Hds	Cyls	RW	WP	Form	Size	Int.	Rec.	Sec	Cap	AA
LT 10	2	615	616					ST412				
LT 20	4	615	616					ST412				
LT 200	4	614	615					ST412				
LT 2000	4	614	615					ST412				
LT 300	4	614	615					ST412				

MagTron, Inc.
5 Fl., Sec. 4
Nan King East Rd.
Taipei, Taiwan, R.O.C.
(02) 716-6777

B

Model #	Hds	Cyls	RW	WP	Form	Size	Int.	Rec.	Sec	Cap	AA
MT4115	4	1600				5.25	ESDI/SCSI			138	33
MT4140	5	1600				5.25	ESDI/SCSI			172	33
MT4170	6	1600				5.25	ESDI/SCSI			207	33

Matsushita Communication
(Panasonic - Japan)

Model #	Hds	Cyls	RW	WP	Form	Size	Int.	Rec.	Sec	Cap	AA
JU-106	2	615				3.50	ST412			20	76
JU-128	7	733				3.50	ST412			53	43
JU-128A	7	733				3.50	ST412			53	38
JU-1381	4	733				3.50	SCSI			40	38
JU-1391	8	733				3.50	SCSI			81	38

Maxtor Corp.
211 River Oaks Pkwy.
San Jose, CA 95134
(408) 432-1700

Model #	Hds	Cyls	RW	WP	Form	Size	Int.	Rec.	Sec	Cap	AA
7040A	2	1159				3.50	PC AT			41	27
7040S	2	1156				3.50	SCSI			40	27
7080A	4	1159				3.50	PC AT			81	27
7080S	4	1156				3.50	SCSI			81	27
LXT-100	8	733				3.50	SCSI/AT			96	37
LXT-200	7	1320				3.50	SCSI/AT		53	207	23

Model #	Hds	Cyls	RW	WP	Form	Size	Int.	Rec.	Sec	Cap	AA
LXT-213	7	1320				3.50	SCSI/AT		55	213	15
LXT-340	7	1560				3.50	SCSI/AT			340	23
XT-1065	7	918	918	918	Full	5.25					
XT-1085	8	1024	1024	1024	Full	5.25	ST412		17	71	28
XT-1105	11	918	918	918	Full	5.25					
XT-1120R	8	1024	1024	1024	Full	5.25	ST412			128	35
XT-1140	15	918	918	918	Full	5.25	ST412		17	120	27
XT-1240R	15	1024	1024	1024	Full	5.25	ST412			240	35
XT-2085	7	1224	1224	1224	Full	5.25					
XT-2140	11	1224	1224	1224	Full	5.25					
XT-2190	15	1224	1224	1224	Full	5.25	ST412		17	160	29
XT-4170E	7	1224	1224	1224	Full	5.25	ESDI		36	158	14
XT-4170S	7	1224			Full	5.25	SCSI			158	14
XT-4175	7	1224	1224	1224	Full	5.25	ESDI				
XT-4230E	9	1224			Full	5.25	ESDI		36	203	16
XT-4280	11	1224	1224	1224	Full	5.25	ESDI				
XT-4280S	11	1224			Full	5.25	SCSI			248	24
XT-4380E	15	1224	1244	1244	Full	5.25	ESDI		36	338	16
XT-4380S	15	1224			Full	5.25	SCSI			338	16
XT-8380E	8	1632			Full	5.25	ESDI		54	361	14
XT-8380S	8	1632			Full	5.25	SCSI			360	14
XT-4170S	7	1224			Full	5.25	SCSI				
XT-8610E	12	1632			Full	5.25	ESDI		54	541	16
XT-8702S					Full	5.25	SCSI			617	16
XT-8760E	15	1632			Full	5.25	ESDI		54	677	16
XT-8760S	15	1632			Full	5.25	SCSI			675	16
XT-8800E	15	1274			Full	5.25	ESDI		71	695	15
XT-81000E	15	1632			Full	5.25	ESDI		71	890	16

Microlab
Brazil

Model #	Hds	Cyls	RW	WP	Form	Size	Int.	Rec.	Sec	Cap	AA
DFW 5025	4	615				5.25			25	73	
DFW 5053	5	1024				5.25			53	36	
DFW 5096	9	1024				5.25			96	36	

Micropolis
21211 Nordhoff St.
Chatsworth, CA 91311
(818) 709-3300

Model #	Hds	Cyls	RW	WP	Form	Size	Int.	Rec.	Sec	Cap	AA
1743-5	5	1140	1141	1141			ESDI				
1744-6	6	1140	1141	1141			ESDI				
1744-7	7	1140	1141	1141			ESDI				
1745-8	8	1140	1141	1141			ESDI				
1745-9	9	1140	1141	1141			ESDI				
1302	3	830	831	831	Full	5.25	MFM				
1303	5	830	831	831	Full	5.25	MFM				
1304	6	830	831	831	Full	5.25	MFM				
1323	4	1024	1025	1025	Full	5.25	MFM				
1323A	5	1024	1025	1025	Full	5.25	MFM				
1324	6	1024	1025	1025	Full	5.25	MFM				
1324A	7	1024	1025	1025	Full	5.25	MFM				
1325	8	1024	1025	1025	Full	5.25	MFM				
1333A	5	1024	1025	1025	Full	5.25	MFM				
1334	6	1024	1025	1025	Full	5.25	MFM				
1335	8	1024	1025	1025	Full	5.25	MFM				
1352	2	1024	1025	1025	Full	5.25	ESDI				
1352A	3	1024	1025	1025	Full	5.25	ESDI				
1353	4	1024	1025	1025	Full	5.25	ESDI				
1353A	5	1024	1025	1025	Full	5.25	ESDI				
1354	6	1024	1025	1025	Full	5.25	ESDI				
1354A	7	1024	1025	1025	Full	5.25	ESDI				
1355	8	1024	1025	1025	Full	5.25	ESDI				
1516-10S	10	1840	1841	1841	Full	5.25	ESDI				
1517-13	13	1925	1926	1926	Full	5.25	ESDI				
1518-14	14	1925	1926	1926	Full	5.25	ESDI				
1518-15	15	1925	1926	1926	Full	5.25	ESDI				
1556-11	11	1224	1225	1225	Full	5.25	ESDI				
1557-12	12	1224	1225	1225	Full	5.25	ESDI				
1557-13	13	1224	1225	1225	Full	5.25	ESDI				
1557-14	14	1224	1225	1225	Full	5.25	ESDI				

B

Model #	Hds	Cyls	RW	WP	Form	Size	Int.	Rec.	Sec	Cap	AA
1557-15	15	1224	1225	1225	Full	5.25	ESDI				
1566-11	11	1632	1633	1633	Full	5.25	ESDI				
1567-12	12	1632	1633	1633	Full	5.25	ESDI				
1567-13	13	1632	1633	1633	Full	5.25	ESDI				
1568-14	14	1632	1633	1633	Full	5.25	ESDI				
1568-15	15	1632	1633	1633	Full	5.25	ESDI				
1653-4	4	1249	1250	1250	Half	5.25	ESDI				
1653-5	5	1249	1250	1250	Half	5.25	ESDI				
1654-6	6	1249	1250	1250	Half	5.25	ESDI				
1654-7	7	1249	1250	1250	Full	5.25	ESDI				
1663-4	4	1780	1781	1781	Half	5.25	ESDI				
1663-5	5	1780	1781	1781	Half	5.25	ESDI				
1664-6	6	1780	1781	1781	Half	5.25	ESDI				
1664-7	7	1780	1781	1781	Half	5.25	ESDI				
1373	4	1016	1017	1017	Full	5.25	SCSI				
1373A	5	1016	1017	1017	Full	5.25	SCSI				
1374	6	1016	1017	1017	Full	5.25	SCSI				
1374A	7	1016	1017	1017	Full	5.25	SCSI				
1375	8	1016	1017	1017	Full	5.25	SCSI				
1576-11	11	1220	1221	1221	Full	5.25	SCSI				
1577-12	12	1220	1221	1221	Full	5.25	SCSI				
1577-13	13	1220	1221	1221	Full	5.25	SCSI				
1578-14	14	1220	1221	1221	Full	5.25	SCSI				
1578-15	15	1220	1221	1221	Full	5.25	SCSI				
1586-11	11	1628	1629	1629	Full	5.25	SCSI				
1587-12	12	1628	1629	1629	Full	5.25	SCSI				
1587-13	13	1628	1629	1629	Full	5.25	SCSI				
1588-14	14	1628	1629	1629	Full	5.25	SCSI				
1588-15	15	1628	1629	1629	Full	5.25	SCSI				
1596-10S	10	1834	1835	1835	Full	5.25	SCSI				
1597-13	13	1919	1920	1920	Full	5.25	SCSI				
1598-14	14	1919	1920	1920	Full	5.25	SCSI				
1598-15	15	1919	1920	1920	Full	5.25	SCSI				
1673-4	4	1249	1250	1250	Full	5.25	SCSI				
1673-5	5	1249	1250	1250	Full	5.25	SCSI				
1674-6	6	1249	1250	1250	Full	5.25	SCSI				
1674-7	7	1249	1250	1250	Full	5.25	SCSI				
1683-4	4	1776	1777	1777	Full	5.25	SCSI				
1683-5	5	1776	1777	1777	Full	5.25	SCSI				

Model #	Hds	Cyls	RW	WP	Form	Size	Int.	Rec.	Sec	Cap	AA
1684-6	6	1776	1777	1777	Full	5.25	SCSI				
1684-7	7	1776	1777	1777	Full	5.25	SCSI				
1773-5	5	1140	1141	1141			SCSI				
1774-6	6	1140	1141	1141			SCSI				
1774-7	7	1140	1141	1141			SCSI				
1775-8	8	1140	1141	1141			SCSI				
1775-9	9	1140	1141	1141			SCSI				

Microscience International
90 Headquarters Dr.
San Jose, CA 95134
(408) 433-9898

Model #	Hds	Cyls	RW	WP	Form	Size	Int.	Rec.	Sec	Cap	AA
4050	5	1024				3.50	ST412			53	26
4060	5	1024				3.50	ST412			80	26
4070	7	1024				3.50	ST412			74	26
4090	7	1024				5.25	ST412			111	26
5100	7	855				3.50	ESDI			124	26
6100	7	855				3.50	SCSI			110	26
7040	3	855				3.50	PC AT			47	26
7100	7	855				3.50	PC AT			110	26
HH-312	4	306	306	306							
HH-325	4	612	612	612		3.50	ST412			25	88
HH-330	4	612	612	612							
HH-612	4	306	306	306							
HH-725	4	612	612	612							
HH-825	4	612	612	612		5.25	ST412			25	73
HH-830	4	612	612	612		5.25	ST412			38	73
HH-1050	5	1024	1024	1024		5.25	ST412			51	36
HH-1060	5	1024	1024	1024		5.25	ST412			80	36
HH-1075	7	1024	1024	1024		5.25	ST412			75	36
HH-1090	7	1314	1314	1314		5.25	ST412			96	36
HH-1095	7	1024	1024	1024		5.25	ST412			112	36
HH-1120	7	1314	1314	1314		5.25	ST412			144	36
HH-2120 F	7	1024	1024	1024		5.25	ESDI			149	26
HH-2160 F	7	1276	1276	1276		5.25	ESDI			186	26
HH-3120 F	7	1314	1314	1314		5.25	SCSI			121	26
HH-3160 F	7	1314	1314	1314		5.25	SCSI			169	26

B

Miltope Business Products, Inc.
1770 Walt Whitman Rd.
Melville, NY 11747
(516) 756-7650

Model #	Hds	Cyls	RW	WP	Form	Size	Int.	Rec.	Sec	Cap	AA
RDS-1500	3	670				5.25	SCSI/NTDS			18	48
RDS-1720	8	1024				5.25	ESDI/NTDS			159	31
RDS-3100	15	1224				5.25	SCSI/NTDS			382	26
RDS-5000	5	1024				5.25	SCSI/NTDS			47	48

MiniScribe - Maxtor Colorado Corp.
1861 Left Hand Circle
Longmont, CO 80501
(800) 356-5333
(303) 651-6000

Model #	Hds	Cyls	RW	WP	Form	Size	Int.	Rec.	Sec	Cap	AA
1006	2	306	153	128	Full	5.25	ST412	MFM	17	5	
1012	4	306	153	128	Full	5.25	ST412	MFM	17	10	
2006	2	306	307	128	Full	5.25	ST412	MFM	17	5	93
2012	4	306	307	128	Full	5.25	ST412	MFM	17	10	85
3012	2	612			Half	5.25	ST412	MFM	19	10	
3053	5	1024	1025	512	Half	5.25	ST412	MFM	17	44	25
3085	7	1170	1171	512	Half	5.25	ST412	MFM	17	68	22
3130E	5	1250			Half	5.25	ESDI	RLL	36	112	17
3130S	5	1250			Half	5.25	SCSI	RLL		115	17
3180E	7	1250			Half	5.25	ESDI	RLL		150	17
3180S	7	1250			Half	5.25	SCSI	RLL		153	17
3212	2	612	613	128	Half	5.25	ST412	MFM	17	10	85
3412	4	306	307	128	Half	5.25	ST412	MFM	17	10	60
3425	4	615	616	128	Half	5.25	ST412	MFM	17	20	85
3425 PLUS	4	615	616	128	Half	5.25	ST412	MFM	17	20	53
3438	4	615	616		Half	5.25	ST412	2,7RLL	26	32	85
3438 PLUS	4	615	616		Half	5.25	ST412	2,7RLL	26	32	53
3650	6	809	810	128	Half	5.25	ST412	MFM	17	40	61
3650F	6	809	810	128	Half	5.25	ST412	MFM	17	40	61
3675	6	809	810	128	Half	5.25	ST412	2,7RLL	26	62	61

Model #	Hds	Cyls	RW	WP	Form	Size	Int.	Rec.	Sec	Cap	AA
4010	2	480	481	481	Full	5.25	ST412	MFM	17	8	
4020	4	480	481	128	Full	5.25	ST412	MFM	17	16	
5330	6	480	481	128			ST412				
5338	6	612	613	128			ST412				
5440	8	480	481	128			ST412				
5451	8	612	643	128			ST412				
6032	3	1024	1025	512	Full	5.25	ST412	MFM	17	26	28
6053	5	1024	1025	512	Full	5.25	ST412	MFM	17	44	28
6074	7	1024	1025	512			ST412				
6079	5	1024	1025	512	Full	5.25	ST412	2,7RLL	26	68	28
6085	8	1024	1025	512	Full	5.25	ST412	MFM	17	71	28
6128	8	1024	1025	512	Full	5.25	ST412	2,7RLL	26	109	28
6170E	8	1024	1025		Full	5.25	ESDI	2,7RLL	26	130	28
6212	8	612	613	128			ST412				
7040A	5	980			1-in	3.50	PC AT			40	19
7080A	10	980			1-in	3.50	PC AT			80	19
7426	4	612	613	128			ST412				
8051A	4	745			Half	3.50	PC AT	2,7RLL	28	40	28
8051S	4	793			Half	3.50	SCSI	2,7RLL	26	43	28
8212	2	615	616	128	Half	3.50	ST412	MFM	17	10	68
8225	2	771	772	128	Half	3.50	ST412	2,7RLL	26	20	68
8225AT	2	747			Half	3.50	PC AT	2,7RLL	26	20	40
8225S	2	804			Half	3.50	SCSI	2,7RLL	26	20	68
8225XT	2	805			Half	3.50	PC XT	2,7RLL	26	20	68
8412	4	306	307	128	Half	3.50	ST412	MFM	17	10	50
8425	4	615	616	128	Half	3.50	ST412	MFM	17	20	68
8425F	4	615	616	128	Half	3.50	ST412	MFM	17	20	40
8425S	4	615	616		Half	3.50	SCSI	MFM	17	20	68
8425XT	4	615	616		Half	3.50	PC XT	MFM	17	20	68
8434F	4	615	616	128			ST412				
8438	4	615	616	128	Half	3.50	ST412	2,7RLL	26	31	68
8438XT	4	615	616	128	Half	3.50	PC XT	2,7RLL	26	32	68
8450	4	771	772	128	Half	3.50	ST412	2,7RLL	26	39	45
8450AT	4	745			Half	3.50	PC AT	2,7RLL	26	41	40
8450XT	4	805			Half	3.50	PC XT	2,7RLL	26	41	68
9380E	15	1224	1225	512	Full	5.25	ESDI	3,9RLL	36	322	16
9780E	15	1661	1662	512	Full	5.25	ESDI	3,9RLL	36	645	17

B

Mitsubishi Electronics
991 Knox St.
Torrance, CA 90502
(213) 217-5732

Model #	Hds	Cyls	RW	WP	Form	Size	Int.	Rec.	Sec	Cap	AA
MR333	4	743				3.50	ST412			30	28
MR335	7	743				3.50	ST412			54	28
MR335R	7	743				3.50	ST412			81	28
MR521	2	612			Half	5.25	ST412				
MR522	4	612			Half	5.25	ST412				
MR535	5	977	300	300	Half	5.25	ST412	MFM		50	28
MR535	5	977	300	300	Half	5.25	ST412	RLL		76	28
MR535S	5	977			Half	5.25	SCSI			51	28
MR3310A	6	921				3.50	PC AT			93	31
MR3310S	6	921				3.50	SCSI			93	31
MR3314A	8	921				3.50	PC AT			124	31
MR3314S	8	921				3.59	SCSI			124	31
MR5310E	5	977			Half	5.25	ESDI			102	25
MR537S	5	977			Half	5.25	SCSI			76	28

Mitsumi Electronics Corp.
35 Pinelawn Rd.
Melville, NY 11747
(516) 752-7730

Model #	Hds	Cyls	RW	WP	Form	Size	Int.	Rec.	Sec	Cap	AA
HD309AA	6	928				3.50	PC AT			90	
HD309AC	6	928				3.50	SCSI			90	
HD313AA	8	963				3.50	PC AT			130	
HD313AC	8	963				3.50	SCSI			130	
HD320	4	612				3.50	ST412			25	
HD354VA	4	615				3.50	PC AT			40	
HD354VC	4	615				3.50	SCSI			40	

MMI
(no longer making drives)

Model #	Hds	Cyls	RW	WP	Form	Size	Int.	Rec.	Sec	Cap	AA
M 106	2	306		128		3.50	ST412				

Model #	Hds	Cyls	RW	WP	Form	Size	Int.	Rec.	Sec	Cap	AA
M 112	4	306		128		3.50	ST412				
M 125	8	306		128		3.50	ST412				
M 306	2	306		128		3.50	ST412				
M 212	4	306		128		5.25	ST412				
M 225	8	306		128		5.25	ST412				
M 312	4	306		128		5.25	ST412				
M 325	8	306		128		5.25	ST412				

Nippon Electric Corp. (NEC)
1414 Massachusetts Avenue
Boxborough, MA 01720
(508) 264-8000

B

Model #	Hds	Cyls	RW	WP	Form	Size	Int.	Rec.	Sec	Cap	AA
5124	4	310	310	310							
5126	4	612	612		Half	5.25	ST412				
5146	8	615	615		Half	5.25					
D3122	4	642				3.50	ST412			27	36
D3126	4	615	615	256		3.50	ST412			25	93
D3126H	4	615				3.50	ST412			25	43
D3142	8	642			Half	3.50	ST412	MFM	16	42	36
D3146H	8	615			Half	3.50	ST412	MFM	16	40	43
D3661	7	915			Half	3.50	ESDI	2,7RLL	36	118	20
D3735	2					3.50	PC AT			45	
D3741	8	440				3.50	PC AT			54	31
D3755	4					3.50	PC AT			104	
D3761	7	915			Half	3.50	PC AT	2,7RLL	35	115	20
D3821	4	440				3.50	SCSI			22	36
D3835	2					3.50	SCSI			45	
D3841	8	440				3.50	SCSI			45	36
D3855	4					3.50	SCSI			104	
D3861	7	915			Half	3.50	SCSI	2,7RLL	35	115	20
D5126H	4	615				5.25	ST412			25	48
D5127	4	615				5.25	ST412			38	93
D5127H	4	615				5.25	ST412			38	48
D5128	4	615				5.25	ST412			25	93
D5146H	8	615				5.25	ST412			51	48
D5147	8	615				5.25	ST412			77	48
D5452	10	823	823	128		5.25	ST412			86	31
D5652	10	823	823	823		5.25	ESDI			172	31

Model #	Hds	Cyls	RW	WP	Form	Size	Int.	Rec.	Sec	Cap	AA
D5655	7	1224			Half	5.25	ESDI	2,7RLL	35	179	26
D5662	15	1224				5.25	ESDI			385	26
D5682	15	1633			Full	5.25	ESDI	1,7RLL	53	665	16
D5882	15	1633			Full	5.25	SCSI	1,7RLL	53	665	16
D5852	10	823				5.25	SCSI			147	31
D5862	15	1221				5.25	SCSI			329	26
D5892	19	1678			Full	5.25	SCSI	1,7RLL	86	1.4	14

Newbury Data, Inc.
9800 North Lamar Blvd.
Austin, TX 78753

Model #	Hds	Cyls	RW	WP	Form	Size	Int.	Rec.	Sec	Cap	AA
PENNY 340	8	615	615	615							
XT-1065	7	918	918	918							
XT-1085	8	1024	1024	1024							
XT-1105	11	918	918	918							
XT-1140	15	918	918	918							
XT-2085	7	1224	1224	1224							
XT-2140	11	1224	1224	1224							
XT-2190	15	1224	1224	1224							
NDR4175	7	1224					ESDI				
NDR4380	15	1224					ESDI				
NDR3170S	9	1224					SCSI				
NDR3280S	15	1224					SCSI				
NDR4380S	15	1224					SCSI				
NDR4175	7	1224					ESDI				
NDR4380	15	1224					ESDI				
NDR3170S	9	1224					SCSI				
NDR3280S	15	1224					SCSI				
NDR4380S	15	1224					SCSI				

Okidata
532 Fellowship Rd.
Mount Laurel, NJ 08054
(609) 235-2600
(800) 654-3282

Model #	Hds	Cyls	RW	WP	Form	Size	Int.	Rec.	Sec	Cap	AA
OD526	4	612	613	613			ST412				

Model #	Hds	Cyls	RW	WP	Form	Size	Int.	Rec.	Sec	Cap	AA
OD540	6	612	613	613			ST412				

Olivetti
765 U.S. Highway 202
Somerville, NJ 08876
(201) 526-8200
See Conner Peripherals, Inc.

Model #	Hds	Cyls	RW	WP	Form	Size	Int.	Rec.	Sec	Cap	AA
HD662/11	2	612					ST412				
HD662/12	4	612					ST412				

Otari
(no longer makes drives)

Model #	Hds	Cyls	RW	WP	Form	Size	Int.	Rec.	Sec	Cap	AA
C 214	4	306	128	128			ST412				
C 519	6	306	128	128			ST412				
C 526	8	306	128	128			ST412				

Panasonic
Two Panasonic Way
Secaucus, NJ 07094
(201) 348-7000

Model #	Hds	Cyls	RW	WP	Form	Size	Int.	Rec.	Sec	Cap	AA
JU-116	4	615	616	616		3.50	ST412				
JU-128	7	733	734	734		3.50	ST412				

Plus Development
1778 McCarthy Blvd.
Milpitas, CA 95035
(408) 434-6900

Model #	Hds	Cyls	RW	WP	Form	Size	Int.	Rec.	Sec	Cap	AA
Hardcard 20	4	615				3.50	IBM PC			21	57
Hardcard 40	4	612				3.50	IBM PC			42	50
Plus Passport	2	612				3.50	IBM PC				50
Plus Passport	4	612				3.50	IBM PC				50

B

PraireTek
1830 Left Hand Circle
Longmont, CO 80501
(303) 772-4011

Model #	Hds	Cyls	RW	WP	Form	Size	Int.	Rec.	Sec	Cap	AA
120	2	615				2.5	PC AT/XT			21	32
220	4	612				2.5	SCSI/PC AT			20	36
240	4	615				2.5	PC AT/XT			43	37

Priam Systems Corp.
1140 Ringwood Court
San Jose, CA 95131
(408) 954-8680

Model #	Hds	Cyls	RW	WP	Form	Size	Int.	Rec.	Sec	Cap	AA
3804	4	771				3.50	PC AT			42	48
519	15	1224				5.25	ST412			191	30
617	7	1225				5.25	ESDI			178	26
628	11	1225				5.25	ESDI			280	26
638	15	1225				5.25	ESDI			382	26
717	7	1225				5.25	SCSI			163	26
728	11	1225				5.25	SCSI			258	26
738	15	1225				5.25	SCSI			353	26
45-AT-D2	5	1017							17	44	
50-AT-D2	5	1158							17	50	
40-PC-W1	5	980							17	42	
40-PC-X2	5	980							17	42	
45H	5	1014							17	44	
62-AT-D2	7	1017							17	70	
70-AT-D2	7	1158							17	70	
60-DP-D1	7	980							17	60	
60-PC-W1	7	980							17	60	
60-PC-X2	7	980							17	60	
130-AT-D2	15	1017							17	133	
160-AT-D2	15	1217							17	159	
75-Rx	5	1165					RLL		25	74	
100-Rx	7	1166					RLL		25	103	

Model #	Hds	Cyls	RW	WP	Form	Size	Int.	Rec.	Sec	Cap	AA
230-Rx	15	1223					RLL		25	234	
120-Ex	7	1023					ESDI		33	120	
150-Ex	7	1275					ESDI		35	159	
160-Ex	7	1224					ESDI		36	157	
250-Ex	11	1224					ESDI		36	247	
330-Ex	15	1224					ESDI		36	337	
160-Sx	7	1224					SCSI		36	156	
250-Sx	11	1224					SCSI		36	246	
330-Sx	15	1224					SCSI		36	336	

Prologica
Brazil

B

Model #	Hds	Cyls	RW	WP	Form	Size	Int.	Rec.	Sec	Cap	AA
W320B	4	612				3.50	ST412			25	56

PTI
(714) 549-0527

Model #	Hds	Cyls	RW	WP	Form	Size	Int.	Rec.	Sec	Cap	AA
PT-238A	4	615				3.50	ST412				
PT-251A	4	820				3.50	ST412				
PT-357A	6	615				3.50	ST412				
PT-376A	6	820				3.50	ST412				
PT-225	4	615				3.50	ST412				
PT-234	4	820				3.50	ST412				
PT-338	6	615				3.50	ST412				
PT-351	6	820				3.50	ST412				
PT-238R	4	615				3.50	ST412				
PT-251R	4	820				3.50	ST412				
PT-257R	6	615				3.50	ST412				
PT-376R	6	820				3.50	ST412				
PT-4102R	8	820				3.50	ST412				
PT-238S	4	615				3.50	SCSI				
PT-251S	4	820				3.50	SCSI				
PT-357S	6	615				3.50	SCSI				
PT-376S	6	820				3.50	SCSI				

Quantum Corp.
1804 McCarthy Blvd.
Milpitas, CA 95035
(408) 432-1100

Model #	Hds	Cyls	RW	WP	Form	Size	Int.	Rec.	Sec	Cap	AA
105AT	4	1219				3.50	PC AT			105	25
105S	4	1219				3.50	SCSI			105	25
120AT	5	1123				3.50	PC AT			120	23
120S	5	1123				3.50	SCSI/SCSI-2			120	23
170AT	7	1123				3.50	PC AT			168	23
170S	7	1123				3.50	SCSI/SCSI-2			168	23
210AT	7	1156				3.50	PC AT			210	23
210S	7	1156				3.50	SCSI/SCSI-2			210	23
330S	7	1512				3.50	SCSI			331	22
331.2AT	7	1511				3.50	PC AT			331	22
40AT	3	834				3.50	PC AT			42	27
40S	3	834				3.50	SCSI			42	27
425.8AT	9	1511				3.50	PC AT			426	22
425S	9	1512				3.50	SCSI			426	22
52AT	2	1219				3.50	PC AT			52	25
52S	2	1219				3.50	SCSI			52	25
80AT	6	834				3.50	PC AT			84	27
80S	6	834				3.50	SCSI			84	27
Q250	4	815				5.25	SCSI			53	34
Q280	6	815				5.25	SCSI			80	34
Q520	4	512	256	256	Full	5.25	ST412				
Q530	6	512	256	256	Full	5.25	ST412				
Q540	8	512	256	256	Full	5.25	ST412				

Ricoh Corp.
5 Dedrick Place
West Caldwell, NJ 07006
(201) 882-2000

Model #	Hds	Cyls	RW	WP	Form	Size	Int.	Rec.	Sec	Cap	AA
RH5130	2	612	613	400		5.25	ST412				106
RH5260	2	1224				5.25	ST506 REMOV.				106

Model #	Hds	Cyls	RW	WP	Form	Size	Int.	Rec.	Sec	Cap	AA
RH5261	2	612				5.25	ST412 REMOV.				
RH5500	2	1285				5.25	SCSI				34

Rodime, Inc.
851 Broken Sound Parkway N.W.
Boca Raton, FL 33487
(407) 994-5585

Model #	Hds	Cyls	RW	WP	Form	Size	Int.	Rec.	Sec	Cap	AA
20 Plus	4	306				3.50	SCSI			21	96
45 Plus	5	680				3.50	SCSI			45	36
60 Plus	7	680				3.50	SCSI			70	36
100 Plus	7	1053				3.50	SCSI			105	32
140 Plus	7	1219				5.25	SCSI			144	32
Cobra 45e	3	868				3.50	SCSI			54	26
Cobra 70e	5	868				3.50	SCSI			90	26
Cobra 100e	7	868				3.50	SCSI			126	26
Cobra 210e	9	1200				3.50	SCSI			250	26
RO102	4	192	96								
RO103	6	192	96								
RO104	8	192	96								
RO201	2	320	132		Full	5.25	ST412				
RO202	4	320	132		Full	5.25	ST412				
RO203	6	320	132		Full	5.25	ST412				
RO204	8	320	132		Full	5.25	ST412				
RO201E	2	640	132		Full	5.25	ST412				
RO202E	4	640	640		Full	5.25	ST412				
RO203E	6	640	640		Full	5.25	ST412				
RO204E	8	640	640		Full	5.25	ST412				
RO252	4	306	80	80	Half	3.50	ST412				
RO351	2	306	80	80	Half	3.50	ST412				
RO352	4	306	80	80	Half	3.50	ST412				
RO652B	4	306				3.50	SCSI			21	96
RO3045	5	872	650			3.50	ST412			45	36
RO3055	6	872	650			3.50	ST412			54	36
RO3057S	5	680					ST412				
RO3065	7	872	650			3.50	ST412			63	36
RO3085S	7	750	751	751			ST412				
RO3259A	9	1235				3.50	PC AT	2,7RLL		213	18

B

Model #	Hds	Cyls	RW	WP	Form	Size	Int.	Rec.	Sec	Cap	AA
RO5090	7	1224	1224			5.25	ST412			89	36
RO5125S	5	1219					ST412				
RO5130R	7	1224	1224			5.25	ST412			134	36
RO5180E	7	1219				5.25	ESDI			178	30
RO5180S	7	1219					ST412				

RMS (Rotating Memory Service)
473 Sapena Court #26
Santa Clara, CA 95954

Model #	Hds	Cyls	RW	WP	Form	Size	Int.	Rec.	Sec	Cap	AA
RMS506	4	153	77	77							
RMS512	8	153	77	77							

Sagem
France

Model #	Hds	Cyls	RW	WP	Form	Size	Int.	Rec.	Sec	Cap	AA
MSA 252-50	4	720				5.25	SCSI			66	25
MSA 252-100	8	720				5.25	SCSI			132	25
MSA 252-200	16	720				5.25	SCSI			265	25

Samsung Electronics
3655 North First St.
San Jose, CA 95134-1708
(408) 434-5400

Model #	Hds	Cyls	RW	WP	Form	Size	Int.	Rec.	Sec	Cap	AA
SHD2040N	4	820				3.50	ST412			51	43
SHD2041B	4	820				3.50	PC AT			47	37

Seagate Technologies
920 Disc Dr.
Scotts Valley, CA 95066-4544
(800) 468-3472
(408) 438-6550

Model #	Hds	Cyls	RW	WP	Form	Size	Int.	Rec.	Sec	Cap	AA
ST125A	4	404					ST412 ESDI				
ST125A-1	4	404					ST412 ESDI				

Model #	Hds	Cyls	RW	WP	Form	Size	Int.	Rec.	Sec	Cap	AA
ST138A	4	604					ST412 ESDI				
ST138A-1	4	604					ST412 ESDI				
ST157A	6	539					ST412 ESDI				
ST157A-1	6	539					ST412 ESDI				
ST125	4	615	616	616			ST412				
ST125-1	4	615	616	616			ST412				
ST138	6	615	616	616			ST412				
ST138-1	6	615	616	616			ST412				
ST151	5	977	978	978			ST412				
ST206	2	306	307	128			ST412				
ST212	4	306	307	128			ST412				
ST213	2	615	613	307			ST412				
ST225	4	615	616	616			ST412				
ST251	6	820	821	821			ST412				
ST251-1	6	820	821	821			ST412				
ST406	2	306	307	307			ST412				
ST412	4	306	307	307			ST412				
ST419	6	306	307	128			ST412				
ST425	8	306	307	128			ST412				
ST506	4	153	128	128			ST412				
ST706	2	306	307	128			ST412				
ST4026	4	615	616	307			ST412				
ST4038	5	733	734	367			ST412				
ST4051	5	977	978	498			ST412				
ST4053	5	1024	1023	1023			ST412				
ST4096	9	1024	1023	1023			ST412				
ST138R	4	615	616	616			ST412				
ST138R-1	4	615	616	616			ST412				
ST157R	6	615	616	616			ST412				
ST157R-1	6	615	616	616			ST412				
ST225R	2	667	668	668			EST412				
ST238R	4	615	616	616			ST412				
ST250R	4	667	668	668			EST412				
ST251R	4	820	821	821			ST412				
ST277R	6	820	821	821			ST412				
ST4077R	5	1024	1025	1025			ST412				
ST4144R	9	1024	1025	1025			ST412				
ST4129E	8	1147	1148	1148			EST412 ESDI				
ST125N	4	407	408	408			ST412 SCSI				
ST125N-1	4	407	408	408			ST412 SCSI				

B

Model #	Hds	Cyls	RW	WP	Form	Size	Int.	Rec.	Sec	Cap	AA
ST138N	4	613	614	614			EST412 SCSI				
ST138N-1	4	613	614	614			EST412 SCSI				
ST157N	6	613	614	614			ST412 SCSI				
ST157N-1	6	613	614	614			ST412 SCSI				
ST177N	5	921	922	922			ST412 SCSI				
ST225N	4	615	616	616			ST412 SCSI				
ST25IN	4	820	821	821			ST412 SCSI				
ST251N-1	4	630	631	631			EST412 SCSI				
ST277N	6	820	821	821			ST412 SCSI				
ST277N-1	6	628	629	629			EST412 SCSI				
ST296N	6	820	821	821			EST412 SCSI				
ST1096N	7	906	907	907			ST412 SCSI				
ST4077N	5	1024	1025	1025			ST412 SCSI				
ST4192N	8	1147	1148	1148			EST412 SCSI				

Shugart Corp.
9292 Jeronimo
Irvine, CA 92718
(714) 770-1100

Model #	Hds	Cyls	RW	WP	Form	Size	Int.	Rec.	Sec	Cap	AA
SA604	4	160	128	128			ST412				
SA606	6	160	128	128			ST412				
SA612	4	360	128	128	Full	5.25	ST412				
SA706	2	320	321	128			ST412				
SA712	4	320	128	128	Half	5.25	ST412				

Siemens Information Systems, Inc.
5500 Broken Sound Blvd.
Boca Raton, FL 33487
(407) 994-8800

Model #	Hds	Cyls	RW	WP	Form	Size	Int.	Rec.	Sec	Cap	AA
1200	8	1216				5.25	ESDI				
1300	12	1216				5.25	ESDI			310	33
2200	8	1216				5.25	ESDI				
2300	12	1216				5.25	SCSI			261	33
4410	11	1100				5.25	ESDI			382	24
4420	11	1100				5.25	SCSI			322	24

Sony

655 River Oaks Parkway
San Jose, CA 95134
Cherry Hill, NJ
(407) 998-5151

Model #	Hds	Cyls	RW	WP	Form	Size	Int.	Rec.	Sec	Cap	AA
SRD2040Z	4	624				3.50	SCSI			42	29

Syquest Technology

47071 Bayside Parkway
Fremont, CA 94538
(415) 226-4000

Model #	Hds	Cyls	RW	WP	Form	Size	Int.	Rec.	Sec	Cap	AA
SQ306RD	2	306	306	306							
SQ312RD	2	615	615	615			ST412				93
SQ319	2	615					IBM PC				93
SQ325F	4	612	612	612							
SQ338F	6	612	612	612							
SQ355/A/S	2	1257				3.50	PC AT/SCSI				27
SQ555	2	1275				5.25	SCSI/SCSI-2			44	29
SQ3100/A/S	2	1609				3.50	PC AT/SCSI				
SQ5200	4	1747				5.25	SCSI/SCSI-2				27
SQ5400	8	1747				5.25	SCSI/SCSI-2				27

Tandon Corp.

405 Science Dr.
Moorpark, CA 93021
(805) 523-0340
See Western Digital

Model #	Hds	Cyls	RW	WP	Form	Size	Int.	Rec.	Sec	Cap	AA
TM252	4	306	306	306	Half	5.25	ST412				
TM262	4	615	615	615	Half	3.50	ST412				
TM270	8	1024			Full	5.25	SCSI				
TM362	4	615	615	615	Half	3.50	ST412				
TM362R	2	782			Half	3.50	ST412				
TM364	4	782			Half	3.50	ST412				
TM501	2	306	128	153	Full	5.25	ST412				
TM502	4	306	128	153	Full	5.25	ST412				

Model #	Hds	Cyls	RW	WP	Form	Size	Int.	Rec.	Sec	Cap	AA
TM503	6	306	128	153	Full	5.25	ST412				
TM602S	4	153	128	153							
TM603S	6	153	128	153							
TM603SE	6	230	128	128							
TM702AT	4	615	615	615	Full	5.25	ST412				
TM703	5	695	695	695	Full	5.25	ST412				
TM703AT	5	733	733	733	Full	5.25	ST412				
TM705	5	962	962	962							
TM755	5	981	981	981							
TM2085	8	1024			Full	5.25	SCSI				
TM2128	8	1024			Full	5.25	SCSI				
TM3085	8	1024			Full	5.25	SCSI				

Teac America, Inc.
7733 Telegraph Rd.
Montebello, CA 90640
(213) 726-0303

Model #	Hds	Cyls	RW	WP	Form	Size	Int.	Rec.	Sec	Cap	AA
SD-340	2	1050				3.50	SCSI-2			43	35
SD-380	4	1050				3.50	SCSI-2			86	32
SD-510	4	306	128	128			ST412				
SD-520	4	615	128	128			ST412				
SD-521	4	615				5.25	ST412			25	48
SD-540	8	615				5.25	ST412			51	48

Texas Instruments
13500 N. Central Expressway
Dallas, TX 75265
(800) 232-3200
(619) 278-9600

Model #	Hds	Cyls	RW	WP	Form	Size	Int.	Rec.	Sec	Cap	AA
ST-506	4	153	64	64			ST412				

Tokico
(Sold only in Japan)

Model #	Hds	Cyls	RW	WP	Form	Size	Int.	Rec.	Sec	Cap	AA
TD3041C	3	928				3.50	SCSI			40	28

Model #	Hds	Cyls	RW	WP	Form	Size	Int.	Rec.	Sec	Cap	AA
TD3081C	5	928				3.50	SCSI			80	28
TD3091A	5	928				3.50	PC AT			90	29
TD3091C	5	963				3.50	SCSI			90	29
TD3135A	7	964				3.50	PC AT			130	29
TD3135C	7	963				3.50	SCSI			130	29

Toshiba
9740 Irvine Blvd.
Irvine, CA 92718
(714) 583-3000
East coast: (617) 431-1811
West coast: (714) 587-6326
Tech. support (714) 455-0407

Model #	Hds	Cyls	RW	WP	Form	Size	Int.	Rec.	Sec	Cap	AA
MK-53FA/B	5	830	830	512		5.25	ST412				
MK-54FA/B	7	830	830	512		5.25	ST412				
MK-56FA/B	10	830	830	512		5.25	ST412			86	33
MK-132FA	3	733				3.50	ST412			22	33
MK-133FA	5	733				3.50	ST412			38	33
MK-134FA	7	733				3.50	ST412			53	33
MK-156FA	10	830				5.25	ESDI			172	31
MK-156FB	10	830				5.25	SCSI			147	33
MK-232FB	3	845				3.50	SCSI			45	33
MK-233FB	5	845				3.50	SCSI			75	33
MK-234FB	7	845				3.50	PC AT/SCSI			106	33
MK-256FA	10	1223				5.25	ESDI			382	26
MK-256FB	10	1223				5.25	SCSI			316	26
MK-355FA	9	1661				5.25	ESDI			459	24
MK-355FB	9	1661				5.25	SCSI/SCSI-2			405	24

Tulin Corp.
2156-H O'Toole Ave.
San Jose, CA 95131
(408) 432-9025

Model #	Hds	Cyls	RW	WP	Form	Size	Int.	Rec.	Sec	Cap	AA
TL226	4	640	640	640	Half	5.25	ST412				
TL326	4	640	640	640							

Model #	Hds	Cyls	RW	WP	Form	Size	Int.	Rec.	Sec	Cap	AA
TL240	6	640	640	640	Half	5.25	ST412				
TL340	6	640	640	640							

Western Digital
15345 Barranca
Irvine, CA 92718
(800) 832-4778

Model #	Hds	Cyls	RW	WP	Form	Size	Int.	Rec.	Sec	Cap	AA
WD20ifc	2	782				3.50	IBM PC			21	70
WD30ifc	4	782				3.50	IBM PC			32	60
WD40ifc	4	782				3.50	IBM PC			43	70
WD93024-X	2	782				3.50	IBM PC			21	37
WD93028-X	2	782	784	784		3.50	IBM PC			21	70
WD93034-X	4	782				3.50	PC XT			32	37
WD93038-X	4	782	784	784		3.50	IBM PC			32	60
WD93044-X	4	782				3.50	PC XT			43	37
WD93048-X	4	782	784	784		3.50	IBM PC			43	70
WD95028-X	2	782	784	784		5.25	ST412				
WD95038-X	3	782	784	784		5.25	ST412				
WD95048-X	4	782	784	784		5.25	ST412				
WD93024-A	2	782				3.50	PC AT			21	28
WD93028-A	2	782				3.50	PC AT			21	70
WD93044-A	4	782				3.50	PC AT			43	28
WD93048-A	4	782				3.50	PC AT			43	70
WD95028-A	2	782				5.25	ST412				
WD95048-A	4	782				5.25	ST412				
WD262	4	615	616	616			ST412				
WD344R	4	782	783	783		3.50	ST412				
WD362	4	615	616	616			ST412				
WD382R	2	782	783	783		3.50	ST412				
WD383R	4	615	616	616		3.50	ST412				
WD384R	4	782	783	783		3.50	ST412				
WD544R	4	782	783	783		3.50	ST412				
WD582R	2	782	783	783		3.50	ST412				
WD583R	4	782	783	783		3.50	ST412				
WD584R	4	782	783	783		3.50	ST412				
WDAC140	2	1079				3.50	PC AT			42	27
WDAC140L	2	1079				3.50	PC AT			42	31
WDAC240	4	820				3.50	PC AT			42	33

Model #	Hds	Cyls	RW	WP	Form	Size	Int.	Rec.	Sec	Cap	AA
WDAC280	4	1079				3.50	PC AT			85	27
WDSC8320	14	949				3.50	SCSI-2			371	19

IO Address Assignments

At the end of this section is a chart of the I/O addresses available in IBM PCs and compatibles. The first two hexidecimal digits of a three-digit address are listed in the left column. The final digit (which replaces the x in each case) is listed across the top. The range of addresses shown is from 000 hex to 3FF hex. This is a *typical chart* — but should not be interpreted as the only way things can be. Consult your computer or motherboard documentation to determine the I/O address assignments for your particular machine.

You can also use this as a "fill-in-the-blank" chart to list the addresses used by your computer and any new addresses added when you install adapter cards. This chart attempts to show the different uses for some addresses based on PC/XT or AT buses, but, again, the best guide for addresses is your computer documentation.

	0 1 2 3 4 5 6 7	8 9 A B C D E F
00x	DMA #1, 8237	DMA #1 (continued)
01x	DMA #1 (continued)	DMA #1 (continued)
02x	Interrupt Controller #1	Interrupt Controller #1
03x	Interrupt Controller #1	8259A is controller
04x	040-043 8253 Timer	
05x		
06x	060-063 8255 PPI (XT)	060-064 8742 Keyboard Controller (AT)
07x	070-071 CMOS RAM	and NMI Mask Reg (AT)
08x	DMA Page Registers	DMA Page registers
09x		
0Ax	NMI Mask Register (XT)	NMI Mask Register (XT)
or 0Ax	Interrupt Controller #2	Interrupt Controller #2
0Bx	Interrupt Controller #2	8259A is controller
0Cx	8237 DMA #2 (AT)	8237 DMA #2 continued
0Dx	8237 DMA #2 continued	8237 DMA #2 continued
0Ex		
0Fx	80287 Numeric	Coprocessor (AT)

B

10x		
11x		
12x		
13x		
14x		
15x		
16x		
17x		
18x		
19x		
1Ax		
1Bx		
1Cx		
1Dx		
1Ex		
1Fx	Hard Disk (AT)	Hard Disk (AT)
20x	Game I/O - Joystick	Game I/O - Joystick
21x	Expansion unit (XT)	Expansion unit (XT)
22x		
23x		238-23B Bus mouse 23C-23F Alt bus mouse
24x		
25x		
26x		
27x		Printer #2 - LPT2
28x		
29x		
2Ax		
2Bx		
2Cx		
2Dx		
2Ex	GPIB (AT)	
2Fx		Serial port #2 - COM2
30x	Prototype card	Prototype card
31x	Prototype card	Prototype card
32x	Hard disk (XT)	Hard disk (XT)
33x		
34x		
35x		
36x	Reserved	Reserved
37x		Printer #1 - LPT1

38x	SDLC · Bisynch 2	SDLC · Bisynch 2
39x		
3Ax	SDLC · Bisynch 1	SDLC · Bisynch 1
3Bx	Monochrome Graphics	and Printer Adapter
3Cx	EGA	EGA
3Dx	CGA	CGA
3Ex		
3Fx	Floppy disk	Serial port #1 · COM1

Hardware Interrupts and Assignments

B

I/O address conflicts and hardware interrupt conflicts are the most likely causes of a malfunctioning computer, especially if they occur right after the installation of a new adapter card. There are eight numbered interrupt lines in the PC/XT and sixteen in the AT. The AT uses two 8259 programmable interrupt controllers; eight interrupts are available from the primary controller; eight more are controlled by the second controller and cascaded through interrupt 2 of the primary controller. Adapter cards will normally have selections of 2 through 7 although some newer cards may let you select from the 8 through 15 range.

The following is a list of the possible interrupts available in your PC.

Interrupt	Description
NMI	Non-Maskable Interrupt—This is a signal line connected directly to the CPU that is triggered in the event of a memory parity error. If a parity error occurs your computer will stop, usually with a parity error message. There is software available to "trap" the error but parity errors are so rare that it's hardly worth the trouble.
IRQ 0	This is your computer timer or clock interrupt. It is not available for general use.
IRQ 1	Keyboard interrupt. Not available.
IRQ 2	Reserved on XT, Int 2 and 8-15 on the AT
IRQ 3	COM2 or SDLC Bisynchronous 2
IRQ 4	COM1 or SDLC Bisynchronous 1

Interrupt	Description
IRQ 5	Hard disk on the XT, LPT2 on AT
IRQ 6	Floppy disk
IRQ 7	LPT1

The following are AT-only interrupts. They are cascaded through the primary interrupt controller on interrupt line 2 so you will still only find IRQ 2 through 7 on the PC/XT/AT bus.

Interrupt	Description
IRQ 8	Real-time clock interrupt
IRQ 9	Redirected to IRQ 2
IRQ 10	Available
IRQ 11	Available
IRQ 12	Available
IRQ 13	80287/80387 math coprocessor
IRQ 14	Hard disk interrupt
IRQ 15	Available

DMA (Direct Memory Access) Channels and Use

There are several direct memory access channels in your computer. The concept of DMA (Direct Memory Access) is simple. If each byte read from a floppy disk must pass through the CPU and then on to memory, a lot of computer time is going to be required. On the other hand, if you tell other hardware how much information you want from the disk and where you want it stored, you can bypass the CPU and send the information directly to memory—direct memory access.

The XT provides four such channels numbered 0 through 3. The AT adds channels 4 through 7. Here is the list.

Channel	Use
0	Memory Refresh
1	SDLC Bisynchronous communication
2	Floppy disk

Channel	Use
3	Available

AT only

4	Available
5	Available
6	Available
7	Available

Displays

B

Monitor	Size	1	2	3	4	5	List	Phone
Acer 7015	13"	X	X	X			$560	(408) 922-0333
Amdek 632	14"	X	X				$595	(800) PC-AMDEK
Amdek 732	12"	X	X				$625	(408) 435-2770
Amdek SmartScan 735	14"	X	X	X			$745	
Amdek SmartScan 738	14"	X	X	X	X		$835	
Casper 5156H	14"	X	X	X	X	X	$680	(415) 770-8500
Casper TM-5157	14"	X	X	X	X		$720	
Casper CDS 1984	19"	X	X	X			$2,495	
Cordata CMC-141M	14"	X	X	X			$599	(213) 603-2901
Dell GPD 16C	16"	X	X	X	X	X	$1,199	(512) 338-4400
Dell GPD 19C	19"	X	X	X	X	X	$2,499	
Electrohome ECM 1310U	14"	X	X	X			$1,259	(519) 744-7111
Goldstar 1450 Plus VGA	14"	X	X	X			$699	(408) 432-1331
Goldstar 1460 3A Plus VGA	14"	X	X	X	X		$799	
Goldstar 1610VGA	16"	X	X	X			$2,995	
Hitachi HM-4317	16"	X	X	X	X	X		(201) 825-8000
Hitachi HM-4319	19"	X	X	X	X	X		
Hitachi Accuvue 20-AS	20"	X	X	X	X	X	$3,535	
Idek MultiFlat MF-5015	15"	X	X	X	X		$1,045	(314) 364-7500
JVC GD-H6116VFW	16"	X	X	X		X	$2,495	(201) 794-3900
JVC GD-H6120VFW	20"	X	X	X		X	$3,995	
Metrics PMV14VC Plus	14"	X	X	X	X		$635	(714) 660-8899
Microvitec 1019/SP	19"	X	X	X	X		$2,395	(404) 991-2246
Mitsuba 710VH	14"	X	X	X	X		$495	(714) 392-2000
Mitsubishi Diamond Scan 14	14"	X	X	X			$889	(213) 515-3993
Mitsubishi FA3415ATK	14"	X	X	X	X		$1,015	

Mitsubishi Diamond Scan 16L	16"	X	X	X	X		$1,945	
Mitsubishi Diamond Scan 20C	20"	X	X	X	X		$2,670	
Mitsubishi Diamond Scan 20L	20"	X	X	X	X	X	$3,480	
Mitsubishi HL-6915SBK	20"	X	X	X	X	X	$3,790	
Monitronix MX-210EZ	19"	X	X	X	X	X	$3,795	
Nanao 8060S	14"	X	X	X			$899	(213) 325-5202
Nanao 9060S	14"	X	X	X	X		$1,069	
Nanao 9070U	16"	X	X	X	X	X	$1,779	
Nanao 9400	20"	X	X	X	X	X	$3,799	
Nanao 9500	20"	X	X	X	X		$3,999	
NEC MultiSync	14"	X	X	X				(708) 860-9500
NEC MultiSync II	14"	X	X	X				
NEC MultiSync 2A	14"	X	X	X			$799	
NEC MultiSync 3D	14"	X	X	X	X		$1,049	
NEC MultiSync 4D	16"	X	X	X	X	X	$1,699	
NEC MultiSync XL	19"	X	X	X	X	X		
NEC MultiSync 5D	20"	X	X	X	X	X	$3,699	
Panasonic PanaSync C1391	14"	X	X	X	X		$899	(201) 348-7000
Pixelink MultiFlat Plus 5115	15"	X	X	X	X	X	$1,395	(508) 562-4803
Pixelink MultiFlat Plus 5121	19"	X	X	X	X	X	$3,295	
Princeton UltraSync	12"	X	X	X			$849	(800) 221-1490
Princeton Ultra 14	14"	X	X	X			$899	
Princeton Ultra II	14"	X	X	X	X	X	$1,295	
Princeton Ultra 16	16"	X	X	X	X		$1,375	
Relisys RE-5155	14"	X	X	X			$799	(408) 945-9000
Relisys RE 1520	13"	X	X	X	X	X	$1,099	
Sampo AlphaScan	14"	X	X	X			$789	(404) 449-
6220Sampo TriSync	20"	X	X	X	X		$1,995	
Samsung VGA-Graphic Master	14"	X	X				$699	(800) 446-0262
Samsung SyncMaster	14"	X	X	X			$799	
Samsung SyncMaster 2	14"	X	X	X	X		$729	
Samsung SyncMaster 3	14"	X	X	X	X		$799	
Samsung SyncMaster 4	17"	X	X	X	X	X	$1,499	
Seiko CM 1440	14"	X	X	X	X		$899	(408) 922-5900
Seiko CM 1450	14"	X	X	X	X	X	$1,099	
Sony CPD-1302	14"	X	X	X	X		$995	(201) 930-1000
Sony MultiScan HG	14"	X	X	X	X	X	$1,095	
Tatung CM-1496X	14"	X	X	X	X		$749	(213) 979-7055
Tatung CM-1595G	15"	X	X	X	X		$1,199	
TVM SuperSync 3A	14"	X	X	X	X		$795	(714) 985-4788
Zenith ZMM-1490	15"	X	X				$995	(708) 808-5000

1 - 512 by 480, 16.7 million colors
2 - 640 by 480, 32,768 colors
3 - 800 by 600, 256 colors
4 - 1024 by 768 interlaced
5 - 1024 by 768 non-interlaced

Display Modes

Mode #	Type	Adapter	Resolution	Box	Char	Colors
00	Text	CGA	320 x 200	8 x 8	40 x 25	16
		EGA	320 x 350	8 x 14	40 x 25	16
		MCGA	320 x 400	8 x 16	40 x 25	16
		VGA	360 x 400	9 x 16	40 x 25	16
01	Text	CGA	320 x 200	8 x 8	40 x 25	16
		EGA	320 x 350	8 x 14	40 x 25	16
		MCGA	320 x 400	8 x 16	40 x 25	16
		VGA	360 x 400	9 x 16	40 x 25	16
02	Text	CGA	640 x 200	8 x 8	80 x 25	16
		EGA	640 x 350	8 x 14	80 x 25	16
		MCGA	640 x 400	8 x 16	80 x 25	16
		VGA	720 x 400	9 x 16	80 x 25	16
03	Text	CGA	640 x 200	8 x 8	80 x 25	16
		EGA	640 x 350	8 x 14	80 x 25	16
		MCGA	640 x 400	8 x 16	80 x 25	16
		VGA	720 x 400	9 x 16	80 x 25	16
04	Graph	CGA/EGA/VGA/MCGA	320 x 200	8 x 8	40 x 25	4
05	Graph	CGA/EGA/VGA/MCGA	320 x 200	8 x 8	40 x 25	4
06	Graph	CGA/EGA/VGA/MCGA	640 x 200	8 x 8	80 x 25	2
07	Text	MDA/EGA	720 x 350	9 x 14	80 x 25	Mono
		VGA	720 x 400	9 x 16	80 x 25	Mono
08	Graph	PCjr	160 x 200	8 x 8	20 x 25	16
09	Graph	PCjr	320 x 200	8 x 8	40 x 25	16
0A	Graph	PCjr	640 x 200	8 x 8	80 x 25	4
0B	***	***	Reserved	***	***	***
0C	***	***	Reserved	***	***	***
0D	Graph	EGA/VGA	320 x 200	8 x 8	40 x 25	16
0E	Graph	EGA/VGA	640 x 200	8 x 8	80 x 25	16

0F	Graph	EGA/VGA	640 x 350	8 x 14	80 x 25	Mono
10	Graph	EGA/VGA	640 x 350	8 x 14	80 x 25	16
11	Graph	MCGA/VGA	640 x 480	8 x 16	80 x 30	2
12	Graph	VGA	640 x 480	8 x 16	80 x 30	16
13	Graph	MCGA/VGA	320 x 200	8 x 8	40 x 25	256
22	Text	8514/A	1188 x 352	9 x 8	132 x 44	16
23	Text	8514/A	1188 x 350	9 x 14	132 x 25	16
24	Text	8514/A	1188 x 364	9 x 13	132 x 28	16
25	Graph	VGA	640 x 480	8 x 16	80 x 30	16
26	Text	VGA	640 x 480	8 x 8	80 x 60	16
29	Graph	SVGA	800 x 600			16
2A	Text	SVGA	800 x 600	8 x 15	100 x 40	16
2D	Graph	VGA	640 x 350			256
2E	Graph	VGA	640 x 480			256
2F	Graph	VGA	640 x 480			256
30	Graph	SVGA	800 x 600			256
37	Graph	8514/A	1024 x 768			16
38	Graph	8514/A	1024 x 768			256

C

Connector Reference

The illustrations and charts in this appendix are all drawn from the same perspective. The connectors are shown as if you were looking at the connector while standing behind your PC. On male connectors, the pins will be sticking out towards you. Female connectors will look like a row of small holes.

The charts accompanying the illustrations give the purpose of each pin of each connector. They also specify whether each individual pin is an output from the computer to the outside world, or an input. Some pins are not used at all, in which case they will be labeled "N/C" for not connected.

Serial Communications Adapter Connector

Perhaps the most commonly used interface connector on the average PC is the serial communications interface. Serial interfaces are used for everything from printers to modems to mice. The early PCs used a 25-pin male connector for the serial interface. This was a very common connector to use

Table C-1.   *Anatomy of a 25-Pin Serial Connector*

Pin	Function	In/Out
1		N/C
2	Transmit Data	Out
3	Receive Data	In
4	Request to Send	Out
5	Clear to Send	In
6	Data Set Ready	In
7	Ground	In
8	Carrier Detect	In
9	Transmit Clock +	Out
10		N/C
11	Transmit Clock –	Out
12		N/C
13		N/C
14		N/C
15		N/C
16		N/C
17		N/C
18	Receive Clock +	In
19		N/C
20	Data Terminal Ready	Out
21		N/C
22	Ring Indicator	In
23		N/C
24		N/C
25	Receive Clock	In

with serial ports, but the majority of the 25 pins weren't used for anything. Then, when the AT was introduced, IBM used a much more compact 9-pin male connector. Virtually all new PCs now use the 9-pin male connector style as well.

The 25-pin male connector shown next

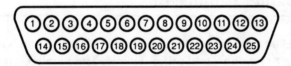

is used for serial ports. Table C-1 lists the function of each pin in the connector.

The 9-pin male connector shown here

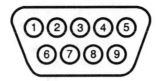

is used for serial ports. Table C-2 lists the function of each pin in this connector.

Table C-2.   *Anatomy of a 9-Pin Serial Connector*

Pin	Function	In/Out
1	Carrier Detect	In
2	Receive Data	In
3	Transmit Data	Out
4	Data Terminal Ready	Out
5	Ground	Out
6	Data Set Ready	In
7	Request to Send	Out
8	Clear to Send	In
9	Ring Indicator	In

Parallel Adapter Connector

The parallel interface is used primarily for printers, but it is also a popular way to interface to scanners and other devices. The parallel interface on IBM

Table C-3.   *Anatomy of a 25-Pin Parallel Connector*

Pin	Function	In/Out
1	Strobe	Out
2	Data Bit 0	Out
3	Data Bit 1	Out
4	Data Bit 2	Out
5	Data Bit 3	Out
6	Data Bit 4	Out
7	Data Bit 5	Out
8	Data Bit 6	Out
9	Data Bit 7	Out
10	Acknowledge	In
11	Busy	In
12	Paper Empty	In
13	Select	In
14	Auto Linefeed	Out
15	Error	In
16	Init Printer	Out
17	Select In	Out
18	Ground	Out
19	Ground	Out
20	Ground	Out
21	Ground	Out
22	Ground	Out
23	Ground	Out
24	Ground	Out
25	Ground	Out

Table C-4.   *Anatomy of a 36-Pin Parallel Connector*

Pin	Function	In/Out
1	Strobe	In
2	Data Bit 0	In
3	Data Bit 1	In
4	Data Bit 2	In
5	Data Bit 3	In
6	Data Bit 4	In
7	Data Bit 5	In
8	Data Bit 6	In
9	Data Bit 7	In
10	Acknowledge	Out
11	Busy	Out
12	Paper Empty	Out
13	Select	Out
14	Auto Linefeed	In
15		N/C
16	Ground	In
17	Ground	In
18	+5 Volts	Out
19	Ground	In
20	Ground	In
21	Ground	In
22	Ground	In
23	Ground	In
24	Ground	In
25	Ground	In
26	Ground	In
27	Ground	In
28	Ground	In
29	Ground	In
30	Ground	In
31	Init Printer	In
32	Error	Out
33	Ground	In
34		N/C
35		N/C
36	Select In	In

Table C-5.   *Anatomy of a 6-Pin Keyboard Connector*

Pin	Function	In/Out
1	Data	Out
2		N/C
3	Ground	In
4	+5 Volts	In
5	Clock	In
6		N/C

computers has always used a 25-pin female connector. This has been copied by other PC makers as well.

The printer manufacturer, Centronics, popularized the use of a 36-pin connector for their printers. Now about half of the printers available with a parallel interface use this kind of connector. (The other half use 25-pin connectors like the ones used by PCs.)

The 25-pin female connector shown here:

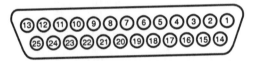

is used for parallel ports. Table C-3 lists the function of each pin in the connector. The 36-pin Centronics connector shown here:

is described in Table C-4. In Table C-4, the input/output description is from the point of view of the printer, not the PC.

Keyboard Connector

Every computer needs a keyboard, of course. Should you find yourself needing to examine a keyboard port closely, the following illustration shows the arrangement of the pins on the connector.

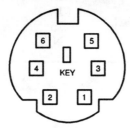

Table C-5 describes the purpose of each pin.

Mouse Connector

There was no dedicated mouse port on most personal computers until the PS/2. Before that, most people used a serial port to attach a mouse, joystick, or trackball. The PS/2 mouse connector has since become something of a de facto standard. An example is shown here:

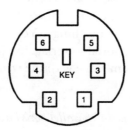

Table C-6 describes the purpose of each pin.

Table C-6. *Anatomy of 6-Pin Mouse Connector*

Pin	Function	In/Out
1	Data	Out
2		N/C
3	Ground	In
4	+5 Volts	In
5	Clock	In
6		N/C

Cabling Woes

The cables between your computer and your peripheral devices can be a constant source of irritation. It can seem that every peripheral device out there needs a different kind of cable, none which you ever have on hand.

Computer stores have serial cables with male connectors on both ends, female connectors on both ends, or a female connector on one end and a male connector on the other. You can also get parallel cables the same way, or with a male 25-pin D-Sub connector on one end and a 36-pin Centronics printer connector on the other.

Another option is to buy short cables called "gender changers" or "gender benders," which have two male connectors or two female connectors back to back. These are useful for many things. You can use them to cable two computer together directly, serial-to-serial, for file transfers, or you might have a printer cable or modem cable with the wrong kind of connector on it.

Remember

Serial ports have male connectors and parallel ports have female connectors. Changing the gender of your cable won't magically transform a serial cable into a parallel cable, or vice versa.

Glossary

AC (Alternating Current)   AC is measured in Hertz (Hz). In the United States, power is 120 volts AC at 60 Hz.

accelerator   Accelerator refers either to cards plugged into a computer to upgrade the CPU or to shortcut keys used with software.

access time   The time it takes to access information in memory or on the hard drive. Access time for memory is measured in nanoseconds. Access time in hard disks is measured in milliseconds.

accumulator   The accumulator in a CPU is a register that allows the accumulation of totals. *See also register.*

adapter bracket   *See bracket.*

adapter cards   The plug-in cards for the computer. There are three types of adapter cards used with the Industry Standard Architecture (ISA) bus. 8-bit adapter cards are used in PC, XT, and AT class computers. 16-bit cards are used in AT class computers; some 16-bit cards can be plugged into 8-bit slots. 32-bit cards are used in 80386 and up AT class computers and are normally a proprietary bus for memory cards made by the computer manufacturer.

adapter socket   The printed circuit edge connector on the motherboard into which adapter cards are inserted.

address   An address specifies a location in computer memory.

ADF (Automatic Document Feed)   A feature on scanners that allows users to load a stack of documents letting the ADF feed them in.

allocation units   The smallest amount of space that can be named as a file on a hard disk. If the allocation unit is 2 Kb, even a 1-byte file will be given 2 Kb of space.

alphanumeric   Numbering systems using the letters A-Z, and a-z, and the numbers 0-9.

Altair 8800   The first desktop computer.

(ALT) **(alternate)**   The (ALT) key is used to modify the meaning of other keys on the keyboard. Like the (SHIFT) key, it is used in conjunction with at least one other key.

ALU (Arithmetic Logic Unit)   The part of the CPU that performs arithmetic functions on data, including comparisons and Boolean operations.

ARLL (Advanced Run Length Limited)   A data encoding scheme for hard drives that increases disk capacity over MFM or RLL.

ASCII (American Standard Code for Information Interchange)   The standard code used to encode character data for a computer.

AT (Advanced Technology)   The name given to any computer running an 80286 or greater CPU.

AUTOEXEC.BAT   A batch file that is automatically run when a PC boots DOS (Disk Operating System). In OS/2 the AUTOEXEC.BAT file is used whenever a DOS session is started.

background   Background processing is processing that continues once started without user intervention and with other programs running in the foreground. For example, the DOS command PRINT will load the file to be printed into memory and then the DOS prompt will reappear. The file is printed (in the background) while the user continues with other work.

backup   The process of saving data and programs to another medium, such as from a hard disk to floppies or tape.

bank   Each row of memory is called a bank of memory. PC/XT motherboards normally have four banks of memory labeled Bank 0 through Bank 3.

BASIC (Beginners All-purpose Symbolic Instruction Code)   A programming language that is included with most versions of DOS.

BAT   The filename extension for batch files.

batch file   A file containing a series of instructions that can be sequentially executed by the operating system's command processor. A batch file must have the filename extension .BAT.

baud   A unit of measure of transmission speed for modems and other serial devices such as terminals. 300 baud is 300 bits per second or 37.5 characters per second. Modem speeds are typically 300, 1200, 2400, and 9600 baud.

bay   The physical compartments in a computer case that are reserved for disk drives.

beep   The sounds generated by the speaker. These beeps are frequently used as a diagnostic aid for identifying problems.

binary   The counting system used by computers. It is based on the numbers 0 and 1.

BIOS (Basic Input Output System)   The BIOS is stored on a ROM on your motherboard. Whenever a system is turned on, this program is loaded and then run.

Gl

bit (Binary Digit)   The counting unit used in binary arithmetic, this can be either a 0 or a 1.

boot   Boot, boot-up, and booting are all terms meaning the same thing—to start the computer.

brackets   The metal piece attached to an adapter card, which in turn is attached to the case. Also called adapter bracket or orb.

burn-in   A period of time (normally 24 hours) that a computer is allowed to run in a heated room. The purpose is to exercise the solder joints and hardware to minimize failures in the field. Burn-in is also used to describe damage to a monitor caused by a high brightness setting or age.

bus   The electrical interface between the computer and adapter cards. The ISA (Industry Standard Architecture) bus is found in PCs, XTs, most ATs, and some PS/2s. The EISA (Extended Industry Standard Architecture) bus is more prevalent in 80386 and 80486 based systems. The MCA (Micro Channel Architecture) Bus is found in PS/2 based systems.

byte   8 bits.

cache   Cache memory is used to speed up disk accesses or instruction access.

CAD (Computer Aided Design)   CAD usually refers to drawing packages such as AutoCAD.

CAE (Computer Aided Engineering)   CAE allows designs to be tested on the computer.

cards   Another term for adapter cards.

carriage return   A term held over from typewriters. The (ENTER) key now replaces carriage return and return, but some manuals still say "press the <CR> key".

cartridge   Cartridge normally refers to the removable portion of a tape, or cartridge backup system.

case The external housing for the system unit containing the power supply, motherboard, adapter cards, and disk drives.

CD-ROM (Compact Disk Read Only Memory) CD-ROM drives act like hard drives but can only be read from (not added to). A CD-ROM platter can store a tremendous amount of information.

Centronics Centronics (actually a company) introduced a printer connector that has become a standard parallel port connection. The terms parallel and Centronics are often used interchangeably.

CGA (Color Graphics Adapter) The first color adapter used on the IBM PC. *See also EGA, VGA, and XGA.*

character A character is any number, letter, or punctuation mark.

chip Jargon for Integrated Circuit (IC).

chip set A group of ICs designed to do a specific task. Some manufacturers will develop a chip set and sell it to other manufacturers so that products are compatible. Video boards, drive controllers, and motherboards are where most of these ICs are found.

CHKDSK The DOS command used to check disks.

CMOS (Complimentary Metal Oxide Semiconductor) CMOS RAM is a type of memory chip that uses battery power to keep your SETUP information intact on your AT-style motherboard.

COM A shortened version of Communications Port, also called a serial port. There are normally only two COM ports, which are called COM1 and COM2. COM is also used as a file extension for some executable files.

COMMAND.COM A program loaded during computer boot. The DOS command line is the result of running this program. It also contains many of the resident commands like DIR and others.

components The conventional name for the individual parts of a computer system and for the parts that are on circuit boards.

CONFIG.SYS   CONFIG.SYS like AUTOEXEC.BAT is used when the computer starts. It contains system setup information, device drivers, and other information. CONFIG.SYS is used with DOS and OS/2. Other operating systems may be different.

connectors   The physical ends on cables used to connect various components together. There are a wide variety of connectors used both inside and outside the computer case.

(CTRL) **(control)**   The (CTRL) keys on the keyboard, like the (SHIFT) and (ALT) keys, are used to modify the meaning of other keys. The (CTRL) key is normally pressed in conjunction with another key.

controller   An adapter card used for controlling hard and floppy drives. Display adapters are sometimes referred to as video controllers.

conventional memory   The first 640 Kilobytes of RAM memory.

coprocessors, math   Math coprocessors are auxiliary chips used for math functions. For 8088 and 8086 processors, the math coprocessor, chip has the number 8087. The 80286 uses an 80287. The 80386 and 80386SX use the 80387 and the 80387SX, respectively. The math coprocessor is built into the 80486.

core   The name of an early type of memory used in mainframe computers.

CP/M (Control Program for Microcomputers)   One of the first operating systems for microcomputers.

CPS (Characters Per Second)   CPS is used to rate the speed at which printers print.

CPU (Central Processing Unit)   CPU is the name used for the actual computer. Some CPUs are the 8086, 8088, 80186, 80286, 80386, 80386DX, 80386SX, 80486, V-20, V-30, and V-50.

crash   Any minor to catastrophic failure of some part of the computer.

crystal   A component that regulates the speed of the computer.

CTRL-ALT-DEL   This keypress sequence is used to reboot (restart) the computer.

CTS (Clear To Send)   One of the control lines found in a serial port.

cursor   A flashing marker on the display indicating the place where a typed character will appear.

cylinders   A cylinder is an imaginary concept. If a disk has only one side, track and cylinder numbers will be identical. If the device has more than one side or more than one platter, all associated tracks at a particular track location are called a cylinder. Let's assume two platters (four sides) labeled side 0, 1, 2, and 3. Track 5 on side 0 is just that—track 5 on side 0. Track 5 - side 0, track 5 - side 1, track 5 - side 2, and track 5 - side 3 would be referred to collectively as cylinder 5. Actually you will normally hear track 5 - head 0, track 5 - head 1, track 5 - head 2, and track 5 - head 3. The meanings are identical.

D-Sub   A type of connector shaped like the letter "D". Also called a D Shell connector.

daisy chain   The process of connecting one peripheral to another through a set of cables.

DC (Direct Current)   Current that flows in one direction. Batteries and power supplies deliver DC voltages.

DEBUG   A program supplied with DOS that allows programs to be examined at the binary or assembly language level.

default   Any setting or answer that is most common for most circumstances.

density   The amount of information that can be stored in a particular area such as a floppy disk. 1.2 MB and 1.44 MB diskettes are said to be high density.

designator   Letter and number markings next to components on a circuit board.

Gl

desktop   Computer cases that sit on your desk are considered to be desktop computers. In Windows and other windowing systems the display area is called the desktop.

device driver   A program that controls a device. Device drivers are programs loaded at boot time by CONFIG.SYS. The most common of these is the mouse device driver. Other operating systems use different methods to load device information.

dialog box   Under Windows and other windowing programs a dialog box is used to request information from the user.

digit   A number such as the digits 0-9.

DIN   A European connector standard. Most keyboard connectors are 5-pin DIN connectors.

diodes   A component that allows current to flow in only one direction.

DIP (Dual Inline Package)   DIP refers to an IC package with 2 rows of pins—one row on each side.

DIP switch   DIP switches use a DIP package with one switch associated with each pair of pins. DIP switches conserve space and are used primarily to set values for adapter cards.

DIR   The DOS directory command for listing files.

directories   Directories are used to split a floppy or hard drive into manageable areas—similar in concept to hanging folders in a filing cabinet.

disable   Disable means to render unusable by the system or to turn off some function.

disk   The magnetic media of a floppy or hard disk system.

DISKCOPY   The DOS command to make a copy of a floppy disk.

display   A display is the television-like unit attached to the computer. Also called the monitor.

DMA (Direct Memory Access)   DMA is used as a fast way to transfer information by not involving the CPU in the transfer.

DOS (Disk Operating System)   The system of programs that allows a user to control the computer. DOS allows reads and writes to the drives and controls the display, the keyboard, and other peripherals.

dot-matrix   A type of printer that utilizes pins, which strike the paper to form the characters.

double-clicking   Clicking the mouse button twice in rapid succession. A double-click is normally used to activate a command of some sort.

downloaded   To receive a file from another computer.

DPI (Dots Per Inch)   DPI designates the resolution of printers and scanners.

DRAM (Dynamic Random Access Memory)   DRAM is the standard memory found in computers. It is normally called simply RAM. DRAM requires a refresh cycle to keep the contents of memory intact.

drive   The physical devices used to read and write to magnetic media such as disks.

DSR (Data Set Ready)   A control line for serial communications.

DTP (DeskTop Publishing)   An acronym for a system that allows you to do writing, illustrations, typesetting, and paste-up work on the computer.

DTR (Data Terminal Ready)   A control line for serial communications.

EBCDIC (Extended Binary Coded Decimal Interchange Code)   An IBM standard like ASCII used mostly on older mainframe computers.

EGA (Enhanced Graphics Adapter)   A graphics adapter that allows higher resolution than CGA. *See also CGA, VGA, and XGA.*

EISA (Extended Industry Standard Architecture)   Early IBM and compatible computers use a system of connections to adapter cards that has

Gl

become known as Industry Standard Architecture or ISA. The PS/2 introduced a new standard called MicroChannel Architecture or MCA. The balance of the computer industry responded by implementing a new type of bus system called Extended Industry Standard Architecture or EISA. This system is available in newer 80386- and 80486-based systems.

EMS (Expanded Memory Specification)   EMS, also known as LIM 4.0, is a memory specification that allows the use of memory above the 640 KB limit.

emulators   Hardware and software that mimic other hardware and software.

enabled   A device or software is said to be enabled when it is usable by the system or turned on.

(ENTER)   A keyboard key—also called Carriage Return or Return key.

EPROM (Erasable Programmable Read Only Memory)   EPROM chips are programmed with special equipment. Once programmed they can only be erased using ultraviolet light. The BIOS is sometimes stored on EPROMs.

ERLL (Enhanced or Expanded Run Length Limited)   *See ARLL.*

ESDI (Extended Small Device Interface)   An interface system for hard drives.

export   Exporting a file usually means to save the file in a different file format.

extended memory   Any memory above the 1 MB boundary in 80286 and higher computer systems.

FAT (File Allocation Table)   The file system used by PC/MS DOS. OS/2 supports the FAT file system but also makes others available.

FDISK   A DOS command used to partition a hard drive into manageable units. Use this command with caution.

file   A named collection of data.

filename   The name of a file. In PCs the filename can be up to eight characters long, followed by a period (.), then up to a three-character extension.

filename extensions   Filename extensions allow files to be differentiated one additional way. Some filename extensions follow:

.$$$	A temporary file, used within a program and then discarded. A file with this filename extension may be erased by any program at anytime.
.ASM	"Assembly" Assembly program source listing.
.BAK	"BackUp" The next oldest copy of a modified file.
.BAS	"BASIC" programs.
.BAT *	"Batch" Contains DOS commands that can be executed as though they were typed at the keyboard.
.C	"C" C language source code.
.COB	"COBOL" COBOL source code.
.COM *	"Command" Contains a program that will be run when the filename is entered as a DOS command.
.DAT	"Data" files.
.DOC	"Document" Word processing file.
.DRW	"Drawing" Graphic files.
.DXF	"Drawing Exchange Format" CAD files.
.EPS	"Encapsulated PostScript" graphic files.
.EXE *	"Executable" Similar to COM.
.GRP	"Group" files.
.INI	"Initialization" files.
.LIB	"Library" Compiler Library file.
.LST	"List" Listing of compilation or assembly.
.MAP	"Map" Memory map for linker.
.OBJ	"Object Code" Compiled programs prior to linking.
.OVR	"Overlay" Program overlay module.
.PAS	"Pascal" Pascal source code.
.PCX	"Paintbrush" Picture file.

Gl

.PRN	"Print" Contains output from a program that would normally have been sent to a printer.
.SYS *	"System" Contains information used by DOS to control some aspect of DOS's operation.
.TIF	"Tagged Information File Format" graphics information files.
.TGA	"Targa" graphics files.
.TMP	"Temporary" Some programs use files with this extension for temporary storage.
.TXT	"Text" files.

* These extensions have special meaning to DOS.

floppy   Floppy, as in floppy disk, refers to the removable media of a floppy drive as opposed to the rigid platters in a hard disk.

floppy drive   Floppy drives are used to read and write to floppy disks.

font   A collection of letters, numbers, and punctuation in a particular typeface and type size.

FORMAT   A DOS command used to prepare a new disk for use.

formatting   The process that prepares a new disk for use.

frame-grabber   *See grabber, frame.*

function keys   The keyboard keys on the left side of a keyboard or along the top, numbered (F1) through (F10) or (F12).

fuse   An electromechanical device to protect against shorts.

game port   The game port on a computer interfaces the computer to a joystick.

gender-bender   Jargon referring to a conversion device allowing a female connector to be changed to a male connector or vice versa.

gigabyte (gb)   One Gigabyte equals roughly one billion bytes.

gigahertz (gHz)   One gigahertz equals one billion hertz.

grabber, frame   A frame-grabber is an adapter card that converts a video image into a file.

graphics   Computer generated images.

gray-scale   A spot of toner or ink on paper or a screen is binary. It's either there or it isn't. Gray-scale refers to any system used to simulate shades of gray.

GUI (Graphical User Interface)   A system that uses pictures or graphics to convey information.

handshaking   Handshaking is a term used in serial communications and other places. When two systems exchange control information to let each other know what is going on, the systems are said to be handshaking. This allows information to be sent over serial communication lines without overrunning the data buffers on either end.

hard drive   Hard drives, so named because the magnetic media used is rigid or hard, are non-removable mass storage devices normally mounted inside the computer. Hard drives can store millions of bytes of data.

hardcard   Adapter cards that have hard drives mounted directly on the card.

hardware   Hardware refers to all pieces of equipment in a computer system (as opposed to software).

head   The read/write unit in both hard and floppy disks.

height   The physical height of the drive. Drives are normally full-height or half-height with some newer one-third height drives.

Hercules   Hercules (a manufacturer) established the first monochrome monitor graphics standard.

hertz (Hz)   Hertz is the unit of measure for frequency in cycles per second (CPS).

Gl

hexadecimal (Hex)   A number system based on the digits 0 through 9, and the letters A through F.

HPFS (High Performance File System)   HPFS is a new file system used with OS/2 (version 1.2 or higher).

ICs   The integrated circuit chips used in computers and other electronic equipment.

I/O   Input/Output.

icon   Icons are small pictures or symbols used to convey information in a GUI.

IDE (Intelligent Drive Electronics)   A hard drive interface system.

import   The act of reading data from a different format or system.

inkjet   Inkjet printers actually shoot jets of ink to form text.

interface   The physical interconnection or interrelation between two devices that allows them to communicate.

interlaced   Interlaced monitors display part of the image, which is called a field. Each field requires 1/60th of a second to paint. The spacing between each horizontal line is wide enough to permit a second field to be painted (like alternate slats in a Venetian blind) in the space between the lines. The result is called a frame and consists of two fields just slightly displaced in the vertical. The problem is that it takes 1/30th of a second (2/60ths) to paint both fields, which may result in noticeable image flicker. The ideal system is non-interlaced, which paints the entire screen in one field time (1/60th of a second) and eliminates flicker.

interleave   If the electronics reading a hard drive were fast enough to read each sector as it came under the read/write head, interleave would not be in the computer vocabulary. The problem is that by the time a computer has read the information in a sector, the next sector has been passed over. This means that the drive must wait a full revolution to read the next sector. If there are 17 sectors, it would take at least 17 revolutions to read a track.

In this circumstance it is normal to format the hard disk in such a way that the sectors alternate. The drive reads a sector, skips one, reads the next and so forth. In this way 8 sectors are read on the first revolution, the second 8 are read on the second revolution (assuming a full track is being read) and the entire track is read in two revolutions by interleaving alternate sectors.

interrupt   A method for passing information to a running system to tell it that a pending operation needs attention. Interrupts can be generated by either hardware or software.

ISA (Industry Standard Architecture)   The bus system found in PCs, XTs, most AT class motherboards, and some PS/2 computers.

jacket   The external plastic cases used for floppy disks.

jumper   The small black plastic blocks used to make connections between two pins on a circuit board. They act much like a switch.

KB   *See kilobyte.*

keyboard   An external input device that resembles the keyboard of a typewriter. There are two basic types of keyboard. The original 84-key keyboard is found mainly with PC/XT-type computers. The 101-key keyboard is found on AT-style computers.

keycap   The tops of the keys on the keyboard.

keylock   Modern computers are fitted with a lock on the front of the case that controls who uses the computer.

keypad   The numeric keypad on the right of the keyboard can be used for numeric entries or it can be used to change the cursor's direction. Also called numeric keypad.

kilobyte   Roughly a thousand bytes, the actual amount is 1024 bytes.

landing zone   An area in the hard drive where the heads can safely contact the disk surface.

Gl

laptop   The new, small computers that can fit on your lap.

laser printer   A high-speed printer that uses copier technology to form an image on paper.

Light Emitting Diode (LED)   LEDs are used extensively as indicator lamps in modern computers. This component lights up when voltage is applied. The drive access lights and the case lights are LEDs.

LIM   *See EMS.*

LPT   A parallel port designation. LPT1 and LPT2 are typical parallel port designations.

magneto-optical   A drive system that uses a laser and a magnetic field to store information on an optical disk.

Megabyte (MB)   Roughly a million bytes. The actual figure is 1,048,576 bytes.

MCA (Micro Channel Architecture)   The MCA bus is found mostly in PS/2- based systems.

MCGA (Multi-Color Graphics Array)

MD   *See MKDIR.*

MDA (Monochrome Display Adapter)

memory   A pseudonym for storage in a computer. It usually refers to the RAM in a microcomputer.

MFM (Modified Frequency Modulation)   A recording method used with disk storage devices.

microcomputer   A computer based on a microprocessor.

microprocessor   Another name for the CPU.

microsecond   One millionth of a second.

MKDIR The DOS command used to create directories. Can also be abbreviated to MD.

Modem (MOdulator-DEModulator) A serial communication device that allows computer data to be sent over telephone lines.

Molex A type of connector. Molex is a manufacturer of connectors that are used in computers. This type of connector is used primarily for drive power connections.

monitor The television-like screen that lets users view input.

monochrome Monchrome means single color. On a monitor, this could be white on black, green on black, or amber on black.

monospace Monospace means having the same amount of space between letters. A typewriter's printing is monospace. *See also proportional.*

motherboard The main board in the computer. This board normally has the processor, memory, and adapter slots on it.

MS-DOS The version of DOS put out by Microsoft.

multifunction card A card that has multiple functions built into it, such as a monochrome graphics adapter with two serial ports, a parallel port, and a game port.

multisynch or multifrequency monitor Multisynch monitors can display CGA, EGA, VGA, and other standard and non-standard graphics and text.

nano Stands for a billionth, as in nanosecond.

nanosecond A billionth of a second. Memory chips are rated in nanoseconds access time.

network Networks use hardware and software to connect computers together to share resources such as printers, large hard drives, and software.

Gl

NLQ (Near Letter Quality)   A printed output that is a little better than dot matrix.

non-interlaced   Non-interlaced monitors are capable of generating a full frame in 1/60th of a second. The result is a flicker-free display.

non-volatile   A type of memory that does not forget what is stored in it when the power is turned off.

OCR (Optical Character Recognition)   OCR software allows a scanned document to be converted to ASCII text.

octal   A numbering system based on the numbers 0-7.

operating system   The software that manages your computer's disk drives, display, keyboard, and other hardware, and furnishes the user a way to interact with these various parts.

orb   *See adapter bracket.*

OS/2 (Operating System/2)   A multitasking operating system.

paper-white   High-resolution desktop publishing monitors that display black characters on a white background.

parallel port   An interface port that sends 8 bits (1 byte) out over 8 lines simultaneously.

parity   A data error-checking scheme.

PC-DOS   The version of DOS distributed by IBM.

peripheral   Any external device attached to the computer system. Printers, plotters, and scanners are all peripherals.

PGA (Pin Grid Array)   A type of IC package that is square in shape with pins on the bottom.

Pixel or Picture Element   This is a single point on the screen. A screen display that is 320 by 200 has a total of 64,000 pixels.

PLCC (Plastic Leaded Chip Carrier)   A type of IC package that is square in shape with leads or pins on all four sides.

PM (Presentation Manager)   The Graphical User Interface (GUI) that comes with OS/2.

port   An interface connection.

POST (Power-On Self-Test)   A series of tests run whenever the system is turned on.

PostScript   A page description language that is very popular for desktop publishing.

printer   Any external device that prints onto paper.

processor   This is the actual computer. Some processors are the 8086, 8088, 80186, 80286, 80386, 80386DX, 80386SX, 80486, V-20, V-30, and V-50. Also called CPU (Central Processing Unit).

proportional   Printing in which the letters take up varying degrees of space— for example, a W takes up more room than an i.

proprietary bus   A bus system supported by a limited number (frequently only one) manufacturer.

PS/2 (Personal System 2)   This is IBM's latest line of computers. The Models 25 and 30 are ISA bus computers. The rest of the line are MCA busses.

rail   Drive installation attachment used in AT-style cases.

RAM (Random Access Memory)   Another term for memory used in computer systems.

RAMDRIVE   A program that allows you to emulate a fast drive using the RAM memory.

read   To load information from a disk into memory.

Gl

read-only   Setting a disk or file so that it cannot be accidentally erased.

reboot   To restart the computer system.

register   A group of flip-flops used to store information temporarily.

reset   To return to the starting condition.

resistor   An electronic component.

RESTORE   A program included with DOS to restore your hard drive from floppies.

RGB (Red Green Blue)   The three colors that make up a color picture.

ribbon   Used in dot matrix printers as the ink source.

RLL (Run Length Limited)   A data encoding scheme for hard drives that increases disk capacity. It is normally implemented using a hard drive controller card.

ROM (Read Only Memory)   A type of IC memory that once programmed cannot be erased.

RPM   Revolutions per minute

RS-232, RS-232C, or RS-422   These are the standards for serial communication ports.

R/W   Acronym for Read/Write.

S-VGA (Super Video Graphics Array)   This is an extended standard for VGA adapter cards. It provides for higher resolutions and more colors than standard VGA. *See also CGA, EGA, VGA, and XGA.*

scanner   A device that converts a picture on paper to an electronic image in the computer.

SCSI (Small Computer System Interface)   An interface for a wide variety of drives and peripherals.

sector　　A portion of a track on a floppy or hard disk—basically the smallest data unit on a disk.

seek　　To search for a sector or track on a disk.

segment　　A part of the memory addressing system.

semiconductor　　Semiconductor material is made of silicon to which various impurities are added to give different parts different characteristics. This material is the basis of the many ICs in a computer.

serial port　　An interface port that sends 8 bits (1 byte) out over a single data line one bit at a time.

SIMM (Single Inline Memory Module)　　A small circuit board with memory chips attached to it.

SIP (Single Inline Pin)　　This can either be a memory module that has a row of pins on the bottom or it can be like the terminating resistors used on drives.

slot　　Another term for an adapter socket.

SMD (Surface Mount Device)　　This is a new style of electronic component that can be mounted on a circuit without the use of through-holes for leads.

software　　The programs used by a computer, including the disk operating system, application programs, and any information supplied on disks.

SPI (Spots Per Inch)　　Refers to the resolution of printers and scanners.

spreadsheet　　An application that calculates columns of numbers.

SRAM (Static Random Access Memory)　　This type of memory will keep the contents of memory intact as long as power is applied. SRAM does not require a refresh cycle.

ST412/506　　The standard hard drive interface.

Gl

stepper motor   A positioning system used to move the heads of a floppy or hard drive.

subdirectory   A subdirectory is a concept similar to hanging folders in a filing cabinet, which allows you to break the hard drive into logical sections.

system   A generic term for a computer system. It is also used when referencing the system unit.

tape   Usually a backup media. It provides for high data capacity.

terabytes   Stands for a trillion bytes.

TIGA (Texas Instruments Graphics Adapter)   A high-resolution color graphics system.

toner   The material that produces the letters on a laser printer.

TPA (Transient Program Area)   This is the actual amount of memory available to run a program. This size will change depending on what DOS is loaded, what device drivers are loaded, and the parameters set up in the CONFIG.SYS file.

track   A circular portion of a floppy or hard disk.

trackball   An input device resembling an upside-down mouse.

transfer rate   The rate at which data is transferred to and from a hard drive.

transistor   One of the most important electronic components, it is basically a solid state switch. The CPU is made up of many transistors.

transmit   To send information to a peripheral or another system.

TSR (Terminate and Stay Resident)   A type of program that stays in memory. It does not run until certain key combinations are pressed, or it can be interrupt driven.

TTL (Transistor Transistor Logic)   A method of connecting transistors internally in an integrated circuit. Developed by Texas Instruments, it is also frequently used to describe the output of display adapters because the circuitry driving the monitor is TTL circuitry.

turbo   A faster running speed for a motherboard.

Tx (Transmit)   This is the transmit line in serial communications.

TYPE   A DOS command that allows you to view the contents of a file.

typeface   The physical appearance of a font excluding its size.

VGA (Video Graphics Array)   A video adapter card that offers high resolution and many colors. *See also CGA, EGA, S-VGA, and XGA.*

video signal   A signal that carries information to form a visual display.

virtual memory   A system that uses the hard drive to give the illusion that more memory is available in the system.

voice-coil   A positioning system used to move the heads of a hard drive.

volt   A measure of electric pressure. In the United States, household power is 110 volts.

watts   The amount of power used by a device.

windows   A graphical user interface.

WORM (Write Once Read Many)   This is a type of drive that allows you to write information to an optical disk only once and then read from it many times.

write   To save information to disk from memory.

write-protect   Setting a floppy disk so that it cannot be erased. This is done by covering the write-protect notch on 5 1/4-inch floppies, or by opening the write-protect shutter on 3 1/2-inch floppies.

GI

XGA (Extended Graphics Adapter)   This is a graphics adapter that provides higher resolutions and more colors than VGA.

XT (Extended Technology)   A computer system based on the 8088 processor that has a hard drive.

Index

Upgrading PCs - The Video

We've prepared a VHS video tape to supplement Upgrading PCs Made Easy. This is a professional tape designed to give you additional information on the subjects covered in our book.

_____ Upgrading PCs - The Video @ $39.95

We can also provide an expanded copy of our vendor list on floppy disk.

_____ Expanded Vendor List @ $39.95

Visual Basic Software

☐ Personal Finance Toolkit with inventory* $29.95
☐ Visual Basic Game Toolkit* $29.95
☐ Home Floor Planner* $29.95
☐ Office Floor Planner* $29.95
☐ Landscape Designer* $29.95
☐ 3-D Kitchen Planner* $39.95
☐ 3-D Interior Design Planner* $39.95
☐ Accounting Software Construction Kit* $495.00
☐ above with runtime distribution license $4995.00

* software includes source code and single user license

Please send the items checked above. I have enclosed a check or have checked the appropriate credit card box below and signed this order. Check here for COD ☐ . Check here for further information ☐ .

Charge my credit card: Exp.__ / __
☐ MasterCard   ☐ Visa
Card # _____

NAME _____

SIGNATURE _____

ADDRESS _____

CITY/STATE/ZIP _____

**CALL TOLL FREE
1-800-437-2886**

Small Packages
4052 Johnson Drive
Oceanside, CA 92056

Upgrade Your Software, Too!

By special arrangement with GLOSSBRENNER'S CHOICE, readers of this book can get two power-packed disks for a total of just $5. The disks contain the three most essential programs in the PC world, after MS-DOS itself. They are FANSI Console, CED, and LIST. Once you've tried these shareware masterpieces, you'll not only want to register them with their authors, you will refuse to use a PC without them from then on. Here's what you get:

• Core Collection Disk 1 (CORE 1) -- FANSI Program, CED, and LIST

Mark Hersey's FANSI ("fancy") Console gives you *complete* control over your system, including: key re-assignments, cursor speed, screen writes and color selection, screen blanking, expanded type-ahead buffer, and more. But the feature you will use every day of your life is FANSI's scroll-recall. Simply tap a key to put everything on hold. Then use your arrow and paging keys to scroll back through previously displayed screens as if they were part of one huge player piano roll. You can even "clip out" portions of this piano roll and record them as files on disk.

CED is the DOS "Command EDitor" by Chris Dunford. The program lets you scroll back through previously issued DOS commands. With CED, you can recall as many commands as you like and edit them as you would with a word processor. Then hit **ENTER** to run them again. You can even use CED to create custom commands and command synonyms.

Vernon Buerg's LIST program is a shareware classic that just keeps getting better. There is no faster way to look at a text file, clip out portions, and write them to disk. There's even a phone dialer and several DOS shell-like features. LIST's FIND function is crucial for locating target words in text files, and it's blazingly fast!

• Core Collection Disk 2 (CORE 2) -- FANSI Documentation, PC-DeskTeam, and PC-Window

The on-disk documentation for FANSI is over 150 pages long. This disk also contains PC-DeskTeam, a top-quality SideKick clone. There is also PC-Window, a pop-up notepad, timer, ASCII table, and alarm that occupies only about 20K of memory. You'll like them both.

To take advantage of this offer, just complete the coupon on the back of this page and mail it with your check or money order to:

Glossbrenner's Choice
699 River Road
Yardley, PA 19067

About Glossbrenner's Choice

Glossbrenner's Choice is shareware with a difference. Every program in the collection has been personally selected as the best in its category by computer writer Alfred Glossbrenner (*Alfred Glossbrenner's Master Guide to FREE Software for IBM's and Compatible Computers*, St. Martin's Press; and *Glossbrenner's Complete Hard Disk Handbook* and *Glossbrenner's Master Guide to GEnie*, both from Osborne McGraw-Hill). Glossbrenner's Choice cuts through the clutter -- and saves you time and money in the process. With Alfred Glossbrenner as your guide, you'll spend your time sampling software instead of plowing your way through catalogues. Truly, this is shareware at its best!

GLOSSBRENNER'S CHOICE COUPON

[Please Print Clearly]

Name:_____

Address:_____

Address:_____

City: _____ State: _____ ZIP:_____

Phone:(_____)_____

Please send me **CORE 1** and **CORE 2** in the format specified:

☐ 5.25-inch format ☐ 3.5-inch format

I've enclosed $5 for shipment to a U.S. address or $8 for shipment outside the U.S.

TOTAL ENCLOSED: _____

☐ Please send me a FREE CATALOGUE of other great shareware available from Glossbrenner's Choice.

Make check payable to **Glossbrenner's Choice**. Check or money order must be in U.S. dollars and drawn on a U.S.-based bank. Mail to:

Glossbrenner's Choice
699 River Road
Yardley, PA 19067

Osborne **McGraw-Hill** assumes NO responsibility for the fulfilment of this offer.

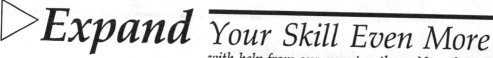

▷ *Expand* *Your Skill Even More*

with help from our expert authors. Now that you've gained greater skills with **Upgrading PCs Made Easy***, let us suggest the following related titles that will help you use your computer to full advantage.*

PCs Made Easy
by James L. Turley

If you are a first-time computer user, no other book meets your needs better than this broad, concise, up-to-date introduction to the use of personal computers. It's designed to help you get maximum information with minimal time invested. Turley explains what PCs are, what they can do, and how to make them do it—without relying on jargon or buzzwords.
$18.95p, ISBN: 0-07-881477-4, 319 pp., 7 3/8 X 9 1/4
Covers All Personal Computers

The Computer Virus Handbook
by Richard B. Levin
Foreword by Alfred Glossbrenner

What can you do to protect your computer data from being invaded by rogue programs? Rich Levin provides you with a practical guide to minimizing the risk of computer viruses and maximizing the recovery process. You'll learn about antiviral policies for the workplace, including how to evaluate and use antivirus software. Levin discusses eight outstanding antiviral and disk management utility programs and provides you with step-by-step instruction for using each of them.
$24.95p, ISBN: 0-07-881647-5, 415 pp., 7 3/8 X 9 1/4

Computer Professional's Dictionary
by Allen Wyatt

For the largest selection of technical terms, concise definitions, and the latest computer jargon, this is the resource to choose. Written with the experienced computer user in mind, over 3,000 terms from "Abbreviated addressing" to "Zmodem" are included covering virtually every aspect of computing. You can quickly locate the meaning or use of a particular word, acronym, or abbreviation. Wyatt gives all programmers, MIS managers, and computer experts a dictionary that truly enlightens.
$19.95p, ISBN: 0-07-881705-6, 350 pp. 7 3/8 X 9 1/4

▶————Osborne **McGraw-Hill** ■ Available at local book and computer stores.

The PC User's Guide
by Nick Anis and Craig Menefee

The PC User's Guide offers comprehensive readable documentation for your IBM PC or PC compatible computer. The book begins by acquainting you with personal computer hardware and how to set it up, before delving into operating system software, applications software, and storage media. You'll also learn about servicing your computer system, optimizing its performance, and adding to or upgrading it. From unpacking to tweaking, from BASIC to BIOS, *The PC User's Guide* is your one-stop source for answers and information.
$29.95p, ISBN: 0-07-881670-X, 700 pp., 7 3/8 X 9 1/4, Dvorak*Osborne/McGraw-Hill

Simply DOS
by Kris Jamsa

Here's the ideal book for everyone who needs to learn the basics of DOS. DOS expert Kris Jamsa makes learning DOS simple, short, and painless. Clear, step-by-step instructions introduce the most essential DOS commands that you need for everyday DOS tasks. All versions of DOS are covered. Filled with helpful illustrations and examples, you'll find a great bonus that makes this book even easier to use—it has a special binding that lays flat when you open to any chosen page.
$14.95p, ISBN: 0-07-881715-3, 200 pp., 5 7/8 X 8 3/4

DOS: The Complete Reference, Second Edition
by Kris Jamsa

Every PC-DOS and MS-DOS user will find essential information — from an overview of the disk operating system to a reference for advanced programming and disk management techniques—in this updated and revised edition of the outstanding bestseller. Each chapter begins with a discussion of specific applications followed by a list of related commands.
$29.95p, ISBN: 0-07-881497-9, 1278 pp., 7 3/8 X 9 1/4, Covers MS-DOS/PC-DOS Versions Through 3.3

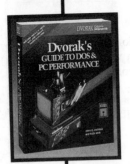

Dvorak's Guide to DOS and PC Performance
(Includes Two 5 1/4" Disks)
by John C. Dvorak and Nick Anis

John Dvorak, the world's most widely read computer columnist, and Nick Anis, author and programming ace, offer all PC owners a wealth of knowledge and experience about IBM-compatible PCs and the DOS operating system, plus a collection of top commercially available DOS-based PC utilities. Whether you want to add a command to your AUTOEXEC file or to install a new motherboard, Dvorak and Anis give you the context, examples, and specific instructions you need for peak PC performance.
$49.95p, ISBN: 0-07-881658-0, 850 pp., 7 3/8 X 9 1/4, Dvorak*Osborne/McGraw-Hill

▶ _____**Osborne McGraw-Hill** ■ Available at local book and computer stores.

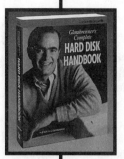

Glossbrenner's Complete Hard Disk Handbook
by Alfred Glossbrenner and Nick Anis
Foreword by John C. Dvorak

This comprehensive volume covers everything from buying a hard disk to installing, loading, organizing, and "tweaking" it for maximum performance. *Glossbrenner's Complete Hard Disk Handbook* also includes two diskettes packed with tutorials, software tools, and utilities. You'll savor the lively style and amazing ability to organize information that Alfred Glossbrenner has brought to dozens of books and articles on computers and software. $39.95p, ISBN: 0-07-881604-1, 450 pp., 7 3/8 X 9 1/4,

Intel's Official Guide to 386™ Computing
by Michael Edelhart

For enhancing your 386 computer, managing memory above 640K, upgrading your 286 system to a 386 system, and learning about the 387 coprocessor and multitasking, this is **the** book. Written by **PC Computing's** Editor-in-Chief Mike Edelhart, with chapters contributed by experts in the field and reviewed by Intel Corporation, this book has the inside information you've been looking for. Filled with exercises, demonstrations, and hands-on examples, this book helps you become more productive with your 386 computer. $29.95p, ISBN: 0-07-881693-9, 366 pp., 7 3/8 X 9 1/4

PC Tools Deluxe™: The Complete Reference
by Hy Bender

Every feature of PC Tools Deluxe, including version 6, is described in detail and accompanied by hundreds of illustrations and examples in this Complete Reference. Simple instructions help you quickly learn the fundamentals of this outstanding DOS-based utility program, then Bender discusses the most important and widely used features, such as managing your files and directories, composing and editing documents, transmitting faxes and electronic mail, and more. $27.95p, ISBN: 0-07-881648-3, 750 pp., 7 3/8 X 9 1/4, Covers Versions Through 6

XTree® Made Easy
by Mike Callahan and Nick Anis

If you're one of the 3.5 million users of any version of XTree, you'll be delighted with this book. Mike Callahan, a.k.a. Dr. File Finder, and Nick Anis complement the XTree documentation by providing you with all the details on this popular DOS shell and utility program. This book includes a step-by-step instruction guide as well as a handy reference. You'll learn everything from basic file management to using XTree on large hard drives and on networks. $19.95p ISBN: 0-07-881711-0, 352 pp., 7 3/8 X 9 1/4, Covers all versions of XTree, including XTreeGold, XTreeEasy, and XTreeNCA.

DOS 5 Made Easy, Second Edition
by Herbert Schildt

DOS 5 delivers the upgrade that DOS users have been waiting for, and you'll find out all about it in the ideal one-volume tutorial on the operating system's features and functions. Written by best-selling author Herb Schildt, this book starts with DOS 5's new graphical user interface and file system basics, works through I/O and configuration options, the editor, and concludes with a discussion of hard disk management.
$19.95p, ISBN: 0-07-881690-4, 412 pp., 7 3/8 X 9 1/4

Windows 3 Made Easy
by Tom Sheldon

Handle Microsoft®'s newest version of Windows effectively and creatively with the skills you learn from *Windows 3 Made Easy*. If you're just beginning to use Windows, Tom Sheldon takes you through all the fundamentals step-by-step, including how to install it and get a fast start. If you're already using Windows, you'll learn all the newest features of the recently released version 3 and how to apply these capabilities through customizing Windows, transferring information between Windows, and more.
$19.95p, ISBN: 0-07-881537-1, 500 pp., 7 3/8 X 9 1/4

F-19 Stealth Air Combat
by Pete Bonanni

In *F-19 Stealth Air Combat*, real-life fighter pilot Bonanni is your co-pilot in a sleek, top-secret Stealth bomber capable of eluding radar detection and delivering deadly payloads over enemy targets. This simulation game is close to real air combat, and Bonanni gives you expert the guidance you need to develop skills and knowledge that lets you excel in complex game scenarios. Aircraft buffs will also enjoy Bonanni's detailed explanations of stealth technology and modern aerial warfare techniques.
$14.95p, ISBN: 0-07-881655-6, 250 pp., 7 3/8 X 9 1/4, Silicon Valley

GW-BASIC Made Easy
by Bob Albrecht and Don Inman

If you've always wanted to learn basic programming skills on your personal computer, but weren't sure where to start, here's the book you need. You can satisfy your curiosity about programming and establishing excellent programming fundamentals for your future ventures in QuickBASIC or Turbo BASIC. The authors emphasize the foundation skills that develop a "clean" style of programming, and make GW—BASIC truly easy to learn.
$19.95p, ISBN:0-07-881473-1, 418 pp., 7 3/8 X 9 1/4
Available in Spanish, ISBN:84-76155387

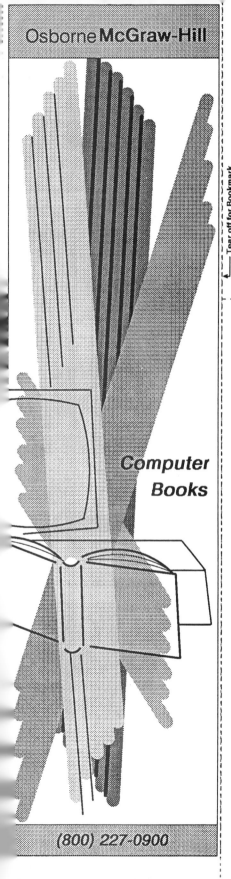

No Postage
Necessary
If Mailed
in the
United States